Simple Machine Learning Models using R Programming

Simple Machine Learning Models using R Programming

Mohsen Nady

ARCLER
PRESS

www.arclerpress.com

Simple Machine Learning Models using R Programming

Mohsen Nady

Arcler Press
4164 Lakeshore Road
Burlington, ON L7L 1A4
Canada
www.arclerpress.com
Email: orders@arclereducation.com

ISBN: 978-1-77956-952-3 (Hardcover)

ABOUT THE AUTHOR

Mohsen Nady is a pharmacist with a M.D. in Microbiology and a Diploma in Industrial Pharmacy. Besides, Mohsen has more than 10 years of experience in Statistics and Data Analytics. Mohsen has applied his skills to different projects related to Genomics, Microbiology, Biostatistics, Six Sigma, Data Analytics, Data Visualization, Building Apps, Geography, Market Analysis, Business Analysis, Machine Learning, etc. Mohsen also published his thesis in a high-impact journal that attracted many citations, where all the statistical analyses were performed by him in addition to the methodological part. Furthermore, Mohsen has earned different certificates, from top universities (Harvard, Johns Hopkins, Denmark, etc) in Statistics, Data Analytics, Data Visualization, and Machine Learning that highlight his outstanding diverse skills.

TABLE OF CONTENTS

Preface ... *ix*

Chapter 1 Linear Regression Modeling ... 1

1.1. Data Used in This Chapter ... 1
1.2. Data Exploration of the Marketing Data ... 4
1.3. Data Exploration of the Heart Attack Data ... 5
1.4. Machine Learning (ML) Steps ... 8
1.5. Simple Linear Regression Modeling ... 9
1.6. Simple Linear Regression Modeling of Marketing Data ... 10
1.7. Simple Linear Regression Modeling of Heart Attack Data ... 29
1.8. Multiple Linear Regression with Many Predictors ... 49
1.9. Multiple Linear Regression of Marketing Data ... 50
1.10. Multiple Linear Regression of Heart Attack Data ... 61

Chapter 2 Linear Classification Modeling ... 73

2.1. Data Used in This Chapter ... 73
2.2. Data Exploration of the Two Class Data ... 75
2.3. Data Exploration of the Iris Data ... 78
2.4. Linear Discriminant Analysis (LDA) ... 80
2.5. Linear Discriminant Analysis (LDA) for the Two Class Data ... 80
2.6. Linear Discriminant Analysis (LDA) for Iris Data ... 104

Chapter 3 Penalized Regression Modeling ... 125

3.1. Data Used in This Chapter ... 125
3.2. Data Exploration ... 132
3.3. Penalized Regression ... 139
3.4. Ridge Regression ... 140
3.5. Lasso Regression ... 184

3.6. Elastic Net Regression 198
3.7. Conclusion 219

Chapter 4 Penalized Classification Modeling 221
4.1. Data Used in This Chapter 221
4.2. Data Exploration 226
4.3. Ridge Classification 230
4.4. Lasso Classification 278
4.5. Elastic Net Classification 297
4.6. Conclusion 316

Chapter 5 K-Nearest Neighbors (KNN) Regression 317
5.1. Data Used in This Chapter 317
5.2. Data Exploration 319
5.3. knn Model 320
5.4. knn Regression 321
5.5. Comparison Between Different Models 345

Chapter 6 K-Nearest Neighbors (KNN) Classification 365
6.1. Data Used in This Chapter 365
6.2. Data Exploration 368
6.3. KNN Model 372
6.4. KNN Classification 372
6.5. Comparison Between Different Models 402

Bibliography 421

Index 423

PREFACE

This book is a continuation of our previous books about Machine Learning (ML) using the R programming language. In this book, we discuss some relatively simple ML models: linear models, penalized models, and K-nearest neighbors (knn) models.

In Chapter 1, we discuss using linear models to predict numerical outcomes in regression models. On the other hand, in Chapter 2, we explain the use of linear models to predict categorical outcomes in categorical models.

In Chapter 3, we explain the use of penalized models used when we have a large number of correlated predictors and select only the most important ones. We have discussed the three types of penalized regression models: Ridge, Lasso, and elastic net, and applied them to an example dataset. Finally, we compared these three approaches to select the best-performing model.

Similarly, in Chapter 4, we discussed the three approaches of penalized models in predicting a categorical outcome and compared the three approaches to select the best-performing model with the highest accuracy.

Chapters 5 and 6 were devoted to using K-nearest neighbors (knn) models to predict numerical and categorical outcomes, respectively. At the end of each chapter, the three modeling approaches of linear, penalized, and knn models were compared visually and statistically to select the best-performing model.

In all these chapters, different datasets per chapter were used to illustrate the different models discussed in each chapter. In addition, all the data preprocessing, analysis, and modeling steps were done using the R programming language with several code chunks to show these complex analyses. I hope that this book with many examples of data modeling will be a great addition to your journey in machine learning.

CHAPTER 1

LINEAR REGRESSION MODELING

Contents

1.1. Data Used in This Chapter 1
1.2. Data Exploration of the Marketing Data 4
1.3. Data Exploration of the Heart Attack Data 5
1.4. Machine Learning (ML) Steps 8
1.5. Simple Linear Regression Modeling 9
1.6. Simple Linear Regression Modeling of Marketing Data 10
1.7. Simple Linear Regression Modeling of Heart Attack Data 29
1.8. Multiple Linear Regression with Many Predictors 49
1.9. Multiple Linear Regression of Marketing Data 50
1.10. Multiple Linear Regression of Heart Attack Data 61

1.1. DATA USED IN THIS CHAPTER

1.1.1. Marketing Data

This data contains the impact of three advertising media (YouTube, Facebook, and newspapers) on sales. The column values are the advertising budget or sales in thousands of dollars. The advertising experiment has been repeated 200 times, so we have 200 rows in this data.

The data is part of the datarium package named "marketing." First, we load the datarium package using the library function; then, we load the marketing data using the data function.

We also load the tidyverse package into our R session because it contains many useful packages for data analysis, and the flextable package to convert the different code outputs into readable tables.

Before loading any package using the library function, we should install the package first using the Tools, then Install Packages in R studio and type the package you want to install.

```
library(datarium)
data("marketing")
library(tidyverse)
library(flextable)
```

To see this data structure, we use the glimpse function.

```
glimpse(marketing)
## Rows: 200
## Columns: 4
## $ youtube <dbl> 276.12, 53.40, 20.64, 181.80, 216.96, 10.44, 69.00, 144.24, …
## $ facebook <dbl> 45.36, 47.16, 55.08, 49.56, 12.96, 58.68, 39.36, 23.52, 2.52…
## $ newspaper <dbl> 83.04, 54.12, 83.16, 70.20, 70.08, 90.00, 28.20, 13.92, 1.20…
## $ sales <dbl> 26.52, 12.48, 11.16, 22.20, 15.48, 8.64, 14.16, 15.84, 5.76,…
```

The glimpse function gives the number of rows, the number of columns, the column names with the prefix "$," the column classes between "<>" parentheses, and the first values of every column.

The data contains 200 rows (200 advertising experiments) and 4 columns:

1. **youtube:** a double (dbl) or numeric column with decimals for advertising budget using youtube. The first column values are 276.12, 53.40, 20.64, 181.80, etc.
2. **facebook:** a double or numeric column with decimals for advertising budget using Facebook. The first column values are 45.36, 47.16, 55.08, 49.56, etc.
3. **newspaper:** a double or numeric column with decimals for advertising budget using the newspaper. The first column values are 83.04, 54.12, 83.16, 70.20, 70.08, etc.

4. **sales:** a double or numeric column with decimals for sales in thousands of dollars. The first column values are 26.52, 12.48, 11.16, 22.20, 15.48, etc. This is the numeric outcome column that will be predicted using the regression models described in the next sections.

1.1.2. Heart Attack Data

Around 72 participants had measures of cholesterol concentration and were treated with three different drugs. The aim is to examine the effect of three drugs in lowering the cholesterol concentration.

The data is also part of the datarium package under the name "heartattack" that is loaded above. So, to load this data into our R session, we use the data function and then use the glimpse function to see the data structure.

data("heartattack")

glimpse(heartattack)

Rows: 72

Columns: 5

$ gender <fct> male, male, male, male, male, male, male, male, male, male…

$ risk <fct> low, low, low, low, low, low, low, low, low, low, low, low…

$ drug <fct> A, A, A, A, A, A, B, B, B, B, B, B, C, C, C, C, C, C, A, A…

$ cholesterol <dbl> 5.238730, 5.075693, 4.678653, 5.361076, 4.957381, 4.828897…

$ id <int> 1, 2, 3, 4, 5, 6, 7, 8, 9, 10, 11, 12, 13, 14, 15, 16, 17,…

The data is composed of 72 rows (participants) and 5 columns:

1. **gender:** a factor column for the participant's gender with two categories: "male" and "female."
2. **risk:** a factor column with two categories: "low" and "high."
3. **drug:** a factor column with three categories: "A," "B," and "C."
4. **cholesterol:** a numeric column for the participant's cholesterol level. This is the numeric outcome column that will be predicted using the regression models described in the next sections.
5. **id:** an integer column for the participant's id. It is a unique number for every participant.

1.2. DATA EXPLORATION OF THE MARKETING DATA

The first step in any data modeling is data exploration using functions from the skimr package.

1.2.1. Numerical Columns

We will use the skim function, from the skimr package, to produce useful information about our data columns. Because the output has too many columns so we use the yank function, from the skimr package too, to look at information related to categorical and numeric columns separately.

To examine all numeric columns at once, we use the following functions on the marketing data:

- The skim function produces information about all data columns.
- The yank function with a "numeric" argument to get only the information related to numeric columns.
- The flextable function converts the result to a table.
- The theme_box function makes all cells in the produced table with complete line boundaries.
- The set_caption function with the caption argument to add a table title.

To use functions from the skimr package, we should first load the skimr package using the library function.

```
library(skimr)
marketing %>% skim() %>% yank("numeric") %>%
flextable() %>% theme_box() %>%
set_caption(caption = "The information gained from skim function on the numeric columns of marketing data")
```

The information gained from skim function on the numeric columns of marketing data:

skim_ variable	n_ miss-ing	com-plete_ rate	mean	sd	p0	p25	p50	p75	p100	hist
youtube	0	1	176.4510	103.025084	0.84	89.25	179.70	262.59	355.68	
facebook	0	1	27.9168	17.816171	0.00	11.97	27.48	43.83	59.52	
newspaper	0	1	36.6648	26.134345	0.36	15.30	30.90	54.12	136.80	
sales	0	1	16.8270	6.260948	1.92	12.45	15.48	20.88	32.40	

We have 11 columns:

1. skim_variable is the column name. We have 4 numeric columns in the marketing data, which are all data columns.
2. n_missing is the number of missings in each column. The value is 0 for all columns, meaning all columns have no missing values.
3. complete_rate is the proportion of present values in each column. All numeric columns have no missing and 1 or 100% complete rate.
4. mean is the mean or average value for each column.
5. sd is the standard deviation for each column.
6. p0 is the 0% percentile or the minimum value for each column.
7. p25 is the 25% percentile or the 1st quartile for each column.
8. p50 is the 50% percentile, the median, or the 2nd quartile for each column.
9. p75 is the 75% percentile or the 3rd quartile for each column.
10. p100 is the 100% percentile or the maximum value for each column.
11. hist is the histogram plot for each column.

1.3. DATA EXPLORATION OF THE HEART ATTACK DATA

1.3.1. Categorical Columns

We will use the same above functions including the yank function with "factor" argument to get only the information related to factor or categorical columns. We use the argument cwidth = 1 within the flextable function to increase slightly the column width of the produced table.

heartattack **%>% skim() %>% yank**("factor") **%>%**

flextable(cwidth = 1) **%>% theme_box() %>%**

set_caption(caption = "The information gained from skim function on the categorical columns of the heart attack data")

The information gained from skim function on the categorical columns of the heart attack data:

skim_variable	n_missing	complete_rate	ordered	n_unique	top_counts
gender	0	1	FALSE	2	mal: 36, fem: 36

risk	0	1	FALSE	2	hig: 36, low: 36
drug	0	1	FALSE	3	A: 24, B: 24, C: 24

- We have 6 columns:
  - The skim_variable is the factor or categorical column name. We have three factor columns which are gender, risk, and drug columns.
  - The n_missing is the number of missing values. The factor columns have zero or no missing values.
  - The complete_rate is the proportion of present values in each column. All columns have no missings so the complete rate = 1 or 100% for all columns.
  - The ordered column denotes if the factor column is an ordered factor column like months where January < February < March…, etc. All factor columns are unordered and so have a FALSE value.
  - The n_unique is the number of unique values in each column. There are 2 different genders in the gender column, 2 risk categories in the risk column, and three drugs in the drug column.
  - The top_counts is the number of rows for the most frequent categories in the categorical columns. However, the categories are trimmed in their names. To see the full names, we can use the count function with the column name for each column. For the gender column:

```
heartattack %>% count(gender) %>% flextable() %>%
theme_box() %>%
set_caption(caption = “The frequency of unique values in the gender column of the heart attack data”)
```

The frequency of unique values in the gender column of the heart attack data:

gender	n
male	36
female	36

- There are 2 unique categories or genders in the "gender" column.
- There are 36 males and 36 females in the data, so the total is 72, which is the total rows in the heart attack data.

For the risk column:

heartattack **%>% count**(risk) **%>% flextable**() **%>%**

theme_box() **%>%**

set_caption(caption = "The frequency of unique values in the risk column of the heart attack data")

The frequency of unique values in the risk column of the heart attack data:

risk	**n**
high	36
low	36

- There are 2 unique risk categories in the "risk" column.
- There are 36 high-risk participants and 36 low-risk participants in the data, so the total is 72, which is the total rows in the heart attack data.

For the drug column, the drug names are not trimmed because every drug name is only 1 letter. We have 24 rows for drug A, 24 rows for drug B, and 24 rows for drug C, with a total of 72, which is the total rows in the heart attack data.

1.3.2. Numeric Columns

We use the same above functions but using the yank function with the "numeric" argument to get useful information about numeric columns in the heart attack data.

heartattack **%>% skim**() **%>% yank**("numeric") **%>%**

flextable() **%>% theme_box**() **%>%**

set_caption(caption = "The information gained from skim function on numerical columns from the heart attack data")

The information gained from skim function on numerical columns from the heart attack data:

skim_ variable	**n_ miss- ing**	**com- plete_ rate**	**mean**	**sd**	**p0**	**p25**	**p50**	**p75**	**p100**	**hist**
cholesterol	0	1	5.128865	0.4955996	4.209694	4.812421	5.146191	5.382391	6.605243	
id	0	1	36.500000	20.9284495	1.000000	18.750000	36.500000	54.250000	72.000000	

We have 11 columns:

1. skim_variable is the column name. We have 2 numeric columns: cholesterol and id columns.
2. n_missing is the number of missings in each column. All numeric columns have 0 missings or no missings.
3. complete_rate is the proportion of present values in each column. All numeric columns have no missings and 1 or 100% complete rate.
4. Other columns from mean to hist have been explained before.

The id column is not a real numeric column and will not be used as a predictor in data modeling.

1.4. MACHINE LEARNING (ML) STEPS

The general steps for data modeling that will be applied in this book, with heavily relying on tidymodels packages, are:

1. Splitting the data into training and testing data.
   - The training data is about 70–80% of the whole data and is used for building the predictive model, while the testing data is about 20–30% of the whole data and is used for evaluating the model performance.
   - This step is called initial split and was explained in the "Statistics with R for Machine Learning: Volume 1 Data Preparation and Splitting with R for Machine Learning" book.
2. Preparing the data for modeling by some preprocessing steps like dropping unnecessary variables, imputing missing values, transformation, dummification, etc.
   - This is done by generating a recipe with the desired preprocessing step(s). The recipe is a description of the steps to be applied to a data set to prepare it for data analysis/modeling. This is followed by looking at the training and testing data after the recipe is applied, if needed.
3. Generate different resamples (different versions) of the training data:
   - The resamples of the training data can be created using different methods and the best method is V-Fold Cross-Validation which was explained in the "Statistics with R for Machine Learning: Volume 1 Data Preparation and Splitting with R for Machine Learning" book.

- The cross-validation overcomes overfitting by providing a more robust estimate of the model's performance on unseen (testing) data. Overfitting means high model performance on training data and low performance on testing data.

4. Define the machine learning (ML) model, like linear regression, decision tree, logistic regression, etc.
5. Define the workflow. The workflow is a container object that aggregates information required to fit and predict from a model. This information is the recipe generated in step 2 and the model defined in step 4.
6. Estimate the different models' performance on the different resamples of the training data.
   - In addition, we can use the grid search to find the best tuning parameters in different ML models that correspond to the best performance metrics. Some models, like the linear regression model in this chapter and the linear discriminant analysis (LDA) model in the next chapter, have no tuning parameters.
7. Fit the best model, found in step 6, on the testing data.

1.4.1. Supervised Learning

In supervised learning, each observation or row of our data contains predictor measurements and an outcome response measurement.

We fit a supervised ML model that relates the response or outcome to the predictors, with 2 main groups:

- Regression models when we have a continuous or numerical outcome.
- Classification models when we have a categorical outcome.

1.5. SIMPLE LINEAR REGRESSION MODELING

Simple linear regression models are models for relating any numerical outcome to a single predictor by a linear equation. We called it simple because we only considered one predictor.

The linear equation of the simple linear regression is written as:

$$y = \beta_o + \beta_1 x_1$$

where; is the mean of the numerical outcome; x_1 is the predictor of interest, which can be numerical or categorical; β_0 is the model intercept and β_1 is the predictor slope. They are also called model coefficients, which are estimated from the data. The result of simple linear regression is a line that relates the predictor (*x*) to the outcome (*y*).

1.6. SIMPLE LINEAR REGRESSION MODELING OF MARKETING DATA

We will create a simple linear model for predicting sales using youtube advertising budget (numerical predictor).

1.6.1. Splitting the Data into Training and Testing Data

As explained in previous books, we first do a stratified splitting of the marketing data using the numerical outcome (sales). This ensures that both the resulting training and testing data have the same sales distribution as the original marketing data.

We create an object called "split_market" by using the initial_split function with the arguments:

- data = marketing, which is the data we want to split.
- strata = sales to make a stratified splitting using the sales outcome column.

To make the splitting reproducible, we use the set.seed function with any number before using the initial_split function. Also, we must load the tidymodels package first using the library function because all following functions, including the initial_split function, are part of the tidymodels packages.

```
library(tidymodels)
set.seed(123)
split_market <- initial_split(data = marketing,
strata = sales)
split_market
## <Training/Testing/Total>
## <148/52/200>
```

- The training data has 148 rows, and the testing data has 52 rows, with a total of 200 which is the total rows of the original data.

To get the actual training and testing data, we use the training and testing functions, respectively, on the split_market object. The resulting data is called train_market for the training data and test_market for the testing data. Finally, we use the dim function to see the data dimensions.

```
train_market<-training(split_market)
test_market<-testing(split_market)
dim(train_market)
## [1] 148 4
dim(test_market)
## [1] 52 4
```

- The training data has 148 rows (1st number) and 4 columns (2nd number), while the testing data has 52 rows (1st number) and 4 columns (2nd number). The same 4 columns of marketing data are present in the training or testing data.

1.6.2. Generating the Recipe

We create an object "rec" by applying the recipe function on the train_market data using the "%>%" operator. The recipe function has the argument sales ~ youtube, meaning predicting the sales outcome column using the youtube predictor column only.

```
rec <- train_market %>%
recipe(sales ~ youtube)
rec
##
## —— Recipe ————————————————————————————————
##
## —— Inputs
## Number of variables by role
## outcome: 1
## predictor: 1
```

- The recipe object "rec" defines the variables by role with 1 variable as an outcome (sales) and 1 variable as a predictor (youtube).

1.6.3. Generate Different Resamples (Different Versions) of the Training Data

We split the train_market data using the vfold_cv function with the arguments:

- v = 10 to split the data to 10 folds.
- repeats = 5 to repeat this process 5 times.

- strata = sales to make stratified resampling using the sales column.
- The result is 50 different resamples of train_market data contained in folds data frame.
- We also use the set.seed function before splitting to make the splitting reproducible.

```
set.seed(123)
folds<-vfold_cv(train_market, v = 10, repeats = 5, strata = sales)
folds
## # 10-fold cross-validation repeated 5 times using stratification
## # A tibble: 50 × 3
## splits id id2
## <list> <chr> <chr>
## 1 <split [132/16]> Repeat1 Fold01
## 2 <split [132/16]> Repeat1 Fold02
## 3 <split [132/16]> Repeat1 Fold03
## 4 <split [132/16]> Repeat1 Fold04
## 5 <split [132/16]> Repeat1 Fold05
## 6 <split [132/16]> Repeat1 Fold06
## 7 <split [134/14]> Repeat1 Fold07
## 8 <split [135/13]> Repeat1 Fold08
## 9 <split [135/13]> Repeat1 Fold09
## 10 <split [136/12]> Repeat1 Fold10
## # i 40 more rows
```

We see that:

- We have 50 different rows. Each row corresponds to 1 resample of train_market data. Each resample has 1 analysis (training) data, with 132, 134, 135, or 136 rows and 1 assessment (testing) data with 16, 14, 13, or 12 rows.
- Each row has 2 id values. id for the repeat number from 1 to 5 and id2 for the resample number from 1 to 10 within that repeat.
- Each row has a total rows of 148 which is the number of rows in original train_market data. 132 + 16 = 134 + 14 = 135 + 13 = 136 + 12 = 148.

1.6.4. Define the Machine Learning (ML) Model

We define a linear regression model by using the functions:

- The linear_reg function to define the model type.
- The set_engine function with the argument "lm" to define the engine that will use the lm function from the stats base R package.
- The set_mode function with the argument "regression" to define the mode of learning. We use regression because we have a numerical outcome (sales).
- All the three functions are applied in sequence using the piping "%>%" operator and the resulting object is called "lm_model."

```
lm_model <- linear_reg() %>%
set_engine("lm") %>%
set_mode("regression")
lm_model
## Linear Regression Model Specification (regression)
##
## Computational engine: lm
```

1.6.5. Generate Workflow

We create the "wflow" object by using the following functions:

- The workflow function to create a workflow.
- The add_recipe function with the argument "rec" to add the above created recipe with no preprocessing steps.
- The add_model function with the argument lm_model to add the above created model.

```
wflow <- workflow() %>%
add_recipe(rec) %>%
add_model(lm_model)
wflow
## == Workflow ==================================================
================================================

## Preprocessor: Recipe
## Model: linear_reg()
##
```

── Preprocessor ──

0 Recipe Steps

##

── Model ──

Linear Regression Model Specification (regression)

##

Computational engine: lm

- The "wflow" object contains no preprocessing steps (0 Recipe Steps) and the linear regression model.

1.6.6. Fit the Model on Training Data

We can fit the linear regression model on whole training data "train_market" to get a 1 model fit. However, we can also fit the linear regression model on the 50 resamples of the training data in the "folds" data frame to get 50 different model fits and obtain more robust estimate of the model performance on testing data.

1.6.6.1. Fitting the Model on Whole Training Data

We create a lin_mod model by using the fit function with the arguments:

- wflow which is the workflow containing no preprocessing steps and the linear regression model.
- train_market which is the whole training data with 148 rows.

Then, we use the following functions:

- The tidy function to see the model results.
- The mutate function with the argument across(is.numeric,round, 5) to round all numeric columns to 5 decimal places.
- The add_significance function, from the rstatix package, with the arguments:

++ p.col = "p.value" to add p-value significance symbols based on the p.value column.

++ output.col = "significance" to create the significance column that will hold the significance symbols.

- The flextable function to convert the result to a table.
- The theme_box function to apply cell boundaries to all cells in the table.

- The set_caption function with the caption = "..." argument to add a table caption or title.

As usual, we first load the rstatix package using the library function.

library(rstatix)

lin_mod<-**fit**(wflow, train_market)

tidy(lin_mod) **%>% mutate**(**across**(is.numeric,round, 5)) **%>%**

add_significance(p.col = "p.value", output.col = "significance") **%>%**

flextable(cwidth = 1) **%>% theme_box**() **%>%**

set_caption(caption = "Linear model results of using youtube advertising for predicting sales in marketing training data")

Linear model results of using youtube advertising for predicting sales in marketing training data:

term	**estimate**	**std.error**	**statistic**	**p.value**	**significance**
(Intercept)	8.71700	0.66083	13.19105	0	****
youtube	0.04515	0.00319	14.13875	0	****

- The linear regression equation will be:

sales = 8.717 + 0.045 × youtube.

- The fitted model results are many columns and we will focus on the estimate and p.value for significance.
- The youtube advertising is a significant predictor of sales with a p.value < 0.05 and an estimate of 0.045.
- This means that each 1 unit increase in youtube advertising budget (1000 USD) is associated with a 0.045 unit increase in sales on the average (0.045 × 1000 = 45 USD).

The linear model can be visualized as a line between the youtube on the x-axis and sales on the y-axis with the following functions applied on train_market data:

- The ggplot function with the arguments aes(x = youtube, y = sales) to plot the youtube values on the x-axis and the sales values on the y-axis.
- The geom_point function to plot a scatter plot.
- The geom_smooth function with the argument method = "lm" to add the best fitting linear regression model line to the plot.

- The labs function with title = "…" argument to add a plot title.
- The theme_classic function to remove the default white grid lines and grey background of a ggplot plot.

```
train_market %>% ggplot(aes(x = youtube, y = sales))+
geom_point()+ geom_smooth(method = "lm")+
labs(title = "Scatter plot of sales vs. youtube with linear regression line")+
theme_classic()
## `geom_smooth()` using formula = 'y ~ x'
```

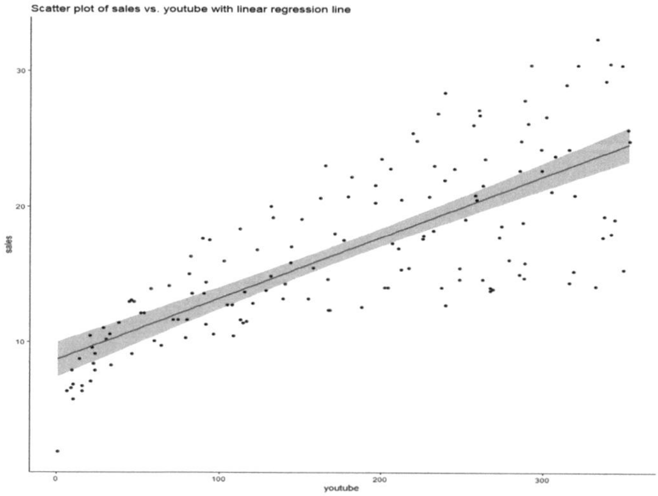

- The blue linear regression line, described by the equation sales = 8.717 + 0.045 × youtube, is plotted with 95% confidence interval as a grey background.

1.6.6.2. Model Performance on Whole Training Data

We use root mean squared error (RMSE) which measures the model prediction error for describing the regression model performance. The lower the RMSE, the better our model is. RMSE has the same scale as the outcome column.

RMSE can be visualized as the dispersion of actual points around the regression line plotted above. The more dispersion of the points, the more RMSE and vice versa.

To get the predicted sales from the fitted "lin_mod," we use the predict function with the argument new_data = train_market to get the predicted sales based on the youtube values in the training data.

```
lin_mod %>%
predict(new_data = train_market)
## # A tibble: 148 × 1
## .pred
## <dbl>
## 1 9.18
## 2 12.3
## 3 10.0
## 4 9.43
## 5 12.1
## 6 14.0
## 7 13.9
## 8 11.1
## 9 10.1
## 10 12.3
## # i 138 more rows
```

- The result is a tibble (data frame) with 148 rows (1st number) and 1 column (2nd number). The column name is called ".pred" which is the predicted sales for every row of the 148 rows of training data.
- To this tibble, we add the actual sales by using the mutate function with the argument truth = train_market$sales to add the "truth" column that contains the actual sales values of the 148 rows of training data.

```
lin_mod %>%
predict(new_data = train_market) %>%
mutate(truth = train_market$sales)
## # A tibble: 148 × 2
## .pred truth
## <dbl> <dbl>
## 1 9.18 5.76
## 2 12.3 10.3
## 3 10.0 11.0
## 4 9.43 6.72
```

```
## 5 12.1 11.6
## 6 14.0 11.5
## 7 13.9 11.4
## 8 11.1 12.1
## 9 10.1 10.2
## 10 12.3 11.6
## # i 138 more rows
```

- The result is a tibble (data frame) with 148 rows (1st number) and 2 columns (2nd number). The column names are ".pred" and "truth."
- For example, the first row has a predicted sales value of 9.18 but the actual sales value is 5.76, while in the 2nd row, the predicted sales value is 12.3 and the actual sales value is 10.3.
- Finally, we use the rmse function, after the mutate function, with the arguments:
- truth = truth which is the column containing the actual sales values.
- estimate = .pred which is the column containing the predicted sales values.

```
lin_mod %>%
predict(new_data = train_market) %>%
mutate(truth = train_market$sales) %>%
rmse(truth = truth, estimate = .pred)
## # A tibble: 1 × 3
## .metric .estimator .estimate
## <chr> <chr> <dbl>
## 1 rmse standard 4.05
```

- The RMSE of linear model using youtube as a single predictor on whole training data = 4.05.

1.6.6.3. Fitting the Model on 50 Resamples of Training Data

We use the fit_resamples function with the arguments:

- wflow which is the workflow containing no preprocessing steps and the linear regression model.
- folds which are the 50 resamples of training data created above, each containing analysis data for fitting the model and assessment data for testing the model performance within each resample.

- = metrics_set(rmse) to get the RMSE performance metric for each linear model on each resample.
- control = control_resamples(save_pred = TRUE) to get the predicted sales values for every assessment (testing) data with 16, 14, 13, or 12 rows within each resample.

```
lin_res<-fit_resamples(wflow, folds, metrics = metric_set(rmse),
control = control_resamples(save_pred = TRUE))
lin_res
## # Resampling results
## # 10-fold cross-validation repeated 5 times using stratification
## # A tibble: 50 × 6
## splits id id2 .metrics .notes .predictions
## <list> <chr> <chr> <list> <list> <list>
## 1 <split [132/16]> Repeat1 Fold01 <tibble [1 × 4]> <tibble> <tibble [16 ×
4]>
## 2 <split [132/16]> Repeat1 Fold02 <tibble [1 × 4]> <tibble> <tibble [16 ×
4]>
## 3 <split [132/16]> Repeat1 Fold03 <tibble [1 × 4]> <tibble> <tibble [16 ×
4]>
## 4 <split [132/16]> Repeat1 Fold04 <tibble [1 × 4]> <tibble> <tibble [16 ×
4]>
## 5 <split [132/16]> Repeat1 Fold05 <tibble [1 × 4]> <tibble> <tibble [16 ×
4]>
## 6 <split [132/16]> Repeat1 Fold06 <tibble [1 × 4]> <tibble> <tibble [16 ×
4]>
## 7 <split [134/14]> Repeat1 Fold07 <tibble [1 × 4]> <tibble> <tibble [14 ×
4]>
## 8 <split [135/13]> Repeat1 Fold08 <tibble [1 × 4]> <tibble> <tibble [13 ×
4]>
## 9 <split [135/13]> Repeat1 Fold09 <tibble [1 × 4]> <tibble> <tibble [13 ×
4]>
## 10 <split [136/12]> Repeat1 Fold10 <tibble [1 × 4]> <tibble> <tibble [12 ×
4]>
## # i 40 more rows
```

The resulting object "lin_res" contains 50 rows for the results of applying this linear model on the 50 resamples of training data. It contains 6 columns:

- The splits column is a list of each combination of analysis and assessment data. The sum is 148, which are total rows of training data.
- The id column is an id column for the repeat number from 1 to 5.
- The id2 column is an id column for the fold number from 1 to 10 so we have 50 resamples because $5 \times 10 = 50$.
- The .metrics column is a list of performance metrics (RMSE) of applying the linear model to the corresponding assessment data (16,14,13, or 12 rows). Each performance metric is saved in 1 row and 4 columns [1×4] tibble or data frame. These will be extracted in the next step. The 1 row is for the RMSE in each resample.
- The .notes column is a list of notes or warnings when applying the linear model to each analysis data (132, 134, 135, or 136 rows). Each note is saved in 0 rows and 3 columns [0×3] tibble or data frame meaning that there are no notes when applying this model to each analysis data.
- The .predictions column is a list of predicted sales for each testing data within each resample.

By using the unnest function with the .predictions argument on the lin_res object, we get the predicted and actual sales for each row within each resample.

```
lin_res %>% unnest(.predictions)
## # A tibble: 740 × 9
## splits id id2 .metrics .notes .pred .row sales .config
## <list> <chr> <chr> <list> <list> <dbl> <int> <dbl> <chr>
## 1 <split [132/16]> Repeat1 Fold01 <tibble> <tibble> 9.15 1 5.76 Preproce...
## 2 <split [132/16]> Repeat1 Fold01 <tibble> <tibble> 9.70 22 8.4 Preproce...
## 3 <split [132/16]> Repeat1 Fold01 <tibble> <tibble> 9.11 23 7.92 Preproce...
## 4 <split [132/16]> Repeat1 Fold01 <tibble> <tibble> 13.0 24 10.6 Preproce...
## 5 <split [132/16]> Repeat1 Fold01 <tibble> <tibble> 19.8 46 15.5 Preproce...
## 6 <split [132/16]> Repeat1 Fold01 <tibble> <tibble> 14.6 49 14.9 Preproce...
## 7 <split [132/16]> Repeat1 Fold01 <tibble> <tibble> 12.7 53 13.6 Preproce...
## 8 <split [132/16]> Repeat1 Fold01 <tibble> <tibble> 20.7 59 13.9 Preproce...
## 9 <split [132/16]> Repeat1 Fold01 <tibble> <tibble> 16.3 81 18 Preproce...
```

10 <split [132/16]> Repeat1 Fold01 <tibble> <tibble> 14.6 91 19.2 Preproce…

i 730 more rows

- The result is a tibble with 740 rows and 9 columns. Each row contains the actual (sales) and predicted sales (.pred) for each row within each resample.

By using the count function after the unnest function with the id,id2 arguments, we get the number of testing rows within each resample.

lin_res **%>%** **unnest**(.predictions) **%>%** **count**(id, id2) **%>%**

flextable(cwidth = 1) **%>%** **theme_box**() **%>%**

set_caption(caption = "The number of testing rows within 50 resamples of marketing training data")

The number of testing rows within 50 resamples of marketing training data:

id	**id2**	**n**
Repeat1	Fold01	16
Repeat1	Fold02	16
Repeat1	Fold03	16
Repeat1	Fold04	16
Repeat1	Fold05	16
Repeat1	Fold06	16
Repeat1	Fold07	14
Repeat1	Fold08	13
Repeat1	Fold09	13
Repeat1	Fold10	12
Repeat2	Fold01	16
Repeat2	Fold02	16
Repeat2	Fold03	16
Repeat2	Fold04	16
Repeat2	Fold05	16
Repeat2	Fold06	16
Repeat2	Fold07	14
Repeat2	Fold08	13
Repeat2	Fold09	13
Repeat2	Fold10	12

Repeat3	Fold01	16
Repeat3	Fold02	16
Repeat3	Fold03	16
Repeat3	Fold04	16
Repeat3	Fold05	16
Repeat3	Fold06	16
Repeat3	Fold07	14
Repeat3	Fold08	13
Repeat3	Fold09	13
Repeat3	Fold10	12
Repeat4	Fold01	16
Repeat4	Fold02	16
Repeat4	Fold03	16
Repeat4	Fold04	16
Repeat4	Fold05	16
Repeat4	Fold06	16
Repeat4	Fold07	14
Repeat4	Fold08	13
Repeat4	Fold09	13
Repeat4	Fold10	12
Repeat5	Fold01	16
Repeat5	Fold02	16
Repeat5	Fold03	16
Repeat5	Fold04	16
Repeat5	Fold05	16
Repeat5	Fold06	16
Repeat5	Fold07	14
Repeat5	Fold08	13
Repeat5	Fold09	13
Repeat5	Fold10	12

- The result is 50 rows because we have 50 resamples. The different resamples may have 16,14,13, or 12 testing rows.

We can plot the actual sales on the x-axis and the predicted sales on the y-axis, after using the unnest function, by using the following functions:

- The ggplot function with the arguments, aes(x = sales, y = .pred, color = id), to plot actual sales on the x-axis, the predicted sales on the y-axis, and a different color for each id or repeat.
- The geom_abline function to plot a diagonal perfect line that corresponds to actual sales equal predicted sales.
- The geom_point function to plot a scatter plot.
- The facet_wrap function with the argument vars(id,id2) to plot a separate plot for each unique combination of id and id2 value.
- The labs function with the arguments, title to add a plot title, *x* to add *x*-axis title, y to add y-axis title. The plot title has "\n" to make it into 2 lines.
- The theme_classic function to remove the grey background and the white background lines from the default ggplot.

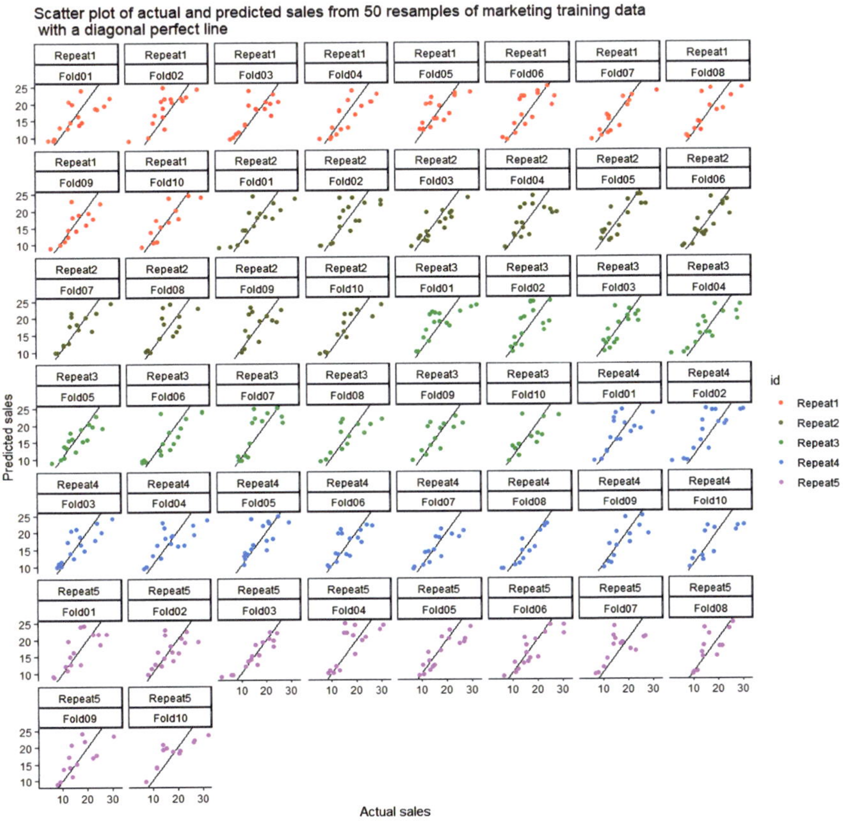

lin_res **%>% unnest**(.predictions) **%>%**

ggplot(**aes**(x = sales, y = .pred, color = id)) +

geom_abline() +

geom_point() +

facet_wrap(**vars**(id,id2))+

labs(title = "Scatter plot of actual and predicted sales from 50 resamples of marketing training data **\n** with a diagonal perfect line",

x = "Actual sales", y = "Predicted sales")+

theme_classic()

- We have 50 plots for 50 resamples. Each plot may contain 16,14,13, or 12 points according to the number of rows in each testing data within each resample.
- The points have distinct colors according to the repeat number from 1 to 5. Each repeat has 10 plots for 10 different resamples within each repeat.

1.6.6.4. Model Performance on 50 Resamples of Training Data

To get the performance metrics (RMSE) on the 50 resamples of training data, we use the following functions on the lin_res object:

- The collect_metrics function with the argument summarize = FALSE to get the RMSE for each resample.
- The arrange function with .estimate argument to arrange by RMSE value in ascending order.
- The flextable, theme_box, and set_caption functions are described previously.

lin_res **%>% collect_metrics**(summarize = FALSE) **%>%**

arrange(.estimate) **%>%**

flextable(cwidth = 1) **%>% theme_box**() **%>%**

set_caption(caption = "The RMSE of 50 resamples of marketing training data when using youtube advertising as a predictor of sales")

The RMSE of 50 resamples of marketing training data when using youtube advertising as a predictor of sales:

id	**id2**	**.metric**	**.estimator**	**.estimate**	**.config**
Repeat4	Fold08	rmse	standard	2.285184	Preprocessor1_ Model1

Repeat5	Fold03	rmse	standard	2.962805	Preprocessor1_ Model1
Repeat2	Fold06	rmse	standard	3.146333	Preprocessor1_ Model1
Repeat3	Fold05	rmse	standard	3.149833	Preprocessor1_ Model1
Repeat3	Fold03	rmse	standard	3.241558	Preprocessor1_ Model1
Repeat2	Fold05	rmse	standard	3.280800	Preprocessor1_ Model1
Repeat4	Fold07	rmse	standard	3.328551	Preprocessor1_ Model1
Repeat2	Fold03	rmse	standard	3.332212	Preprocessor1_ Model1
Repeat1	Fold07	rmse	standard	3.356172	Preprocessor1_ Model1
Repeat1	Fold10	rmse	standard	3.439336	Preprocessor1_ Model1
Repeat1	Fold09	rmse	standard	3.585174	Preprocessor1_ Model1
Repeat2	Fold10	rmse	standard	3.650804	Preprocessor1_ Model1
Repeat5	Fold08	rmse	standard	3.652446	Preprocessor1_ Model1
Repeat4	Fold05	rmse	standard	3.702400	Preprocessor1_ Model1
Repeat5	Fold06	rmse	standard	3.711295	Preprocessor1_ Model1
Repeat4	Fold06	rmse	standard	3.711773	Preprocessor1_ Model1
Repeat4	Fold09	rmse	standard	3.755332	Preprocessor1_ Model1
Repeat2	Fold07	rmse	standard	3.756602	Preprocessor1_ Model1
Repeat5	Fold05	rmse	standard	3.798168	Preprocessor1_ Model1
Repeat3	Fold09	rmse	standard	3.817086	Preprocessor1_ Model1
Repeat1	Fold03	rmse	standard	3.838473	Preprocessor1_ Model1
Repeat4	Fold03	rmse	standard	3.847348	Preprocessor1_ Model1

Repeat1	Fold05	rmse	standard	3.964193	Preprocessor1_Model1
Repeat1	Fold08	rmse	standard	4.019667	Preprocessor1_Model1
Repeat3	Fold10	rmse	standard	4.064210	Preprocessor1_Model1
Repeat1	Fold04	rmse	standard	4.098921	Preprocessor1_Model1
Repeat5	Fold02	rmse	standard	4.127897	Preprocessor1_Model1
Repeat5	Fold01	rmse	standard	4.142697	Preprocessor1_Model1
Repeat3	Fold06	rmse	standard	4.159880	Preprocessor1_Model1
Repeat3	Fold07	rmse	standard	4.219432	Preprocessor1_Model1
Repeat2	Fold08	rmse	standard	4.313118	Preprocessor1_Model1
Repeat1	Fold02	rmse	standard	4.350496	Preprocessor1_Model1
Repeat3	Fold02	rmse	standard	4.391531	Preprocessor1_Model1
Repeat5	Fold09	rmse	standard	4.396327	Preprocessor1_Model1
Repeat3	Fold04	rmse	standard	4.465977	Preprocessor1_Model1
Repeat5	Fold10	rmse	standard	4.482891	Preprocessor1_Model1
Repeat1	Fold06	rmse	standard	4.488216	Preprocessor1_Model1
Repeat5	Fold04	rmse	standard	4.496817	Preprocessor1_Model1
Repeat4	Fold01	rmse	standard	4.581585	Preprocessor1_Model1
Repeat3	Fold01	rmse	standard	4.582007	Preprocessor1_Model1
Repeat2	Fold01	rmse	standard	4.605101	Preprocessor1_Model1
Repeat3	Fold08	rmse	standard	4.622281	Preprocessor1_Model1
Repeat2	Fold09	rmse	standard	4.659222	Preprocessor1_Model1

Repeat2	Fold04	rmse	standard	4.677185	Preprocessor1_Model1
Repeat4	Fold10	rmse	standard	4.734401	Preprocessor1_Model1
Repeat2	Fold02	rmse	standard	4.821271	Preprocessor1_Model1
Repeat4	Fold04	rmse	standard	4.878059	Preprocessor1_Model1
Repeat4	Fold02	rmse	standard	4.889413	Preprocessor1_Model1
Repeat5	Fold07	rmse	standard	4.931747	Preprocessor1_Model1
Repeat1	Fold01	rmse	standard	5.016266	Preprocessor1_Model1

- The result is 50 rows with 1 RMSE value for each resample.
- The lowest RMSE (2.285) was achieved in repeat 4 and fold 8, while the highest RMSE (5.016) was achieved in repeat 1 and fold 1.

If we used the collect_metrics function with the argument summarize = TRUE, we will get the mean RMSE value across the 50 resamples of the training data.

```
lin_res %>% collect_metrics(summarize = TRUE)
## # A tibble: 1 × 6
## .metric .estimator mean n std_err .config
## <chr> <chr> <dbl> <int> <dbl> <chr>
## 1 rmse standard 4.03 50 0.0849 Preprocessor1_Model1
```

- The mean RMSE of linear model using youtube as a single predictor on 50 resamples of training data (n = 50) = 4.03, while the RMSE on whole training data = 4.05.

1.6.7. Model Performance on Testing Data

To get the predicted sales from the fitted "lin_mod" based on youtube values in testing data, we use the predict function with the argument new_data = test_market to get the predicted sales based on the youtube values in the testing data.

```
lin_mod %>%
predict(new_data = test_market)
## # A tibble: 52 × 1
## .pred
## <dbl>
```

```
## 1 21.2
## 2 11.1
## 3 9.65
## 4 9.19
## 5 14.0
## 6 21.7
## 7 12.5
## 8 14.8
## 9 21.1
## 10 19.7
## # i 42 more rows
```

- The result is a tibble (data frame) with 52 rows (1st number) and 1 column (2nd number). The column name is called ".pred" which is the predicted sales for every row of the 52 rows of testing data.
- To this tibble, we add the actual sales by using the mutate function with the argument truth = test_market$sales to add the "truth" column that contains the actual sales values of the 52 rows of testing data.

```
lin_mod %>%
predict(new_data = test_market) %>%
mutate(truth = test_market$sales)
## # A tibble: 52 × 2
## .pred truth
## <dbl> <dbl>
## 1 21.2 26.5
## 2 11.1 12.5
## 3 9.65 11.2
## 4 9.19 8.64
## 5 14.0 11.6
## 6 21.7 19.1
## 7 12.5 12.6
## 8 14.8 14.3
## 9 21.1 25.8
```

```
## 10 19.7 19.9
## # i 42 more rows
```

- The result is a tibble (data frame) with 52 rows (1st number) and 2 columns (2nd number). The column names are ".pred" and "truth."
- For example, the first row has a predicted sales value of 21.2 but the actual sales value is 26.5, while in the 2nd row, the predicted sales value is 11.1 and the actual sales value is 12.5.

Finally, we use the rmse function, after the mutate function, with the arguments:

- truth = truth which is the column containing the actual sales values.
- estimate = .pred which is the column containing the predicted sales values.

```
lin_mod %>%
predict(new_data = test_market) %>%
mutate(truth = test_market$sales) %>%
rmse(truth = truth, estimate = .pred)
## # A tibble: 1 × 3
## .metric .estimator .estimate
## <chr> <chr> <dbl>
## 1 rmse standard 3.45
```

- The RMSE of linear model using youtube as a single predictor on testing data = 3.45.
- The RMSE on testing data (3.45) is nearer to that of cross-validated training data (4.03) than to the whole training data (4.05). This is the advantage of using cross-validation to obtain more robust estimate of model performance on future unseen data.

1.7. SIMPLE LINEAR REGRESSION MODELING OF HEART ATTACK DATA

We will create a simple linear model for predicting cholesterol using participant's gender (categorical predictor).

1.7.1. Splitting the Data into Training and Testing Data

We create an object called "split_heart" by using the initial_split function with the arguments:

- data = heartattack which is the data we want to split.

- strata = cholesterol to make a stratified splitting using the cholesterol outcome column.

To make the splitting reproducible, we use the set.seed function with any number before using the initial_split function.

```
set.seed(123)
split_heart <- initial_split(data = heartattack,
strata = cholesterol)
split_heart
## <Training/Testing/Total>
## <54/18/72>
```

- The training data has 54 rows and the testing data has 18 rows with a total of 72 which is the total rows of original data.

To get the actual training and testing data, we use the training and testing functions, respectively, on the split_heart object. The resulting data is called train_heart for the training data and test_heart for the testing data. Finally, we use the dim function to see the data dimensions.

```
train_heart<-training(split_heart)
test_heart<-testing(split_heart)
dim(train_heart)
## [1] 54 5
dim(test_heart)
## [1] 18 5
```

- The training data has 54 rows (1st number) and 5 columns (2nd number), while the testing data has 18 rows (1st number) and 5 columns (2nd number). The same 5 columns of heart attack data are present in the training or testing data.

1.7.2. Generating the Recipe

We create an object "rec2" by applying the recipe function on the train_heart data using the "%>%" operator. The recipe function has the argument cholesterol ~ gender meaning predicting the cholesterol column using the gender column only.

```
rec2 <- train_heart %>%
recipe(cholesterol ~ gender)
rec2
```

```
##
## ── Recipe ──────────────────────────────────────────────────
##
## ── Inputs
## Number of variables by role
## outcome: 1
## predictor: 1
```

- ·The recipe object "rec2" defines the variables by role with 1 variable as an outcome (cholesterol) and 1 variable as a predictor (gender).

1.7.3. Generate Different Resamples (Different Versions) of the Training Data

We split the train_heart data using the vfold_cv function with the arguments:

- v = 10 to split the data to 10 folds.
- repeats = 5 to repeat this process 5 times.
- strata = cholesterol to make stratified resampling using the cholesterol column.

The result is 50 different resamples of train_heart data contained in folds2 data frame.

- We also use the set.seed function before splitting to make the splitting reproducible.

```
set.seed(123)
folds2<-vfold_cv(train_heart, v = 10, repeats = 5, strata = cholesterol)
folds2
## # 10-fold cross-validation repeated 5 times using stratification
## # A tibble: 50 × 3
## splits id id2
## <list> <chr> <chr>
## 1 <split [48/6]> Repeat1 Fold01
## 2 <split [48/6]> Repeat1 Fold02
## 3 <split [48/6]> Repeat1 Fold03
## 4 <split [48/6]> Repeat1 Fold04
## 5 <split [48/6]> Repeat1 Fold05
```

```
## 6 <split [48/6]> Repeat1 Fold06
## 7 <split [48/6]> Repeat1 Fold07
## 8 <split [50/4]> Repeat1 Fold08
## 9 <split [50/4]> Repeat1 Fold09
## 10 <split [50/4]> Repeat1 Fold10
## # i 40 more rows
```

We see that:

- We have 50 different rows. Each row corresponds to 1 resample of train_heart data. Each resample has 1 analysis (training) data, with 48 or 50 rows and 1 assessment (testing) data with 6 or 4 rows.
- Each row has 2 id values. id for the repeat number from 1 to 5 and id2 for the resample number from 1 to 10 within that repeat.
- Each row has a total rows of 54 which is the number of rows in the original train_heart data. 48 + 6 = 50 + 4 = 54.

1.7.4. Define the Machine Learning (ML) Model

We use the same "lm_model" defined in Section 1.6.4.

1.7.5. Generate Workflow

We create the "wflow2" object by using the following functions:

- The workflow function to create a workflow.
- The add_recipe function with the argument "rec2" to add the above created recipe with no preprocessing steps.
- The add_model function with the argument lm_model to add the above created model.

```
wflow2 <- workflow() %>%
add_recipe(rec2) %>%
add_model(lm_model)
wflow2
## ══ Workflow ══════════════════════════════════════════════
═════════════════════════════════════
## Preprocessor: Recipe
## Model: linear_reg()
##
```

— Preprocessor ──

0 Recipe Steps

##

— Model ──

Linear Regression Model Specification (regression)

##

Computational engine: lm

- The "wflow2" object contains no preprocessing steps (0 Recipe Steps) and the linear regression model.

1.7.6. Fit the Model on Training Data

1.7.6.1. Fitting the Model on Whole Training Data

We create a lin_mod2 model by using the fit function with the arguments:

- which is the workflow containing no preprocessing steps and the linear regression model.
- train_heart which is the whole training data with 54 rows.

Then, we use the following functions:

- The tidy function to see the model results.
- The mutate function with the argument across(is.numeric,round, 5) to round all numeric columns to 5 decimal places.
- The add_significance function, from the rstatix package, with the arguments:

++ p.col = "p.value" to add p-value significance symbols based on the p.value column.

++ output.col = "significance" to create the significance column that will hold the significance symbols.

- The flextable function to convert the result to a table.
- The theme_box function to apply cell boundaries to all cells in the table.
- The set_caption function with the caption = "…" argument to add a table caption or title.

lin_mod2<-**fit**(wflow2, train_heart)

tidy(lin_mod2) **%>% mutate**(**across**(is.numeric,round, 5)) **%>%**

add_significance(p.col = "p.value", output.col = "significance") **%>%**

flextable(cwidth = 1) **%>% theme_box**() **%>%**

set_caption(caption = "Linear model results of using gender for predicting cholesterol in heart attack training data")

Linear model results of using gender for predicting cholesterol in heart attack training data:

term	**estimate**	**std.error**	**statistic**	**p.value**	**signifi-cance**
(Intercept)	5.25211	0.08542	61.48458	0.00000	****
genderfemale	–0.27173	0.12080	–2.24935	0.02875	*

- The linear regression equation will be:

cholesterol = 5.25 – 0.272 × genderfemale.

- The female gender is a significant predictor of cholesterol with a p.value < 0.05 and an estimate of –0.272.
- This means that females have lower cholesterol level than males (reference category) by 0.272 unit on the average.

The linear model can be visualized as a line between the gender on the x-axis and cholesterol on the y-axis with the following functions applied on train_heart data:

- The mutate function with the argument gender = as.numeric(gender=="female") so if gender value is "female," it will be converted to 1, otherwise, the gender will be converted to 0.
- The ggplot function with the arguments aes(x = gender, y = cholesterol) to plot the numeric gender values on the x-axis and the cholesterol values on the y-axis.
- The geom_point function to plot a scatter plot.
- The geom_smooth function with the argument method = "lm" to add the best fitting linear regression model line to the plot.
- The labs function with title = "…" argument to add a plot title.
- The theme_classic function explained before.

train_heart **%>% mutate**(gender = **as.numeric**(gender=="female")) **%>%**

ggplot(**aes**(x = gender, y = cholesterol))+

geom_point()+ **geom_smooth**(method = "lm")+

labs(title = "Scatter plot of gender values coded as 1 for females and 0 for males**n** vs. cholesterol with linear regression line")+

theme_classic()

`geom_smooth()` using formula = 'y ~ x'

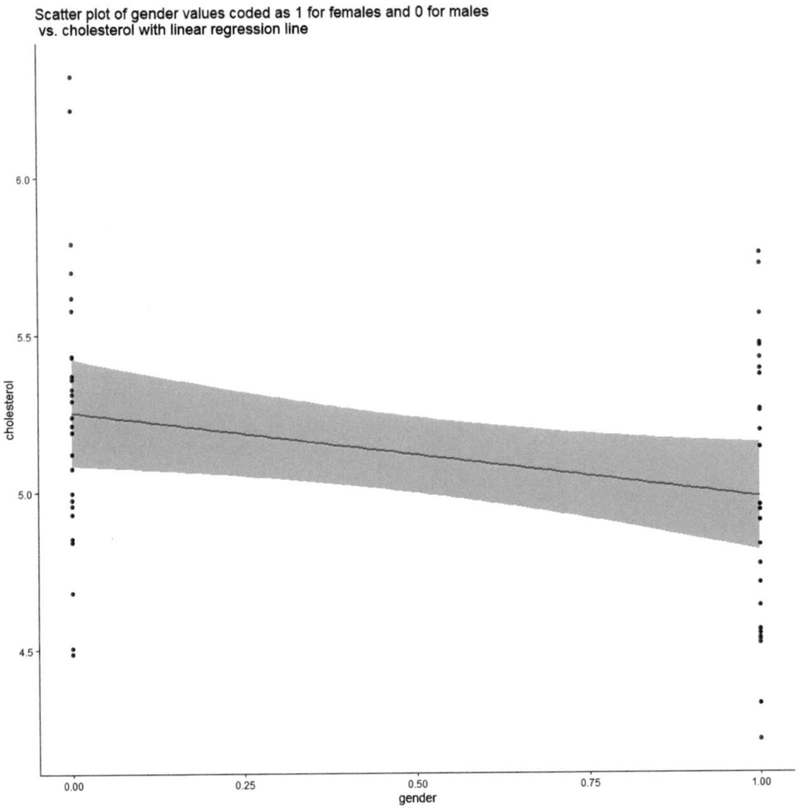

- The blue linear regression line, described by the equation cholesterol = 5.25 – 0.272 × genderfemale, is plotted with 95% confidence interval as a grey background.
- This means that this regression line predicts only 1 cholesterol value for each gender.
- For all females, the predicted cholesterol value = 5.25–0.272 = 4.98.
- For all males, the predicted cholesterol value = 5.25–0.272X0 = 5.25.

- These 2 values are connected by the regression line plotted above. The black dots denote the actual cholesterol level of females and males in the data.

1.7.6.2. Model Performance on Whole Training Data

To get the predicted cholesterol from the fitted "lin_mod2," we use the predict function with the argument new_data = train_heart to get the predicted cholesterol value based on the gender values in the training data.

```
lin_mod2 %>% predict(new_data = train_heart)
## # A tibble: 54 × 1
## .pred
## <dbl>
## 1 5.25
## 2 5.25
## 3 5.25
## 4 5.25
## 5 5.25
## 6 4.98
## 7 4.98
## 8 4.98
## 9 4.98
## 10 4.98
## # i 44 more rows
```

- The result is a tibble (data frame) with 54 rows (1st number) and 1 column (2nd number). The column name is called ".pred" which is the predicted cholesterol for every row of the 54 rows of training data.
- As deduced above, there are only 2 predicted cholesterol values: 5.25 for males and 4.98 for females.
- To this tibble, we add the actual cholesterol by using the mutate function with the argument truth = train_heart$cholesterol to add the "truth" column that contains the actual cholesterol values of the 54 rows of training data.

```
lin_mod2 %>% predict(new_data = train_heart) %>%
mutate(truth = train_heart$cholesterol)
```

```
## # A tibble: 54 × 2
## .pred truth
## <dbl> <dbl>
## 1 5.25 4.68
## 2 5.25 4.50
## 3 5.25 4.85
## 4 5.25 4.84
## 5 5.25 4.49
## 6 4.98 4.53
## 7 4.98 4.91
## 8 4.98 4.71
## 9 4.98 4.21
## 10 4.98 4.53
## # i 44 more rows
```

- The result is a tibble (data frame) with 54 rows (1st number) and 2 columns (2nd number). The column names are ".pred" and "truth."
- For example, the 1st to 5th rows have a predicted cholesterol value of 5.25 but the actual cholesterol values are 4.68, 4.50, 4.85, 4.84, and 4.49, respectively.
- Finally, we use the rmse function, after the mutate function, with the arguments:
- truth = truth which is the column containing the actual cholesterol values.
- estimate = .pred which is the column containing the predicted cholesterol values.

```
lin_mod2 %>%
predict(new_data = train_heart) %>%
mutate(truth = train_heart$cholesterol) %>%
rmse(truth = truth, estimate = .pred)
## # A tibble: 1 × 3
## .metric .estimator .estimate
## <chr> <chr> <dbl>
## 1 rmse standard 0.436
```

- The RMSE of linear model using gender as a single predictor on whole training data = 0.436.

1.7.6.3. Fitting the Model on 50 Resamples of Training Data

We use the fit_resamples function with the arguments:

- wflow2 which is the workflow containing no preprocessing steps and the linear regression model.
- folds2 which are the 50 resamples of training data created above.
- metrics = metrics_set(rmse) to get the RMSE performance metric for each linear model on each resample.
- control = control_resamples(save_pred = TRUE) to get the predicted sales values for every assessment (testing) data with 6 or 4 rows within each resample.

```
lin_res2<-fit_resamples(wflow2, folds2, metrics = metric_set(rmse),
control = control_resamples(save_pred = TRUE))
lin_res2
## # Resampling results
## # 10-fold cross-validation repeated 5 times using stratification
## # A tibble: 50 × 6
## splits id id2 .metrics .notes .predictions
## <list> <chr> <chr> <list> <list> <list>
## 1 <split [48/6]> Repeat1 Fold01 <tibble [1 × 4]> <tibble [0 × 3]> <tibble>
## 2 <split [48/6]> Repeat1 Fold02 <tibble [1 × 4]> <tibble [0 × 3]> <tibble>
## 3 <split [48/6]> Repeat1 Fold03 <tibble [1 × 4]> <tibble [0 × 3]> <tibble>
## 4 <split [48/6]> Repeat1 Fold04 <tibble [1 × 4]> <tibble [0 × 3]> <tibble>
## 5 <split [48/6]> Repeat1 Fold05 <tibble [1 × 4]> <tibble [0 × 3]> <tibble>
## 6 <split [48/6]> Repeat1 Fold06 <tibble [1 × 4]> <tibble [0 × 3]> <tibble>
## 7 <split [48/6]> Repeat1 Fold07 <tibble [1 × 4]> <tibble [0 × 3]> <tibble>
## 8 <split [50/4]> Repeat1 Fold08 <tibble [1 × 4]> <tibble [0 × 3]> <tibble>
## 9 <split [50/4]> Repeat1 Fold09 <tibble [1 × 4]> <tibble [0 × 3]> <tibble>
## 10 <split [50/4]> Repeat1 Fold10 <tibble [1 × 4]> <tibble [0 × 3]> <tibble>
## # i 40 more rows
```

The resulting object "lin_res2" contains 50 rows for the results of applying this linear model on the 50 resamples of training data. It contains 6 columns:

- The splits column is a list of each combination of analysis and assessment data. The sum is 54, which are total rows of training data.
- The id column is an id column for the repeat number from 1 to 5.
- The id2 column is an id column for the fold number from 1 to 10 so we have 50 resamples because 5 × 10 = 50.
- The .metrics column is a list of performance metrics (RMSE) for applying the linear model to the corresponding assessment data (6 or 4 rows). Each performance metric is saved in 1 row and 4 columns [1 × 4] tibble or data frame. These will be extracted in the next step. The 1 row is for the RMSE in each resample.
- The .notes column is a list of notes or warnings when applying the linear model to each analysis data (48 or 50 rows). Each note is saved in 0 rows and 3 columns [0 × 3] tibble or data frame meaning that there are no notes when applying this model to each analysis data within each resample.
- The .predictions column is a list of predicted cholesterol for each testing data within each resample.

By using the unnest function with the .predictions argument on the lin_res2 object, we get the predicted and actual cholesterol for each row within each resample.

```
lin_res2 %>% unnest(.predictions)
## # A tibble: 270 × 9
## splits id id2 .metrics .notes .pred .row cholesterol .config
## <list> <chr> <chr> <list> <list> <dbl> <int> <dbl> <chr>
## 1 <split [48/6]> Repea… Fold… <tibble> <tibble> 4.97 7 4.91 Prepro…
## 2 <split [48/6]> Repea… Fold… <tibble> <tibble> 5.25 26 4.93 Prepro…
## 3 <split [48/6]> Repea… Fold… <tibble> <tibble> 5.25 28 5.12 Prepro…
## 4 <split [48/6]> Repea… Fold… <tibble> <tibble> 4.97 34 5.19 Prepro…
## 5 <split [48/6]> Repea… Fold… <tibble> <tibble> 5.25 43 5.58 Prepro…
## 6 <split [48/6]> Repea… Fold… <tibble> <tibble> 5.25 45 5.37 Prepro…
## 7 <split [48/6]> Repea… Fold… <tibble> <tibble> 5.24 30 5.00 Prepro…
## 8 <split [48/6]> Repea… Fold… <tibble> <tibble> 4.94 31 5.14 Prepro…
## 9 <split [48/6]> Repea… Fold… <tibble> <tibble> 4.94 32 4.95 Prepro…
## 10 <split [48/6]> Repea… Fold… <tibble> <tibble> 5.24 37 5.36 Prepro…
## # i 260 more rows
```

- The result is a tibble with 270 rows and 9 columns. Each row contains the actual (cholesterol) and predicted cholesterol (.pred) for each row within each resample.

By using the count function after the unnest function with the id,id2 arguments, we get the number of testing rows within each resample.

lin_res2 **%>% unnest**(.predictions) **%>% count**(id, id2) **%>%**

flextable(cwidth = 1) **%>% theme_box**() **%>%**

set_caption(caption = "The number of testing rows within 50 resamples of heart attack training data")

The number of testing rows within 50 resamples of heart attack training data:

id	**id2**	**n**
Repeat1	Fold01	6
Repeat1	Fold02	6
Repeat1	Fold03	6
Repeat1	Fold04	6
Repeat1	Fold05	6
Repeat1	Fold06	6
Repeat1	Fold07	6
Repeat1	Fold08	4
Repeat1	Fold09	4
Repeat1	Fold10	4
Repeat2	Fold01	6
Repeat2	Fold02	6
Repeat2	Fold03	6
Repeat2	Fold04	6
Repeat2	Fold05	6
Repeat2	Fold06	6
Repeat2	Fold07	6
Repeat2	Fold08	4
Repeat2	Fold09	4
Repeat2	Fold10	4
Repeat3	Fold01	6
Repeat3	Fold02	6
Repeat3	Fold03	6

Repeat3	Fold04	6
Repeat3	Fold05	6
Repeat3	Fold06	6
Repeat3	Fold07	6
Repeat3	Fold08	4
Repeat3	Fold09	4
Repeat3	Fold10	4
Repeat4	Fold01	6
Repeat4	Fold02	6
Repeat4	Fold03	6
Repeat4	Fold04	6
Repeat4	Fold05	6
Repeat4	Fold06	6
Repeat4	Fold07	6
Repeat4	Fold08	4
Repeat4	Fold09	4
Repeat4	Fold10	4
Repeat5	Fold01	6
Repeat5	Fold02	6
Repeat5	Fold03	6
Repeat5	Fold04	6
Repeat5	Fold05	6
Repeat5	Fold06	6
Repeat5	Fold07	6
Repeat5	Fold08	4
Repeat5	Fold09	4
Repeat5	Fold10	4

- The result is 50 rows because we have 50 resamples. The different resamples may have 6 or 4 testing rows. The sum of n column = 270 which is the result of unnest function above.

We can plot the actual cholesterol on the x-axis and the predicted cholesterol on the y-axis, after using the unnest function, by using the following functions:

- The ggplot function with the arguments, aes(x = cholesterol, y = .pred, color = id), to plot actual cholesterol on the x-axis, the predicted cholesterol on the y-axis, and a distinct color for each id or repeat.

- The geom_abline function to plot a diagonal perfect line that corresponds to actual cholesterol equal predicted cholesterol.
- The geom_point function to plot a scatter plot.
- facet_wrap function with the argument vars(id,id2) to plot a separate plot for each unique combination of id and id2 value.
- labs function with the arguments, title to add a plot title, *x* to add *x*-axis title, y to add y-axis title. The plot title has "\n" to make it into 2 lines.
- The theme_classic function to remove the grey background and the white background lines from the default ggplot.

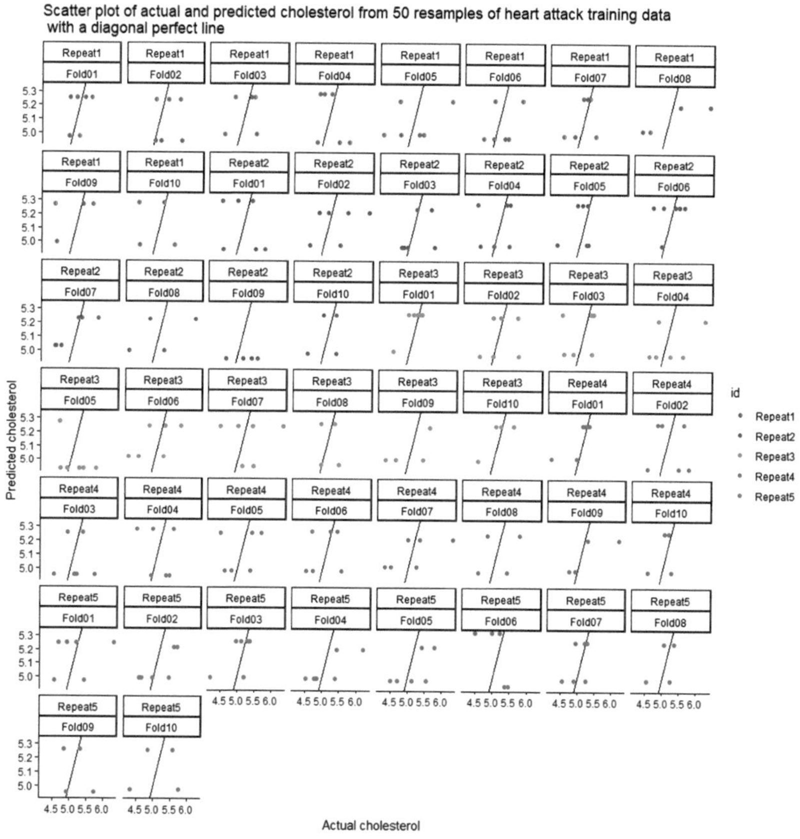

lin_res2 **%>%** **unnest**(.predictions) **%>%**

ggplot(**aes**(x = cholesterol, y = .pred, color = id)) +

geom_abline() +

geom_point() +

facet_wrap(**vars**(id,id2))+

labs(title = "Scatter plot of actual and predicted cholesterol from 50 resamples of heart attack training data **n** with a diagonal perfect line",

x = "Actual cholesterol", y = "Predicted cholesterol")+

theme_classic()

- We have 50 plots for 50 resamples. Each plot may contain 4 or 6 points according to the number of rows in each testing data within each resample.
- The points have distinct colors according to the repeat number from 1 to 5. Each repeat has 10 plots for 10 different resamples within each repeat.
- The predicted cholesterol values within each plot on the y-axis are 2 values only corresponding to males and females.

1.7.6.4. Model Performance on 50 Resamples of Training Data

To get the performance metrics (RMSE) on the 50 resamples of training data, we use the following functions on the lin_res2 object:

- The collect_metrics function with the argument summarize = FALSE to get the RMSE for each resample.
- The arrange function with .estimate argument to arrange by RMSE value in ascending order.
- The flextable, theme_box, and set_caption functions are described previously.

lin_res2 **%>% collect_metrics**(summarize = FALSE) **%>%**

arrange(.estimate) **%>%**

flextable(cwidth = 1) **%>% theme_box**() **%>%**

set_caption(caption = "The RMSE of 50 resamples of heart attack training data when using gender as a predictor of cholesterol levels")

The RMSE of 50 resamples of heart attack training data when using gender as a predictor of cholesterol levels:

id	id2	.metric	.estimator	.estimate	.config
Repeat1	Fold01	rmse	standard	0.2208376	Preprocessor1_ Model1

Repeat3	Fold01	rmse	standard	0.2379474	Preprocessor1_Model1
Repeat5	Fold07	rmse	standard	0.2493365	Preprocessor1_Model1
Repeat4	Fold10	rmse	standard	0.2722364	Preprocessor1_Model1
Repeat5	Fold08	rmse	standard	0.2829956	Preprocessor1_Model1
Repeat1	Fold07	rmse	standard	0.2909134	Preprocessor1_Model1
Repeat3	Fold10	rmse	standard	0.2986413	Preprocessor1_Model1
Repeat3	Fold08	rmse	standard	0.3042824	Preprocessor1_Model1
Repeat2	Fold06	rmse	standard	0.3060001	Preprocessor1_Model1
Repeat2	Fold10	rmse	standard	0.3300342	Preprocessor1_Model1
Repeat4	Fold01	rmse	standard	0.3352007	Preprocessor1_Model1
Repeat2	Fold05	rmse	standard	0.3440419	Preprocessor1_Model1
Repeat1	Fold06	rmse	standard	0.3480303	Preprocessor1_Model1
Repeat2	Fold03	rmse	standard	0.3587948	Preprocessor1_Model1
Repeat5	Fold03	rmse	standard	0.3605000	Preprocessor1_Model1
Repeat1	Fold03	rmse	standard	0.3710653	Preprocessor1_Model1
Repeat2	Fold07	rmse	standard	0.3874167	Preprocessor1_Model1
Repeat5	Fold02	rmse	standard	0.3947646	Preprocessor1_Model1
Repeat4	Fold03	rmse	standard	0.4036207	Preprocessor1_Model1
Repeat1	Fold02	rmse	standard	0.4049303	Preprocessor1_Model1

Repeat3	Fold03	rmse	standard	0.4059521	Preprocessor1_ Model1
Repeat4	Fold06	rmse	standard	0.4077203	Preprocessor1_ Model1
Repeat5	Fold05	rmse	standard	0.4115717	Preprocessor1_ Model1
Repeat2	Fold04	rmse	standard	0.4123129	Preprocessor1_ Model1
Repeat3	Fold02	rmse	standard	0.4131810	Preprocessor1_ Model1
Repeat2	Fold09	rmse	standard	0.4199758	Preprocessor1_ Model1
Repeat4	Fold05	rmse	standard	0.4285834	Preprocessor1_ Model1
Repeat5	Fold09	rmse	standard	0.4370714	Preprocessor1_ Model1
Repeat1	Fold04	rmse	standard	0.4420556	Preprocessor1_ Model1
Repeat4	Fold08	rmse	standard	0.4546721	Preprocessor1_ Model1
Repeat4	Fold04	rmse	standard	0.4590951	Preprocessor1_ Model1
Repeat1	Fold09	rmse	standard	0.4750994	Preprocessor1_ Model1
Repeat3	Fold09	rmse	standard	0.4793873	Preprocessor1_ Model1
Repeat3	Fold05	rmse	standard	0.4826510	Preprocessor1_ Model1
Repeat3	Fold06	rmse	standard	0.4873499	Preprocessor1_ Model1
Repeat4	Fold02	rmse	standard	0.4967602	Preprocessor1_ Model1
Repeat5	Fold04	rmse	standard	0.5038713	Preprocessor1_ Model1
Repeat4	Fold09	rmse	standard	0.5174444	Preprocessor1_ Model1
Repeat3	Fold04	rmse	standard	0.5374092	Preprocessor1_ Model1
Repeat1	Fold10	rmse	standard	0.5437015	Preprocessor1_ Model1

Repeat2	Fold01	rmse	standard	0.5551921	Preprocessor1_Model1
Repeat5	Fold01	rmse	standard	0.5712053	Preprocessor1_Model1
Repeat5	Fold06	rmse	standard	0.5721828	Preprocessor1_Model1
Repeat5	Fold10	rmse	standard	0.5725193	Preprocessor1_Model1
Repeat2	Fold02	rmse	standard	0.5820719	Preprocessor1_Model1
Repeat4	Fold07	rmse	standard	0.5891487	Preprocessor1_Model1
Repeat3	Fold07	rmse	standard	0.5944267	Preprocessor1_Model1
Repeat1	Fold05	rmse	standard	0.6037996	Preprocessor1_Model1
Repeat2	Fold08	rmse	standard	0.6717551	Preprocessor1_Model1
Repeat1	Fold08	rmse	standard	0.7144109	Preprocessor1_Model1

- The result is 50 rows with 1 RMSE value for each resample.
- The lowest RMSE (0.22) was achieved in repeat 1 and fold 1, while the highest RMSE (0.714) was achieved in repeat 1 and fold 8.

If we used the collect_metrics function with the argument summarize = TRUE, we will get the mean RMSE value across the 50 resamples of the training data.

```
lin_res2 %>% collect_metrics(summarize = TRUE)
## # A tibble: 1 × 6
## .metric .estimator mean n std_err .config
## <chr> <chr> <dbl> <int> <dbl> <chr>
## 1 rmse standard 0.435 50 0.0163 Preprocessor1_Model1
```

- The mean RMSE of linear model using gender as a single predictor on 50 resamples of training data (n = 50) = 0.435, while the performance on whole training data = 0.436.

1.7.7. Model Performance on Testing Data

To get the predicted cholesterol from the fitted "lin_mod2" based on gender values in testing data, we use the predict function with the argument new_data

= test_heart to get the predicted cholesterol based on the gender values in the testing data.

```
lin_mod2 %>%
predict(new_data = test_heart)
## # A tibble: 18 × 1
## .pred
## <dbl>
## 1 5.25
## 2 5.25
## 3 5.25
## 4 5.25
## 5 5.25
## 6 5.25
## 7 5.25
## 8 5.25
## 9 5.25
## 10 4.98
## 11 4.98
## 12 4.98
## 13 4.98
## 14 4.98
## 15 4.98
## 16 4.98
## 17 4.98
## 18 4.98
```

- The result is a tibble (data frame) with 18 rows (1st number) and 1 column (2nd number). The column name is called ".pred" which is the predicted cholesterol for every row of the 18 rows of testing data.
- To this tibble, we add the actual cholesterol by using the mutate function with the argument truth = test_heart$cholesterol to add the "truth" column that contains the actual cholesterol values of the 18 rows of testing data.

```
lin_mod2 %>%
predict(new_data = test_heart) %>%
```

```
mutate(truth = test_heart$cholesterol)
## # A tibble: 18 × 2
## .pred truth
## <dbl> <dbl>
## 1 5.25 4.83
## 2 5.25 4.96
## 3 5.25 4.51
## 4 5.25 4.58
## 5 5.25 6.61
## 6 5.25 6.12
## 7 5.25 6.02
## 8 5.25 4.92
## 9 5.25 5.25
## 10 4.98 5.16
## 11 4.98 4.63
## 12 4.98 4.24
## 13 4.98 5.38
## 14 4.98 5.37
## 15 4.98 5.34
## 16 4.98 4.83
## 17 4.98 4.95
## 18 4.98 5.31
```

- The result is a tibble (data frame) with 18 rows (1st number) and 2 columns (2nd number). The column names are ".pred" and "truth."
- The predicted values are 5.25 or 4.98 for the reasons explained above.

Finally, we use the rmse function, after the mutate function, with the arguments:

- truth = truth which is the column containing the actual cholesterol values.
- estimate = .pred which is the column containing the predicted cholesterol values.

```
lin_mod2 %>%
```

```
predict(new_data = test_heart) %>%
mutate(truth = test_heart$cholesterol) %>%
rmse(truth = truth, estimate = .pred)
## # A tibble: 1 × 3
## .metric .estimator .estimate
## <chr> <chr> <dbl>
## 1 rmse standard 0.570
```

- The RMSE of linear model using gender as a single predictor on testing data = 0.57.

1.8. MULTIPLE LINEAR REGRESSION WITH MANY PREDICTORS

Multiple linear regression models are models for relating any numerical outcome to several predictors by a linear equation.

The linear equation of the multiple regression with three predictors is written as:

$$y = \beta_o + \beta_1 x_1 + \beta_2 x_2 + \beta_3 x_3$$

where; y is the mean of numerical outcome; x_1, x_2, x_3 are the predictors of interest; β_0 is the model intercept; β_1, β_2, β_3 are the effect of the corresponding predictor on the outcome when the value of the other 2 predictors is constant.

1.8.1. Advantages of Multiple Regression Over Simple Regression

- Improves the prediction of an outcome by taking multiple predictors in one model.
- Allows for the adjustment of important confounders or predictors. Confounders are variables that are related to both the predictor and the outcome of interest. Ignoring the effect of confounders may lead to over-estimate or under-estimate the association between the predictor and the outcome.

For example, in the above simple regression, we are considering the effect of 1 predictor (youtube advertising) on the sales, but of course, this outcome depends on other factors like the facebook and newspaper advertising.

1.9. MULTIPLE LINEAR REGRESSION OF MARKETING DATA

1.9.1. Splitting the Data into Training and Testing Data

We will use the same train_market and test_market data generated above.

1.9.2. Generating the Recipe

We create an object "rec3" by applying the recipe function on the train_market data using the "%>%" operator. The recipe function has the argument sales ~. meaning predicting the sales outcome column using all other columns in the data (youtube, facebook, and newspaper).

```
rec3 <- train_market %>%
recipe(sales ~ .)
rec3
##
## ── Recipe ──────────────────────────────────────────────────────────────
##
## ── Inputs
## Number of variables by role
## outcome: 1
## predictor: 3
```

- The recipe object "rec3" defines the variables by role with 1 variable as an outcome (sales) and 3 variables as a predictors (YouTube, Facebook, and newspaper).

1.9.3. Generate Different Resamples of the Training Data

We will use the same folds data frame generated above with 50 resamples of the training data stratified by the sales column.

1.9.4. Define the Machine Learning (ML) Model

We will use the same lm_model generated above.

1.9.5. Generate Workflow

We create the "wflow3" object by using the following functions:

- The workflow function to create a workflow.
- The add_recipe function with the argument "rec3" to add the above created recipe with three predictors for predicting the sales column.
- The add_model function with the argument lm_model to add the above created model.

```
wflow3 <- workflow() %>%
add_recipe(rec3) %>%
add_model(lm_model)
wflow3
## == Workflow ==========================================================
## Preprocessor: Recipe
## Model: linear_reg()
##
## -- Preprocessor ------------------------------------------------------
## 0 Recipe Steps
##
## -- Model -------------------------------------------------------------
## Linear Regression Model Specification (regression)
##
## Computational engine: lm
```

- The "wflow3" object contains no preprocessing steps (0 Recipe Steps) and the linear regression model.

1.9.6. Fit the Model on Training Data

As before, we can fit the linear model on whole training data "train_market" or the 50 resamples of the training data in the "folds" data frame.

1.9.6.1. Fitting the Model on the Whole Training Data

We create a lin_mod3 model by using the fit function with the arguments:

- wflow3 which is the workflow containing no preprocessing steps and the linear regression model.
- train_market which is the whole training data with 148 rows.

Then, we use the following functions:

- The tidy function to see the model results.
- The mutate function with the argument across(is.numeric,round, 5) to round all numeric columns to 5 decimal places.
- The add_significance function with the arguments:

  ++ p.col = "p.value" to add p-value significance symbols based on the p.value column.

  ++ output.col = "significance" to create the significance column that will hold the significance symbols.
- The flextable function to convert the result to a table.
- The theme_box function to apply cell boundaries to all cells in the table.
- The set_caption function with the caption = "..." argument to add a table caption or title.

```
lin_mod3<-fit(wflow3, train_market)
tidy(lin_mod3) %>% mutate(across(is.numeric,round, 5)) %>%
add_significance(p.col = "p.value", output.col = "significance") %>%
flextable(cwidth = 1) %>% theme_box() %>%
set_caption(caption = "Linear model results of using youtube, facebook, and newspaper advertising for predicting sales in marketing training data")
```

Linear model results of using youtube, facebook, and newspaper advertising for predicting sales in marketing training data:

term	estimate	std.error	statistic	p.value	significance
(Intercept)	3.31844	0.45555	7.28442	0.00000	****
youtube	0.04489	0.00163	27.46871	0.00000	****
facebook	0.19029	0.01026	18.55362	0.00000	****
newspaper	0.00415	0.00745	0.55723	0.57824	ns

- The linear regression equation will be:

  sales = 3.318 + 0.045 × youtube + 0.19 × facebook + 0.004 × newspaper.
- The youtube advertising is a significant predictor of sales with a p.value < 0.05 and an estimate of 0.045.

- This means that each 1 unit increase in youtube advertising budget (1000 USD) is associated with a 0.045 unit increase in sales on the average (0.045 × 1000 = 45 USD) when we have the same facebook and newspaper advertising budgets.
- The facebook advertising is a significant predictor of sales with a p.value < 0.05 and an estimate of 0.19.
- This means that each 1 unit increase in facebook advertising budget (1000 USD) is associated with a 0.19 unit increase in sales on the average (0.19 × 1000 = 190 USD) when we have the same youtube and newspaper advertising budgets.
- This also means that Facebook advertising has a greater effect on sales than YouTube advertising.
- The newspaper advertising is a non-significant predictor of sales with a p.value > 0.05 and an estimate of 0.004.
- This means that the increase in the newspaper advertising budget has no effect on sales and the observed effect of 0.004 is due to sampling error.

1.9.6.2. Model Performance on the Whole Training Data

We use the same functions above on the lin_mod3 object.

```
lin_mod3 %>%
predict(new_data = train_market) %>%
mutate(truth = train_market$sales) %>%
rmse(truth = truth, estimate = .pred)
## # A tibble: 1 × 3
## .metric .estimator .estimate
## <chr> <chr> <dbl>
## 1 rmse standard 2.06
```

- The RMSE of linear model using youtube, facebook, and newspaper as predictors on whole training data = 2.06.
- The RMSE of multiple model (2.06) is much lower than that of simple model (4.05) which illustrates the advantages of multiple models over simple models.

1.9.6.3. Fitting the Model on 50 Resamples of Training Data

We create an object "lin_res3" by using the fit_resamples function with the arguments:

- wflow3 which is the workflow containing the recipe with three predictors and the linear regression model.
- folds which are the 50 resamples of training data created above.
- metrics = metrics_set(rmse) to get the RMSE performance metric for each linear model on each resample.
- control = control_resamples(save_pred = TRUE) to get the predicted sales values for every assessment (testing) data within each resample.

```
lin_res3<-fit_resamples(wflow3, folds, metrics = metric_set(rmse),
control = control_resamples(save_pred = TRUE))
lin_res3
## # Resampling results
## # 10-fold cross-validation repeated 5 times using stratification
## # A tibble: 50 × 6
## splits id id2 .metrics .notes .predictions
## <list> <chr> <chr> <list> <list> <list>
## 1 <split [132/16]> Repeat1 Fold01 <tibble [1 × 4]> <tibble> <tibble [16 ×
4]>
## 2 <split [132/16]> Repeat1 Fold02 <tibble [1 × 4]> <tibble> <tibble [16 ×
4]>
## 3 <split [132/16]> Repeat1 Fold03 <tibble [1 × 4]> <tibble> <tibble [16 ×
4]>
## 4 <split [132/16]> Repeat1 Fold04 <tibble [1 × 4]> <tibble> <tibble [16 ×
4]>
## 5 <split [132/16]> Repeat1 Fold05 <tibble [1 × 4]> <tibble> <tibble [16 ×
4]>
## 6 <split [132/16]> Repeat1 Fold06 <tibble [1 × 4]> <tibble> <tibble [16 ×
4]>
## 7 <split [134/14]> Repeat1 Fold07 <tibble [1 × 4]> <tibble> <tibble [14 ×
4]>
## 8 <split [135/13]> Repeat1 Fold08 <tibble [1 × 4]> <tibble> <tibble [13 ×
4]>
## 9 <split [135/13]> Repeat1 Fold09 <tibble [1 × 4]> <tibble> <tibble [13 ×
4]>
## 10 <split [136/12]> Repeat1 Fold10 <tibble [1 × 4]> <tibble> <tibble [12 ×
4]>
```

```
## # i 40 more rows
```

The resulting object "lin_res3" contains the results of applying this linear model on the 50 resamples of training data. It contains 6 columns that were described before.

By using the unnest function with the .predictions argument on the lin_res3 object, we get the predicted and actual sales for each row within each resample.

```
lin_res3 %>% unnest(.predictions)
## # A tibble: 740 × 9
## splits id id2 .metrics .notes .pred .row sales .config
## <list> <chr> <chr> <list> <list> <dbl> <int> <dbl> <chr>
## 1 <split [132/16]> Repeat1 Fold01 <tibble> <tibble> 4.31 1 5.76 Preproce…
## 2 <split [132/16]> Repeat1 Fold01 <tibble> <tibble> 9.54 22 8.4 Preproce…
## 3 <split [132/16]> Repeat1 Fold01 <tibble> <tibble> 12.8 23 7.92 Preproce…
## 4 <split [132/16]> Repeat1 Fold01 <tibble> <tibble> 7.73 24 10.6 Preproce…
## 5 <split [132/16]> Repeat1 Fold01 <tibble> <tibble> 16.5 46 15.5 Preproce…
## 6 <split [132/16]> Repeat1 Fold01 <tibble> <tibble> 12.7 49 14.9 Preproce…
## 7 <split [132/16]> Repeat1 Fold01 <tibble> <tibble> 12.2 53 13.6 Preproce…
## 8 <split [132/16]> Repeat1 Fold01 <tibble> <tibble> 16.0 59 13.9 Preproce…
## 9 <split [132/16]> Repeat1 Fold01 <tibble> <tibble> 17.7 81 18 Preproce…
## 10 <split [132/16]> Repeat1 Fold01 <tibble> <tibble> 18.8 91 19.2
Preproce…
## # i 730 more rows
```

- The result is a tibble with 740 rows and 9 columns. Each row contains the actual (sales) and predicted sales (.pred) for each row within each resample.

  We can plot the actual sales on the x-axis and the predicted sales on the y-axis, after using the unnest function, by using the following functions:

- The ggplot function with the arguments, aes(x = sales, y = .pred, color = id), to plot actual sales on the x-axis, the predicted sales on the y-axis, and a distinct color for each id or repeat.
- The geom_abline function to plot a diagonal perfect line that corresponds to actual sales equal predicted sales.
- The geom_point function to plot a scatter plot.

- The facet_wrap function with the argument vars(id,id2) to plot a separate plot for each unique combination of id and id2 value.
- The labs function with the arguments, title to add a plot title, *x* to add *x*-axis title, y to add y-axis title. The plot title has "\n" to make it into 2 lines.
- The theme_classic function to remove the grey background and the white background lines from the default ggplot.

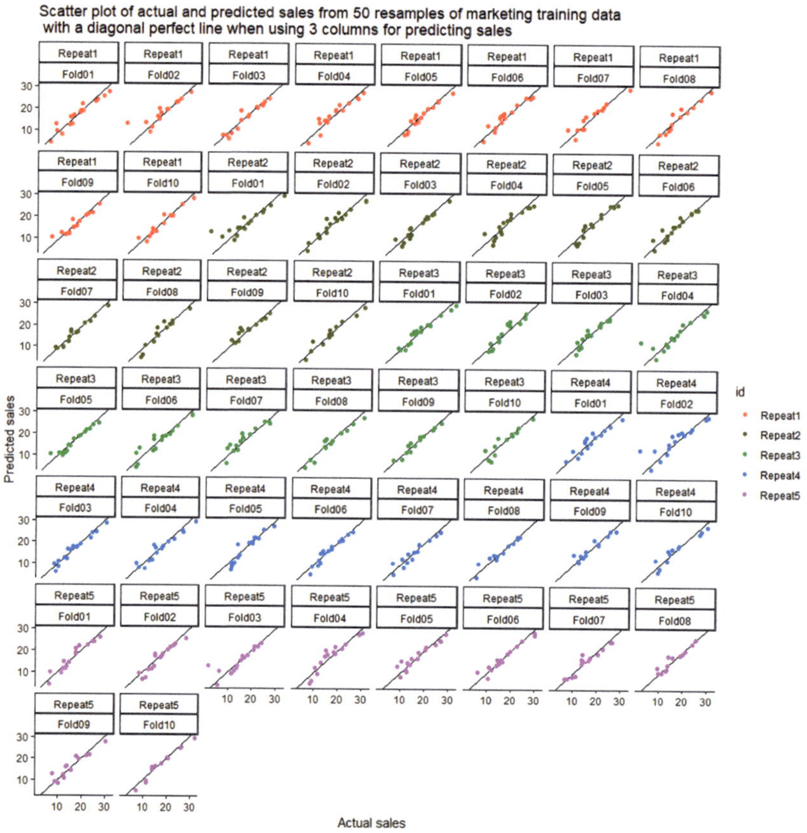


```
lin_res3 %>% unnest(.predictions) %>%
ggplot(aes(x = sales, y = .pred, color = id)) +
geom_abline() +
geom_point() +
facet_wrap(vars(id,id2))+
```

labs(title = "Scatter plot of actual and predicted sales from 50 resamples of marketing training data **\n** with a diagonal perfect line when using 3 columns for predicting sales,"

x = "Actual sales", y = "Predicted sales")+

theme_classic()

- We have 50 plots for 50 resamples.
- A remarkable note is that the points are nearer to the diagonal line than that of the simple model and so a lower RMSE or error as expected with the multiple model.

1.9.6.4. Model Performance on 50 Resamples of Training Data

To get the performance metrics (RMSE) on the 50 resamples of training data, we use the same above functions on the lin_res3 object.

lin_res3 **%>% collect_metrics**(summarize = FALSE) **%>%**

arrange(.estimate) **%>%**

flextable() **%>% theme_box**() **%>%**

set_caption(caption = "The RMSE of 50 resamples of marketing training data when using three columns as predictors of sales")

The RMSE of 50 resamples of marketing training data when using three columns as predictors of sales:

id	**id2**	**.metric**	**.estimator**	**.estimate**	**.config**
Repeat3	Fold09	rmse	standard	1.350809	Preprocessor1_ Model1
Repeat3	Fold05	rmse	standard	1.400088	Preprocessor1_ Model1
Repeat4	Fold06	rmse	standard	1.441738	Preprocessor1_ Model1
Repeat4	Fold03	rmse	standard	1.451275	Preprocessor1_ Model1
Repeat2	Fold07	rmse	standard	1.455446	Preprocessor1_ Model1
Repeat4	Fold08	rmse	standard	1.561059	Preprocessor1_ Model1
Repeat5	Fold10	rmse	standard	1.610608	Preprocessor1_ Model1

Repeat3	Fold03	rmse	standard	1.638860	Preprocessor1_ Model1
Repeat1	Fold05	rmse	standard	1.676374	Preprocessor1_ Model1
Repeat1	Fold10	rmse	standard	1.687139	Preprocessor1_ Model1
Repeat5	Fold08	rmse	standard	1.699893	Preprocessor1_ Model1
Repeat5	Fold06	rmse	standard	1.702985	Preprocessor1_ Model1
Repeat2	Fold03	rmse	standard	1.703712	Preprocessor1_ Model1
Repeat2	Fold09	rmse	standard	1.760913	Preprocessor1_ Model1
Repeat1	Fold03	rmse	standard	1.764593	Preprocessor1_ Model1
Repeat2	Fold10	rmse	standard	1.765286	Preprocessor1_ Model1
Repeat1	Fold09	rmse	standard	1.768533	Preprocessor1_ Model1
Repeat3	Fold01	rmse	standard	1.770712	Preprocessor1_ Model1
Repeat2	Fold05	rmse	standard	1.809197	Preprocessor1_ Model1
Repeat4	Fold09	rmse	standard	1.810250	Preprocessor1_ Model1
Repeat3	Fold08	rmse	standard	1.833094	Preprocessor1_ Model1
Repeat5	Fold01	rmse	standard	1.870432	Preprocessor1_ Model1
Repeat4	Fold07	rmse	standard	1.928457	Preprocessor1_ Model1
Repeat3	Fold02	rmse	standard	1.930982	Preprocessor1_ Model1
Repeat1	Fold06	rmse	standard	1.933486	Preprocessor1_ Model1
Repeat2	Fold08	rmse	standard	1.947309	Preprocessor1_ Model1
Repeat5	Fold02	rmse	standard	1.950470	Preprocessor1_ Model1

Repeat5	Fold07	rmse	standard	1.964223	Preprocessor1_Model1
Repeat4	Fold04	rmse	standard	1.976037	Preprocessor1_Model1
Repeat2	Fold06	rmse	standard	1.989128	Preprocessor1_Model1
Repeat4	Fold05	rmse	standard	2.013996	Preprocessor1_Model1
Repeat1	Fold08	rmse	standard	2.056267	Preprocessor1_Model1
Repeat2	Fold02	rmse	standard	2.083976	Preprocessor1_Model1
Repeat1	Fold07	rmse	standard	2.121357	Preprocessor1_Model1
Repeat4	Fold01	rmse	standard	2.123148	Preprocessor1_Model1
Repeat5	Fold05	rmse	standard	2.172129	Preprocessor1_Model1
Repeat1	Fold04	rmse	standard	2.187684	Preprocessor1_Model1
Repeat1	Fold01	rmse	standard	2.201453	Preprocessor1_Model1
Repeat3	Fold10	rmse	standard	2.242961	Preprocessor1_Model1
Repeat2	Fold04	rmse	standard	2.258303	Preprocessor1_Model1
Repeat4	Fold10	rmse	standard	2.277209	Preprocessor1_Model1
Repeat5	Fold04	rmse	standard	2.279852	Preprocessor1_Model1
Repeat5	Fold09	rmse	standard	2.330450	Preprocessor1_Model1
Repeat3	Fold07	rmse	standard	2.443212	Preprocessor1_Model1
Repeat3	Fold06	rmse	standard	2.522965	Preprocessor1_Model1
Repeat5	Fold03	rmse	standard	3.144103	Preprocessor1_Model1
Repeat3	Fold04	rmse	standard	3.318964	Preprocessor1_Model1

Repeat1	Fold02	rmse	standard	3.369519	Preprocessor1_Model1
Repeat2	Fold01	rmse	standard	3.561038	Preprocessor1_Model1
Repeat4	Fold02	rmse	standard	3.625243	Preprocessor1_Model1

- The result is 50 rows with 1 RMSE value for each resample.
- The lowest RMSE (1.35) was achieved in repeat 3 and fold 9, while the highest RMSE (3.63) was achieved in repeat 4 and fold 2.

If we used the collect_metrics function with the argument summarize = TRUE, we will get the mean RMSE value across the 50 resamples of the training data.

```
lin_res3 %>% collect_metrics(summarize = TRUE)
## # A tibble: 1 × 6
## .metric .estimator mean n std_err .config
## <chr> <chr> <dbl> <int> <dbl> <chr>
## 1 rmse standard 2.05 50 0.0754 Preprocessor1_Model1
```

- The mean RMSE of linear model using 3 columns on 50 resamples of training data (n = 50) = 2.05, while the RMSE on whole training data = 2.06.

1.9.7. Model Performance on Testing Data

To get the RMSE from applying the model with three predictors on the testing data, we use the same above functions on the lin_mod3 object.

```
lin_mod3 %>%
predict(new_data = test_market) %>%
mutate(truth = test_market$sales) %>%
rmse(truth = truth, estimate = .pred)
## # A tibble: 1 × 3
## .metric .estimator .estimate
## <chr> <chr> <dbl>
## 1 rmse standard 1.88
```

- The RMSE of linear model using 3 columns as predictors on testing data = 1.88.
- The RMSE on testing data (1.88) is nearer to that of cross-validated training data (2.05) than to the whole training data (2.06). This is the

advantage of using cross-validation to obtain more robust estimate of model performance on future unseen data.

1.10. MULTIPLE LINEAR REGRESSION OF HEART ATTACK DATA

1.10.1. Splitting the Data into Training and Testing Data

We will use the same train_heart and test_heart data generated above.

1.10.2. Generating the Recipe

We create an object "rec4" by applying the recipe function on the train_heart data using the "%>%" operator. The recipe function has the argument cholesterol ~gender+risk+drug meaning predicting the cholesterol outcome column using the three other columns in the data (gender, risk, and drug).

```
rec4 <- train_heart %>%
recipe(cholesterol ~ gender+risk+drug)
rec4
##
## — Recipe ——————————————————————————————————————
##
## — Inputs
## Number of variables by role
## outcome: 1
## predictor: 3
```

- The recipe object "rec4" defines the variables by role with 1 variable as an outcome (cholesterol) and 3 variables as a predictors (gender, risk, and drug).

1.10.3. Generate Different Resamples of the Training Data

We will use the same folds2 data frame generated above with 50 resamples of the training data stratified by the cholesterol column.

1.10.4. Define the Machine Learning (ML) Model

We will use the same lm_model generated above.

1.10.5. Generate Workflow

We create the "wflow4" object by using the following functions:

- The workflow function to create a workflow.
- The add_recipe function with the argument "rec4" to add the above created recipe with three predictors for predicting the cholesterol level.
- The add_model function with the argument lm_model to add the above created model.

```
wflow4 <- workflow() %>%
add_recipe(rec4) %>%
add_model(lm_model)
wflow4
## ══ Workflow ════════════════════════════════════════════════════════════
## Preprocessor: Recipe
## Model: linear_reg()
##
## ── Preprocessor ────────────────────────────────────────────────────────
## 0 Recipe Steps
##
## ── Model ───────────────────────────────────────────────────────────────
## Linear Regression Model Specification (regression)
##
## Computational engine: lm
```

- The "wflow4" object contains no preprocessing steps (0 Recipe Steps) and the linear regression model.

1.10.6. Fit the Model on Training Data

1.10.6.1. Fitting the Model on the Whole Training Data

We create a lin_mod4 model by using the fit function with the arguments:

- wflow4 which is the workflow containing no preprocessing steps and the linear regression model.

- train_heart which is the whole training data with 54 rows.

Then, we use the following functions:

- The tidy function to see the model results.
- The mutate function with the argument across(is.numeric,round, 5) to round all numeric columns to 5 decimal places.
- The add_significance function with the arguments:

  ++ p.col = "p.value" to add p-value significance symbols based on the p.value column.

  ++ output.col = "significance" to create the significance column that will hold the significance symbols.
- The flextable function to convert the result to a table.
- The theme_box function to apply cell boundaries to all cells in the table.
- The set_caption function with the caption = "…" argument to add a table caption or title.

lin_mod4<-**fit**(wflow4, train_heart)

tidy(lin_mod4) **%>% mutate**(**across**(is.numeric,round, 5)) **%>%**

add_significance(p.col = "p.value", output.col = "significance") **%>%**

flextable(cwidth = 1) **%>% theme_box**() **%>%**

set_caption(caption = "Linear model results of using gender, risk, and drug for predicting cholesterol in heart attack training data")

Linear model results of using gender, risk, and drug for predicting cholesterol in heart attack training data:

term	**estimate**	**std.error**	**statistic**	**p.value**	**significance**
(Intercept)	5.71180	0.09641	59.24486	0.00000	****
genderfemale	–0.24829	0.08370	–2.96659	0.00464	**
risklow	–0.63785	0.08354	–7.63526	0.00000	****
drugB	–0.22299	0.10091	–2.20971	0.03183	*
drugC	–0.14698	0.10523	–1.39680	0.16877	ns

- The linear regression equation will be:

  cholesterol = 5.71 – 0.25 × genderfemale –0.64 × risklow –0.22 × drugB –0.15 × drugC.

- The female gender is a significant predictor of cholesterol with a p.value < 0.05 and an estimate of –0.25.
- This means that females have lower cholesterol level than males by 0.25 unit on the average when they have the same risk and same drug treatment.
- The low risk is a significant predictor of cholesterol with a p.value < 0.05 and an estimate of –0.64.
- This means that low risk participants have lower cholesterol level than high risk participants by 0.64 unit on the average when they have the same gender and same drug treatment.
- This also means that low risk has greater effect on lowering cholesterol than gender.
- Drug B is a significant predictor of cholesterol with a p.value < 0.05 and an estimate of –0.22.
- This means that participants taking drug B have lower cholesterol level than participants taking drug A by 0.22 unit on the average when they have the same gender and the same risk category.
- Drug C is a non-significant predictor of cholesterol with a p.value > 0.05 and an estimate of –0.15.
- This means that participants taking drug C have equivalent cholesterol level to participants taking drug A when they have the same gender and the same risk category.

1.10.6.2. Model Performance on the Whole Training Data

We use the same functions above on the lin_mod4 object.

```
lin_mod4 %>%
predict(new_data = train_heart) %>%
mutate(truth = train_heart$cholesterol) %>%
rmse(truth = truth, estimate = .pred)
## # A tibble: 1 × 3
## .metric .estimator .estimate
## <chr> <chr> <dbl>
## 1 rmse standard 0.291
```

- The RMSE of linear model using gender, risk, and drug as predictors on whole training data = 0.291.

1.10.6.3. Fitting the Model on 50 Resamples of Training Data

We create an object "lin_res4" by using the fit_resamples function with the arguments:

- wflow4 which is the workflow containing the recipe with three predictors and the linear regression model.
- folds2 which are the 50 resamples of training data created above.
- metrics = metrics_set(rmse) to get the RMSE performance metric for each linear model on each resample.
- control = control_resamples(save_pred = TRUE) to get the predicted cholesterol values for every assessment (testing) data within each resample.

```
lin_res4<-fit_resamples(wflow4, folds2, metrics = metric_set(rmse),
control = control_resamples(save_pred = TRUE))
lin_res4
## # Resampling results
## # 10-fold cross-validation repeated 5 times using stratification
## # A tibble: 50 × 6
## splits id id2 .metrics .notes .predictions
## <list> <chr> <chr> <list> <list> <list>
## 1 <split [48/6]> Repeat1 Fold01 <tibble [1 × 4]> <tibble [0 × 3]> <tibble>
## 2 <split [48/6]> Repeat1 Fold02 <tibble [1 × 4]> <tibble [0 × 3]> <tibble>
## 3 <split [48/6]> Repeat1 Fold03 <tibble [1 × 4]> <tibble [0 × 3]> <tibble>
## 4 <split [48/6]> Repeat1 Fold04 <tibble [1 × 4]> <tibble [0 × 3]> <tibble>
## 5 <split [48/6]> Repeat1 Fold05 <tibble [1 × 4]> <tibble [0 × 3]> <tibble>
## 6 <split [48/6]> Repeat1 Fold06 <tibble [1 × 4]> <tibble [0 × 3]> <tibble>
## 7 <split [48/6]> Repeat1 Fold07 <tibble [1 × 4]> <tibble [0 × 3]> <tibble>
## 8 <split [50/4]> Repeat1 Fold08 <tibble [1 × 4]> <tibble [0 × 3]> <tibble>
## 9 <split [50/4]> Repeat1 Fold09 <tibble [1 × 4]> <tibble [0 × 3]> <tibble>
## 10 <split [50/4]> Repeat1 Fold10 <tibble [1 × 4]> <tibble [0 × 3]> <tibble>
## # i 40 more rows
```

The resulting object "lin_res4" contains the results of applying this linear model on the 50 resamples of training data. It contains 6 columns that were described before. By using the unnest function with the .predictions argument on the lin_res4 object, we get the predicted and actual cholesterol for each row within each resample.

```
lin_res4 %>% unnest(.predictions)
## # A tibble: 270 × 9
## splits id id2 .metrics .notes .pred .row cholesterol .config
## <list> <chr> <chr> <list> <list> <dbl> <int> <dbl> <chr>
## 1 <split [48/6]> Repea… Fold… <tibble> <tibble> 4.82 7 4.91 Prepro…
## 2 <split [48/6]> Repea… Fold… <tibble> <tibble> 4.93 26 4.93 Prepro…
## 3 <split [48/6]> Repea… Fold… <tibble> <tibble> 5.53 28 5.12 Prepro…
## 4 <split [48/6]> Repea… Fold… <tibble> <tibble> 5.49 34 5.19 Prepro…
## 5 <split [48/6]> Repea… Fold… <tibble> <tibble> 5.53 43 5.58 Prepro…
## 6 <split [48/6]> Repea… Fold… <tibble> <tibble> 5.61 45 5.37 Prepro…
## 7 <split [48/6]> Repea… Fold… <tibble> <tibble> 5.63 30 5.00 Prepro…
## 8 <split [48/6]> Repea… Fold… <tibble> <tibble> 4.73 31 5.14 Prepro…
## 9 <split [48/6]> Repea… Fold… <tibble> <tibble> 4.73 32 4.95 Prepro…
## 10 <split [48/6]> Repea… Fold… <tibble> <tibble> 5.03 37 5.36 Prepro…
## # ℹ 260 more rows
```

- The result is a tibble with 270 rows and 9 columns. Each row contains the actual (cholesterol) and predicted cholesterol (.pred) for each row within each resample.

  We can plot the actual cholesterol on the x-axis and the predicted cholesterol on the y-axis, after using the unnest function, by using the following functions:
- The ggplot function with the arguments, aes(x = cholesterol, y = .pred, color = id), to plot actual cholesterol on the x-axis, the predicted cholesterol on the y-axis, and a different color for each id or repeat.
- The geom_abline function to plot a diagonal perfect line that corresponds to actual cholesterol equal predicted cholesterol.
- The geom_point function to plot a scatter plot.
- The facet_wrap function with the argument vars(id,id2) to plot a separate plot for each unique combination of id and id2 value.
- The labs function with the arguments, title to add a plot title, *x* to add *x*-axis title, y to add y-axis title. The plot title has "\n" to make it into 2 lines.

- The theme_classic function to remove the grey background and the white background lines from the default ggplot.

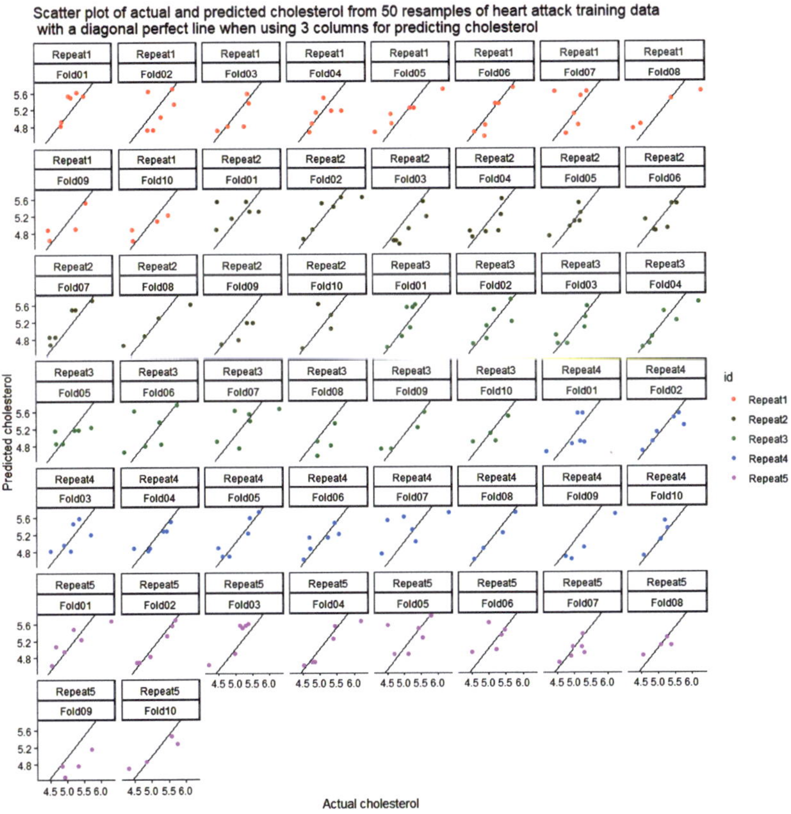


```
lin_res4 %>% unnest(.predictions) %>%
ggplot(aes(x = cholesterol, y = .pred, color = id)) +
geom_abline() +
geom_point() +
facet_wrap(vars(id,id2))+
labs(title = "Scatter plot of actual and predicted cholesterol from 50 resamples of heart attack training data \n with a diagonal perfect line when using 3 columns for predicting cholesterol",
x = "Actual cholesterol", y = "Predicted cholesterol")+
theme_classic()
```

- We have 50 plots for 50 resamples.
- A remarkable note is that the points are nearer to the diagonal line than that of the simple model with gender only and so a lower RMSE or error as expected with the multiple model.

1.10.6.4. Model Performance on 50 Resamples of Training Data

To get the performance metrics (RMSE) on the 50 resamples of training data, we use the same above functions on the lin_res4 object.

lin_res4 **%>% collect_metrics**(summarize = FALSE) **%>%**

arrange(.estimate) **%>%**

flextable() **%>% theme_box**() **%>%**

set_caption(caption = "The RMSE of 50 resamples of heart attack training data when using 3 columns as predictors of cholesterol")

The RMSE of 50 resamples of heart attack training data when using three columns as predictors of cholesterol:

id	id2	.metric	.estimator	.estimate	.config
Repeat5	Fold02	rmse	standard	0.1032422	Preprocessor1_Model1
Repeat4	Fold08	rmse	standard	0.1104720	Preprocessor1_Model1
Repeat1	Fold06	rmse	standard	0.1710928	Preprocessor1_Model1
Repeat4	Fold10	rmse	standard	0.1765728	Preprocessor1_Model1
Repeat4	Fold05	rmse	standard	0.1894235	Preprocessor1_Model1
Repeat4	Fold04	rmse	standard	0.1928800	Preprocessor1_Model1
Repeat5	Fold07	rmse	standard	0.2051204	Preprocessor1_Model1
Repeat2	Fold05	rmse	standard	0.2127004	Preprocessor1_Model1
Repeat5	Fold08	rmse	standard	0.2136800	Preprocessor1_Model1
Repeat4	Fold02	rmse	standard	0.2183098	Preprocessor1_Model1

Repeat3	Fold03	rmse	standard	0.2203575	Preprocessor1_ Model1
Repeat2	Fold07	rmse	standard	0.2248146	Preprocessor1_ Model1
Repeat3	Fold09	rmse	standard	0.2273761	Preprocessor1_ Model1
Repeat1	Fold01	rmse	standard	0.2327617	Preprocessor1_ Model1
Repeat3	Fold10	rmse	standard	0.2368913	Preprocessor1_ Model1
Repeat1	Fold03	rmse	standard	0.2419249	Preprocessor1_ Model1
Repeat3	Fold01	rmse	standard	0.2459256	Preprocessor1_ Model1
Repeat4	Fold06	rmse	standard	0.2480871	Preprocessor1_ Model1
Repeat5	Fold04	rmse	standard	0.2497942	Preprocessor1_ Model1
Repeat2	Fold06	rmse	standard	0.2510969	Preprocessor1_ Model1
Repeat3	Fold02	rmse	standard	0.2622767	Preprocessor1_ Model1
Repeat1	Fold10	rmse	standard	0.2738664	Preprocessor1_ Model1
Repeat2	Fold09	rmse	standard	0.2749384	Preprocessor1_ Model1
Repeat2	Fold04	rmse	standard	0.2797994	Preprocessor1_ Model1
Repeat1	Fold04	rmse	standard	0.2812196	Preprocessor1_ Model1
Repeat3	Fold04	rmse	standard	0.2822213	Preprocessor1_ Model1
Repeat1	Fold09	rmse	standard	0.2861093	Preprocessor1_ Model1
Repeat5	Fold10	rmse	standard	0.3015015	Preprocessor1_ Model1
Repeat3	Fold05	rmse	standard	0.3047595	Preprocessor1_ Model1
Repeat4	Fold03	rmse	standard	0.3094625	Preprocessor1_ Model1

Repeat5	Fold03	rmse	standard	0.3173284	Preprocessor1_ Model1
Repeat2	Fold02	rmse	standard	0.3201685	Preprocessor1_ Model1
Repeat2	Fold03	rmse	standard	0.3236409	Preprocessor1_ Model1
Repeat3	Fold08	rmse	standard	0.3430675	Preprocessor1_ Model1
Repeat5	Fold01	rmse	standard	0.3431095	Preprocessor1_ Model1
Repeat1	Fold05	rmse	standard	0.3472099	Preprocessor1_ Model1
Repeat2	Fold10	rmse	standard	0.3520580	Preprocessor1_ Model1
Repeat4	Fold01	rmse	standard	0.3562849	Preprocessor1_ Model1
Repeat5	Fold06	rmse	standard	0.3628463	Preprocessor1_ Model1
Repeat2	Fold08	rmse	standard	0.3704612	Preprocessor1_ Model1
Repeat1	Fold02	rmse	standard	0.3900164	Preprocessor1_ Model1
Repeat4	Fold09	rmse	standard	0.3909872	Preprocessor1_ Model1
Repeat1	Fold08	rmse	standard	0.4336578	Preprocessor1_ Model1
Repeat3	Fold07	rmse	standard	0.4422324	Preprocessor1_ Model1
Repeat5	Fold09	rmse	standard	0.4549545	Preprocessor1_ Model1
Repeat5	Fold05	rmse	standard	0.4602897	Preprocessor1_ Model1
Repeat2	Fold01	rmse	standard	0.4979322	Preprocessor1_ Model1
Repeat1	Fold07	rmse	standard	0.4990760	Preprocessor1_ Model1
Repeat3	Fold06	rmse	standard	0.5221029	Preprocessor1_ Model1
Repeat4	Fold07	rmse	standard	0.5857764	Preprocessor1_ Model1

- The result is 50 rows with 1 RMSE value for each resample.
- The lowest RMSE (0.103) was achieved in repeat 5 and fold 2, while the highest RMSE (0.586) was achieved in repeat 4 and fold 7.

If we used the collect_metrics function with the argument summarize = TRUE, we will get the mean RMSE value across the 50 resamples of the training data.

```
lin_res4 %>% collect_metrics(summarize = TRUE)
## # A tibble: 1 × 6
## .metric .estimator mean n std_err .config
## <chr> <chr> <dbl> <int> <dbl> <chr>
## 1 rmse standard 0.303 50 0.0149 Preprocessor1_Model1
```

- The mean RMSE of linear model using 3 columns on 50 resamples of training data (n = 50) = 0.303, while the RMSE on whole training data = 0.291.

1.10.7. Model Performance on Testing Data

To get the RMSE from applying the model with three predictors on the testing data, we use the same above functions on the lin_mod4 object.

```
lin_mod4 %>%
predict(new_data = test_heart) %>%
mutate(truth = test_heart$cholesterol) %>%
rmse(truth = truth, estimate = .pred)
## # A tibble: 1 × 3
## .metric .estimator .estimate
## <chr> <chr> <dbl>
## 1 rmse standard 0.387
```

- The RMSE of linear model using three columns as predictors on testing data = 0.387.
- The RMSE on testing data (0.387) is nearer to that of cross-validated training data (0.303) than to the whole training data (0.291). This is the advantage of using cross-validation to obtain more robust estimate of model performance on future unseen data.

CHAPTER 2

LINEAR CLASSIFICATION MODELING

Contents

2.1. Data Used in This Chapter 73
2.2. Data Exploration of the Two Class Data 75
2.3. Data Exploration of the Iris Data 78
2.4. Linear Discriminant Analysis (LDA) 80
2.5. Linear Discriminant Analysis (LDA) for the Two Class Data 80
2.6. Linear Discriminant Analysis (LDA) for Iris Data 104

2.1. DATA USED IN THIS CHAPTER

2.1.1. Two Class Data

This is an artifical data with two predictors (A and B) and a factor or categorical outcome variable (Class).

The data is part of modeldata package under the name "two_class_dat." The modeldata package is part of tidymodels package which is a collection of different packages for data modeling.

First, we load the tidymodels package using the library function then, we load the two_class_dat using the data function.

We also load the tidyverse package into our R session because it contains many useful packages for data analysis, and the flextable package to make the different code outputs into readable tables.

Before loading any package using the library function, we should install the package first using the Tools then Install Packages in R studio and type the package you want to install.

```
library(tidymodels)
data(two_class_dat)
library(tidyverse)
library(flextable)
```

To see the data structure, we use the glimpse function.

```
glimpse(two_class_dat)
## Rows: 791
## Columns: 3
## $ A <dbl> 2.0697297, 2.0164150, 1.6885554, 3.4345378, 2.8845957, 3.3135895...
## $ B <dbl> 1.6316467, 1.0366289, 1.3666097, 1.9797759, 1.9758911, 2.4058755...
## $ Class <fct> Class1, Class1, Class2, Class2, Class1, Class2, Class2, Class2, ...
```

- The glimpse function gives the number of rows, the number of columns, the column names with the prefix "$," the column classes between "<>" parentheses, and the first values of every column.
- The data contains 791 rows and 3 columns:
  - **A:** A double or numeric column (dbl).
  - **B:** A double or numeric column too.
  - **Class:** A factor or categorical column (fct). This is the categorical outcome column with 2 classes that we want to predict using the A and B columns.

2.1.2. Edgar Anderson's Iris Data

The iris data gives measurements in centimeters of sepal length, sepal width, petal length and petal width for 50 flowers from each of 3 species of iris. The species are *Iris setosa*, *versicolor*, and *virginica*.

The data is part of datasets package which is part of core R programming under the name "iris" so to load this data into our R session, we will only load this data using the data function. Then, to see its structure, we will use the glimpse function.

data("iris")

glimpse(iris)

Rows: 150

Columns: 5

$ Sepal.Length <dbl> 5.1, 4.9, 4.7, 4.6, 5.0, 5.4, 4.6, 5.0, 4.4, 4.9, 5.4, 4...

$ Sepal.Width <dbl> 3.5, 3.0, 3.2, 3.1, 3.6, 3.9, 3.4, 3.4, 2.9, 3.1, 3.7, 3...

$ Petal.Length <dbl> 1.4, 1.4, 1.3, 1.5, 1.4, 1.7, 1.4, 1.5, 1.4, 1.5, 1.5, 1...

$ Petal.Width <dbl> 0.2, 0.2, 0.2, 0.2, 0.2, 0.4, 0.3, 0.2, 0.2, 0.1, 0.2, 0...

$ Species <fct> setosa, setosa, setosa, setosa, setosa, setosa, setosa, s...

The data contains 150 rows (150 flowers) and 5 columns:

1. **Sepal.Length:** A numeric (dbl) column with decimals for the sepal length.
2. **Sepal.Width:** A numeric column with decimals for the sepal width.
3. **Petal.Length:** A numeric column with decimals for the petal length.
4. **Petal.Width:** A numeric column with decimals for the petal width.
5. **Species:** A factor (fct) or categorical column for the species. This is the categorical column with three species that we want to predict using the other 4 columns.

2.2. DATA EXPLORATION OF THE TWO CLASS DATA

2.2.1. Categorical Columns

We will use the skim function, from the skimr package, to produce useful information about our data columns. Because the output has too many columns so we use the yank function, from the skimr package too, to look at information related to categorical and numeric columns separately.

To examine all factor categorical columns at once, we use the following functions on the two_class_dat data:

- The skim function that produces information about all data columns.
- The yank function with "factor" argument to get only the information related to factor or categorical columns.

Then, we convert the result to a table as explained in previous chapters using functions from the flextable package. To use functions from the skimr package, we should first load the skimr package first using the library function.

library(skimr)

two_class_dat **%>% skim**() **%>% yank**("factor") **%>%**

flextable(cwidth = 1) **%>% theme_box**() **%>%**

set_caption(caption = "The information gained from skim function on the categorical columns of two class data")

The information gained from skim function on the categorical columns of two class data:

skim_ variable	n_missing	complete_ rate	ordered	n_ unique	top_counts
Class	0	1	FALSE	2	Cla: 437, Cla: 354

- We have 6 columns:
  - The skim_variable is the factor or categorical column name. We have only 1 factor column which is the class column.
  - The n_missing is the number of missing values. The factor column has zero or no missing values.
  - The complete_rate is the proportion of present values in each column. Because we have 791 rows, so each column must have 791 values and because there are no missings so the complete rate = 791/791 = 1 or 100% for the class column.
  - The ordered column denotes if the factor column is an ordered factor column like months where January < February < March < ... December in order. The class factor column is unordered and so has a FALSE value.
  - The n_unique is the number of unique values in the class column. There are 2 different classes in the class column.
  - The top_counts is the number of rows for the most frequent categories in the class column. However, note that the top

frequent categories are trimmed in their names. To see the full names, we can use the count function with the specific column name.

two_class_dat **%>% count**(Class) **%>% flextable**(cwidth = 1) **%>%**

theme_box() %>%

set_caption(caption = "The frequency of unique values in the class column of the 2 class data")

The frequency of unique values in the class column of the 2 class data:

Class	n
Class1	437
Class2	354

- There are 2 unique categories in the "Class" column.
- The class1 has a count or frequency of 437 where the class2 has a count of 354. The total is 791 which is the total rows in the two class data.

2.2.2. Numeric Columns

We use the same above functions but use the yank function with the "numeric" argument to get useful information about numeric columns in the two class data.

two_class_dat **%>% skim() %>% yank**("numeric") **%>%**

flextable() %>% theme_box() %>%

set_caption(caption = "The information gained from skim function on numerical columns from the two class data")

The information gained from skim function on numerical columns from the two class data:

skim_variable	n_missing	complete_rate	mean	sd	p0	p25	p50	p75	p100	hist
A	0	1	2.025899	0.8974531	0.4122137	1.2783392	1.865892	2.737398	3.932072	
B	0	1	1.540352	0.7304615	0.1461280	0.9344985	1.471292	2.034217	3.809708	

We have 11 columns:

1. skim_variable is the column name.
2. n_missing is the number of missings in each column.
3. complete_rate is the proportion of present values in each column. All numeric columns have no missings and 1 or 100% complete rate.

4. mean is the mean or average value for each column.
5. sd is the standard deviation for each column.
6. p0 is the 0% percentile or the minimum value for each column.
7. p25 is the 25% percentile or the 1st quartile for each column.
8. p50 is the 50% percentile, the median, or the 2nd quartile for each column.
9. p75 is the 75% percentile or the 3rd quartile for each column.
10. p100 is the 100% percentile or the maximum value for each column.
11. hist is the histogram plot for each column.

2.3. DATA EXPLORATION OF THE IRIS DATA

2.3.1. Categorical Columns

We will use the same above functions including the yank function with "factor" argument to get only the information related to factor or categorical columns.

iris **%>% skim**() **%>% yank**("factor") **%>%**

flextable(cwidth = 1) **%>% theme_box**() **%>%**

set_caption(caption = "The information gained from skim function on the categorical columns of the iris data")

The information gained from skim function on the categorical columns of the iris data:

skim_ variable	**n_missing**	**com- plete_rate**	**ordered**	**n_ unique**	**top_counts**
Species	0	1	FALSE	3	set: 50, ver: 50, vir: 50

- We have 6 columns:
  - The skim_variable is the factor or categorical column name. We have only 1 factor column which is the species column.
  - The n_missing is the number of missing values. The factor column has zero or no missing values.
  - The complete_rate is the proportion of present values in each column. Because we have 150 rows, so each column must have 150 values and because there are no missings so the complete rate = 150/150 = 1 or 100% for the species column.

- The ordered column denotes if the factor column is an ordered factor column. The species factor column is unordered and so has a FALSE value.
- The n_unique is the number of unique values in the species column. There are three distinct species in the species column.
- The top_counts is the number of rows for the most frequent categories in the species column. As noted before, the categories are trimmed in their names. To see the full names, we can use the count function with the species column name.

```
iris %>% count(Species) %>% flextable(cwidth = 1) %>%
theme_box() %>%
set_caption(caption = "The frequency of unique values in the species column of the iris data")
```

The frequency of unique values in the species column of the iris data:

Species	n
setosa	50
versicolor	50
virginica	50

- There are three unique categories in the "Species" column.
- All three categories setosa, versicolor, and virginica have a count or frequency of 50, so the total is 150 which is the total rows in the iris data.

2.3.2. Numeric Columns

We use the same above functions but using the yank function with the "numeric" argument to get useful information about numeric columns in the iris data.

```
iris %>% skim() %>% yank("numeric") %>%
flextable() %>% theme_box() %>%
set_caption(caption = "The information gained from skim function on numerical columns from the iris data")
```

The information gained from skim function on numerical columns from the iris data:

skim_variable	n_missing	complete_rate	mean	sd	p0	p25	p50	p75	p100	hist
Sepal.Length	0	1	5.843333	0.8280661	4.3	5.1	5.80	6.4	7.9	

Sepal.Width	0	1	3.057333	0.4358663	2.0	2.8	3.00	3.3	4.4	
Petal.Length	0	1	3.758000	1.7652982	1.0	1.6	4.35	5.1	6.9	
Petal.Width	0	1	1.199333	0.7622377	0.1	0.3	1.30	1.8	2.5	

We have 11 columns:

1. skim_variable is the column name. We have 4 numeric columns.
2. n_missing is the number of missings in each column. All columns have 0 missings.
3. complete_rate is the proportion of present values in each column. All numeric columns have no missings and 1 or 100% complete rate.
4. mean is the mean or average value for each column.
5. sd is the standard deviation for each column.
6. p0 is the 0% percentile or the minimum value for each column.
7. p25 is the 25% percentile or the 1st quartile for each column.
8. p50 is the 50% percentile, the median, or the 2nd quartile for each column.
9. p75 is the 75% percentile or the 3rd quartile for each column.
10. p100 is the 100% percentile or the maximum value for each column.
11. hist is the histogram plot for each column.

2.4. LINEAR DISCRIMINANT ANALYSIS (LDA)

The LDA algorithm tries to find directions that maximize the separation between classes. These directions, called linear discriminants, are linear combinations of predictor variables.

Before performing LDA, we should normalize the variables to make their scale comparable. This step will be included in the preprocessing recipe applied to each training data.

2.5. LINEAR DISCRIMINANT ANALYSIS (LDA) FOR THE TWO CLASS DATA

2.5.1. Splitting the Data into Training and Testing Data

As explained in the first chapter, we first do a stratified splitting of the data using the categorical outcome (class). This ensures that both the resulting training and testing data have the same class distribution (proportion) as the original two class data.

We create an object called "split_class" by using the initial_split function with the arguments:

- data = two_class_dat which is the data we want to split.
- strata = Class to make a stratified splitting using the class outcome column. The column name is with capital "C" as present in the original data.

To make the splitting reproducible, we use the set.seed function with any number before using the initial_split function.

```
set.seed(123)
split_class <- initial_split(data = two_class_dat,
strata = Class)
split_class
## <Training/Testing/Total>
## <592/199/791>
```

The training data has 592 rows and the testing data has 199 rows with a total of 791 which is the total rows of original data.

To get the actual training and testing data, we use the training and testing functions, respectively, on the split_class object. The resulting data is called train_class for the training data and test_class for the testing data. Finally, we use the dim function to see the data dimensions.

```
train_class<-training(split_class)
test_class<-testing(split_class)
dim(train_class)
## [1] 592 3
dim(test_class)
## [1] 199 3
```

The training data has 592 rows (1st number) and 3 columns (2nd number), while the testing data has 199 rows (1st number) and 3 columns (2nd number). The same 3 columns of two class data are present in the training and testing data.

2.5.2. Generating the Recipe

We create an object "rec" by applying the following functions on the train_class data using the "%>%" operator:

- The recipe function with the argument Class ~. meaning define the class column as an outcome and all other columns (A and B) as predictors.

- The step_normalize function with the arguments:

  ++ all_numeric_predictors to convert all numeric predictors (A and B) into columns with 0 mean and 1 standard deviation so the 2 predictors have a common scale.

```
rec <- train_class %>%
recipe(Class ~ .) %>%
step_normalize(all_numeric_predictors())
rec
##
## — Recipe ——————————————————————————————————————
##
## — Inputs
## Number of variables by role
## outcome: 1
## predictor: 2
##
## — Operations
## • Centering and scaling for: all_numeric_predictors()
```

- The recipe object "rec:

  ++ Defines the variables by role: 1 outcome and 2 predictors.

  ++ Contains 1 preprocessing operation: centering and scaling or normalization for all numeric predictors.

2.5.3. Look at Preprocessed Data

First, we prepare the recipe using the prep function on the "rec" recipe. The resulting object is called "prep_rec."

```
prep_rec <- prep(rec)
prep_rec
##
## — Recipe ——————————————————————————————————————
```

```
##
## ── Inputs
## Number of variables by role
## outcome: 1
## predictor: 2
##
## ── Training information
## Training data contained 592 data points and no incomplete rows.
##
## ── Operations
## • Centering and scaling for: A and B | Trained
```

- The recipe has normalized the 2 predictor numeric columns: A and B.

We can use the tidy function on the prepared recipe with the argument, number = 1, to see the result of 1st preprocessing step (normalization).

tidy(prep_rec, number = 1) **%>% flextable**(cwidth = 1) **%>% theme_box**() **%>%**

set_caption(caption = "The mean and standard deviation of numeric predictors of the 2 class data by using step_normalize function")

The mean and standard deviation of numeric predictors of the 2 class data by using step_normalize function:

terms	statistic	value	id
A	mean	2.0589766	normalize_IGMe8
B	mean	1.5537614	normalize_IGMe8
A	sd	0.8900098	normalize_IGMe8
B	sd	0.7408061	normalize_IGMe8

- The step_normalize function will estimate the predictors' means (m) and standard deviation (sd) from the training data to apply the predictor normalization. The formula for normalization is (data value – m)/sd.

- The mean and standard deviations estimated from the training data are also used to normalize the predictors in the testing data.

Second, to get the preprocessed training data, we use the bake function with the arguments:

- prep_rec which is the prepared recipe.
- new_data = NULL to apply the prepared recipe to training data contained in the original recipe.

The resulting data is called "train_class2" and we use the glimpse function to see the data structure.

```
train_class2 <- bake(prep_rec, new_data = NULL)
glimpse(train_class2)
## Rows: 592
## Columns: 3
## $ A <dbl> –0.04782144, 0.91794683, –0.69175198, 1.34154480, –1.13185204, 0…
## $ B <dbl> –0.69806730, –1.31475406, 0.16717677, –0.92403356, –0.95661115, …
## $ Class <fct> Class1, Class1, Class1, Class1, Class1, Class1, Class1, Class1, …
```

- The training data has the same 592 rows and 3 columns of the original training data. However, the column values in A and B columns have some negative values because of normalization.

We can use the skim function again on the train_class2 data with the yank function with the "numeric" argument to get useful information about numeric columns in the two class training data after normalization.

```
train_class2 %>% skim() %>% yank("numeric") %>%
flextable() %>% theme_box() %>%
set_caption(caption = "The information gained from skim function on numerical columns from the two class training data after normalization")
```

The information gained from skim function on numerical columns from the two class training data after normalization:

skim_ variable	n_ miss- ing	com- plete_ rate	mean	sd	p0	p25	p50	p75	p100	hist
A	0	1	–0.00000000000 000016327261	1	–1.850 275	–0.8699 539	–0.1442 194	0.8331503	2.104578	

B	0	1	–0.000000000000 00008034753	1	–1.900 137	–0.8138 577	–0.1103356	0.6322811	3.045259	

- The mean of the 2 predictors is extremely low and nearly equals zero.
- The standard deviation of the 2 predictors = 1. So, the 2 predictors are now on a comparable scale.

Finally, to get the preprocessed testing data, we use the bake function with the arguments:

- prep_rec which is the prepared recipe.
- new_data = test_class to apply the prepared recipe to the testing data.

The resulting data is called "test_class2" and we use the glimpse function to see the data structure.

```
test_class2 <- bake(prep_rec, new_data = test_class)
glimpse(test_class2)
## Rows: 199
## Columns: 3
## $ A <dbl> 0.012081972, 0.927651619, 1.409661835, –1.359872042, –1.31770981...
## $ B <dbl> 0.1051359, 0.5698249, 1.1502526, –1.0000566, –1.4379076, 1.23677...
## $ Class <fct> Class1, Class1, Class2, Class1, Class1, Class2, Class1, Class1, ...
```

- The testing data has the same 199 rows and 3 columns of the original testing data. However, the column values in A and B columns have some negative values because of normalization.

We can use the skim function again on the test_class2 data with the yank function with the "numeric" argument to get useful information about numeric columns in the two class testing data after normalization.

```
test_class2 %>% skim() %>% yank("numeric") %>%
flextable() %>% theme_box() %>%
set_caption(caption = "The information gained from skim function on numerical columns from the two class testing data after normalization")
```

The information gained from skim function on numerical columns from the two class testing data after normalization:

skim_ variable	n_ miss- ing	com- plete_ rate	mean	sd	p0	p25	p50	p75	p100	hist
A	0	1	–0.14772772	1.0274481	–1.835332	–0.9399451	–0.3469792	0.5051348	2.104578	
B	0	1	–0.07194882	0.9436658	–1.900137	–0.8853746	–0.1172962	0.6987014	2.217475	

- The mean of the 2 predictors is exceptionally low and nearly equals zero.
- The standard deviation of the 2 predictors nearly equals 1. However, they are not perfect as that of the training data because the mean and standard deviation of training data are used to normalize the columns in testing data because the testing data represents future unseen data.

2.5.4. Generate Different Resamples of the Training Data

We split the train_class data using the vfold_cv function with the arguments:

- v = 10 to split the data to 10 folds.
- repeats = 5 to repeat this process 5 times.
- strata = Class to make stratified resampling using the class column.

The result is 50 different resamples of train_class data contained in folds data frame.

- We also use the set.seed function before the splitting to make the splitting reproducible.

```
set.seed(123)
folds<-vfold_cv(train_class, v = 10, repeats = 5, strata = Class)
folds
## # 10-fold cross-validation repeated 5 times using stratification
## # A tibble: 50 × 3
## splits id id2
## <list> <chr> <chr>
## 1 <split [532/60]> Repeat1 Fold01
## 2 <split [532/60]> Repeat1 Fold02
## 3 <split [532/60]> Repeat1 Fold03
## 4 <split [532/60]> Repeat1 Fold04
## 5 <split [532/60]> Repeat1 Fold05
## 6 <split [533/59]> Repeat1 Fold06
## 7 <split [533/59]> Repeat1 Fold07
```

```
## 8 <split [534/58]> Repeat1 Fold08
## 9 <split [534/58]> Repeat1 Fold09
## 10 <split [534/58]> Repeat1 Fold10
## # i 40 more rows
```

- There are 50 different rows. Each row corresponds to 1 resample of train_class data. Each resample has 1 analysis (training) data, with 532, 533, or 534 rows and 1 assessment (testing) data with 60, 59, or 58 rows.
- Each resample has 2 id values. id for the repeat number from 1 to 5 and id2 for the resample number from 1 to 10 within that repeat.
- Each resample has a total rows of 592 which is the number of rows in original train_class data. 532 + 60 = 533 + 59 = 534 + 58 = 592.

2.5.5. Define the Machine Learning (ML) Model

We define a linear discriminant model by using the functions:

- The discrim_linear function defines the linear discriminant model type. The discrim package is required to fit this model so we must first load this package using the library function.
- The set_engine function with the argument "MASS" to define the engine that will use the lda function from the MASS package.
- The set_mode function with the argument "classification" to define the mode of learning. We use classification because we have a categorical outcome (class).
- All the three functions are applied in sequence using the piping "%>%" operator and the resulting object is called "discrim_model."

```
library(discrim)
discrim_model <- discrim_linear() %>%
set_engine("MASS") %>%
set_mode("classification")
discrim_model
## Linear Discriminant Model Specification (classification)
##
## Computational engine: MASS
```

2.5.6. Generate the Workflow

We create the "wflow" object by using the following functions:

- The workflow function to create a workflow.
- The add_recipe function with the argument "rec" to add the above created recipe with normalization preprocessing step.
- The add_model function with the argument discrim_model to add the above created model.

```
wflow <- workflow() %>%
add_recipe(rec) %>%
add_model(discrim_model)
wflow
## ══ Workflow ════════════════════════════════════════════════════════════════
## Preprocessor: Recipe
## Model: discrim_linear()
##
## ── Preprocessor ────────────────────────────────────────────────────────────
## 1 Recipe Step
##
## • step_normalize()
##
## ── Model ───────────────────────────────────────────────────────────────────
## Linear Discriminant Model Specification (classification)
##
## Computational engine: MASS
```

- The "wflow" object contains 1 preprocessing step (step_normalize) and the linear discriminant model.

2.5.7. Fit the Model on Training Data

We can fit the linear discriminant model on whole training data "train_class" to get a 1 model fit. However, we can also fit the linear discriminant model on the 50 resamples of the training data in the "folds" data frame to get 50 different model fits and obtain more robust estimate of the model performance on testing data.

2.5.7.1. Fit the Model on Whole Training Data

We create a fit_mod model by using the fit function with the arguments:

- wflow which is the workflow containing normalization preprocessing step and the linear discriminant model.
- train_class which is the whole training data with 592 rows.

```
fit_mod<-fit(wflow, train_class)
fit_mod
## ══ Workflow [trained] ══════════════════════════════════════════════
## Preprocessor: Recipe
## Model: discrim_linear()
##
## ── Preprocessor ────────────────────────────────────────────────────
## 1 Recipe Step
##
## • step_normalize()
##
## ── Model ───────────────────────────────────────────────────────────
## Call:
## lda(..y ~ ., data = data)
##
## Prior probabilities of groups:
## Class1 Class2
## 0.5523649 0.4476351
##
## Group means:
## A B
## Class1 –0.2996268 –0.5543266
## Class2 0.3697282 0.6840181
```

##

Coefficients of linear discriminants:

LD1

A –0.5838379

B 1.6852499

The fitted model outputs contain the following elements:

- Prior probabilities of groups which is the proportion of training rows in each class. There are 55.2% of the training rows in the class1 group and 44.8% of the training rows in the class2 group.
- To confirm that, we can use the following functions on the train_class2 data which is the preprocessed data:

    ++ The count function with "Class" argument to get the number of rows in each class.

    ++ The mutate function with the argument "proportion = n/sum(n)" to create a "proportion" column by dividing n or count by sum of counts.

train_class2 **%>% count**(Class) **%>% mutate**(proportion = n/**sum**(n)) **%>%**
flextable(cwidth = 1) **%>% theme_box**() **%>%**

set_caption(caption = "The count and proportion of training rows in the class1 and class2 groups")

The count and proportion of training rows in the class1 and class2 groups:

Class	**n**	**proportion**
Class1	327	0.5523649
Class2	265	0.4476351

- Again, there are 55.2% of the training rows (327/592 = 0.552) in the class 1 group and 44.8% of the training rows (265/592 = 0.448) in the class 2 group.
- Group means in the fitted model output are the mean of each normalized predictor in each class.
- Coefficients of linear discriminants in the fitted model output are the linear combination of predictor variables that are used to form the LDA decision rule. There is only 1 linear discriminant (LD1) that is defined by the equation:

$$LD1 = -0.5838379 \times A + 1.6852499 \times B.$$

2.5.7.2. Plotting the Boundary Line on the Whole Training Data

To see how this LD1 will separate between the 2 classes, we use the following functions on the preprocessed training data (train_class2):

- The mutate function with the argument "ld1 = –0.5838379*A + 1.6852499*B" to create a new column "ld1" by multiplying the coefficients by the corresponding A and B column values.

```
train_class2 %>% mutate(ld1 = –0.5838379*A + 1.6852499*B)
## # A tibble: 592 × 4
## A B Class ld1
## <dbl> <dbl> <fct> <dbl>
## 1 –0.0478 –0.698 Class1 –1.15
## 2 0.918 –1.31 Class1 –2.75
## 3 –0.692 0.167 Class1 0.686
## 4 1.34 –0.924 Class1 –2.34
## 5 –1.13 –0.957 Class1 –0.951
## 6 0.953 –0.0215 Class1 –0.593
## 7 –1.04 –0.886 Class1 –0.885
## 8 –1.23 –1.09 Class1 –1.11
## 9 –0.622 –0.790 Class1 –0.968
## 10 –0.470 –1.42 Class1 –2.12
## # i 582 more rows
```

We have 4 columns instead of 3 with the additional ld1 column.

- The mutate function with the predict function as an argument. The predict function has the following arguments:

  ++ fit_mod which is the fitted workflow with normalization preprocessing step.

  ++ train_class which is the training data without preprocessing since it will be preprocessed and modelled using the fit_mod object.

  ++ type = "class" to get the predicted class for each row of training data.

```
train_class2 %>% mutate(ld1 = –0.5838379*A + 1.6852499*B) %>%
mutate(predict(fit_mod, train_class, type = "class"))
## # A tibble: 592 × 5
## A B Class ld1 .pred_class
```

```
## <dbl> <dbl> <fct> <dbl> <fct>
## 1 –0.0478 –0.698 Class1 –1.15 Class1
## 2 0.918 –1.31 Class1 –2.75 Class1
## 3 –0.692 0.167 Class1 0.686 Class2
## 4 1.34 –0.924 Class1 –2.34 Class1
## 5 –1.13 –0.957 Class1 –0.951 Class1
## 6 0.953 –0.0215 Class1 –0.593 Class1
## 7 –1.04 –0.886 Class1 –0.885 Class1
## 8 –1.23 –1.09 Class1 –1.11 Class1
## 9 –0.622 –0.790 Class1 –0.968 Class1
## 10 –0.470 –1.42 Class1 –2.12 Class1
## # i 582 more rows
```

There are 5 columns with an additional column ".pred_class" containing the predicted class for every row in the training data.

- The group_by function with the argument ".pred_class" to split the data into 2 data each containing a single class.
- The get_summary_stats function, from the rstatix package, with the arguments "ld1, show = c("min","max")" to get the minimum and maximum ld1 value in each data with a single class.

```
library(rstatix)
train_class2 %>% mutate(ld1 = –0.5838379*A + 1.6852499*B) %>%
mutate(predict(fit_mod, train_class, type = "class")) %>%
group_by(.pred_class) %>%
get_summary_stats(ld1, show = c("min","max")) %>%
flextable(cwidth = 1) %>% theme_box() %>%
set_caption(caption = "The minimum and maximum LD1 in each predicted class of the 2 class training data")
```

The minimum and maximum LD1 in each predicted class of the 2 class training data:

.pred_class	variable	n	min	max
Class1	ld1	335	–3.073	0.204
Class2	ld1	257	0.213	3.946

The maximum ld1 in class1 = 0.204 while the minimum ld1 in class2 = 0.213 so a line at ld1 = 0.210 would separate the 2 predicted classes.

To plot the boundary line, we use the following functions after creating the ".pred_class" column:

- The ggplot function with the arguments "aes(x= ld1, y = .pred_class, colour = .pred_class)" to plot ld1 values on x-axis, the predicted class on the y-axis and a different color for each class.
- The geom_jitter function to add a small amount of random variation to the location of each point and so overcomes overplotting. Since a random variation is added to each point location we must use set. seed function before using these functions.
- The geom_vline function with the argument "xintercept = 0.210" to add a vertical line at x-axis value = 0.210.
- The labs function with the arguments "title" to add a plot title, "x" to add an x-axis title, "y" to add a y-axis title, and "color" to add a legend title.
- The theme_classic function as explained before.

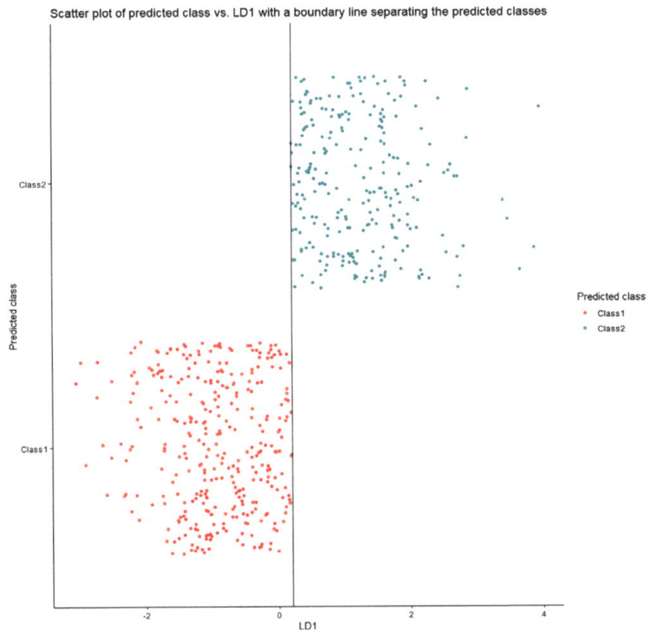

set.seed(123)

train_class2 **%>% mutate**(ld1 = –0.5838379*A + 1.6852499*B) **%>%**

mutate(**predict**(fit_mod, train_class, type = "class")) **%>%**

ggplot(**aes**(x= ld1, y = .pred_class, colour = .pred_class))+
geom_jitter()+ **geom_vline**(xintercept = 0.210)+
labs(title = "Scatter plot of predicted class vs. LD1 with a boundary line separating the predicted classes",
x = "LD1", y = "Predicted class", color = "Predicted class")+
theme_classic()

The LD1 boundary line completely separates the class1, on the left-hand side of the line or red points, from the class2 on the right-hand side of the line or blue points.

We can produce the same plot but use the actual classes to see how this boundary line separate the actual classes.

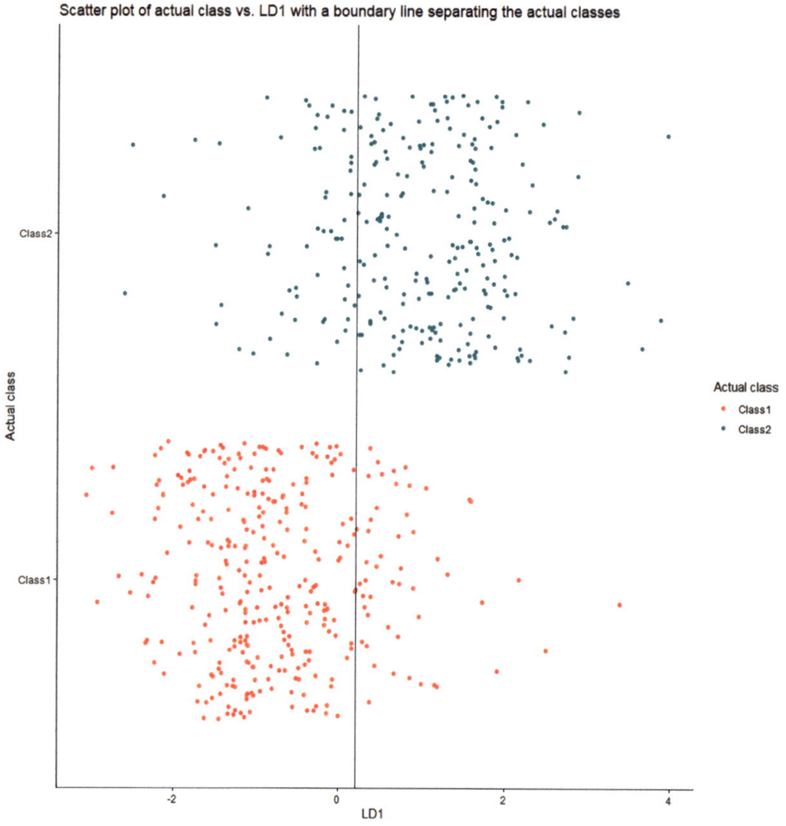

```
set.seed(123)
train_class2 %>% mutate(ld1 = –0.5838379*A + 1.6852499*B) %>%
mutate(predict(fit_mod, train_class, type = "class")) %>%
ggplot(aes(x= ld1, y = Class, colour = Class))+
geom_jitter()+ geom_vline(xintercept = 0.210)+
labs(title = "Scatter plot of actual class vs. LD1 with a boundary line separating the actual classes",
x = "LD1", y = "Actual class", color = "Actual class")+
theme_classic()
```

The majority of actual class1 (red points) are on the left-hand side of the line, while the majority of actual class2 (blue points) are on the right-hand side of the line.

The incorrectly separated blue or red points represent the model prediction error on the training data.

2.5.7.3. The Model Performance on the Whole Training Data

The performance of any classification model is assessed through its accuracy. The accuracy is the proportion of true predictions to all rows in the data.

To get the predicted class for every row in the training data, we use the same predict function mentioned in the previous section.

```
predict(fit_mod, train_class, type = "class")
## # A tibble: 592 × 1
## .pred_class
## <fct>
## 1 Class1
## 2 Class1
## 3 Class2
## 4 Class1
## 5 Class1
## 6 Class1
## 7 Class1
## 8 Class1
## 9 Class1
```

```
## 10 Class1
## # i 582 more rows
```

The result is 592 rows (same row number as class training data) and 1 column ".pred_class."

By using the mutate function, we can add a truth column containing the actual classes in the training data by using the argument "truth = train_class$Class."

```
predict(fit_mod, train_class, type = "class") %>%
mutate(truth = train_class$Class)
## # A tibble: 592 × 2
## .pred_class truth
## <fct> <fct>
## 1 Class1 Class1
## 2 Class1 Class1
## 3 Class2 Class1
## 4 Class1 Class1
## 5 Class1 Class1
## 6 Class1 Class1
## 7 Class1 Class1
## 8 Class1 Class1
## 9 Class1 Class1
## 10 Class1 Class1
## # i 582 more rows
```

We have 2 columns: ".pred_class" for the predicted class and "truth" for the actual class.

To see how many actual classes are predicted correctly, we create a confusion matrix by using the conf_mat function with the arguments:

- truth = truth which is the column containing the actual classes.
- estimate = .pred_class which is the column containing the predicted classes.

```
predict(fit_mod, train_class, type = "class") %>%
mutate(truth = train_class$Class) %>%
conf_mat(truth = truth, estimate = .pred_class)
## Truth
```

Prediction Class1 Class2
Class1 277 58
Class2 50 207

- The true classes are in columns and the predicted classes are in rows.
- There are 277 class1 rows that are predicted correctly as class1.
- There are 58 class2 rows that are predicted correctly as class1.
- There are 50 class1 rows that are predicted incorrectly as class2.
- There are 207 class2 rows that are predicted correctly as class2.
- The model accuracy = (277 + 207)/(277 + 58 + 50 + 207) = (277 + 207)/592 = 0.818 or 81.8%.

The confusion matrix can be plotted directly as a heatmap using the autoplot function with type = "heatmap" argument. Then, we use the labs function to add a plot title.

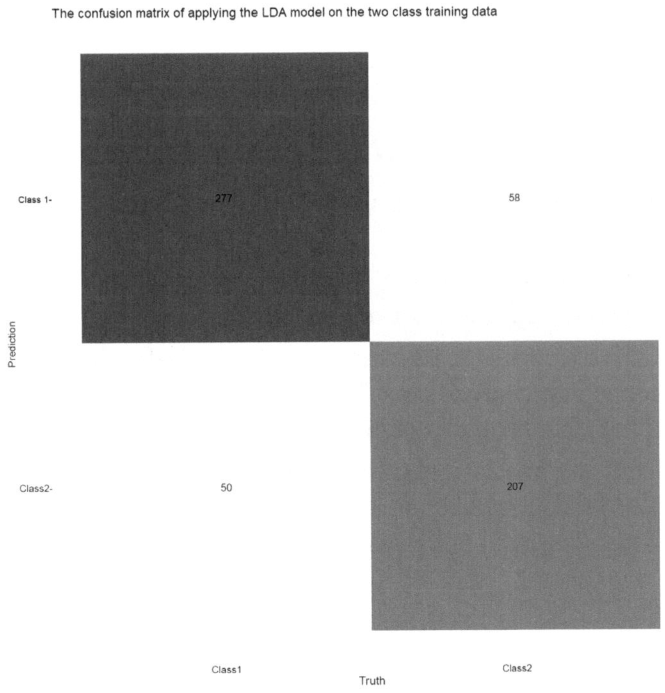

predict(fit_mod, train_class, type = "class") **%>%**

mutate(truth = train_class$Class) **%>%**

conf_mat(truth = truth, estimate = .pred_class) **%>%**

autoplot(type = “heatmap”)+

labs(title = “The confusion matrix of applying the LDA model on the two class training data”)

We get the same numbers mentioned above. Alternatively, we can use the accuracy function to get the model accuracy directly with the same arguments as that used with the conf_mat function.

fit_mod **%>%** **predict**(new_data = train_class) **%>%**

mutate(truth = train_class$Class) **%>%**

accuracy(truth = truth, estimate = .pred_class)

A tibble: 1 × 3

.metric .estimator .estimate

<chr> <chr> <dbl>

1 accuracy binary 0.818

The model accuracy on training data = 0.818 or 81.8% as calculated previously.

2.5.7.4. Fit the Model on 50 Resamples of the Training Data

We create an object “lda_res” by using the fit_resamples function with the arguments:

- wflow which is the workflow containing normalization preprocessing step and the linear discriminant model.
- folds which are the 50 resamples of training data created above, each containing analysis data for fitting the model and assessment data for testing the model performance within each resample.
- metrics = metrics_set(accuracy) to get the accuracy of the linear discriminant model on each resample.

lda_res<-**fit_resamples**(wflow, folds, metrics = **metric_set**(accuracy))

lda_res

Resampling results

10-fold cross-validation repeated 5 times using stratification

A tibble: 50 × 5

splits id id2 .metrics .notes

<list> <chr> <chr> <list> <list>

```
## 1 <split [532/60]> Repeat1 Fold01 <tibble [1 × 4]> <tibble [0 × 3]>
## 2 <split [532/60]> Repeat1 Fold02 <tibble [1 × 4]> <tibble [0 × 3]>
## 3 <split [532/60]> Repeat1 Fold03 <tibble [1 × 4]> <tibble [0 × 3]>
## 4 <split [532/60]> Repeat1 Fold04 <tibble [1 × 4]> <tibble [0 × 3]>
## 5 <split [532/60]> Repeat1 Fold05 <tibble [1 × 4]> <tibble [0 × 3]>
## 6 <split [533/59]> Repeat1 Fold06 <tibble [1 × 4]> <tibble [0 × 3]>
## 7 <split [533/59]> Repeat1 Fold07 <tibble [1 × 4]> <tibble [0 × 3]>
## 8 <split [534/58]> Repeat1 Fold08 <tibble [1 × 4]> <tibble [0 × 3]>
## 9 <split [534/58]> Repeat1 Fold09 <tibble [1 × 4]> <tibble [0 × 3]>
## 10 <split [534/58]> Repeat1 Fold10 <tibble [1 × 4]> <tibble [0 × 3]>
## # ℹ 40 more rows
```

The resulting object "lda_res" contains 50 rows (for 50 resamples) and 5 columns:

- The splits column is a list of each combination of analysis and assessment data withing each resample. The sum is 592, which are total rows of training data.
- The id column is an id column for the repeat number from 1 to 5.
- The id2 column is an id column for the fold number from 1 to 10 so we have 50 resamples because 5 × 10 = 50.
- The .metrics column is a list of performance metric (accuracy) of applying the LDA model to the corresponding assessment data (60,59, or 58 rows) within each resample. Each performance metric is saved in 1 row and 4 columns [1 × 4] tibble or data frame. These will be extracted in the next step. The 1 row is for the accuracy in the assessment data within each resample.
- The .notes column is a list of notes or warnings when applying the linear model to each analysis data (532,533, or 534 rows) within each resample. Each note is saved in 0 rows and 3 columns [0 × 3] tibble or data frame meaning that there are no notes when applying this model to each analysis data.

2.5.7.5. The Model Performance on 50 Resamples of the Training Data

To get the performance metric (accuracy) on the 50 resamples of training data, we use the following functions on the "lda_res" object:

- The collect_metrics function with the argument summarize = FALSE to get the accuracy for each resample.
- The arrange function with .estimate argument to arrange by accuracy value in ascending order.
- The flextable, theme_box, and set_caption functions are described previously.

lda_res **%>% collect_metrics**(summarize = FALSE) **%>%**

arrange(.estimate) **%>%**

flextable(cwidth = 1) **%>% theme_box**() **%>%**

set_caption(caption = "The accuracy of 50 resamples of two class training data when using LDA model")

The accuracy of 50 resamples of two class training data when using LDA model:

id	**id2**	**.metric**	**.estimator**	**.estimate**	**.config**
Repeat3	Fold06	accuracy	binary	0.6779661	Preprocessor1_Model1
Repeat2	Fold10	accuracy	binary	0.7068966	Preprocessor1_Model1
Repeat1	Fold06	accuracy	binary	0.7457627	Preprocessor1_Model1
Repeat2	Fold05	accuracy	binary	0.7500000	Preprocessor1_Model1
Repeat1	Fold08	accuracy	binary	0.7586207	Preprocessor1_Model1
Repeat4	Fold06	accuracy	binary	0.7627119	Preprocessor1_Model1
Repeat1	Fold01	accuracy	binary	0.7666667	Preprocessor1_Model1
Repeat2	Fold02	accuracy	binary	0.7666667	Preprocessor1_Model1
Repeat5	Fold05	accuracy	binary	0.7666667	Preprocessor1_Model1
Repeat2	Fold09	accuracy	binary	0.7758621	Preprocessor1_Model1
Repeat4	Fold08	accuracy	binary	0.7758621	Preprocessor1_Model1
Repeat4	Fold07	accuracy	binary	0.7796610	Preprocessor1_Model1
Repeat3	Fold04	accuracy	binary	0.7833333	Preprocessor1_Model1
Repeat5	Fold01	accuracy	binary	0.7833333	Preprocessor1_Model1
Repeat5	Fold04	accuracy	binary	0.7833333	Preprocessor1_Model1
Repeat3	Fold09	accuracy	binary	0.7931034	Preprocessor1_Model1
Repeat3	Fold10	accuracy	binary	0.7931034	Preprocessor1_Model1
Repeat4	Fold09	accuracy	binary	0.7931034	Preprocessor1_Model1
Repeat5	Fold09	accuracy	binary	0.7931034	Preprocessor1_Model1
Repeat1	Fold07	accuracy	binary	0.7966102	Preprocessor1_Model1
Repeat4	Fold03	accuracy	binary	0.8000000	Preprocessor1_Model1

Repeat4	Fold05	accuracy	binary	0.8000000	Preprocessor1_Model1
Repeat5	Fold02	accuracy	binary	0.8000000	Preprocessor1_Model1
Repeat2	Fold06	accuracy	binary	0.8135593	Preprocessor1_Model1
Repeat3	Fold07	accuracy	binary	0.8135593	Preprocessor1_Model1
Repeat1	Fold04	accuracy	binary	0.8166667	Preprocessor1_Model1
Repeat4	Fold02	accuracy	binary	0.8166667	Preprocessor1_Model1
Repeat1	Fold09	accuracy	binary	0.8275862	Preprocessor1_Model1
Repeat1	Fold10	accuracy	binary	0.8275862	Preprocessor1_Model1
Repeat3	Fold08	accuracy	binary	0.8275862	Preprocessor1_Model1
Repeat5	Fold08	accuracy	binary	0.8275862	Preprocessor1_Model1
Repeat5	Fold06	accuracy	binary	0.8305085	Preprocessor1_Model1
Repeat1	Fold02	accuracy	binary	0.8333333	Preprocessor1_Model1
Repeat2	Fold01	accuracy	binary	0.8333333	Preprocessor1_Model1
Repeat3	Fold02	accuracy	binary	0.8333333	Preprocessor1_Model1
Repeat2	Fold08	accuracy	binary	0.8448276	Preprocessor1_Model1
Repeat4	Fold10	accuracy	binary	0.8448276	Preprocessor1_Model1
Repeat5	Fold10	accuracy	binary	0.8448276	Preprocessor1_Model1
Repeat5	Fold07	accuracy	binary	0.8474576	Preprocessor1_Model1
Repeat2	Fold04	accuracy	binary	0.8500000	Preprocessor1_Model1
Repeat2	Fold07	accuracy	binary	0.8644068	Preprocessor1_Model1
Repeat3	Fold03	accuracy	binary	0.8666667	Preprocessor1_Model1
Repeat4	Fold04	accuracy	binary	0.8666667	Preprocessor1_Model1
Repeat5	Fold03	accuracy	binary	0.8666667	Preprocessor1_Model1
Repeat1	Fold03	accuracy	binary	0.8833333	Preprocessor1_Model1
Repeat1	Fold05	accuracy	binary	0.8833333	Preprocessor1_Model1
Repeat2	Fold03	accuracy	binary	0.8833333	Preprocessor1_Model1
Repeat3	Fold05	accuracy	binary	0.8833333	Preprocessor1_Model1
Repeat3	Fold01	accuracy	binary	0.9000000	Preprocessor1_Model1
Repeat4	Fold01	accuracy	binary	0.9000000	Preprocessor1_Model1

- The result is 50 rows with 1 accuracy value for each resample.
- The lowest accuracy (0.678) was achieved in repeat 3 and fold 6, while the highest accuracy (0.90) was achieved in repeat 3 and fold 1 or repeat 4 and fold 1.

If we used the collect_metrics function with the argument summarize = TRUE, we will get the mean accuracy value across the 50 resamples of the training data.

lda_res **%>% collect_metrics**(summarize = TRUE)

A tibble: 1 × 6

.metric .estimator mean n std_err .config

<chr> <chr> <dbl> <int> <dbl> <chr>

1 accuracy binary 0.814 50 0.00679 Preprocessor1_Model1

- The mean accuracy of LDA model on 50 resamples of training data (n = 50) = 0.814, while the accuracy on whole training data = 0.818.

2.5.8. Model Performance on Testing Data

We use the same above functions to get the confusion matrix of the testing data so we use:

- The "test_class" argument within the predict function.
- The truth column = test_class$Class. within the mutate function.

predict(fit_mod, test_class, type = "class") **%>%**

mutate(truth = test_class$Class) **%>%**

conf_mat(truth = truth, estimate = .pred_class)

Truth

Prediction Class1 Class2

Class1 92 15

Class2 18 74

- The true classes are in columns and the predicted classes are in rows.
- There are 92 class1 rows that are predicted correctly as class1.
- There are 15 class2 rows that are predicted correctly as class1.
- There are 18 class1 rows that are predicted incorrectly as class2.
- There are 74 class2 rows that are predicted correctly as class2.
- The model accuracy = (92 + 74)/(92 + 15 + 18 + 74) = (92 + 74)/199 = 0.834 or 83.4%.

The confusion matrix can be plotted directly as a heatmap using the autoplot function with type = "heatmap" argument.

predict(fit_mod, test_class, type = "class") **%>%**

mutate(truth = test_class$Class) **%>%**

conf_mat(truth = truth, estimate = .pred_class) **%>%**

autoplot(type = "heatmap")+

labs(title = "The confusion matrix of applying the LDA model on the two class testing data")

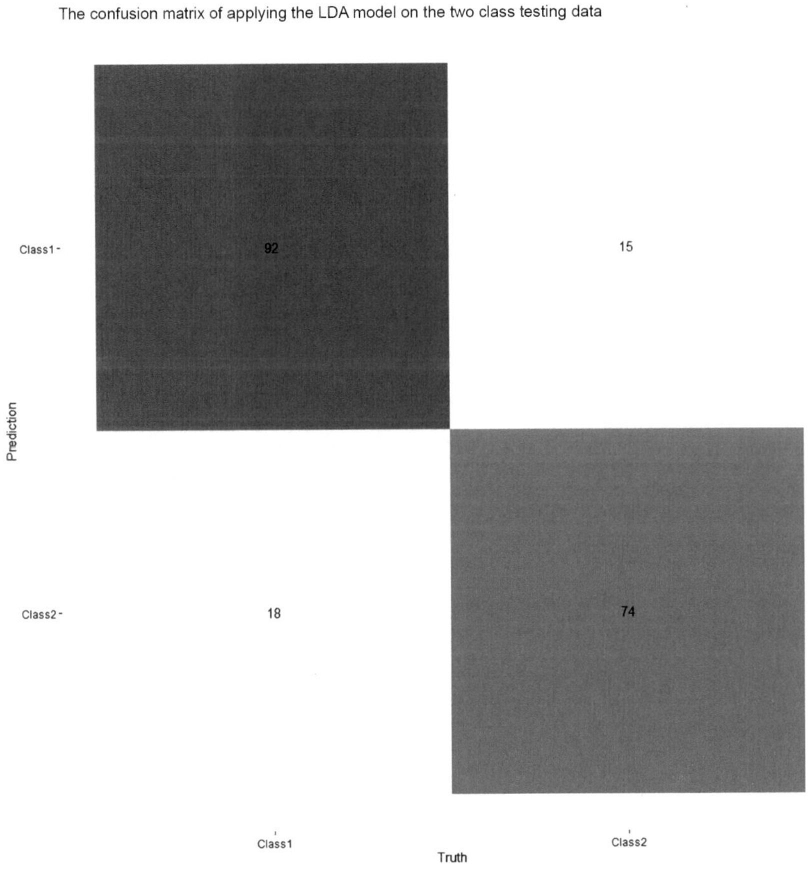

We get the same numbers mentioned above. Alternatively, we can use the accuracy function to get the model accuracy directly.

```
fit_mod %>% predict(new_data = test_class) %>%
mutate(truth = test_class$Class) %>%
accuracy(truth = truth, estimate = .pred_class)
## # A tibble: 1 × 3
## .metric .estimator .estimate
## <chr> <chr> <dbl>
## 1 accuracy binary 0.834
```

The model accuracy on testing data = 0.834 or 83.4% as calculated previously.

2.6. LINEAR DISCRIMINANT ANALYSIS (LDA) FOR IRIS DATA

The iris data contains the species categorical outcome with three categories: setosa, versicolor, and virginica.

2.6.1. Splitting the Data into Training and Testing Data

We create an object "split_iris" by using the initial_split function with the arguments:

- data = iris which is the data we want to split.
- strata = Species to make a stratified splitting using the species outcome column. The column name is with capital "S" as present in the original data.

To make the splitting reproducible, we use the set.seed function with any number before using the initial_split function.

```
set.seed(123)
split_iris <- initial_split(data = iris,
strata = Species)
split_iris
## <Training/Testing/Total>
## <111/39/150>
```

The training data has 111 rows and the testing data has 39 rows with a total of 150 which is the total rows of original iris data.

To get the actual training and testing data, we use the training and testing functions, respectively, on the split_iris object. The resulting data is called train_iris for the training data and test_iris for the testing data. Finally, we use the dim function to see the data dimensions.

```
train_iris<-training(split_iris)
test_iris<-testing(split_iris)
dim(train_iris)
## [1] 111 5
dim(test_iris)
## [1] 39 5
```

The training data has 111 rows (1st number) and 5 columns (2nd number), while the testing data has 39 rows (1st number) and 5 columns (2nd number). The same 5 columns of iris data are present in the training and testing data.

2.6.2. Generating the Recipe

We create an object "rec2" by applying the following functions on the train_iris data using the "%>%" operator:

- The recipe function with the argument Species ~. meaning define the species column as an outcome and all other columns (4 columns: Sepal.Length, Sepal.Width, Petal.Length, and Petal.Width) as predictors.
- The step_normalize function with the arguments:

  ++ all_numeric_predictors to convert all numeric predictors (Sepal. Length, Sepal.Width, Petal.Length, and Petal.Width) into columns with 0 mean and 1 standard deviation so the 4 predictors have a common scale.

```
rec2 <- train_iris %>%
recipe(Species ~ .) %>%
step_normalize(all_numeric_predictors())
rec2
##
## — Recipe ——————————————————————————————————————————————
##
## — Inputs
## Number of variables by role
## outcome: 1
## predictor: 4
##
## — Operations
## • Centering and scaling for: all_numeric_predictors()
```

The recipe object "rec2":

++ Defines the variables by role: 1 outcome and 4 predictors.

++ Contains 1 preprocessing operation: centering and scaling or normalization for all numeric predictors.

2.6.3. Look at Preprocessed Data

First, we prepare the recipe using the prep function on the "rec2" recipe. The resulting object is called "prep_rec2."

```
prep_rec2 <- prep(rec2)
prep_rec2
##
## — Recipe ——————————————————————————————————————
##
## — Inputs
## Number of variables by role
## outcome: 1
## predictor: 4
##
## — Training information
## Training data contained 111 data points and no incomplete rows.
##
## — Operations
## • Centering and scaling for: Sepal.Length and Sepal.Width, … | Trained
```

The recipe has normalized the 4 predictor numeric columns: Sepal.Length, Sepal.Width, Petal.Length, and Petal.Width.

Second, to get the preprocessed training data, we use the bake function with the arguments:

- prep_rec2 which is the prepared recipe.
- new_data = NULL to apply the prepared recipe to training data contained in the original recipe.

The resulting data is called "train_iris2" and we use the glimpse function to see the data structure.

```
train_iris2 <- bake(prep_rec2, new_data = NULL)
glimpse(train_iris2)
## Rows: 111
## Columns: 5
## $ Sepal.Length <dbl> –1.35570543, –1.47308711, –1.00356042, –1.47308711, –1.00…
## $ Sepal.Width <dbl> 0.39769063, 0.16162828, 1.34194005, 0.86981534, 0.8698153…
```

```
## $ Petal.Length <dbl> –1.390967, –1.278392, –1.334680, –1.334680, –1.278392, –1…
## $ Petal.Width <dbl> –1.2980199, –1.2980199, –1.2980199, –1.1681009, –1.298019…
## $ Species <fct> setosa, setosa, setosa, setosa, setosa, setosa, setosa, s…
```

The training data has the same 111 rows and 5 columns of the original training data. However, the column values in the 4 numeric predictors have some negative values because of normalization.

Finally, to get the preprocessed testing data, we use the bake function with the arguments:

- prep_rec2 which is the prepared recipe.
- new_data = test_iris to apply the prepared recipe to the testing data.

The resulting data is called "test_iris2" and we use the glimpse function to see the data structure.

```
test_iris2 <- bake(prep_rec2, new_data = test_iris)
glimpse(test_iris2)
## Rows: 39
## Columns: 5
## $ Sepal.Length <dbl> –0.8861787, –1.1209421, –0.5340337, –0.1818887, –0.886178…
## $ Sepal.Width <dbl> 1.10587769, –0.07443408, 2.05012711, 3.23043887, 1.578002…
## $ Petal.Length <dbl> –1.33467970, –1.33467970, –1.16581634, –1.27839191, –1.27…
## $ Petal.Width <dbl> –1.298019897, –1.298019897, –1.038181829, –1.038181829, –…
## $ Species <fct> setosa, setosa, setosa, setosa, setosa, setosa, setosa, s…
```

The testing data has the same 39 rows and 5 columns of the original testing data. However, the numeric column values have some negative values because of normalization.

2.6.4. Generate Different Resamples (Different Versions) of the Training Data

We split the train_iris data using the vfold_cv function with the arguments:

- v = 10 to split the data to 10 folds.

- repeats = 5 to repeat this process 5 times.
- strata = Species to make stratified resampling using the species column.

The result is 50 different resamples of train_iris data contained in folds2 data frame.

- We also use the set.seed function before splitting to make the splitting reproducible.

```
set.seed(123)
folds2<-vfold_cv(train_iris, v = 10, repeats = 5, strata = Species)
folds2
## # 10-fold cross-validation repeated 5 times using stratification
## # A tibble: 50 × 3
## splits id id2
## <list> <chr> <chr>
## 1 <split [99/12]> Repeat1 Fold01
## 2 <split [99/12]> Repeat1 Fold02
## 3 <split [99/12]> Repeat1 Fold03
## 4 <split [99/12]> Repeat1 Fold04
## 5 <split [99/12]> Repeat1 Fold05
## 6 <split [99/12]> Repeat1 Fold06
## 7 <split [99/12]> Repeat1 Fold07
## 8 <split [102/9]> Repeat1 Fold08
## 9 <split [102/9]> Repeat1 Fold09
## 10 <split [102/9]> Repeat1 Fold10
## # i 40 more rows
```

- There are 50 different rows. Each row corresponds to 1 resample of train_iris data. Each resample has 1 analysis (training) data, with 99 or 102 rows and 1 assessment (testing) data with 12 or 9 rows.
- Each resample has 2 id values. id for the repeat number from 1 to 5 and id2 for the resample number from 1 to 10 within that repeat.
- Each resample has a total rows of 111 which is the number of rows in the original train_iris data. 99 + 12 = 102 + 9 = 111.

2.6.5. Define the Machine Learning (ML) Model

We will use the same discrim_model generated above.

2.6.6. Generate the Workflow

We create the "wflow2" object by using the following functions:

- The workflow function to create a workflow.
- The add_recipe function with the argument "rec2" to add the above created recipe with normalization preprocessing step.
- The add_model function with the argument discrim_model to add the above created model.

```
wflow2 <- workflow() %>%
add_recipe(rec2) %>%
add_model(discrim_model)
wflow2
## ══ Workflow ════════════════════════════════════════════════════════════

## Preprocessor: Recipe
## Model: discrim_linear()
##
## ── Preprocessor ────────────────────────────────────────────────────────

## 1 Recipe Step
##
## • step_normalize()
##
## ── Model ───────────────────────────────────────────────────────────────

## Linear Discriminant Model Specification (classification)
##
## Computational engine: MASS
```

2.6.7. Fit the Model on Training Data

2.6.7.1. Fit the Model on Whole Training Data

We create a "fit_mod2" model by using the fit function with the arguments:

- wflow2 which is the workflow containing normalization preprocessing step and the linear discriminant model.
- train_iris which is the whole training data with 111 rows.

```
fit_mod2<-fit(wflow2, train_iris)
fit_mod2
## ══ Workflow [trained] ══════════════════════════════════════════════════════════
## Preprocessor: Recipe
## Model: discrim_linear()
##
## ── Preprocessor ────────────────────────────────────────────────────────────────
## 1 Recipe Step
##
## • step_normalize()
##
## ── Model ───────────────────────────────────────────────────────────────────────
## Call:
## lda(..y ~ ., data = data)
##
## Prior probabilities of groups:
## setosa versicolor virginica
## 0.3333333 0.3333333 0.3333333
##
## Group means:
## Sepal.Length Sepal.Width Petal.Length Petal.Width
## setosa –1.0067329 0.8251549 –1.2951261 –1.2523727
## versicolor 0.1258416 –0.6677800 0.2763679 0.1697141
## virginica 0.8808913 –0.1573749 1.0187582 1.0826586
##
```

Coefficients of linear discriminants:
LD1 LD2
Sepal.Length 0.7118590 0.3123855
Sepal.Width 0.6597131 –1.0872690
Petal.Length –3.8026706 1.0395145
Petal.Width –2.2835793 –1.8660639
##
Proportion of trace:
LD1 LD2
0.9911 0.0089

The fitted model outputs contain the following elements:

- Prior probabilities of groups, which is the proportion of training rows in each species. There are 33.33% of the training rows in each of the 3 species.
- Group means which are the mean of each normalized predictor in each species.
- Coefficients of linear discriminants which is the linear combination of predictor variables that are used to form the LDA decision rule. There are 2 linear discriminants (LD1 and LD2) that are defined by the equations:

LD1 = 0.7118590 × Sepal.Length + 0.6597131 × Sepal.Width –3.8026706 × Petal.Length –2.2835793 × Petal.Width

LD2 = 0.3123855 × Sepal.Length –1.0872690 × Sepal.Width+ 1.0395145 × Petal.Length –1.8660639 × Petal.Width

2.6.7.2. Plotting Boundary Line on Whole Training Data

To see how these 2 linear discriminants will separate the 3 species, we use the following functions on the preprocessed training data (train_iris2):

- The mutate function with the arguments LD1 and LD2 to create 2 new columns by using the equations generated above.

train_iris2 **%>%** **mutate**(LD1 = 0.7118590*Sepal.Length + 0.6597131*Sepal.Width –3.8026706* Petal.Length –2.2835793 *Petal.Width,

LD2 = 0.3123855* Sepal.Length –1.0872690*Sepal.Width+ 1.0395145*Petal.Length –1.8660639*Petal.Width)

A tibble: 111 × 7

```
## Sepal.Length Sepal.Width Petal.Length Petal.Width Species LD1 LD2
## <dbl> <dbl> <dbl> <dbl> <fct> <dbl> <dbl>
## 1 –1.36 0.398 –1.39 –1.30 setosa 7.55 0.120
## 2 –1.47 0.162 –1.28 –1.30 setosa 6.88 0.457
## 3 –1.00 1.34 –1.33 –1.30 setosa 8.21 –0.738
## 4 –1.47 0.870 –1.33 –1.17 setosa 7.27 –0.614
## 5 –1.00 0.870 –1.28 –1.30 setosa 7.68 –0.166
## 6 –1.71 –0.310 –1.33 –1.30 setosa 6.62 0.839
## 7 –1.12 0.162 –1.28 –1.43 setosa 7.43 0.810
## 8 –0.534 1.58 –1.28 –1.30 setosa 8.49 –0.789
## 9 –1.24 0.870 –1.22 –1.30 setosa 7.30 –0.181
## 10 –1.24 –0.0744 –1.33 –1.43 setosa 7.41 0.971
## # i 101 more rows
```

Then, we use the mutate function again with the predict function as an argument. The predict function has the following arguments:

- fit_mod2 which is the fitted workflow with normalization preprocessing step.
- train_iris which is the training data without preprocessing since it will be preprocessed and modelled using the fit_mod2 object.
- type = "class" to get the predicted class or species for each row of training data.

```
train_iris2 %>% mutate(LD1 = 0.7118590*Sepal.Length + 0.6597131*Sepal.
Width –3.8026706* Petal.Length –2.2835793 *Petal.Width,
LD2 = 0.3123855* Sepal.Length –1.0872690*Sepal.Width+ 1.0395145*Petal.
Length –1.8660639*Petal.Width) %>%
mutate(predict(fit_mod2, train_iris, type = "class"))
## # A tibble: 111 × 8
## Sepal.Length Sepal.Width Petal.Length Petal.Width Species LD1 LD2
## <dbl> <dbl> <dbl> <dbl> <fct> <dbl> <dbl>
## 1 –1.36 0.398 –1.39 –1.30 setosa 7.55 0.120
## 2 –1.47 0.162 –1.28 –1.30 setosa 6.88 0.457
## 3 –1.00 1.34 –1.33 –1.30 setosa 8.21 –0.738
## 4 –1.47 0.870 –1.33 –1.17 setosa 7.27 –0.614
## 5 –1.00 0.870 –1.28 –1.30 setosa 7.68 –0.166
```

6 –1.71 –0.310 –1.33 –1.30 setosa 6.62 0.839

7 –1.12 0.162 –1.28 –1.43 setosa 7.43 0.810

8 –0.534 1.58 –1.28 –1.30 setosa 8.49 –0.789

9 –1.24 0.870 –1.22 –1.30 setosa 7.30 –0.181

10 –1.24 –0.0744 –1.33 –1.43 setosa 7.41 0.971

i 101 more rows

i 1 more variable: .pred_class <fct>

Then, we use the following functions:

- The group_by function with the argument ".pred_class" to split the data into 3 data each containing a single class or species.
- The get_summary_stats function, from the rstatix package, with the arguments "LD1,LD2, show = c("min","max")" to get the minimum and maximum LD1 and LD2 values in each data with a single species.

```
train_iris2 %>% mutate(LD1 = 0.7118590*Sepal.Length + 0.6597131*Sepal.Width –3.8026706* Petal.Length –2.2835793 *Petal.Width,
LD2 = 0.3123855* Sepal.Length –1.0872690*Sepal.Width+ 1.0395145*Petal.Length –1.8660639*Petal.Width) %>%
mutate(predict(fit_mod2, train_iris, type = "class")) %>%
group_by(.pred_class) %>%
get_summary_stats(LD1,LD2, show = c("min","max")) %>%
flextable(cwidth = 1) %>% theme_box() %>%
set_caption(caption = "The minimum and maximum LD1 and LD2 in each predicted species of the iris training data")
```

The minimum and maximum LD1 and LD2 in each predicted species of the iris training data:

.pred_class	variable	n	min	max
setosa	LD1	37	5.685	9.930
setosa	LD2	37	-1.904	2.115
versicolor	LD1	35	-3.765	0.486
versicolor	LD2	35	-0.954	2.804
virginica	LD1	39	-9.094	-3.685
virginica	LD2	39	-2.757	2.177

- The maximum LD1 in virginica = –3.685 while the minimum LD1 in versicolor = –3.765 so a line at LD1 = –3.7 would nearly separate these 2 species.
- The maximum LD1 in versicolor = 0.486 while the minimum LD1 in setosa = 5.685 so a line at LD1 = 4 would separate these 2 species.

To plot the 2 boundary lines, we use the following functions after creating the ".pred_class" column:

- The ggplot function with the arguments "aes(x= LD1, y = LD2, colour = .pred_class)" to plot LD1 values on x-axis, the LD2 values on the y-axis and a different color for each species.
- The geom_point function to plot a scatter plot.
- The geom_vline function with the argument "xintercept = c(–3.7,4)" to add 2 vertical lines at the x-axis values –3.7 and 4.0.
- The labs function with the arguments "title" to add a plot title, and "color" to add a legend title. We add "\n" inside the plot title to make it into 2 lines.
- The theme_classic function as explained before.

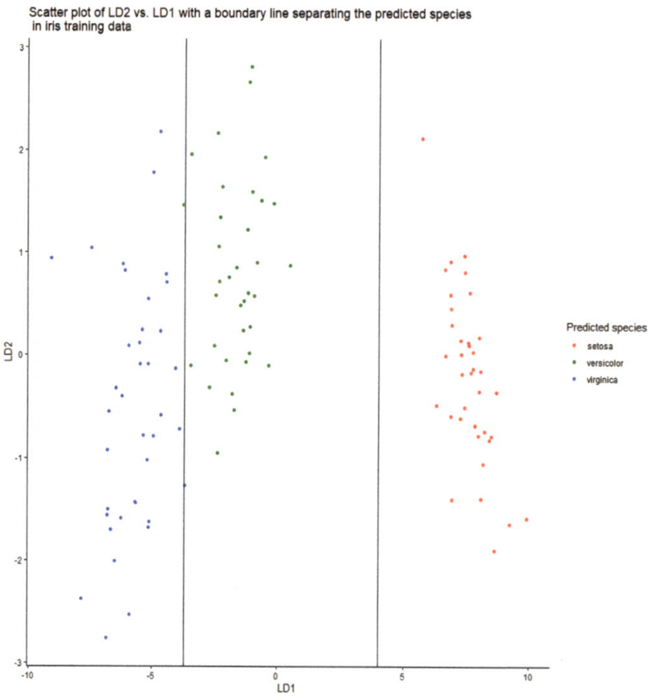

```
train_iris2 %>% mutate(LD1 = 0.7118590*Sepal.Length + 0.6597131*Sepal.Width –3.8026706* Petal.Length –2.2835793 *Petal.Width,
LD2 = 0.3123855* Sepal.Length –1.0872690*Sepal.Width+ 1.0395145*Petal.Length –1.8660639*Petal.Width) %>%
mutate(predict(fit_mod2, train_iris, type = "class")) %>%
ggplot(aes(x= LD1, y = LD2, colour = .pred_class))+
geom_point()+ geom_vline(xintercept = c(–3.7,4))+
labs(title = "Scatter plot of LD2 vs. LD1 with a boundary line separating the predicted species\n in iris training data",
color = "Predicted species")+
theme_classic()
```

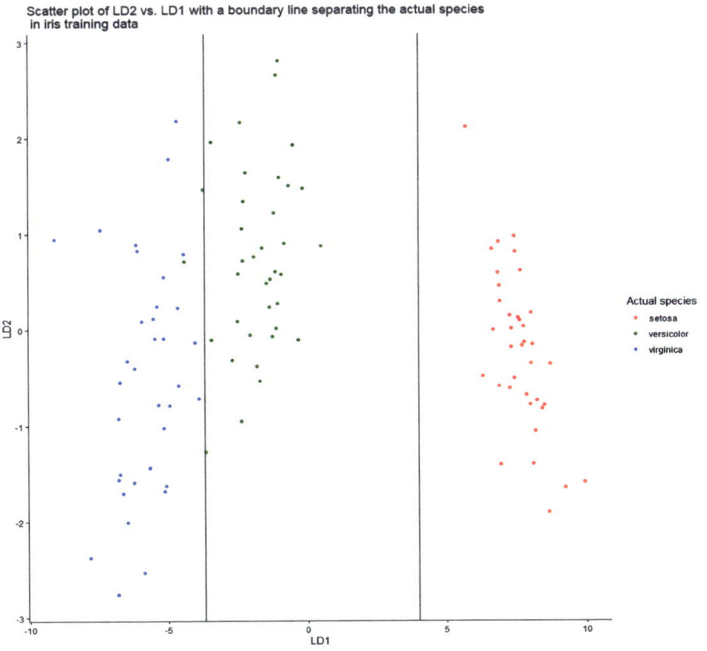

We can produce the same plot but use the actual classes to see how this boundary line separate the actual classes.

```
train_iris2 %>% mutate(LD1 = 0.7118590*Sepal.Length + 0.6597131*Sepal.Width –3.8026706* Petal.Length –2.2835793 *Petal.Width,
LD2 = 0.3123855* Sepal.Length –1.0872690*Sepal.Width+ 1.0395145*Petal.Length –1.8660639*Petal.Width) %>%
```

mutate(**predict**(fit_mod2, train_iris, type = "class")) **%>%**

ggplot(**aes**(x= LD1, y = LD2, colour = Species))+

geom_point()+ **geom_vline**(xintercept = **c**(–3.7,4))+

labs(title = "Scatter plot of LD2 vs. LD1 with a boundary line separating the actual species**n** in iris training data",

color = "Actual species")+

theme_classic()

The lines nearly separates the 3 species perfectly.

2.6.7.3. Model Performance on Whole Training Data

We use the same above functions to generate the confusion matrix.

predict(fit_mod2, train_iris, type = "class") **%>%**

mutate(truth = train_iris$Species) **%>%**

conf_mat(truth = truth, estimate = .pred_class)

Truth

Prediction setosa versicolor virginica

setosa 37 0 0

versicolor 0 35 0

virginica 0 2 37

- The true species are in columns and the predicted species are in rows.
- There are 37 setosa flowers that are predicted correctly as setosa.
- There are 35 versicolor flowers that are predicted correctly as versicolor.
- There are 2 versicolor flowers that are predicted incorrectly as virginica.
- There are 37 virginica flowers that are predicted correctly as virginica.
- The model accuracy = (37 + 35 + 37)/(37 + 35 + 37 + 2) = 0.982 or 98.2%.

The confusion matrix can be plotted directly as a heatmap using the autoplot function with type = "heatmap" argument.

predict(fit_mod2, train_iris, type = "class") **%>%**

mutate(truth = train_iris$Species) **%>%**

conf_mat(truth = truth, estimate = .pred_class) **%>%**

autoplot(type = "heatmap")+

labs(title = "The confusion matrix of applying the LDA model on the iris training data")

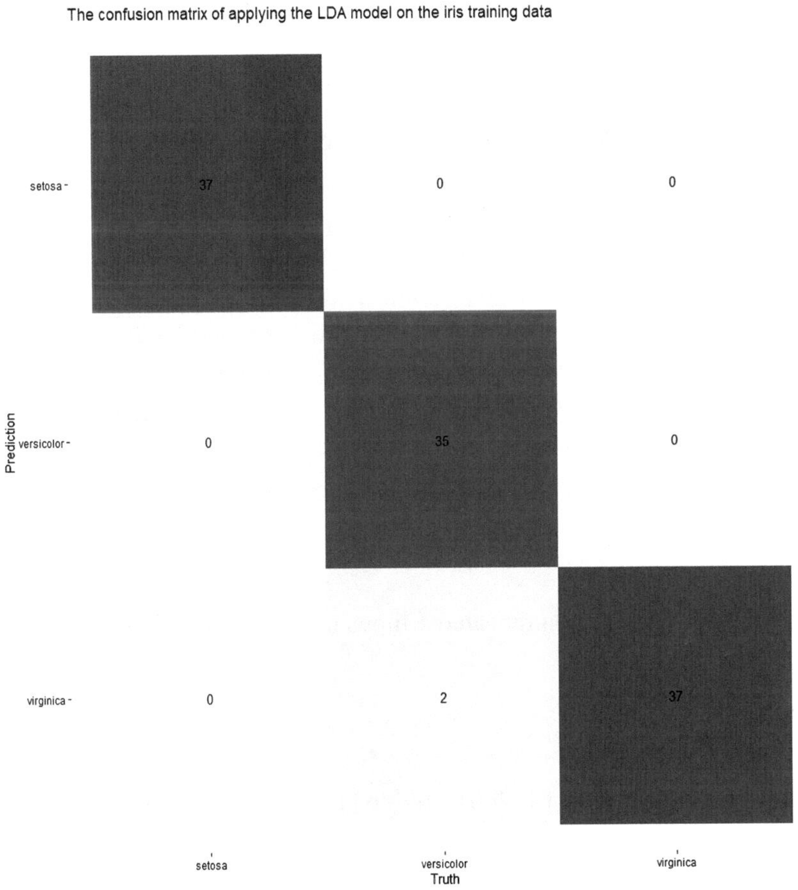

We get the same numbers mentioned above. Alternatively, we can use the accuracy function to get the model accuracy directly with the same arguments as that used with the conf_mat function.

predict(fit_mod2, train_iris, type = "class") **%>%**

mutate(truth = train_iris$Species) **%>%**

accuracy(truth = truth, estimate = .pred_class)

A tibble: 1 × 3

```
## .metric .estimator .estimate
## <chr> <chr> <dbl>
## 1 accuracy multiclass 0.982
```

The model accuracy on training data = 0.982 or 98.2% as calculated previously.

2.6.7.4. Fit the Model on 50 Resamples of Training Data

We create an object "lda_res2" by using the fit_resamples function with the arguments:

- wflow2 which is the workflow containing normalization preprocessing step and the linear discriminant model.
- folds2 which are the 50 resamples of iris training data created above, each containing analysis data for fitting the model and assessment data for testing the model performance within each resample.
- metrics = metrics_set(accuracy) to get the accuracy of the linear discriminant model on each resample.

```
lda_res2<-fit_resamples(wflow2, folds2, metrics = metric_set(accuracy))
lda_res2
## # Resampling results
## # 10-fold cross-validation repeated 5 times using stratification
## # A tibble: 50 × 5
## splits id id2 .metrics .notes
## <list> <chr> <chr> <list> <list>
## 1 <split [99/12]> Repeat1 Fold01 <tibble [1 × 4]> <tibble [0 × 3]>
## 2 <split [99/12]> Repeat1 Fold02 <tibble [1 × 4]> <tibble [0 × 3]>
## 3 <split [99/12]> Repeat1 Fold03 <tibble [1 × 4]> <tibble [0 × 3]>
## 4 <split [99/12]> Repeat1 Fold04 <tibble [1 × 4]> <tibble [0 × 3]>
## 5 <split [99/12]> Repeat1 Fold05 <tibble [1 × 4]> <tibble [0 × 3]>
## 6 <split [99/12]> Repeat1 Fold06 <tibble [1 × 4]> <tibble [0 × 3]>
## 7 <split [99/12]> Repeat1 Fold07 <tibble [1 × 4]> <tibble [0 × 3]>
## 8 <split [102/9]> Repeat1 Fold08 <tibble [1 × 4]> <tibble [0 × 3]>
## 9 <split [102/9]> Repeat1 Fold09 <tibble [1 × 4]> <tibble [0 × 3]>
## 10 <split [102/9]> Repeat1 Fold10 <tibble [1 × 4]> <tibble [0 × 3]>
## # i 40 more rows
```

The resulting object "lda_res2" contains 50 rows (for 50 resamples) and 5 columns:

- The splits column is a list of each combination of analysis and assessment data withing each resample. The sum is 111 which are total rows of iris training data.
- The id column is an id column for the repeat number from 1 to 5.
- The id2 column is an id column for the fold number from 1 to 10 so we have 50 resamples because 5 × 10 = 50.
- The .metrics column is a list of performance metric (accuracy) of applying the LDA model to the corresponding assessment data (12 or 9 rows) within each resample. Each performance metric is saved in 1 row and 4 columns [1 × 4] tibble or data frame. These will be extracted in the next step.
- The .notes column is a list of notes or warnings when applying the linear model to each analysis data (99 or 102 rows) within each resample. Each note is saved in 0 rows and 3 columns [0 × 3] tibble or data frame meaning that there are no notes when applying this model to each analysis data.

2.6.7.5. Model Performance on 50 Resamples of Training Data

To get the performance metric (accuracy) on the 50 resamples of training data, we use the same above functions on the "lda_res2."

lda_res2 **%>% collect_metrics**(summarize = FALSE) **%>%**

arrange(.estimate) **%>%**

flextable(cwidth = 1) **%>% theme_box() %>%**

set_caption(caption = "The accuracy of 50 resamples of iris training data when using LDA model")

The accuracy of 50 resamples of iris training data when using LDA model:

id	**id2**	**.metric**	**.estimator**	**.estimate**	**.config**
Repeat5	Fold08	accuracy	multiclass	0.8888889	Preprocessor1_Model1
Repeat1	Fold02	accuracy	multiclass	0.9166667	Preprocessor1_Model1
Repeat1	Fold03	accuracy	multiclass	0.9166667	Preprocessor1_Model1

Repeat2	Fold03	accuracy	multiclass	0.9166667	Preprocessor1_Model1
Repeat2	Fold06	accuracy	multiclass	0.9166667	Preprocessor1_Model1
Repeat3	Fold02	accuracy	multiclass	0.9166667	Preprocessor1_Model1
Repeat3	Fold04	accuracy	multiclass	0.9166667	Preprocessor1_Model1
Repeat4	Fold01	accuracy	multiclass	0.9166667	Preprocessor1_Model1
Repeat4	Fold04	accuracy	multiclass	0.9166667	Preprocessor1_Model1
Repeat5	Fold05	accuracy	multiclass	0.9166667	Preprocessor1_Model1
Repeat5	Fold06	accuracy	multiclass	0.9166667	Preprocessor1_Model1
Repeat1	Fold01	accuracy	multiclass	1.0000000	Preprocessor1_Model1
Repeat1	Fold04	accuracy	multiclass	1.0000000	Preprocessor1_Model1
Repeat1	Fold05	accuracy	multiclass	1.0000000	Preprocessor1_Model1
Repeat1	Fold06	accuracy	multiclass	1.0000000	Preprocessor1_Model1
Repeat1	Fold07	accuracy	multiclass	1.0000000	Preprocessor1_Model1
Repeat1	Fold08	accuracy	multiclass	1.0000000	Preprocessor1_Model1
Repeat1	Fold09	accuracy	multiclass	1.0000000	Preprocessor1_Model1
Repeat1	Fold10	accuracy	multiclass	1.0000000	Preprocessor1_Model1
Repeat2	Fold01	accuracy	multiclass	1.0000000	Preprocessor1_Model1
Repeat2	Fold02	accuracy	multiclass	1.0000000	Preprocessor1_Model1

Repeat2	Fold04	accuracy	multiclass	1.0000000	Preprocessor1_Model1
Repeat2	Fold05	accuracy	multiclass	1.0000000	Preprocessor1_Model1
Repeat2	Fold07	accuracy	multiclass	1.0000000	Preprocessor1_Model1
Repeat2	Fold08	accuracy	multiclass	1.0000000	Preprocessor1_Model1
Repeat2	Fold09	accuracy	multiclass	1.0000000	Preprocessor1_Model1
Repeat2	Fold10	accuracy	multiclass	1.0000000	Preprocessor1_Model1
Repeat3	Fold01	accuracy	multiclass	1.0000000	Preprocessor1_Model1
Repeat3	Fold03	accuracy	multiclass	1.0000000	Preprocessor1_Model1
Repeat3	Fold05	accuracy	multiclass	1.0000000	Preprocessor1_Model1
Repeat3	Fold06	accuracy	multiclass	1.0000000	Preprocessor1_Model1
Repeat3	Fold07	accuracy	multiclass	1.0000000	Preprocessor1_Model1
Repeat3	Fold08	accuracy	multiclass	1.0000000	Preprocessor1_Model1
Repeat3	Fold09	accuracy	multiclass	1.0000000	Preprocessor1_Model1
Repeat3	Fold10	accuracy	multiclass	1.0000000	Preprocessor1_Model1
Repeat4	Fold02	accuracy	multiclass	1.0000000	Preprocessor1_Model1
Repeat4	Fold03	accuracy	multiclass	1.0000000	Preprocessor1_Model1
Repeat4	Fold05	accuracy	multiclass	1.0000000	Preprocessor1_Model1
Repeat4	Fold06	accuracy	multiclass	1.0000000	Preprocessor1_Model1

Repeat4	Fold07	accuracy	multiclass	1.0000000	Preproces-sor1_Model1
Repeat4	Fold08	accuracy	multiclass	1.0000000	Preproces-sor1_Model1
Repeat4	Fold09	accuracy	multiclass	1.0000000	Preproces-sor1_Model1
Repeat4	Fold10	accuracy	multiclass	1.0000000	Preproces-sor1_Model1
Repeat5	Fold01	accuracy	multiclass	1.0000000	Preproces-sor1_Model1
Repeat5	Fold02	accuracy	multiclass	1.0000000	Preproces-sor1_Model1
Repeat5	Fold03	accuracy	multiclass	1.0000000	Preproces-sor1_Model1
Repeat5	Fold04	accuracy	multiclass	1.0000000	Preproces-sor1_Model1
Repeat5	Fold07	accuracy	multiclass	1.0000000	Preproces-sor1_Model1
Repeat5	Fold09	accuracy	multiclass	1.0000000	Preproces-sor1_Model1
Repeat5	Fold10	accuracy	multiclass	1.0000000	Preproces-sor1_Model1

- The result is 50 rows with 1 accuracy value for each resample.
- The lowest accuracy (0.888) was achieved in repeat 5 and fold 8, while the highest accuracy (1.00 or 100%) was achieved in many resamples.

If we used the collect_metrics function with the argument summarize = TRUE, we will get the mean accuracy value across the 50 resamples of the iris training data.

lda_res2 **%>% collect_metrics**(summarize = TRUE)

A tibble: 1 × 6

.metric .estimator mean n std_err .config

<chr> <chr> <dbl> <int> <dbl> <chr>

1 accuracy multiclass 0.981 50 0.00511 Preprocessor1_Model1

- The mean accuracy of LDA model on 50 resamples of iris training data (n = 50) = 0.981, while the accuracy on whole training data = 0.982.

2.6.8. Model Performance on Testing Data

We use the same above functions to get the confusion matrix of the testing data so we use:

- The "test_iris" argument within the predict function.
- The truth column = test_iris$Species within the mutate function.

```
predict(fit_mod2, test_iris, type = "class") %>%
mutate(truth = test_iris$Species) %>%
conf_mat(truth = truth, estimate = .pred_class)
## Truth
## Prediction setosa versicolor virginica
## setosa 13 0 0
## versicolor 0 13 1
## virginica 0 0 12
```

- The true species are in columns and the predicted species are in rows.
- There arc 13 setosa flowers that are predicted correctly as setosa.
- There are 13 versicolor flowers that are predicted correctly as versicolor.
- There is 1 virginica flower that is predicted incorrectly as versicolor.
- There are 12 virginica flowers that are predicted correctly as virginica.
- The model accuracy = (13 + 13 + 12)/(13 + 13 + 12 + 1) = 0.974 or 97.4%.

The confusion matrix can be plotted directly as a heatmap using the autoplot function with type = "heatmap" argument.

```
predict(fit_mod2, test_iris, type = "class") %>%
mutate(truth = test_iris$Species) %>%
conf_mat(truth = truth, estimate = .pred_class) %>%
autoplot(type = "heatmap")+
labs(title = "The confusion matrix of applying the LDA model on the iris testing data")
```

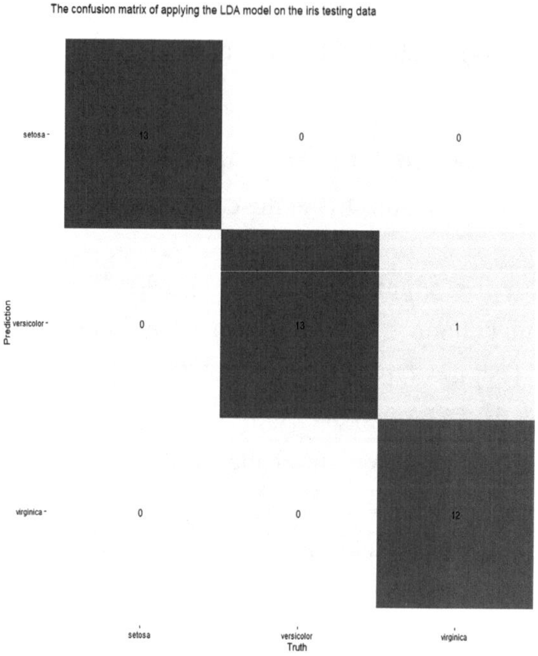

We get the same numbers mentioned above. Alternatively, we can use the accuracy function to get the model accuracy directly.

```
fit_mod2 %>% predict(new_data = test_iris) %>%
mutate(truth = test_iris$Species) %>%
accuracy(truth = truth, estimate = .pred_class)
## # A tibble: 1 × 3
## .metric .estimator .estimate
## <chr> <chr> <dbl>
## 1 accuracy multiclass 0.974
```

The model accuracy on testing data = 0.974 or 97.4% as calculated previously.

CHAPTER 3

PENALIZED REGRESSION MODELING

Contents

3.1. Data Used in This Chapter 125
3.2. Data Exploration 132
3.3. Penalized Regression 139
3.4. Ridge Regression 140
3.5. Lasso Regression 184
3.6. Elastic Net Regression 198
3.7. Conclusion 219

3.1. DATA USED IN THIS CHAPTER

3.1.1. Ames Housing Data

This data contains 74 characteristics that were recorded for 2,930 properties in Ames Iowa.

The data is part of the modeldata package under the name "ames." The modeldata package is part of tidymodels package which is a collection of different packages for data modeling.

First, we load the tidymodels package using the library function then, we load the ames data using the data function.

We also load the tidyverse and flextable packages for the reasons described above.

```
library(tidymodels)
data(ames)
library(tidyverse)
library(flextable)
```

Then, to see the data structure, we use the glimpse function.

```
glimpse(ames)
## Rows: 2,930
## Columns: 74
## $ MS_SubClass <fct> One_Story_1946_and_Newer_All_Styles, One_Story_1946…
## $ MS_Zoning <fct> Residential_Low_Density, Residential_High_Density, …
## $ Lot_Frontage <dbl> 141, 80, 81, 93, 74, 78, 41, 43, 39, 60, 75, 0, 63,…
## $ Lot_Area <int> 31770, 11622, 14267, 11160, 13830, 9978, 4920, 5005…
## $ Street <fct> Pave, Pave, Pave, Pave, Pave, Pave, Pave, Pave, Pav…
## $ Alley <fct> No_Alley_Access, No_Alley_Access, No_Alley_Access, …
## $ Lot_Shape <fct> Slightly_Irregular, Regular, Slightly_Irregular, Re…
## $ Land_Contour <fct> Lvl, Lvl, Lvl, Lvl, Lvl, Lvl, Lvl, HLS, Lvl, Lvl, L…
## $ Utilities <fct> AllPub, AllPub, AllPub, AllPub, AllPub, AllPub, All…
## $ Lot_Config <fct> Corner, Inside, Corner, Corner, Inside, Inside, Ins…
## $ Land_Slope <fct> Gtl, Gtl, Gtl, Gtl, Gtl, Gtl, Gtl, Gtl, Gtl, Gtl, G…
## $ Neighborhood <fct> North_Ames, North_Ames, North_Ames, North_Ames, Gil…
## $ Condition_1 <fct> Norm, Feedr, Norm, Norm, Norm, Norm, Norm, Norm, No…
## $ Condition_2 <fct> Norm, Norm, Norm, Norm, Norm, Norm, Norm, Norm,
```

Nor…

$ Bldg_Type <fct> OneFam, OneFam, OneFam, OneFam, OneFam, OneFam, Twn…

$ House_Style <fct> One_Story, One_Story, One_Story, One_Story, Two_Sto…

$ Overall_Cond <fct> Average, Above_Average, Above_Average, Average, Ave…

$ Year_Built <int> 1960, 1961, 1958, 1968, 1997, 1998, 2001, 1992, 199…

$ Year_Remod_Add <int> 1960, 1961, 1958, 1968, 1998, 1998, 2001, 1992, 199…

$ Roof_Style <fct> Hip, Gable, Hip, Hip, Gable, Gable, Gable, Gable, G…

$ Roof_Matl <fct> CompShg, CompShg, CompShg, CompShg, CompShg, CompSh…

$ Exterior_1st <fct> BrkFace, VinylSd, Wd Sdng, BrkFace, VinylSd, VinylS…

$ Exterior_2nd <fct> Plywood, VinylSd, Wd Sdng, BrkFace, VinylSd, VinylS…

$ Mas_Vnr_Type <fct> Stone, None, BrkFace, None, None, BrkFace, None, No…

$ Mas_Vnr_Area <dbl> 112, 0, 108, 0, 0, 20, 0, 0, 0, 0, 0, 0, 0, 0, 0, 6…

$ Exter_Cond <fct> Typical, Typical, Typical, Typical, Typical, Typica…

$ Foundation <fct> CBlock, CBlock, CBlock, CBlock, PConc, PConc, PConc…

$ Bsmt_Cond <fct> Good, Typical, Typical, Typical, Typical, Typical, …

$ Bsmt_Exposure <fct> Gd, No, No, No, No, No, Mn, No, No, No, No, No, No,…

$ BsmtFin_Type_1 <fct> BLQ, Rec, ALQ, ALQ, GLQ, GLQ, GLQ, ALQ, GLQ, Unf, U…

$ BsmtFin_SF_1 <dbl> 2, 6, 1, 1, 3, 3, 3, 1, 3, 7, 7, 1, 7, 3, 3, 1, 3, …

$ BsmtFin_Type_2 <fct> Unf, LwQ, Unf, Unf, Unf, Unf, Unf, Unf, Unf, Unf, U…

$ BsmtFin_SF_2 <dbl> 0, 144, 0, 0, 0, 0, 0, 0, 0, 0, 0, 0, 0, 0, 1120, 0…

$ Bsmt_Unf_SF <dbl> 441, 270, 406, 1045, 137, 324, 722, 1017, 415, 994,…

$ Total_Bsmt_SF <dbl> 1080, 882, 1329, 2110, 928, 926, 1338, 1280, 1595, …

```
## $ Heating <fct> GasA, GasA, GasA, GasA, GasA, GasA, GasA, GasA, Gas…
## $ Heating_QC <fct> Fair, Typical, Typical, Excellent, Good, Excellent,…
## $ Central_Air <fct> Y, Y, Y, Y, Y, Y, Y, Y, Y, Y, Y, Y, Y, Y, Y, Y, Y, …
## $ Electrical <fct> SBrkr, SBrkr, SBrkr, SBrkr, SBrkr, SBrkr, SBrkr, SB…
## $ First_Flr_SF <int> 1656, 896, 1329, 2110, 928, 926, 1338, 1280, 1616, …
## $ Second_Flr_SF <int> 0, 0, 0, 0, 701, 678, 0, 0, 0, 776, 892, 0, 676, 0,…
## $ Gr_Liv_Area <int> 1656, 896, 1329, 2110, 1629, 1604, 1338, 1280, 1616…
## $ Bsmt_Full_Bath <dbl> 1, 0, 0, 1, 0, 0, 1, 0, 1, 0, 0, 1, 0, 1, 1, 1, 0, …
## $ Bsmt_Half_Bath <dbl> 0, 0, 0, 0, 0, 0, 0, 0, 0, 0, 0, 0, 0, 0, 0, 0, 0, …
## $ Full_Bath <int> 1, 1, 1, 2, 2, 2, 2, 2, 2, 2, 2, 2, 2, 1, 1, 3, 2, …
## $ Half_Bath <int> 0, 0, 1, 1, 1, 1, 0, 0, 0, 1, 1, 0, 1, 1, 1, 1, 0, …
## $ Bedroom_AbvGr <int> 3, 2, 3, 3, 3, 3, 2, 2, 2, 3, 3, 3, 3, 2, 1, 4, 4, …
## $ Kitchen_AbvGr <int> 1, 1, 1, 1, 1, 1, 1, 1, 1, 1, 1, 1, 1, 1, 1, 1, 1, …
## $ TotRms_AbvGrd <int> 7, 5, 6, 8, 6, 7, 6, 5, 5, 7, 7, 6, 7, 5, 4, 12, 8,…
## $ Functional <fct> Typ, Typ, Typ, Typ, Typ, Typ, Typ, Typ, Typ, Typ, T…
## $ Fireplaces <int> 2, 0, 0, 2, 1, 1, 0, 0, 1, 1, 1, 0, 1, 1, 0, 1, 0, …
## $ Garage_Type <fct> Attchd, Attchd, Attchd, Attchd, Attchd, Attchd, Att…
## $ Garage_Finish <fct> Fin, Unf, Unf, Fin, Fin, Fin, Fin, RFn, RFn, Fin, F…
## $ Garage_Cars <dbl> 2, 1, 1, 2, 2, 2, 2, 2, 2, 2, 2, 2, 2, 2, 2, 3, 2, …
## $ Garage_Area <dbl> 528, 730, 312, 522, 482, 470, 582, 506, 608, 442, 4…
## $ Garage_Cond <fct> Typical, Typical, Typical, Typical, Typical, Typica…
## $ Paved_Drive <fct> Partial_Pavement, Paved, Paved, Paved, Paved, Paved…
## $ Wood_Deck_SF <int> 210, 140, 393, 0, 212, 360, 0, 0, 237, 140, 157, 48…
## $ Open_Porch_SF <int> 62, 0, 36, 0, 34, 36, 0, 82, 152, 60, 84, 21, 75, 0…
## $ Enclosed_Porch <int> 0, 0, 0, 0, 0, 0, 170, 0, 0, 0, 0, 0, 0, 0, 0, 0, 0…
## $ Three_season_porch <int> 0, 0, 0, 0, 0, 0, 0, 0, 0, 0, 0, 0, 0, 0, 0, 0, …
## $ Screen_Porch <int> 0, 120, 0, 0, 0, 0, 0, 144, 0, 0, 0, 0, 0, 0, 140, …
## $ Pool_Area <int> 0, 0, 0, 0, 0, 0, 0, 0, 0, 0, 0, 0, 0, 0, 0, 0, …
## $ Pool_QC <fct> No_Pool, No_Pool, No_Pool, No_Pool, No_Pool, No_Poo…
```

$ Fence <fct> No_Fence, Minimum_Privacy, No_Fence, No_Fence, Mini…

$ Misc_Feature <fct> None, None, Gar2, None, None, None, None, None, Non…

$ Misc_Val <int> 0, 0, 12500, 0, 0, 0, 0, 0, 0, 0, 0, 500, 0, 0, 0, …

$ Mo_Sold <int> 5, 6, 6, 4, 3, 6, 4, 1, 3, 6, 4, 3, 5, 2, 6, 6, 6, …

$ Year_Sold <int> 2010, 2010, 2010, 2010, 2010, 2010, 2010, 2010, 201…

$ Sale_Type <fct> WD, WD, WD, WD, WD, WD, WD, WD, WD, WD, W…

$ Sale_Condition <fct> Normal, Normal, Normal, Normal, Normal, Normal, Nor…

$ Sale_Price <int> 215000, 105000, 172000, 244000, 189900, 195500, 213…

$ Longitude <dbl> –93.61975, –93.61976, –93.61939, –93.61732, –93.638…

$ Latitude <dbl> 42.05403, 42.05301, 42.05266, 42.05125, 42.06090, 4…

The data has 2930 rows (properties) and 74 columns:

1. **MS_SubClass:** a factor column for the type of dwelling involved in the sale.
2. **MS_Zoning:** a factor column for the general zoning classification of the sale.
3. **Lot_Frontage:** a numeric column for the linear feet of street connected to property.
4. **Lot_Area:** a numeric column for the lot size in square feet.
5. **Street:** a factor column for the type of road access to property.
6. **Alley:** a factor column for the type of alley access to property.
7. **Lot_Shape:** a factor column for the general shape of property.
8. **Land_Contour:** a factor column for the flatness of the property.
9. **Utilities:** a factor column for the type of utilities available.
10. **Lot_Config:** a factor column for the lot configuration.
11. **Land_Slope:** a factor column for the slope of property.
12. **Neighborhood:** a factor column for the physical locations within Ames city limits.
13. **Condition_1:** a factor column for the proximity to various conditions.
14. **Condition_2:** a factor column for the proximity to various conditions (if more than one is present).

15. **Bldg_Type:** a factor column for the type of dwelling.
16. **House_Style:** a factor column for the style of dwelling.
17. **Overall_Cond:** a factor column for the rate of the overall condition of the house.
18. **Year_Built:** a numeric column for the original construction year.
19. **Year_Remod_Add:** a numeric column for the remodeling year (same as construction year if no remodeling or additions were done).
20. **Roof_Style:** a factor column for the Type of roof.
21. **Roof_Matl:** a factor column for the roof material.
22. **Exterior_1st:** a factor column for the exterior covering on house.
23. **Exterior_2nd:** a factor column for the exterior covering on house (if more than one material).
24. **Mas_Vnr_Type:** a factor column for the masonry veneer type.
25. **Mas_Vnr_Area:** a numeric column for the masonry veneer area in square feet.
26. **Exter_Cond:** a factor column that evaluates the present condition of the material on the exterior.
27. **Foundation:** a factor column for the type of foundation.
28. **Bsmt_Cond:** a factor column that evaluates the general condition of the basement.
29. **Bsmt_Exposure:** a factor column that refers to walkout or garden level walls.
30. **BsmtFin_Type_1:** a factor column containing the rating of basement finished area.
31. **BsmtFin_SF_1:** a numeric column for type 1 finished square feet.
32. **BsmtFin_Type_2:** a factor column containing the rating of basement finished area (if multiple types).
33. **BsmtFin_SF_2:** a numeric column containing type 2 finished square feet.
34. **Bsmt_Unf_SF:** a numeric column containing the unfinished square feet of basement area.
35. **Total_Bsmt_SF:** a numeric column containing the total square feet of basement area.
36. **Heating:** a factor column for the type of heating.
37. **Heating_QC:** a factor column for the heating quality and condition.

38. **Central_Air:** a factor column for the presence of central air conditioning.
39. **Electrical:** a factor column containing the electrical system.
40. **First_Flr_SF:** a numeric column holding the first-floor square feet.
41. **Second_Flr_SF:** a numeric column holding the second-floor square feet.
42. **Gr_Liv_Area:** a numeric column holding the above grade (ground) living area square feet.
43. **Bsmt_Full_Bath:** a numeric column holding the number of basement full bathrooms.
44. **Bsmt_Half_Bath:** a numeric column holding the number of basement half bathrooms.
45. **Full_Bath:** a numeric column holding the number of full bathrooms above grade.
46. **Half_Bath:** a numeric column holding the number of half baths above grade.
47. **Bedroom_AbvGr:** a numeric column holding the number of bedrooms above grade (does not include basement bedrooms).
48. **Kitchen_AbvGr:** a numeric column holding the number of kitchens above grade.
49. **TotRms_AbvGrd:** a numeric column holding the number of total rooms above grade (does not include bathrooms).
50. **Functional:** a factor column for the home functionality (assume typical unless deductions are warranted).
51. **Fireplaces:** a numeric column holding the number of fireplaces.
52. **Garage_Type:** a factor column for the garage type.
53. **Garage_Finish:** a factor column for the interior finish of the garage.
54. **Garage_Cars:** a numeric column for the size of garage in car capacity.
55. **Garage_Area:** a numeric column for the size of garage in square feet.
56. **Garage_Cond:** a factor column holding the garage condition.
57. **Paved_Drive:** a factor column for the type of paved driveway.
58. **Wood_Deck_SF:** a numeric column for the wood deck area in square feet.

59. **Open_Porch_SF:** a numeric column for the open porch area in square feet.
60. **Enclosed_Porch:** a numeric column for the enclosed porch area in square feet.
61. **Three_season_porch:** a numeric column holding the three-season porch area in square feet.
62. **Screen_Porch:** a numeric column holding the screen porch area in square feet.
63. **Pool_Area:** a numeric column for the pool area in square feet.
64. **Pool_QC:** a factor column for the pool quality.
65. **Fence:** a factor column for the fence quality.
66. **Misc_Feature:** a factor column for miscellaneous feature not covered in other columns.
67. **Misc_Val:** a numeric column holding the dollar value of miscellaneous feature.
68. **Mo_Sold:** a numeric column holding the month in which the selling was done.
69. **Year_Sold:** a numeric column holding the year in which the selling was done.
70. **Sale_Type:** a factor column holding the type of sale.
71. **Sale_Condition:** a factor column holding the condition of the sale.
72. **Sale_Price:** a numeric column holding the sold price in dollars.

- The Sale_Price column is our numerical outcome that will be modeled using a penalized regression model.

73. **Longitude:** a numeric column holding the longitude of the property.
74. **Latitude:** a numeric column holding the latitude of the property.

The data reference is De Cock (2011).

3.2. DATA EXPLORATION

The first step in any data modeling is exploring the data using the functions from the skimr package as described in previous chapters.

3.2.1. Categorical Columns

To examine all factor categorical columns at once, we use the following functions on the ames data:

- The skim function that produces information about all data columns.
- The yank function with "factor" argument to get only the information related to factor or categorical columns.

Then, we convert the result to a table as explained in previous chapters using functions from the flextable package. To use functions from the skimr package, we should first load the skimr package first using the library function.

library(skimr)

ames **%>% skim**() **%>% yank**("factor") **%>%**

flextable(cwidth = 1) **%>% theme_box**() **%>%**

set_caption(caption = "The information gained from skim function on the categorical columns of the ames data")

The information gained from skim function on the categorical columns of the ames data:

skim_variable	**n_missing**	**complete_rate**	**ordered**	**n_unique**	**top_counts**
MS_SubClass	0	1	FALSE	16	One: 1079, Two: 575, One: 287, One: 192
MS_Zoning	0	1	FALSE	7	Res: 2273, Res: 462, Flo: 139, Res: 27
Street	0	1	FALSE	2	Pav: 2918, Grv: 12
Alley	0	1	FALSE	3	No_: 2732, Gra: 120, Pav: 78
Lot_Shape	0	1	FALSE	4	Reg: 1859, Sli: 979, Mod: 76, Irr: 16
Land_Contour	0	1	FALSE	4	Lvl: 2633, HLS: 120, Bnk: 117, Low: 60
Utilities	0	1	FALSE	3	All: 2927, NoS: 2, NoS: 1
Lot_Config	0	1	FALSE	5	Ins: 2140, Cor: 511, Cul: 180, FR2: 85
Land_Slope	0	1	FALSE	3	Gtl: 2789, Mod: 125, Sev: 16

Neighbor-hood	0	1	FALSE	28	Nor: 443, Col: 267, Old: 239, Edw: 194
Condition_1	0	1	FALSE	9	Nor: 2522, Fee: 164, Art: 92, RRA: 50
Condition_2	0	1	FALSE	8	Nor: 2900, Fee: 13, Art: 5, Pos: 4
Bldg_Type	0	1	FALSE	5	One: 2425, Twn: 233, Dup: 109, Twn: 101
House_Style	0	1	FALSE	8	One: 1481, Two: 873, One: 314, SLv: 128
Overall_Cond	0	1	FALSE	9	Ave: 1654, Abo: 533, Goo: 390, Ver: 144
Roof_Style	0	1	FALSE	6	Gab: 2321, Hip: 551, Gam: 22, Fla: 20
Roof_Matl	0	1	FALSE	8	Com: 2887, Tar: 23, WdS: 9, WdS: 7
Exterior_1st	0	1	FALSE	16	Vin: 1026, Met: 450, HdB: 442, Wd: 420
Exterior_2nd	0	1	FALSE	17	Vin: 1015, Met: 447, HdB: 406, Wd: 397
Mas_Vnr_Type	0	1	FALSE	5	Non: 1775, Brk: 880, Sto: 249, Brk: 25
Exter_Cond	0	1	FALSE	5	Typ: 2549, Goo: 299, Fai: 67, Exc: 12
Foundation	0	1	FALSE	6	PCo: 1310, CBl: 1244, Brk: 311, Sla: 49
Bsmt_Cond	0	1	FALSE	6	Typ: 2616, Goo: 122, Fai: 104, No_: 80

Bsmt_Expo-sure	0	1	FALSE	5	No: 1906, Av: 418, Gd: 284, Mn: 239
BsmtFin_Type_1	0	1	FALSE	7	GLQ: 859, Unf: 851, ALQ: 429, Rec: 288
BsmtFin_Type_2	0	1	FALSE	7	Unf: 2499, Rec: 106, LwQ: 89, No_: 81
Heating	0	1	FALSE	6	Gas: 2885, Gas: 27, Gra: 9, Wal: 6
Heating_QC	0	1	FALSE	5	Exc: 1495, Typ: 864, Goo: 476, Fai: 92
Central_Air	0	1	FALSE	2	Y: 2734, N: 196
Electrical	0	1	FALSE	6	SBr: 2682, Fus: 188, Fus: 50, Fus: 8
Functional	0	1	FALSE	8	Typ: 2728, Min: 70, Min: 65, Mod: 35
Garage_Type	0	1	FALSE	7	Att: 1731, Det: 782, Bui: 186, No_: 157
Garage_Fin-ish	0	1	FALSE	4	Unf: 1231, RFn: 812, Fin: 728, No_: 159
Garage_Cond	0	1	FALSE	6	Typ: 2665, No_: 159, Fai: 74, Goo: 15
Paved_Drive	0	1	FALSE	3	Pav: 2652, Dir: 216, Par: 62
Pool_QC	0	1	FALSE	5	No_: 2917, Exc: 4, Goo: 4, Typ: 3
Fence	0	1	FALSE	5	No_: 2358, Min: 330, Goo: 118, Goo: 112
Misc_Feature	0	1	FALSE	6	Non: 2824, She: 95, Gar: 5, Oth: 4

Sale_Type	0	1	FALSE	10	WD: 2536, New: 239, COD: 87, Con: 26
Sale_Condition	0	1	FALSE	6	Nor: 2413, Par: 245, Abn: 190, Fam: 46

We have 6 columns:

1. The skim_variable is the factor or categorical column name. We have 40 different factor columns.
2. The n_missing is the number of missing values. All factor columns have zero or no missing values.
3. The complete_rate is the proportion of present values in each column. All factor columns have a complete rate of 1 or 100%.
4. The ordered column denotes if the factor column is an ordered factor. All factor columns are unordered and so have a FALSE value.
5. The n_unique is the number of unique values in each factor column.
6. The top_counts is the number of rows for the most frequent categories in the factor columns. Some categories have very low frequency and so should be removed in the preprocessing steps because of low variability after dummification.

3.2.2. Numerical Columns

We use the same above functions but use the yank function with the "numeric" argument to get useful information about numeric columns in the ames data.

ames **%>% skim**() **%>% yank**("numeric") **%>%**

flextable() **%>% theme_box**() **%>%**

set_caption(caption = "The information gained from skim function on numerical columns from the ames data")

The information gained from skim function on numerical columns from the ames data:

skim_variable	n_missing	complete_rate	mean	sd	p0	p25	p50	p75	p100	hist
Lot_Frontage	0	1	57.64778157	33.49944079	0.00000	43.00000	63.00000	78.00000	313.00000	
Lot_Area	0	1	10,147.92184300	7,880.01775944	1,300.00000	7,440.25000	9,436.50000	11,555.25000	215,245.00000	
Year_Built	0	1	1,971.35631399	30.24536063	1,872.00000	1,954.00000	1,973.00000	2,001.00000	2,010.00000	
Year_Remod_Add	0	1	1,984.26655290	20.86028588	1,950.00000	1,965.00000	1,993.00000	2,004.00000	2,010.00000	
Mas_Vnr_Area	0	1	101.09692833	178.63454483	0.00000	0.00000	0.00000	162.75000	1,600.00000	
BsmtFin_SF_1	0	1	4.17747440	2.23337248	0.00000	3.00000	3.00000	7.00000	7.00000	
BsmtFin_SF_2	0	1	49.70546075	169.14208929	0.00000	0.00000	0.00000	0.00000	1,526.00000	
Bsmt_Unf_SF	0	1	559.07167235	439.54057106	0.00000	219.00000	465.50000	801.75000	2,336.00000	
Total_Bsmt_SF	0	1	1,051.25563140	440.96801766	0.00000	793.00000	990.00000	1,301.50000	6,110.00000	
First_Flr_SF	0	1	1,159.55767918	391.89088525	334.00000	876.25000	1,084.00000	1,384.00000	5,095.00000	
Second_Flr_SF	0	1	335.45597270	428.39571501	0.00000	0.00000	0.00000	703.75000	2,065.00000	
Gr_Liv_Area	0	1	1,499.69044369	505.50888747	334.00000	1,126.00000	1,442.00000	1,742.75000	5,642.00000	
Bsmt_Full_Bath	0	1	0.43105802	0.52476196	0.00000	0.00000	0.00000	1.00000	3.00000	
Bsmt_Half_Bath	0	1	0.06109215	0.24517502	0.00000	0.00000	0.00000	0.00000	2.00000	
Full_Bath	0	1	1.56655290	0.55294061	0.00000	1.00000	2.00000	2.00000	4.00000	
Half_Bath	0	1	0.37952218	0.50262925	0.00000	0.00000	0.00000	1.00000	2.00000	

Bedroom_ AbvGr	0	1	2.85426621	0.82773114	0.00000	2.00000	3.00000	3.00000	8.00000	
Kitchen_Ab- vGr	0	1	1.04436860	0.21407624	0.00000	1.00000	1.00000	1.00000	3.00000	
TotRms_Ab- vGrd	0	1	6.44300341	1.57296440	2.00000	5.00000	6.00000	7.00000	15.00000	
Fireplaces	0	1	0.59931741	0.64792092	0.00000	0.00000	1.00000	1.00000	4.00000	
Garage_Cars	0	1	1.76621160	0.76113672	0.00000	1.00000	2.00000	2.00000	5.00000	
Garage_Area	0	1	472.65836177	215.18719571	0.00000	320.00000	480.00000	576.00000	1,488.00000	
Wood_Deck_ SF	0	1	93.75187713	126.36156188	0.00000	0.00000	0.00000	168.00000	1,424.00000	
Open_Porch_ SF	0	1	47.53344710	67.48340014	0.00000	0.00000	27.00000	70.00000	742.00000	
Enclosed_ Porch	0	1	23.01160410	64.13905921	0.00000	0.00000	0.00000	0.00000	1,012.00000	
Three_sea- son_porch	0	1	2.59249147	25.14133103	0.00000	0.00000	0.00000	0.00000	508.00000	
Screen_Porch	0	1	16.00204778	56.08737023	0.00000	0.00000	0.00000	0.00000	576.00000	
Pool_Area	0	1	2.24334471	35.59718062	0.00000	0.00000	0.00000	0.00000	800.00000	
Misc_Val	0	1	50.63515358	566.34428826	0.00000	0.00000	0.00000	0.00000	17,000.00000	
Mo_Sold	0	1	6.21604096	2.71449243	1.00000	4.00000	6.00000	8.00000	12.00000	
Year_Sold	0	1	2,007.79044369	1.31661292	2,006.00000	2,007.00000	2,008.00000	2,009.00000	2,010.00000	
Sale_Price	0	1	180,796.06006826	79,886.69235666	12,789.00000	129,500.00000	160,000.0 0000	213,500.00000	755,000.00000	
Longitude	0	1	–93.64289690	0.02569957	–93.69315	–93.66022	–93.64181	–93.62211	–93.57743	
Latitude	0	1	42.03448223	0.01841007	41.98650	42.02209	42.03466	42.04985	42.06339	

We have 11 columns:

1. skim_variable is the column name. There are 34 numeric columns.
2. n_missing is the number of missings in each column. All numeric columns have 0 or no missings.
3. complete_rate is the proportion of present values in each column. All numeric columns have no missings and 1 or 100% complete rate.
4. mean is the mean or average value for each column.
5. sd is the standard deviation for each column.
6. p0 is the 0% percentile or the minimum value for each column.
7. p25 is the 25% percentile or the 1st quartile for each column.
8. p50 is the 50% percentile, the median, or the 2nd quartile for each column.
9. p75 is the 75% percentile or the 3rd quartile for each column.
10. p100 is the 100% percentile or the maximum value for each column.
11. hist is the histogram plot for each column.

- The longitude and latitude columns are not numeric columns and will be removed in the preprocessing steps.

3.3. PENALIZED REGRESSION

3.3.1. Ridge Regression

Ridge regression shrinks the regression coefficients so predictors, with minor contribution to the outcome, have their coefficients close to zero.

The shrinkage of the coefficients is achieved by a penalty value that can be fine-tuned using the tune function.

The disadvantage of the ridge regression is including all the predictors in the final model as it will not set any of predictors' coefficients to zero. Lasso regression is an alternative that overcomes this disadvantage.

3.3.2. Lasso (Least Absolute Shrinkage and Selection Operator) Regression

In lasso regression, the penalty makes some of the predictors' coefficients, with a minor contribution to the outcome, to be exactly equal to zero. So, some predictors will be removed and arrive at a simpler regression model.

As in ridge regression, the penalty value can be fine-tuned using the tune function.

Lasso might perform better in situations where some of the predictors have large coefficients, and the remaining predictors have very small coefficients. Ridge regression will perform better when the outcome is a function of many predictors, all with coefficients of roughly equal size (James et al., 2014).

In addition, both ridge and lasso regression can deal with correlated predictors. Ridge regression shrinks the coefficients of correlated predictors towards each other, allowing them to borrow strength from each other. In the extreme case of k identical predictors, they each get identical coefficients with 1/kth the size that any single one would get if fit alone. Lasso regression, on the other hand, deals with very correlated predictors by picking one and ignoring the rest (Friedman et al., 2010).

3.3.3. Elastic Net

Elastic net combines the penalties of the lasso and ridge methods. The result is to shrink coefficients (like in ridge regression) and to set some coefficients to zero (as in lasso).

All three penalized regressions are highly affected by the scale of the predictors. Therefore, it is better to normalize the predictors before applying any of these penalized regression methods (James et al., 2014), so that all the predictors have the same mean and standard deviation as we did in LDA classification models.

Cross-validation methods can be used for identifying which of these 3 techniques is better on a particular data set.

3.4. RIDGE REGRESSION

3.4.1. Split the Data

We first do a stratified splitting of the data using the numerical outcome (Sale_Price). This ensures that both the resulting training and testing data have the same price distribution as the original ames data.

We create an object called "split_ames" by using the initial_split function with the arguments:

- data = ames which is the data we want to split.
- strata = Sale_Price to make a stratified splitting using the price outcome column.

To make the splitting reproducible, we use the set.seed function with any number before using the initial_split function.

```
set.seed(123)
split_ames <- initial_split(data = ames,
strata = Sale_Price)
split_ames
## <Training/Testing/Total>
## <2197/733/2930>
```

The training data has 2197 rows and the testing data has 733 rows with a total of 2930 which is the total rows of original data.

To get the actual training and testing data, we use the training and testing functions, respectively, on the split_ames object. The resulting data is called train_ames for the training data and test_ames for the testing data. Finally, we use the dim function to see the data dimensions.

```
train_ames<-training(split_ames)
test_ames<-testing(split_ames)
dim(train_ames)
## [1] 2197 74
dim(test_ames)
## [1] 733 74
```

- The training data has 2197 rows (1st number) and 74 columns, while the testing data has 733 rows (1st number) and 74 columns. The same 74 columns are present in training, testing, and original data.

3.4.2. Generate the Recipe

We create an object "rec" by applying the following functions on the train_ames data using the "%>%" operator:

- The recipe function with the argument Sale_Price ~ . meaning define the price column as an outcome and all other columns as predictors.
- The step_rm function with the arguments Longitude, Latitude to remove these 2 columns form the data as they are not real numeric predictors.
- The step_dummy with the arguments:

  ++ all_nominal_predictors() to convert all categorical or factor predictors into numerical columns containing 1 and 0 values.

  ++ one_hot = FALSE to convert any categorical predictor with n categories into n–1 columns so the resulting numerical columns will not be perfectly correlated and can be used in linear models.

- The step_nzv function with the argument all_predictors() to remove near zero variance predictors or predictors with low variability.
- The step_normalize function with the argument all_predictors to convert all (now numeric) predictors into columns having 0 mean and 1 standard deviation so all predictors will have a common scale.

```
rec <- train_ames %>%
recipe(Sale_Price ~ .) %>%
step_rm(Longitude, Latitude) %>%
step_dummy(all_nominal_predictors(), one_hot = FALSE) %>%
step_nzv(all_predictors()) %>%
step_normalize(all_predictors())
rec
##
## ── Recipe ──────────────────────────────────────────────────────
##
## ── Inputs
## Number of variables by role
## outcome: 1
## predictor: 73
##
## ── Operations
## • Variables removed: Longitude and Latitude
## • Dummy variables from: all_nominal_predictors()
## • Sparse, unbalanced variable filter on: all_predictors()
## • Centering and scaling for: all_predictors()
```

- The recipe object "rec":

  ++ Defines the variables by role: 1 outcome and 73 predictors.

  ++ Contains 4 preprocessing operations of removing longitude and latitude, dummification for all categorical predictors, removing predictors with low variability, and normalizing all (numeric) predictors.

3.4.3. Look at Preprocessed Data

First, we prepare the recipe using the prep function on the "rec" recipe. The resulting object is called "prep_rec."

```
prep_rec <- prep(rec)
prep_rec
##
## ── Recipe ──────────────────────────────────────────
##
## ── Inputs
## Number of variables by role
## outcome: 1
## predictor: 73
##
## ── Training information
## Training data contained 2197 data points and no incomplete rows.
##
## ── Operations
## • Variables removed: Longitude and Latitude | Trained
## • Dummy variables from: MS_SubClass, MS_Zoning, Street, Alley, ... | Trained
## • Sparse, unbalanced variable filter removed: BsmtFin_SF_2, ... | Trained
## • Centering and scaling for: Lot_Frontage and Lot_Area, ... | Trained
```

Second, to get the preprocessed training data, we use the bake function with the arguments:

- prep_rec which is the prepared recipe.
- new_data = NULL to apply the prepared recipe to training data contained in the original recipe.

The resulting data is called "train_ames2" and we use the glimpse function to see the data structure.

```
train_ames2 <- bake(prep_rec, new_data = NULL)
glimpse(train_ames2)
## Rows: 2,197
```

```
## Columns: 99
## $ Lot_Frontage <dbl> 0.36988074, –1.084951…
## $ Lot_Area <dbl> –0.20459440, –0.98396…
## $ Year_Built <dbl> –0.05555905, –0.02252…
## $ Year_Remod_Add <dbl> –0.69017890, –0.64221…
## $ Mas_Vnr_Area <dbl> –0.56135250, 2.110295…
## $ BsmtFin_SF_1 <dbl> –1.4273777, 0.8106674…
## $ Bsmt_Unf_SF <dbl> –1.26061912, –0.75399…
## $ Total_Bsmt_SF <dbl> –0.36424940, –1.16150…
## $ First_Flr_SF <dbl> –0.6958220444, –1.598…
## $ Second_Flr_SF <dbl> –0.78663287, 0.527358…
## $ Gr_Liv_Area <dbl> –1.20792407, –0.79888…
## $ Bsmt_Full_Bath <dbl> 1.0905034, –0.8109537…
## $ Bsmt_Half_Bath <dbl> –0.2518688, –0.251868…
## $ Full_Bath <dbl> –1.0481912, –1.048191…
## $ Half_Bath <dbl> –0.7489047, 1.2430367…
## $ Bedroom_AbvGr <dbl> –1.0405629, 0.1626564…
## $ TotRms_AbvGrd <dbl> –1.5335141, –0.284531…
## $ Fireplaces <dbl> –0.9220114, –0.922011…
## $ Garage_Cars <dbl> 0.3023882, –1.0028118…
## $ Garage_Area <dbl> 0.2405208, –0.6984888…
## $ Wood_Deck_SF <dbl> 1.15922645, –0.753806…
## $ Open_Porch_SF <dbl> –0.69380079, –0.69380…
## $ Mo_Sold <dbl> –0.79073528, –1.15825…
## $ Year_Sold <dbl> 1.669834, 1.669834, 1…
## $ Sale_Price <int> 126000, 105500, 88000…
## $ MS_SubClass_One_and_Half_Story_Finished_All_Ages <dbl> –0.3309775, –0.330977…
## $ MS_SubClass_Two_Story_1946_and_Newer <dbl> –0.4974675, –0.497467…
## $ MS_SubClass_One_Story_PUD_1946_and_Newer <dbl> –0.2744905, –0.274490…
```

```
## $ MS_Zoning_Residential_Low_Density <dbl> 0.5440867, –1.8371056…
## $ MS_Zoning_Residential_Medium_Density <dbl> –0.4352129, 2.2966804…
## $ Alley_No_Alley_Access <dbl> 0.2744905, 0.2744905,…
## $ Lot_Shape_Slightly_Irregular <dbl> –0.7234225, –0.723422…
## $ Land_Contour_Lvl <dbl> 0.3468313, 0.3468313,…
## $ Lot_Config_CulDSac <dbl> –0.2497013, –0.249701…
## $ Lot_Config_Inside <dbl> –1.6538286, 0.6043824…
## $ Neighborhood_College_Creek <dbl> –0.3198619, –0.319861…
## $ Neighborhood_Old_Town <dbl> –0.2941234, –0.294123…
## $ Neighborhood_Edwards <dbl> –0.266744, –0.266744,…
## $ Neighborhood_Somerset <dbl> –0.2628085, –0.262808…
## $ Neighborhood_Northridge_Heights <dbl> –0.2445188, –0.244518…
## $ Neighborhood_Gilbert <dbl> –0.242422, –0.242422,…
## $ Condition_1_Feedr <dbl> –0.2476383, –0.247638…
## $ Condition_1_Norm <dbl> 0.4097796, 0.4097796,…
## $ Bldg_Type_TwnhsE <dbl> –0.3049467, –0.304946…
## $ House_Style_One_Story <dbl> 0.9902613, –1.0093748…
## $ House_Style_Two_Story <dbl> –0.6558526, 1.5240388…
## $ Overall_Cond_Average <dbl> 0.8645646, 0.8645646,…
## $ Overall_Cond_Above_Average <dbl> –0.4615679, –0.461567…
## $ Overall_Cond_Good <dbl> –0.3883242, –0.388324…
## $ Overall_Cond_Very_Good <dbl> –0.2306245, –0.230624…
## $ Roof_Style_Gable <dbl> 0.5088299, 0.5088299,…
## $ Roof_Style_Hip <dbl> –0.4810373, –0.481037…
## $ Exterior_1st_HdBoard <dbl> –0.428538, 2.332453, …
## $ Exterior_1st_MetalSd <dbl> –0.4270494, –0.427049…
## $ Exterior_1st_Plywood <dbl> 3.4744616, –0.2876834…
## $ Exterior_1st_VinylSd <dbl> –0.7285388, –0.728538…
## $ Exterior_1st_Wd.Sdng <dbl> –0.4029391, –0.402939…
## $ Exterior_2nd_HdBoard <dbl> –0.4014121, 2.4900713…
```

```
## $ Exterior_2nd_MetalSd <dbl> –0.4225716, –0.422571…
## $ Exterior_2nd_Plywood <dbl> 3.0998630, –0.3224481…
## $ Exterior_2nd_VinylSd <dbl> –0.7256135, –0.725613…
## $ Exterior_2nd_Wd.Sdng <dbl> –0.3898745, –0.389874…
## $ Mas_Vnr_Type_BrkFace <dbl> –0.6544337, 1.5273431…
## $ Mas_Vnr_Type_None <dbl> 0.8072069, –1.2382759…
## $ Mas_Vnr_Type_Stone <dbl> –0.3076127, –0.307612…
## $ Exter_Cond_Good <dbl> –0.3326673, –0.332667…
## $ Exter_Cond_Typical <dbl> 0.3805275, 0.3805275,…
## $ Foundation_CBlock <dbl> 1.1691170, 1.1691170,…
## $ Foundation_PConc <dbl> –0.906284, –0.906284,…
## $ Bsmt_Cond_Typical <dbl> 0.3468313, 0.3468313,…
## $ Bsmt_Exposure_Gd <dbl> –0.318997, –0.318997,…
## $ Bsmt_Exposure_Mn <dbl> –0.2950355, –0.295035…
## $ Bsmt_Exposure_No <dbl> 0.7256135, 0.7256135,…
## $ BsmtFin_Type_1_BLQ <dbl> –0.3172626, –0.317262…
## $ BsmtFin_Type_1_GLQ <dbl> –0.6508892, –0.650889…
## $ BsmtFin_Type_1_LwQ <dbl> –0.2295283, –0.229528…
## $ BsmtFin_Type_1_Rec <dbl> –0.3181305, 3.1419329…
## $ BsmtFin_Type_1_Unf <dbl> –0.6487642, –0.648764…
## $ BsmtFin_Type_2_Unf <dbl> –2.4347279, 0.4105366…
## $ Heating_QC_Good <dbl> –0.4403787, –0.440378…
## $ Heating_QC_Typical <dbl> 1.5767592, 1.5767592,…
## $ Central_Air_Y <dbl> 0.2706374, 0.2706374,…
## $ Electrical_SBrkr <dbl> 0.3049467, 0.3049467,…
## $ Functional_Typ <dbl> 0.278305, 0.278305, 0…
## $ Garage_Type_BuiltIn <dbl> –0.2588287, –0.258828…
## $ Garage_Type_Detchd <dbl> –0.6064879, 1.6480871…
## $ Garage_Type_No_Garage <dbl> –0.242422, –0.242422,…
## $ Garage_Finish_No_Garage <dbl> –0.2445188, –0.244518…
```

```
## $ Garage_Finish_RFn <dbl> –0.6240589, –0.624058…
## $ Garage_Finish_Unf <dbl> –0.8485933, 1.1778844…
## $ Garage_Cond_No_Garage <dbl> –0.2445188, –0.244518…
## $ Garage_Cond_Typical <dbl> 0.3172626, 0.3172626,…
## $ Paved_Drive_Paved <dbl> 0.3267299, 0.3267299,…
## $ Fence_Minimum_Privacy <dbl> 2.8819334, –0.3468313…
## $ Fence_No_Fence <dbl> –2.0655852, 0.4839039…
## $ Sale_Type_New <dbl> –0.2968541, –0.296854…
## $ Sale_Type_WD. <dbl> 0.3906485, 0.3906485,…
## $ Sale_Condition_Normal <dbl> 0.4695265, 0.4695265,…
## $ Sale_Condition_Partial <dbl> –0.3013679, –0.301367…
```

- The training data has the same 2197 rows of the original training data but 99 numeric columns (98 predictors + 1 outcome) because of dummification.
- All columns have negative values because of normalization.

We can use the skim and yank functions again on the train_ames2 data to get useful information about numeric columns in the ames training data after normalization.

```
train_ames2 %>% skim() %>% yank("numeric") %>%
flextable() %>% theme_box() %>%
set_caption(caption = "The information gained from skim function on all columns from the ames training data after normalization")
```

The information gained from skim function on all columns from the ames training data after normalization:

skim_variable	n_missing	complete_rate	mean	sd	p0	p25	p50	p75	p100	hist
Lot_Frontage	0	1	0.0000000000000000444416790	1.00	–1.7084517	–0.4317618	0.16204750	0.6074045	7.5846635	
Lot_Area	0	1	0.0000000000000000461741077	1.00	–1.0280360	–0.3228916	–0.09441560	0.1523849	23.7848096	
Year_Built	0	1	0.0000000000000030266540472	1.00	–3.2929598	–0.5841143	0.07657976	0.9685167	1.2658290	
Year_Remod_Add	0	1	0.0000000000000013505548681	1.00	–1.6493610	–0.9299744	0.41288053	0.9404307	1.2281853	
Mas_Vnr_Area	0	1	0.0000000000000000244103900	1.00	–0.5613525	–0.5613525	–0.56135250	0.3400573	8.1269343	
BsmtFin_SF_1	0	1	0.0000000000000001756386299	1.00	–1.8749867	–0.5321596	–0.53215965	1.2582764	1.2582764	
Bsmt_Unf_SF	0	1	–0.0000000000000000586752746	1.00	–1.2606191	–0.7720101	–0.22710965	0.5362013	3.9992461	
Total_Bsmt_SF	0	1	–0.0000000000000002445005687	1.00	–2.3339370	–0.5875700	–0.14316202	0.5692307	11.3109509	
First_Flr_SF	0	1	–0.0000000000000000300623551	1.00	–2.0820569	–0.7211183	–0.20254506	0.5715204	9.9614905	
Second_Flr_SF	0	1	0.0000000000000000639962053	1.00	–0.7866329	–0.7866329	–0.78663287	0.8633881	3.5516245	
Gr_Liv_Area	0	1	–0.0000000000000000838562525	1.00	–2.2753302	–0.7307078	–0.10156155	0.4633066	8.0637055	
Bsmt_Full_Bath	0	1	0.0000000000000000112456983	1.00	–0.8109537	–0.8109537	–0.81095375	1.0905034	4.8934178	
Bsmt_Half_Bath	0	1	–0.0000000000000000344643788	1.00	–0.2518688	–0.2518688	–0.25186884	–0.2518688	7.9459956	
Full_Bath	0	1	–0.0000000000000000109207337	1.00	–2.8686466	–1.0481912	0.77226419	0.7722642	4.4131750	

Half_Bath	0	1	–0.0000000000000 000011793968	1.00	–0.7489047	–0.7489047	–0.74890468	1.2430367	3.2349781	
Bedroom_AbvGr	0	1	–0.000000000000 0001073008784	1.00	–3.4470017	–1.0405629	0.16265642	0.1626564	6.1787533	
TotRms_AbvGrd	0	1	0.0000000000000 000895057009	1.00	–2.7824966	–0.9090228	–0.28453152	0.3399597	5.3358899	
Fireplaces	0	1	–0.0000000000000 000079042632	1.00	–0.9220114	–0.9220114	0.63140809	0.6314081	5.2916664	
Garage_Cars	0	1	–0.000000000000 0000315707631	1.00	–2.3080118	–1.0028118	0.30238816	0.3023882	2.9127881	
Garage_Area	0	1	–0.000000000000 0000928804467	1.00	–2.1642600	–0.6984888	0.02523568	0.4741281	4.6515759	
Wood_Deck_SF	0	1	–0.0000000000000 000336936675	1.00	–0.7538063	–0.7538063	–0.75380631	0.5853166	6.1809374	
Open_Porch_SF	0	1	–0.000000000000 0000204302527	1.00	–0.6938008	–0.6938008	–0.31299068	0.3168107	10.1739339	
Mo_Sold	0	1	0.0000000000000 001491554250	1.00	–1.8932815	–0.7907353	–0.05570443	0.6793264	2.1493881	
Year_Sold	0	1	0.0000000000000 720339700094	1.00	–1.3689943	–0.6092872	0.15041993	0.9101270	1.6698341	
Sale_Price	0	1	180,466.5785161 583917215466499329	79,558.12	12,789.0000000	129,500.0000000	160,000.00000000	213,500.0000000	755,000.0000000	
MS_SubClass_ One_and_Half_ Story_Finished_ All_Ages	0	1	0.000000000000 0000233769188	1.00	–0.3309775	–0.3309775	–0.33097745	–0.3309775	3.0199786	
MS_SubClass_ Two_Story_1946_ and_Newer	0	1	–0.000000000000 0000459471507	1.00	–0.4974675	–0.4974675	–0.49746749	–0.4974675	2.0092666	
MS_Sub- Class_One_Story_ PUD_1946_and_ Newer	0	1	–0.000000000000 0000214087735	1.00	–0.2744905	–0.2744905	–0.27449050	–0.2744905	3.6414551	

MS_Zoning_Residential_Low_Density	0	1	0.0000000000000 000930516885	1.00	–1.8371056	0.5440867	0.54408675	0.5440867	0.5440867	
MS_Zoning_Residential_Medium_Density	0	1	–0.00000000000 00000681577996	1.00	–0.4352129	–0.4352129	–0.43521285	–0.4352129	2.2966804	
Alley_No_Alley_Access	0	1	0.000000000 0000001258874940	1.00	–3.6414551	0.2744905	0.27449050	0.2744905	0.2744905	
Lot_Shape_Slightly_Irregular	0	1	0.0000000000000 000068025420	1.00	–0.7234225	–0.7234225	–0.72342245	1.3816890	1.3816890	
Land_Contour_Lvl	0	1	–0.000000000000 0000401317903	1.00	–2.8819334	0.3468313	0.34683135	0.3468313	0.3468313	
Lot_Config_CulD-Sac	0	1	–0.00000000000 00000056798105	1.00	–0.2497013	–0.2497013	–0.24970126	–0.2497013	4.0029628	
Lot_Config_Inside	0	1	–0.00000000000 00000471528753	1.00	–1.6538286	–1.6538286	0.60438236	0.6043824	0.6043824	
Neighborhood_College_Creek	0	1	–0.00000000000 00000302107976	1.00	–0.3198619	–0.3198619	–0.31986195	–0.3198619	3.1249258	
Neighborhood_Old_Town	0	1	–0.00000000000 00000608613213	1.00	–0.2941234	–0.2941234	–0.29412341	–0.2941234	3.3983859	
Neighborhood_Edwards	0	1	–0.0000000000 000000170112653	1.00	–0.2667440	–0.2667440	–0.26674405	–0.2667440	3.7472058	
Neighborhood_Somerset	0	1	0.000000000000 0000000000000	1.00	–0.2628085	–0.2628085	–0.26280849	–0.2628085	3.8033201	
Neighborhood_Northridge_Heights	0	1	–0.00000000000 00000075768065	1.00	–0.2445188	–0.2445188	–0.24451884	–0.2445188	4.0878029	
Neighborhood_Gilbert	0	1	–0.00000000000 00000025406578	1.00	–0.2424220	–0.2424220	–0.24242199	–0.2424220	4.1231608	
Condition_1_Feedr	0	1	–0.000000000000 0000108289812	1.00	–0.2476383	–0.2476383	–0.24763831	–0.2476383	4.0363094	
Condition_1_Norm	0	1	0.0000000000 000001194345417	1.00	–2.4392257	0.4097796	0.40977955	0.4097796	0.4097796	

Bldg_Type_ TwnhsE	0	1	–0.00000000000 00000184525337	1.00	–0.3049467	–0.3049467	–0.30494658	–0.3049467	3.2777692	
House_Style_ One_Story	0	1	0.000000000000 0000634027317	1.00	–1.0093748	–1.0093748	0.99026132	0.9902613	0.9902613	
House_Style_ Two_Story	0	1	0.00000000000 00000152453532	1.00	–0.6558526	–0.6558526	–0.65585253	1.5240388	1.5240388	
Overall_Cond_ Average	0	1	–0.0000000000 000001428365053	1.00	–1.1561252	–1.1561252	0.86456455	0.8645646	0.8645646	
Overall_Cond_ Above_Average	0	1	0.00000000000 00000159892432	1.00	–0.4615679	–0.4615679	–0.46156787	–0.4615679	2.1655425	
Overall_Cond_ Good	0	1	0.0000000000000 000309108408	1.00	–0.3883242	–0.3883242	–0.38832417	–0.3883242	2.5739960	
Overall_Cond_ Very_Good	0	1	0.00000000000 00000204073917	1.00	–0.2306245	–0.2306245	–0.23062452	–0.2306245	4.3340788	
Roof_Style_Gable	0	1	–0.00000000000 00000154793671	1.00	–1.9643987	0.5088299	0.50882992	0.5088299	0.5088299	
Roof_Style_Hip	0	1	–0.00000000000 00000431675317	1.00	–0.4810373	–0.4810373	–0.48103729	–0.4810373	2.0778947	
Exterior_1st_Hd- Board	0	1	–0.00000000000 00000583335560	1.00	–0.4285380	–0.4285380	–0.42853800	–0.4285380	2.3324532	
Exterior_1st_Met- alSd	0	1	0.00000000000 00000151626192	1.00	–0.4270494	–0.4270494	–0.42704942	–0.4270494	2.3405835	
Exterior_1st_Ply- wood	0	1	–0.00000000000 00000084447851	1.00	–0.2876834	–0.2876834	–0.28768337	–0.2876834	3.4744616	
Exterior_1st_Vi- nylSd	0	1	0.000000000000 0000373281382	1.00	–0.7285388	–0.7285388	–0.72853878	1.3719858	1.3719858	
Exterior_1st_ Wd.Sdng	0	1	–0.00000000000 00000006877553	1.00	–0.4029391	–0.4029391	–0.40293911	–0.4029391	2.4806349	
Exterior_2nd_Hd- Board	0	1	0.000000000000 0000308100697	1.00	–0.4014121	–0.4014121	–0.40141213	–0.4014121	2.4900713	
Exterior_2nd_ MetalSd	0	1	0.000000000000 0000476481933	1.00	–0.4225716	–0.4225716	–0.42257160	–0.4225716	2.3653858	

Exterior_2nd_Plywood	0	1	–0.0000000000000000017899452	1.00	–0.3224481	–0.3224481	–0.32244806	–0.3224481	3.0998630	
Exterior_2nd_VinylSd	0	1	–0.0000000000000000209224864	1.00	–0.7256135	–0.7256135	–0.72561349	1.3775169	1.3775169	
Exterior_2nd_Wd.Sdng	0	1	0.0000000000000000640267771	1.00	–0.3898745	–0.3898745	–0.38987447	–0.3898745	2.5637607	
Mas_Vnr_Type_BrkFace	0	1	0.0000000000000000315358239	1.00	–0.6544337	–0.6544337	–0.65443374	1.5273431	1.5273431	
Mas_Vnr_Type_None	0	1	0.0000000000000000748072850	1.00	–1.2382759	–1.2382759	0.80720690	0.8072069	0.8072069	
Mas_Vnr_Type_Stone	0	1	–0.0000000000000000245853083	1.00	–0.3076127	–0.3076127	–0.30761269	–0.3076127	3.2493615	
Exter_Cond_Good	0	1	–0.0000000000000000253872083	1.00	–0.3326673	–0.3326673	–0.33266725	–0.3326673	3.0046385	
Exter_Cond_Typical	0	1	0.0000000000000000175798423	1.00	–2.6267348	0.3805275	0.38052750	0.3805275	0.3805275	
Foundation_CBlock	0	1	–0.0000000000000000411795974	1.00	–0.8549571	–0.8549571	–0.85495709	1.1691170	1.1691170	
Foundation_PConc	0	1	–0.0000000000000000834836660	1.00	–0.9062840	–0.9062840	–0.90628400	1.1029046	1.1029046	
Bsmt_Cond_Typical	0	1	–0.0000000000000000389398094	1.00	–2.8819334	0.3468313	0.34683135	0.3468313	0.3468313	
Bsmt_Exposure_Gd	0	1	0.0000000000000000236805151	1.00	–0.3189970	–0.3189970	–0.31899699	–0.3189970	3.1333990	
Bsmt_Exposure_Mn	0	1	–0.0000000000000000043374009	1.00	–0.2950355	–0.2950355	–0.29503553	–0.2950355	3.3878796	
Bsmt_Exposure_No	0	1	–0.0000000000000000448409635	1.00	–1.3775169	–1.3775169	0.72561349	0.7256135	0.7256135	
BsmtFin_Type_1_BLQ	0	1	–0.0000000000000000047212637	1.00	–0.3172626	–0.3172626	–0.31726262	–0.3172626	3.1505283	
BsmtFin_Type_1_GLQ	0	1	0.0000000000000000368368175	1.00	–0.6508892	–0.6508892	–0.65088918	1.5356606	1.5356606	

BsmtFin_Type_1_LwQ	0	1	–0.0000000000 000000255734645	1.00	–0.2295283	–0.2295283	–0.22952831	–0.2295283	4.3547780	
BsmtFin_Type_1_Rec	0	1	0.00000000000 00000199190936	1.00	–0.3181305	–0.3181305	–0.31813055	–0.3181305	3.1419329	
BsmtFin_Type_1_Unf	0	1	–0.00000000000000 00510943475	1.00	–0.6487642	–0.6487642	–0.64876422	1.5406904	1.5406904	
BsmtFin_Type_2_Unf	0	1	–0.00000000000000 00420349673	1.00	–2.4347279	0.4105366	0.41053657	0.4105366	0.4105366	
Heating_QC_Good	0	1	–0.00000000000000 00091107527	1.00	–0.4403787	–0.4403787	–0.44037873	–0.4403787	2.2697391	
Heating_QC_Typical	0	1	0.00000000000000 00256916929	1.00	–0.6339236	–0.6339236	–0.63392359	1.5767592	1.5767592	
Central_Air_Y	0	1	0.00000000000000 01859646069	1.00	–3.6932987	0.2706374	0.27063742	0.2706374	0.2706374	
Electrical_SBrkr	0	1	0.00000000000000 01214534673	1.00	–3.2777692	0.3049467	0.30494668	0.3049467	0.3049467	
Functional_Typ	0	1	0.0000000000000 000785598731	1.00	–3.5915441	0.2783050	0.27830504	0.2783050	0.2783050	
Garage_Type_BuiltIn	0	1	0.0000000000000 000561994494	1.00	–0.2588287	–0.2588287	–0.25882875	–0.2588287	3.8617999	
Garage_Type_Detchd	0	1	–0.00000000000 00000423376260	1.00	–0.6064879	–0.6064879	–0.60648786	1.6480871	1.6480871	
Garage_Type_No_Garage	0	1	–0.000000000000 0000030294124	1.00	–0.2424220	–0.2424220	–0.24242199	–0.2424220	4.1231608	
Garage_Finish_No_Garage	0	1	–0.00000000000 00000074109931	1.00	–0.2445188	–0.2445188	–0.24451884	–0.2445188	4.0878029	
Garage_Finish_RFn	0	1	–0.00000000000 00000740643327	1.00	–0.6240589	–0.6240589	–0.62405887	1.6016836	1.6016836	
Garage_Finish_Unf	0	1	0.000000000000 0000090426014	1.00	–0.8485933	–0.8485933	–0.84859331	1.1778844	1.1778844	
Garage_Cond_No_Garage	0	1	–0.0000000000000 000074109931	1.00	–0.2445188	–0.2445188	–0.24451884	–0.2445188	4.0878029	

Garage_Cond_ Typical	0	1	0.000000000000 0000068310412	1.00	−3.1505283	0.3172626	0.31726262	0.3172626	0.3172626	
Paved_Drive_ Paved	0	1	0.0000000000000 001062532934	1.00	−3.0592394	0.3267299	0.32672985	0.3267299	0.3267299	
Fence_Minimum_ Privacy	0	1	0.000000000000 0000384358553	1.00	−0.3468313	−0.3468313	−0.34683135	−0.3468313	2.8819334	
Fence_No_Fence	0	1	0.000000000000 0000652453078	1.00	−2.0655852	0.4839039	0.48390395	0.4839039	0.4839039	
Sale_Type_New	0	1	0.000000000000 0000270916313	1.00	−0.2968541	−0.2968541	−0.29685405	−0.2968541	3.3671255	
Sale_Type_WD.	0	1	0.000000000000 0001307173753	1.00	−2.5586807	0.3906485	0.39064852	0.3906485	0.3906485	
Sale_Condi- tion_Normal	0	1	−0.000000000000 0001060523434	1.00	−2.1288357	0.4695265	0.46952653	0.4695265	0.4695265	
Sale_Condi- tion_Partial	0	1	0.0000000000000 000105066445	1.00	−0.3013679	−0.3013679	−0.30136787	−0.3013679	3.3166934	

- The mean of all 98 predictors is extremely low and nearly equals zero.
- The standard deviation of all 98 predictors = 1. So, all 98 predictors are now on a comparable scale.

Finally, to get the preprocessed testing data, we use the bake function with the arguments:

- prep_rec which is the prepared recipe.
- new_data = test_ames to apply the prepared recipe to the testing data.

The resulting data is called "test_ames2" and we use the glimpse function to see the data structure.

```
test_ames2 <- bake(prep_rec, new_data = test_ames)
glimpse(test_ames2)
## Rows: 733
## Columns: 99
## $ Lot_Frontage <dbl> 0.66678538, 0.6964758…
## $ Lot_Area <dbl> 0.16908570, 0.4758466…
## $ Year_Built <dbl> –0.35287136, –0.45197…
## $ Year_Remod_Add <dbl> –1.1218108, –1.265688…
## $ Mas_Vnr_Area <dbl> –0.56135250, 0.025106…
## $ BsmtFin_SF_1 <dbl> 0.8106674, –1.4273777…
## $ Bsmt_Unf_SF <dbl> –0.65267238, –0.34644…
## $ Total_Bsmt_SF <dbl> –0.36424940, 0.633993…
## $ First_Flr_SF <dbl> –0.660407286, 0.43492…
## $ Second_Flr_SF <dbl> –0.7866329, –0.786632…
## $ Gr_Liv_Area <dbl> –1.1806546, –0.337247…
## $ Bsmt_Full_Bath <dbl> –0.8109537, –0.810953…
## $ Bsmt_Half_Bath <dbl> –0.2518688, –0.251868…
## $ Full_Bath <dbl> –1.0481912, –1.048191…
## $ Half_Bath <dbl> –0.7489047, 1.2430367…
## $ Bedroom_AbvGr <dbl> –1.0405629, 0.1626564…
## $ TotRms_AbvGrd <dbl> –0.9090228, –0.284531…
## $ Fireplaces <dbl> –0.9220114, –0.922011…
```

```
## $ Garage_Cars <dbl> –1.0028118, –1.002811…
## $ Garage_Area <dbl> 1.179530472, –0.73513…
## $ Wood_Deck_SF <dbl> 0.36212947, 2.3787848…
## $ Open_Porch_SF <dbl> –0.693800794, –0.1665…
## $ Mo_Sold <dbl> –0.05570443, –0.05570…
## $ Year_Sold <dbl> 1.669834, 1.669834, 1…
## $ Sale_Price <int> 105000, 172000, 18990…
## $ MS_SubClass_One_and_Half_Story_Finished_All_Ages <dbl> –0.3309775, –0.330977…
## $ MS_SubClass_Two_Story_1946_and_Newer <dbl> –0.4974675, –0.497467…
## $ MS_SubClass_One_Story_PUD_1946_and_Newer <dbl> –0.2744905, –0.274490…
## $ MS_Zoning_Residential_Low_Density <dbl> –1.8371056, 0.5440867…
## $ MS_Zoning_Residential_Medium_Density <dbl> –0.4352129, –0.435212…
## $ Alley_No_Alley_Access <dbl> 0.2744905, 0.2744905,…
## $ Lot_Shape_Slightly_Irregular <dbl> –0.7234225, 1.3816890…
## $ Land_Contour_Lvl <dbl> 0.3468313, 0.3468313,…
## $ Lot_Config_CulDSac <dbl> –0.2497013, –0.249701…
## $ Lot_Config_Inside <dbl> 0.6043824, –1.6538286…
## $ Neighborhood_College_Creek <dbl> –0.3198619, –0.319861…
## $ Neighborhood_Old_Town <dbl> –0.2941234, –0.294123…
## $ Neighborhood_Edwards <dbl> –0.266744, –0.266744,…
## $ Neighborhood_Somerset <dbl> –0.2628085, –0.262808…
## $ Neighborhood_Northridge_Heights <dbl> –0.2445188, –0.244518…
## $ Neighborhood_Gilbert <dbl> –0.242422, –0.242422,…
## $ Condition_1_Feedr <dbl> 4.0363094, –0.2476383…
## $ Condition_1_Norm <dbl> –2.4392257, 0.4097796…
## $ Bldg_Type_TwnhsE <dbl> –0.3049467, –0.304946…
## $ House_Style_One_Story <dbl> 0.9902613, 0.9902613,…
## $ House_Style_Two_Story <dbl> –0.6558526, –0.655852…
## $ Overall_Cond_Average <dbl> –1.1561252, –1.156125…
```

```
## $ Overall_Cond_Above_Average <dbl> 2.1655425, 2.1655425,…
## $ Overall_Cond_Good <dbl> –0.3883242, –0.388324…
## $ Overall_Cond_Very_Good <dbl> –0.2306245, –0.230624…
## $ Roof_Style_Gable <dbl> 0.5088299, –1.9643987…
## $ Roof_Style_Hip <dbl> –0.4810373, 2.0778947…
## $ Exterior_1st_HdBoard <dbl> –0.428538, –0.428538,…
## $ Exterior_1st_MetalSd <dbl> –0.4270494, –0.427049…
## $ Exterior_1st_Plywood <dbl> –0.2876834, –0.287683…
## $ Exterior_1st_VinylSd <dbl> 1.3719858, –0.7285388…
## $ Exterior_1st_Wd.Sdng <dbl> –0.4029391, 2.4806349…
## $ Exterior_2nd_HdBoard <dbl> –0.4014121, –0.401412…
## $ Exterior_2nd_MetalSd <dbl> –0.4225716, –0.422571…
## $ Exterior_2nd_Plywood <dbl> –0.3224481, –0.322448…
## $ Exterior_2nd_VinylSd <dbl> 1.3775169, –0.7256135…
## $ Exterior_2nd_Wd.Sdng <dbl> –0.3898745, 2.5637607…
## $ Mas_Vnr_Type_BrkFace <dbl> –0.6544337, 1.5273431…
## $ Mas_Vnr_Type_None <dbl> 0.8072069, –1.2382759…
## $ Mas_Vnr_Type_Stone <dbl> –0.3076127, –0.307612…
## $ Exter_Cond_Good <dbl> –0.3326673, –0.332667…
## $ Exter_Cond_Typical <dbl> 0.3805275, 0.3805275,…
## $ Foundation_CBlock <dbl> 1.1691170, 1.1691170,…
## $ Foundation_PConc <dbl> –0.906284, –0.906284,…
## $ Bsmt_Cond_Typical <dbl> 0.3468313, 0.3468313,…
## $ Bsmt_Exposure_Gd <dbl> –0.318997, –0.318997,…
## $ Bsmt_Exposure_Mn <dbl> –0.2950355, –0.295035…
## $ Bsmt_Exposure_No <dbl> 0.7256135, 0.7256135,…
## $ BsmtFin_Type_1_BLQ <dbl> –0.3172626, –0.317262…
## $ BsmtFin_Type_1_GLQ <dbl> –0.6508892, –0.650889…
## $ BsmtFin_Type_1_LwQ <dbl> –0.2295283, –0.229528…
## $ BsmtFin_Type_1_Rec <dbl> 3.1419329, –0.3181305…
## $ BsmtFin_Type_1_Unf <dbl> –0.6487642, –0.648764…
## $ BsmtFin_Type_2_Unf <dbl> –2.4347279, 0.4105366…
```

```
## $ Heating_QC_Good <dbl> –0.4403787, –0.440378…
## $ Heating_QC_Typical <dbl> 1.5767592, 1.5767592,…
## $ Central_Air_Y <dbl> 0.2706374, 0.2706374,…
## $ Electrical_SBrkr <dbl> 0.3049467, 0.3049467,…
## $ Functional_Typ <dbl> 0.278305, 0.278305, 0…
## $ Garage_Type_BuiltIn <dbl> –0.2588287, –0.258828…
## $ Garage_Type_Detchd <dbl> –0.6064879, –0.606487…
## $ Garage_Type_No_Garage <dbl> –0.242422, –0.242422,…
## $ Garage_Finish_No_Garage <dbl> –0.2445188, –0.244518…
## $ Garage_Finish_RFn <dbl> –0.6240589, –0.624058…
## $ Garage_Finish_Unf <dbl> 1.1778844, 1.1778844,…
## $ Garage_Cond_No_Garage <dbl> –0.2445188, –0.244518…
## $ Garage_Cond_Typical <dbl> 0.3172626, 0.3172626,…
## $ Paved_Drive_Paved <dbl> 0.3267299, 0.3267299,…
## $ Fence_Minimum_Privacy <dbl> 2.8819334, –0.3468313…
## $ Fence_No_Fence <dbl> –2.0655852, 0.4839039…
## $ Sale_Type_New <dbl> –0.2968541, –0.296854…
## $ Sale_Type_WD. <dbl> 0.3906485, 0.3906485,…
## $ Sale_Condition_Normal <dbl> 0.4695265, 0.4695265,…
## $ Sale_Condition_Partial <dbl> –0.3013679, –0.301367…
```

- The testing data has the same 733 rows of the original testing data but 99 numeric columns (98 predictors + 1 outcome) as that of the preprocessed training data.

3.4.4. Generate Different Resamples of Training Data

We split the train_ames data using the vfold_cv function with the arguments:

- v = 10 to split the data into 10 folds.
- repeats = 5 to repeat this process 5 times.
- strata = Sale_Price to make stratified resampling using the price column.

The result is 50 different resamples of train_ames data contained in folds data frame.

- We also use the set.seed function before splitting to make the splitting reproducible.

```
set.seed(123)
folds<-vfold_cv(train_ames, v = 10, repeats = 5, strata = Sale_Price)
folds
## # 10-fold cross-validation repeated 5 times using stratification
## # A tibble: 50 × 3
## splits id id2
## <list> <chr> <chr>
## 1 <split [1976/221]> Repeat1 Fold01
## 2 <split [1976/221]> Repeat1 Fold02
## 3 <split [1976/221]> Repeat1 Fold03
## 4 <split [1976/221]> Repeat1 Fold04
## 5 <split [1977/220]> Repeat1 Fold05
## 6 <split [1977/220]> Repeat1 Fold06
## 7 <split [1978/219]> Repeat1 Fold07
## 8 <split [1978/219]> Repeat1 Fold08
## 9 <split [1979/218]> Repeat1 Fold09
## 10 <split [1980/217]> Repeat1 Fold10
## # i 40 more rows
```

- There are 50 different rows. Each row corresponds to 1 resample of train_ames data. Each resample has 1 analysis (training) data, with 1976, 1977, 1978, 1979, or 1980 rows and 1 assessment (testing) data with 221, 220, 219, 218, or 217 rows.
- Each resample has 2 id values. id for the repeat number from 1 to 5 and id2 for the resample number from 1 to 10 within that repeat.
- Each resample has a total rows of 2197 which is the number of rows in original train_ames data. 1976 + 221 = 1977 + 220 = 1978 + 219 = 1979 + 218 = 1980 + 217 = 2197.

3.4.5. Define Machine Learning (ML) Model

We define a linear regression model by using the functions:

- The linear_reg function to define the linear regression model type with the following arguments:
  - mixture = 0 to indicate a ridge regression models.
  - penalty = tune() to tune the penalty term on the different resamples of training data.

- The set_engine function with the argument "glmnet" to define the engine that will use the glmnet function from the glmnet package.
- The set_mode function with the argument "regression" to define the mode of learning. We use regression because we have a numerical outcome (price).
- All the three functions are applied in sequence using the piping "%>%" operator and the resulting object is called "rid_model."

```
rid_model <- linear_reg(mixture = 0, penalty = tune()) %>%
set_engine("glmnet") %>%
set_mode("regression")
rid_model
## Linear Regression Model Specification (regression)
##
## Main Arguments:
## penalty = tune()
## mixture = 0
##
## Computational engine: glmnet
```

3.4.6. Generate Workflow

We create the "wflow" object by using the following functions:

- The workflow function to create a workflow.
- The add_recipe function with the argument "rec" to add the above created recipe with 4 preprocessing steps.
- The add_model function with the argument rid_model to add the above created ridge model.

```
wflow <- workflow() %>%
add_recipe(rec) %>%
add_model(rid_model)
wflow
## ══ Workflow ════════════════════════════════════════════════════════════════
════════════════════════════════════════════════════════════

## Preprocessor: Recipe
```

```
## Model: linear_reg()
##
## ── Preprocessor ────────────────────────────────────────────────
##
## 4 Recipe Steps
##
## • step_rm()
## • step_dummy()
## • step_nzv()
## • step_normalize()
##
## ── Model ──────────────────────────────────────────────────────
##
## Linear Regression Model Specification (regression)
##
## Main Arguments:
## penalty = tune()
## mixture = 0
##
## Computational engine: glmnet
```

- The "wflow" object contains 4 preprocessing steps and the linear regression model with 0 mixture and tuned penalty (ridge regression).

3.4.7. Fit Model on Different Resamples with Tuning

We can train many models using 50 resamples of training data in the folds data fame and see which models turn out best. We can use the grid_regular function to choose sensible values for the penalty term.

We create a grid of penalty values "my_grid" by using the grid_regular function with the arguments:

- penalty() to choose sensible values for the penalty term.
- levels = 50 to choose 50 different penalty values.

- my_grid <- **grid_regular**(**penalty**(), levels = 50)
- my_grid **%>% flextable**(cwidth = 2) **%>% theme_box**() **%>%**
- **set_caption**(caption = "The different 50 penalty values chosen by using the grid_regular function")

The different 50 penalty values chosen by using the grid_regular function:

penalty
0.0000000001000000
0.0000000001599859
0.0000000002559548
0.0000000004094915
0.0000000006551286
0.0000000010481131
0.0000000016768329
0.0000000026826958
0.0000000042919343
0.0000000068664885
0.0000000109854114
0.0000000175751062
0.0000000281176870
0.0000000449843267
0.0000000719685673
0.0000001151395399
0.0000001842069969
0.0000002947051703
0.0000004714866363
0.0000007543120063
0.0000012067926406
0.0000019306977289
0.0000030888435965
0.0000049417133613
0.0000079060432109
0.0000126485521686
0.0000202358964773
0.0000323745754282
0.0000517947467923

0.0000828642772855
0.0001325711365590
0.0002120950887920
0.0003393221771895
0.0005428675439324
0.0008685113737514
0.0013894954943731
0.0022229964825262
0.0035564803062231
0.0056898660290183
0.0091029817799152
0.0145634847750124
0.0232995181051537
0.0372759372031494
0.0596362331659464
0.0954095476349996
0.1526417967175236
0.2442053094548655
0.3906939937054621
0.6250551925273976
1.0000000000000000

- The penalty values range from 0.0000000001 to 1.00.

To try all these 50 different penalties on the 50 resamples of the training data, we use the tune_grid function with the arguments:

- wflow which is the workflow containing 4 preprocessing steps and the linear ridge model.
- folds which are the 50 resamples of training data created above.
- metrics = metrics_set(rmse) to get the RMSE of the linear ridge model on each resample using the 50 penalty values. Since we have 50 resamples × 50 penalty values = 2500 different ridge models.
- grid = my_grid to use the 50 penalty values in the my_grid data in tuning.
- control = control_grid(verbose = TRUE) to monitor the training process.

set.seed(123)

rid_res <- **tune_grid**(wflow, folds,

```
metrics = metric_set(rmse),
grid = my_grid,
control = control_grid(verbose = TRUE))
## i Fold01, Repeat1: preprocessor 1/1
## ✓ Fold01, Repeat1: preprocessor 1/1
## i Fold01, Repeat1: preprocessor 1/1, model 1/1
## ✓ Fold01, Repeat1: preprocessor 1/1, model 1/1
## i Fold01, Repeat1: preprocessor 1/1, model 1/1 (extracts)
## i Fold01, Repeat1: preprocessor 1/1, model 1/1 (predictions)
## i Fold02, Repeat1: preprocessor 1/1
## ✓ Fold02, Repeat1: preprocessor 1/1
## i Fold02, Repeat1: preprocessor 1/1, model 1/1
## ✓ Fold02, Repeat1: preprocessor 1/1, model 1/1
## i Fold02, Repeat1: preprocessor 1/1, model 1/1 (extracts)
## i Fold02, Repeat1: preprocessor 1/1, model 1/1 (predictions)
## i Fold03, Repeat1: preprocessor 1/1
## ✓ Fold03, Repeat1: preprocessor 1/1
## i Fold03, Repeat1: preprocessor 1/1, model 1/1
## ✓ Fold03, Repeat1: preprocessor 1/1, model 1/1
## i Fold03, Repeat1: preprocessor 1/1, model 1/1 (extracts)
## i Fold03, Repeat1: preprocessor 1/1, model 1/1 (predictions)
## i Fold04, Repeat1: preprocessor 1/1
## ✓ Fold04, Repeat1: preprocessor 1/1
## i Fold04, Repeat1: preprocessor 1/1, model 1/1
## ✓ Fold04, Repeat1: preprocessor 1/1, model 1/1
## i Fold04, Repeat1: preprocessor 1/1, model 1/1 (extracts)
## i Fold04, Repeat1: preprocessor 1/1, model 1/1 (predictions)
## i Fold05, Repeat1: preprocessor 1/1
## ✓ Fold05, Repeat1: preprocessor 1/1
## i Fold05, Repeat1: preprocessor 1/1, model 1/1
## ✓ Fold05, Repeat1: preprocessor 1/1, model 1/1
## i Fold05, Repeat1: preprocessor 1/1, model 1/1 (extracts)
```

```
## i Fold05, Repeat1: preprocessor 1/1, model 1/1 (predictions)
## i Fold06, Repeat1: preprocessor 1/1
## ✓ Fold06, Repeat1: preprocessor 1/1
## i Fold06, Repeat1: preprocessor 1/1, model 1/1
## ✓ Fold06, Repeat1: preprocessor 1/1, model 1/1
## i Fold06, Repeat1: preprocessor 1/1, model 1/1 (extracts)
## i Fold06, Repeat1: preprocessor 1/1, model 1/1 (predictions)
## i Fold07, Repeat1: preprocessor 1/1
## ✓ Fold07, Repeat1: preprocessor 1/1
## i Fold07, Repeat1: preprocessor 1/1, model 1/1
## ✓ Fold07, Repeat1: preprocessor 1/1, model 1/1
## i Fold07, Repeat1: preprocessor 1/1, model 1/1 (extracts)
## i Fold07, Repeat1: preprocessor 1/1, model 1/1 (predictions)
## i Fold08, Repeat1: preprocessor 1/1
## ✓ Fold08, Repeat1: preprocessor 1/1
## i Fold08, Repeat1: preprocessor 1/1, model 1/1
## ✓ Fold08, Repeat1: preprocessor 1/1, model 1/1
## i Fold08, Repeat1: preprocessor 1/1, model 1/1 (extracts)
## i Fold08, Repeat1: preprocessor 1/1, model 1/1 (predictions)
## i Fold09, Repeat1: preprocessor 1/1
## ✓ Fold09, Repeat1: preprocessor 1/1
## i Fold09, Repeat1: preprocessor 1/1, model 1/1
## ✓ Fold09, Repeat1: preprocessor 1/1, model 1/1
## i Fold09, Repeat1: preprocessor 1/1, model 1/1 (extracts)
## i Fold09, Repeat1: preprocessor 1/1, model 1/1 (predictions)
## i Fold10, Repeat1: preprocessor 1/1
## ✓ Fold10, Repeat1: preprocessor 1/1
## i Fold10, Repeat1: preprocessor 1/1, model 1/1
## ✓ Fold10, Repeat1: preprocessor 1/1, model 1/1
## i Fold10, Repeat1: preprocessor 1/1, model 1/1 (extracts)
## i Fold10, Repeat1: preprocessor 1/1, model 1/1 (predictions)
## i Fold01, Repeat2: preprocessor 1/1
```

```
## ✓ Fold01, Repeat2: preprocessor 1/1
## i Fold01, Repeat2: preprocessor 1/1, model 1/1
## ✓ Fold01, Repeat2: preprocessor 1/1, model 1/1
## i Fold01, Repeat2: preprocessor 1/1, model 1/1 (extracts)
## i Fold01, Repeat2: preprocessor 1/1, model 1/1 (predictions)
## i Fold02, Repeat2: preprocessor 1/1
## ✓ Fold02, Repeat2: preprocessor 1/1
## i Fold02, Repeat2: preprocessor 1/1, model 1/1
## ✓ Fold02, Repeat2: preprocessor 1/1, model 1/1
## i Fold02, Repeat2: preprocessor 1/1, model 1/1 (extracts)
## i Fold02, Repeat2: preprocessor 1/1, model 1/1 (predictions)
## i Fold03, Repeat2: preprocessor 1/1
## ✓ Fold03, Repeat2: preprocessor 1/1
## i Fold03, Repeat2: preprocessor 1/1, model 1/1
## ✓ Fold03, Repeat2: preprocessor 1/1, model 1/1
## i Fold03, Repeat2: preprocessor 1/1, model 1/1 (extracts)
## i Fold03, Repeat2: preprocessor 1/1, model 1/1 (predictions)
## i Fold04, Repeat2: preprocessor 1/1
## ✓ Fold04, Repeat2: preprocessor 1/1
## i Fold04, Repeat2: preprocessor 1/1, model 1/1
## ✓ Fold04, Repeat2: preprocessor 1/1, model 1/1
## i Fold04, Repeat2: preprocessor 1/1, model 1/1 (extracts)
## i Fold04, Repeat2: preprocessor 1/1, model 1/1 (predictions)
## i Fold05, Repeat2: preprocessor 1/1
## ✓ Fold05, Repeat2: preprocessor 1/1
## i Fold05, Repeat2: preprocessor 1/1, model 1/1
## ✓ Fold05, Repeat2: preprocessor 1/1, model 1/1
## i Fold05, Repeat2: preprocessor 1/1, model 1/1 (extracts)
## i Fold05, Repeat2: preprocessor 1/1, model 1/1 (predictions)
## i Fold06, Repeat2: preprocessor 1/1
## ✓ Fold06, Repeat2: preprocessor 1/1
## i Fold06, Repeat2: preprocessor 1/1, model 1/1
```

```
## ✓ Fold06, Repeat2: preprocessor 1/1, model 1/1
## i Fold06, Repeat2: preprocessor 1/1, model 1/1 (extracts)
## i Fold06, Repeat2: preprocessor 1/1, model 1/1 (predictions)
## i Fold07, Repeat2: preprocessor 1/1
## ✓ Fold07, Repeat2: preprocessor 1/1
## i Fold07, Repeat2: preprocessor 1/1, model 1/1
## ✓ Fold07, Repeat2: preprocessor 1/1, model 1/1
## i Fold07, Repeat2: preprocessor 1/1, model 1/1 (extracts)
## i Fold07, Repeat2: preprocessor 1/1, model 1/1 (predictions)
## i Fold08, Repeat2: preprocessor 1/1
## ✓ Fold08, Repeat2: preprocessor 1/1
## i Fold08, Repeat2: preprocessor 1/1, model 1/1
## ✓ Fold08, Repeat2: preprocessor 1/1, model 1/1
## i Fold08, Repeat2: preprocessor 1/1, model 1/1 (extracts)
## i Fold08, Repeat2: preprocessor 1/1, model 1/1 (predictions)
## i Fold09, Repeat2: preprocessor 1/1
## ✓ Fold09, Repeat2: preprocessor 1/1
## i Fold09, Repeat2: preprocessor 1/1, model 1/1
## ✓ Fold09, Repeat2: preprocessor 1/1, model 1/1
## i Fold09, Repeat2: preprocessor 1/1, model 1/1 (extracts)
## i Fold09, Repeat2: preprocessor 1/1, model 1/1 (predictions)
## i Fold10, Repeat2: preprocessor 1/1
## ✓ Fold10, Repeat2: preprocessor 1/1
## i Fold10, Repeat2: preprocessor 1/1, model 1/1
## ✓ Fold10, Repeat2: preprocessor 1/1, model 1/1
## i Fold10, Repeat2: preprocessor 1/1, model 1/1 (extracts)
## i Fold10, Repeat2: preprocessor 1/1, model 1/1 (predictions)
## i Fold01, Repeat3: preprocessor 1/1
## ✓ Fold01, Repeat3: preprocessor 1/1
## i Fold01, Repeat3: preprocessor 1/1, model 1/1
## ✓ Fold01, Repeat3: preprocessor 1/1, model 1/1
## i Fold01, Repeat3: preprocessor 1/1, model 1/1 (extracts)
```

```
## i Fold01, Repeat3: preprocessor 1/1, model 1/1 (predictions)
## i Fold02, Repeat3: preprocessor 1/1
## ✓ Fold02, Repeat3: preprocessor 1/1
## i Fold02, Repeat3: preprocessor 1/1, model 1/1
## ✓ Fold02, Repeat3: preprocessor 1/1, model 1/1
## i Fold02, Repeat3: preprocessor 1/1, model 1/1 (extracts)
## i Fold02, Repeat3: preprocessor 1/1, model 1/1 (predictions)
## i Fold03, Repeat3: preprocessor 1/1
## ✓ Fold03, Repeat3: preprocessor 1/1
## i Fold03, Repeat3: preprocessor 1/1, model 1/1
## ✓ Fold03, Repeat3: preprocessor 1/1, model 1/1
## i Fold03, Repeat3: preprocessor 1/1, model 1/1 (extracts)
## i Fold03, Repeat3: preprocessor 1/1, model 1/1 (predictions)
## i Fold04, Repeat3: preprocessor 1/1
## ✓ Fold04, Repeat3: preprocessor 1/1
## i Fold04, Repeat3: preprocessor 1/1, model 1/1
## ✓ Fold04, Repeat3: preprocessor 1/1, model 1/1
## i Fold04, Repeat3: preprocessor 1/1, model 1/1 (extracts)
## i Fold04, Repeat3: preprocessor 1/1, model 1/1 (predictions)
## i Fold05, Repeat3: preprocessor 1/1
## ✓ Fold05, Repeat3: preprocessor 1/1
## i Fold05, Repeat3: preprocessor 1/1, model 1/1
## ✓ Fold05, Repeat3: preprocessor 1/1, model 1/1
## i Fold05, Repeat3: preprocessor 1/1, model 1/1 (extracts)
## i Fold05, Repeat3: preprocessor 1/1, model 1/1 (predictions)
## i Fold06, Repeat3: preprocessor 1/1
## ✓ Fold06, Repeat3: preprocessor 1/1
## i Fold06, Repeat3: preprocessor 1/1, model 1/1
## ✓ Fold06, Repeat3: preprocessor 1/1, model 1/1
## i Fold06, Repeat3: preprocessor 1/1, model 1/1 (extracts)
## i Fold06, Repeat3: preprocessor 1/1, model 1/1 (predictions)
## i Fold07, Repeat3: preprocessor 1/1
```

```
## ✓ Fold07, Repeat3: preprocessor 1/1
## i Fold07, Repeat3: preprocessor 1/1, model 1/1
## ✓ Fold07, Repeat3: preprocessor 1/1, model 1/1
## i Fold07, Repeat3: preprocessor 1/1, model 1/1 (extracts)
## i Fold07, Repeat3: preprocessor 1/1, model 1/1 (predictions)
## i Fold08, Repeat3: preprocessor 1/1
## ✓ Fold08, Repeat3: preprocessor 1/1
## i Fold08, Repeat3: preprocessor 1/1, model 1/1
## ✓ Fold08, Repeat3: preprocessor 1/1, model 1/1
## i Fold08, Repeat3: preprocessor 1/1, model 1/1 (extracts)
## i Fold08, Repeat3: preprocessor 1/1, model 1/1 (predictions)
## i Fold09, Repeat3: preprocessor 1/1
## ✓ Fold09, Repeat3: preprocessor 1/1
## i Fold09, Repeat3: preprocessor 1/1, model 1/1
## ✓ Fold09, Repeat3: preprocessor 1/1, model 1/1
## i Fold09, Repeat3: preprocessor 1/1, model 1/1 (extracts)
## i Fold09, Repeat3: preprocessor 1/1, model 1/1 (predictions)
## i Fold10, Repeat3: preprocessor 1/1
## ✓ Fold10, Repeat3: preprocessor 1/1
## i Fold10, Repeat3: preprocessor 1/1, model 1/1
## ✓ Fold10, Repeat3: preprocessor 1/1, model 1/1
## i Fold10, Repeat3: preprocessor 1/1, model 1/1 (extracts)
## i Fold10, Repeat3: preprocessor 1/1, model 1/1 (predictions)
## i Fold01, Repeat4: preprocessor 1/1
## ✓ Fold01, Repeat4: preprocessor 1/1
## i Fold01, Repeat4: preprocessor 1/1, model 1/1
## ✓ Fold01, Repeat4: preprocessor 1/1, model 1/1
## i Fold01, Repeat4: preprocessor 1/1, model 1/1 (extracts)
## i Fold01, Repeat4: preprocessor 1/1, model 1/1 (predictions)
## i Fold02, Repeat4: preprocessor 1/1
## ✓ Fold02, Repeat4: preprocessor 1/1
## i Fold02, Repeat4: preprocessor 1/1, model 1/1
```

```
## ✓ Fold02, Repeat4: preprocessor 1/1, model 1/1
## i Fold02, Repeat4: preprocessor 1/1, model 1/1 (extracts)
## i Fold02, Repeat4: preprocessor 1/1, model 1/1 (predictions)
## i Fold03, Repeat4: preprocessor 1/1
## ✓ Fold03, Repeat4: preprocessor 1/1
## i Fold03, Repeat4: preprocessor 1/1, model 1/1
## ✓ Fold03, Repeat4: preprocessor 1/1, model 1/1
## i Fold03, Repeat4: preprocessor 1/1, model 1/1 (extracts)
## i Fold03, Repeat4: preprocessor 1/1, model 1/1 (predictions)
## i Fold04, Repeat4: preprocessor 1/1
## ✓ Fold04, Repeat4: preprocessor 1/1
## i Fold04, Repeat4: preprocessor 1/1, model 1/1
## ✓ Fold04, Repeat4: preprocessor 1/1, model 1/1
## i Fold04, Repeat4: preprocessor 1/1, model 1/1 (extracts)
## i Fold04, Repeat4: preprocessor 1/1, model 1/1 (predictions)
## i Fold05, Repeat4: preprocessor 1/1
## ✓ Fold05, Repeat4: preprocessor 1/1
## i Fold05, Repeat4: preprocessor 1/1, model 1/1
## ✓ Fold05, Repeat4: preprocessor 1/1, model 1/1
## i Fold05, Repeat4: preprocessor 1/1, model 1/1 (extracts)
## i Fold05, Repeat4: preprocessor 1/1, model 1/1 (predictions)
## i Fold06, Repeat4: preprocessor 1/1
## ✓ Fold06, Repeat4: preprocessor 1/1
## i Fold06, Repeat4: preprocessor 1/1, model 1/1
## ✓ Fold06, Repeat4: preprocessor 1/1, model 1/1
## i Fold06, Repeat4: preprocessor 1/1, model 1/1 (extracts)
## i Fold06, Repeat4: preprocessor 1/1, model 1/1 (predictions)
## i Fold07, Repeat4: preprocessor 1/1
## ✓ Fold07, Repeat4: preprocessor 1/1
## i Fold07, Repeat4: preprocessor 1/1, model 1/1
## ✓ Fold07, Repeat4: preprocessor 1/1, model 1/1
## i Fold07, Repeat4: preprocessor 1/1, model 1/1 (extracts)
```

```
## i Fold07, Repeat4: preprocessor 1/1, model 1/1 (predictions)
## i Fold08, Repeat4: preprocessor 1/1
## ✓ Fold08, Repeat4: preprocessor 1/1
## i Fold08, Repeat4: preprocessor 1/1, model 1/1
## ✓ Fold08, Repeat4: preprocessor 1/1, model 1/1
## i Fold08, Repeat4: preprocessor 1/1, model 1/1 (extracts)
## i Fold08, Repeat4: preprocessor 1/1, model 1/1 (predictions)
## i Fold09, Repeat4: preprocessor 1/1
## ✓ Fold09, Repeat4: preprocessor 1/1
## i Fold09, Repeat4: preprocessor 1/1, model 1/1
## ✓ Fold09, Repeat4: preprocessor 1/1, model 1/1
## i Fold09, Repeat4: preprocessor 1/1, model 1/1 (extracts)
## i Fold09, Repeat4: preprocessor 1/1, model 1/1 (predictions)
## i Fold10, Repeat4: preprocessor 1/1
## ✓ Fold10, Repeat4: preprocessor 1/1
## i Fold10, Repeat4: preprocessor 1/1, model 1/1
## ✓ Fold10, Repeat4: preprocessor 1/1, model 1/1
## i Fold10, Repeat4: preprocessor 1/1, model 1/1 (extracts)
## i Fold10, Repeat4: preprocessor 1/1, model 1/1 (predictions)
## i Fold01, Repeat5: preprocessor 1/1
## ✓ Fold01, Repeat5: preprocessor 1/1
## i Fold01, Repeat5: preprocessor 1/1, model 1/1
## ✓ Fold01, Repeat5: preprocessor 1/1, model 1/1
## i Fold01, Repeat5: preprocessor 1/1, model 1/1 (extracts)
## i Fold01, Repeat5: preprocessor 1/1, model 1/1 (predictions)
## i Fold02, Repeat5: preprocessor 1/1
## ✓ Fold02, Repeat5: preprocessor 1/1
## i Fold02, Repeat5: preprocessor 1/1, model 1/1
## ✓ Fold02, Repeat5: preprocessor 1/1, model 1/1
## i Fold02, Repeat5: preprocessor 1/1, model 1/1 (extracts)
## i Fold02, Repeat5: preprocessor 1/1, model 1/1 (predictions)
## i Fold03, Repeat5: preprocessor 1/1
```

```
## ✓ Fold03, Repeat5: preprocessor 1/1
## i Fold03, Repeat5: preprocessor 1/1, model 1/1
## ✓ Fold03, Repeat5: preprocessor 1/1, model 1/1
## i Fold03, Repeat5: preprocessor 1/1, model 1/1 (extracts)
## i Fold03, Repeat5: preprocessor 1/1, model 1/1 (predictions)
## i Fold04, Repeat5: preprocessor 1/1
## ✓ Fold04, Repeat5: preprocessor 1/1
## i Fold04, Repeat5: preprocessor 1/1, model 1/1
## ✓ Fold04, Repeat5: preprocessor 1/1, model 1/1
## i Fold04, Repeat5: preprocessor 1/1, model 1/1 (extracts)
## i Fold04, Repeat5: preprocessor 1/1, model 1/1 (predictions)
## i Fold05, Repeat5: preprocessor 1/1
## ✓ Fold05, Repeat5: preprocessor 1/1
## i Fold05, Repeat5: preprocessor 1/1, model 1/1
## ✓ Fold05, Repeat5: preprocessor 1/1, model 1/1
## i Fold05, Repeat5: preprocessor 1/1, model 1/1 (extracts)
## i Fold05, Repeat5: preprocessor 1/1, model 1/1 (predictions)
## i Fold06, Repeat5: preprocessor 1/1
## ✓ Fold06, Repeat5: preprocessor 1/1
## i Fold06, Repeat5: preprocessor 1/1, model 1/1
## ✓ Fold06, Repeat5: preprocessor 1/1, model 1/1
## i Fold06, Repeat5: preprocessor 1/1, model 1/1 (extracts)
## i Fold06, Repeat5: preprocessor 1/1, model 1/1 (predictions)
## i Fold07, Repeat5: preprocessor 1/1
## ✓ Fold07, Repeat5: preprocessor 1/1
## i Fold07, Repeat5: preprocessor 1/1, model 1/1
## ✓ Fold07, Repeat5: preprocessor 1/1, model 1/1
## i Fold07, Repeat5: preprocessor 1/1, model 1/1 (extracts)
## i Fold07, Repeat5: preprocessor 1/1, model 1/1 (predictions)
## i Fold08, Repeat5: preprocessor 1/1
## ✓ Fold08, Repeat5: preprocessor 1/1
## i Fold08, Repeat5: preprocessor 1/1, model 1/1
```

```
## ✓ Fold08, Repeat5: preprocessor 1/1, model 1/1
## i Fold08, Repeat5: preprocessor 1/1, model 1/1 (extracts)
## i Fold08, Repeat5: preprocessor 1/1, model 1/1 (predictions)
## i Fold09, Repeat5: preprocessor 1/1
## ✓ Fold09, Repeat5: preprocessor 1/1
## i Fold09, Repeat5: preprocessor 1/1, model 1/1
## ✓ Fold09, Repeat5: preprocessor 1/1, model 1/1
## i Fold09, Repeat5: preprocessor 1/1, model 1/1 (extracts)
## i Fold09, Repeat5: preprocessor 1/1, model 1/1 (predictions)
## i Fold10, Repeat5: preprocessor 1/1
## ✓ Fold10, Repeat5: preprocessor 1/1
## i Fold10, Repeat5: preprocessor 1/1, model 1/1
## ✓ Fold10, Repeat5: preprocessor 1/1, model 1/1
## i Fold10, Repeat5: preprocessor 1/1, model 1/1 (extracts)
## i Fold10, Repeat5: preprocessor 1/1, model 1/1 (predictions)
rid_res
## # Tuning results
## # 10-fold cross-validation repeated 5 times using stratification
## # A tibble: 50 × 5
## splits id id2 .metrics .notes
## <list> <chr> <chr> <list> <list>
## 1 <split [1976/221]> Repeat1 Fold01 <tibble [50 × 5]> <tibble [0 × 3]>
## 2 <split [1976/221]> Repeat1 Fold02 <tibble [50 × 5]> <tibble [0 × 3]>
## 3 <split [1976/221]> Repeat1 Fold03 <tibble [50 × 5]> <tibble [0 × 3]>
## 4 <split [1976/221]> Repeat1 Fold04 <tibble [50 × 5]> <tibble [0 × 3]>
## 5 <split [1977/220]> Repeat1 Fold05 <tibble [50 × 5]> <tibble [0 × 3]>
## 6 <split [1977/220]> Repeat1 Fold06 <tibble [50 × 5]> <tibble [0 × 3]>
## 7 <split [1978/219]> Repeat1 Fold07 <tibble [50 × 5]> <tibble [0 × 3]>
## 8 <split [1978/219]> Repeat1 Fold08 <tibble [50 × 5]> <tibble [0 × 3]>
## 9 <split [1979/218]> Repeat1 Fold09 <tibble [50 × 5]> <tibble [0 × 3]>
## 10 <split [1980/217]> Repeat1 Fold10 <tibble [50 × 5]> <tibble [0 × 3]>
## # i 40 more rows
```

- Every fold within each repeat or every resample is monitored during model fitting on it.

The resulting object "rid_res" contains 50 rows (for 50 resamples) and 5 columns:

- The splits column is a list of each combination of analysis and assessment data withing each resample. The sum is 2197, which are total rows of training data.
- The id column is an id column for the repeat number from 1 to 5.
- The id2 column is an id column for the fold number from 1 to 10 so we have 50 resamples because 5 × 10 = 50.
- The .metrics column is a list of performance metric (RMSE) of applying the ridge model to the corresponding assessment data (221,220,219,218, or 217 rows) within each resample. Each performance metric is saved in 50 rows and 5 columns [50 × 5] tibble or data frame. The 50 rows are for the RMSE of applying the 50 penalty values in the assessment data within each resample.
- The .notes column is a list of notes or warnings when applying the ridge model to each analysis data (1976, 1977, 1978, 1979, or 1980 rows) within each resample. Each note is saved in 0 rows and 3 columns [0 × 3] tibble or data frame meaning that there are no rows or no notes when applying this model to each analysis data.

3.4.8. The Model Performance on 50 Resamples of the Training Data

To get the performance metric (RMSE) on the 50 resamples of training data using the 50 penalty values, we will use the unnest function with the ".metrics" argument to expand the .metrics list column of the rid_res object into rows and columns.

```
rid_res %>% unnest(.metrics)
## # A tibble: 2,500 × 9
## splits id id2 penalty .metric .estimator .estimate .config
## <list> <chr> <chr> <dbl> <chr> <chr> <dbl> <chr>
## 1 <split [1976/221]> Repea... Fold... 1 e-10 rmse standard 28216. Prepro...
## 2 <split [1976/221]> Repea... Fold... 1.60e-10 rmse standard 28216. Prepro...
## 3 <split [1976/221]> Repea... Fold... 2.56e-10 rmse standard 28216. Prepro...
```

4 <split [1976/221]> Repea… Fold… 4.09e-10 rmse standard 28216. Prepro…

5 <split [1976/221]> Repea… Fold… 6.55e-10 rmse standard 28216. Prepro…

6 <split [1976/221]> Repea… Fold… 1.05e-9 rmse standard 28216. Prepro…

7 <split [1976/221]> Repea… Fold… 1.68e-9 rmse standard 28216. Prepro…

8 <split [1976/221]> Repea… Fold… 2.68e-9 rmse standard 28216. Prepro…

9 <split [1976/221]> Repea… Fold… 4.29e-9 rmse standard 28216. Prepro…

10 <split [1976/221]> Repea… Fold… 6.87e-9 rmse standard 28216. Prepro…

i 2,490 more rows

i 1 more variable: .notes <list>

- result is 2500 rows because we have applied the 50 penalties to 50 resamples of the training data so we have 50 × 50 rows or 2500 different models. Each row contains the RMSE of the ridge model on 1 resample using 1 penalty.

To get the mean RMSE of each penalty value on the 50 resamples of the training data, we use the following functions on the "rid_res" object:

- The collect_metrics function to get the mean for each penalty across the 50 resamples of the training data.
- The arrange function with mean argument to arrange by mean RMSE value in ascending order.
- The flextable, theme_box, and set_caption functions are described previously.

rid_res **%>% collect_metrics**() **%>%**

arrange(mean) **%>%**

flextable(cwidth = 1) **%>% theme_box**() **%>%**

set_caption(caption = "The mean RMSE of applying 50 penalties on 50 resamples of ames training data when using ridge regression model")

The mean RMSE of applying 50 penalties on 50 resamples of ames training data when using ridge regression model:

penalty	**.metric**	**.estimator**	**mean**	**n**	**std_err**	**.config**
0.0000000001000000	rmse	standard	34,206.08	50	986.5667	Preprocessor1_Model01
0.0000000001599859	rmse	standard	34,206.08	50	986.5667	Preprocessor1_Model02
0.0000000002559548	rmse	standard	34,206.08	50	986.5667	Preprocessor1_Model03

0.0000000004094915	rmse	standard	34,206.08	50	986.5667	Preprocessor1_Model04
0.0000000006551286	rmse	standard	34,206.08	50	986.5667	Preprocessor1_Model05
0.0000000010481131	rmse	standard	34,206.08	50	986.5667	Preprocessor1_Model06
0.0000000016768329	rmse	standard	34,206.08	50	986.5667	Preprocessor1_Model07
0.0000000026826958	rmse	standard	34,206.08	50	986.5667	Preprocessor1_Model08
0.0000000042919343	rmse	standard	34,206.08	50	986.5667	Preprocessor1_Model09
0.0000000068664885	rmse	standard	34,206.08	50	986.5667	Preprocessor1_Model10
0.0000000109854114	rmse	standard	34,206.08	50	986.5667	Preprocessor1_Model11
0.0000000175751062	rmse	standard	34,206.08	50	986.5667	Preprocessor1_Model12
0.0000000281176870	rmse	standard	34,206.08	50	986.5667	Preprocessor1_Model13
0.0000000449843267	rmse	standard	34,206.08	50	986.5667	Preprocessor1_Model14
0.0000000719685673	rmse	standard	34,206.08	50	986.5667	Preprocessor1_Model15
0.0000001151395399	rmse	standard	34,206.08	50	986.5667	Preprocessor1_Model16
0.0000001842069969	rmse	standard	34,206.08	50	986.5667	Preprocessor1_Model17
0.0000002947051703	rmse	standard	34,206.08	50	986.5667	Preprocessor1_Model18
0.0000004714866363	rmse	standard	34,206.08	50	986.5667	Preprocessor1_Model19
0.0000007543120063	rmse	standard	34,206.08	50	986.5667	Preprocessor1_Model20
0.0000012067926406	rmse	standard	34,206.08	50	986.5667	Preprocessor1_Model21
0.0000019306977289	rmse	standard	34,206.08	50	986.5667	Preprocessor1_Model22
0.0000030888435965	rmse	standard	34,206.08	50	986.5667	Preprocessor1_Model23
0.0000049417133613	rmse	standard	34,206.08	50	986.5667	Preprocessor1_Model24
0.0000079060432109	rmse	standard	34,206.08	50	986.5667	Preprocessor1_Model25
0.0000126485521686	rmse	standard	34,206.08	50	986.5667	Preprocessor1_Model26
0.0000202358964773	rmse	standard	34,206.08	50	986.5667	Preprocessor1_Model27
0.0000323745754282	rmse	standard	34,206.08	50	986.5667	Preprocessor1_Model28
0.0000517947467923	rmse	standard	34,206.08	50	986.5667	Preprocessor1_Model29
0.0000828642772855	rmse	standard	34,206.08	50	986.5667	Preprocessor1_Model30
0.0001325711365590	rmse	standard	34,206.08	50	986.5667	Preprocessor1_Model31
0.0002120950887920	rmse	standard	34,206.08	50	986.5667	Preprocessor1_Model32
0.0003393221771895	rmse	standard	34,206.08	50	986.5667	Preprocessor1_Model33
0.0005428675439324	rmse	standard	34,206.08	50	986.5667	Preprocessor1_Model34
0.0008685113737514	rmse	standard	34,206.08	50	986.5667	Preprocessor1_Model35
0.0013894954943731	rmse	standard	34,206.08	50	986.5667	Preprocessor1_Model36
0.0022229964825262	rmse	standard	34,206.08	50	986.5667	Preprocessor1_Model37
0.0035564803062231	rmse	standard	34,206.08	50	986.5667	Preprocessor1_Model38
0.0056898660290183	rmse	standard	34,206.08	50	986.5667	Preprocessor1_Model39
0.0091029817799152	rmse	standard	34,206.08	50	986.5667	Preprocessor1_Model40
0.0145634847750124	rmse	standard	34,206.08	50	986.5667	Preprocessor1_Model41
0.0232995181051537	rmse	standard	34,206.08	50	986.5667	Preprocessor1_Model42
0.0372759372031494	rmse	standard	34,206.08	50	986.5667	Preprocessor1_Model43
0.0596362331659464	rmse	standard	34,206.08	50	986.5667	Preprocessor1_Model44

0.0954095476349996	rmse	standard	34,206.08	50	986.5667	Preprocessor1_Model45
0.1526417967175236	rmse	standard	34,206.08	50	986.5667	Preprocessor1_Model46
0.2442053094548655	rmse	standard	34,206.08	50	986.5667	Preprocessor1_Model47
0.3906939937054621	rmse	standard	34,206.08	50	986.5667	Preprocessor1_Model48
0.6250551925273976	rmse	standard	34,206.08	50	986.5667	Preprocessor1_Model49
1.0000000000000000	rmse	standard	34,206.08	50	986.5667	Preprocessor1_Model50

- The result is 50 rows with 1 mean RMSE value for each penalty across the 50 resamples (n = 50).
- All penalties have the same mean RMSE value (34206.08) across the 50 resamples with the same standard error (986.5667).

We can plot the 50 mean RMSE values from the 50 penalties by using the following functions after the collect_metrics function:

- The ggplot function with the argument aes(x = penalty, y = mean) to plot the penalty on the x-axis and the mean RMSE value on the y-axis.

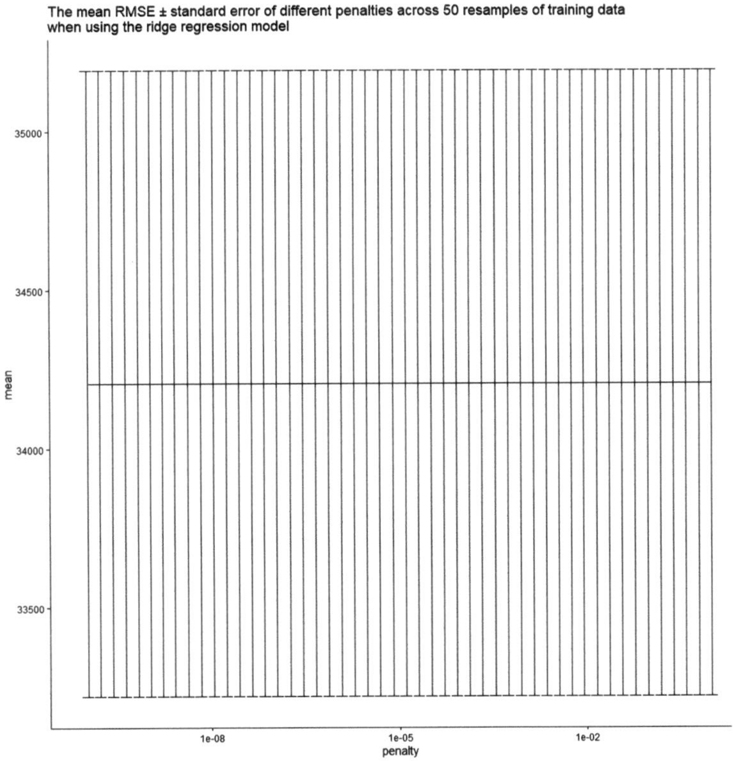

- The geom_errorbar function with the argument aes(ymin = mean–std_err, ymax = mean + std_err) to plot an error bar that represents mean–standard error at the lower end and the mean+ standard error at the upper end.
- The geom_line function to connect the 50 mean values by a line.
- The scale_x_log10() to plot the x-axis values after being log transformed with the base 10.
- The labs function with title = "…" argument to add a plot title. We use the "\n" inside the title to make it into 2 lines.
- The theme_classic function as explained before.

```
rid_res %>% collect_metrics() %>%
ggplot(aes(x = penalty, y = mean)) +
geom_errorbar(aes(ymin = mean–std_err, ymax = mean + std_err)) +
geom_line() + scale_x_log10()+
labs(title = "The mean RMSE ± standard error of different penalties across 50 resamples of training data \nwhen using the ridge regression model")+
theme_classic()
```

- As we have seen before, all penalties have the same mean RMSE value (34206.08) and the same standard error (986.5667).

We can use the select_best function to create an object "best_pen" that contains the best penalty value for the best ridge model.

```
best_pen<-rid_res %>% select_best()
best_pen
## # A tibble: 1 × 2
## penalty .config
## <dbl> <chr>
## 1 0.0000000001 Preprocessor1_Model01
```

- Because all penalties are the same, so the function selects the 1st tried penalty = 0.0000000001.

To get the final workflow with the best penalty, we use the finalize_workflow function with the arguments:

- wflow which is the original workflow with tuned penalty.
- best_pen which is the data of 1 row containing the best penalty value.

The resulting workflow "rid_final" is the final workflow containing the best penalty.

```
rid_final <- finalize_workflow(wflow, best_pen)
rid_final
## == Workflow ==========================================
## Preprocessor: Recipe
## Model: linear_reg()
##
## -- Preprocessor ---------------------------------------
## 4 Recipe Steps
##
## • step_rm()
## • step_dummy()
## • step_nzv()
## • step_normalize()
##
## -- Model ----------------------------------------------
## Linear Regression Model Specification (regression)
##
## Main Arguments:
## penalty = 1e-10
## mixture = 0
##
## Computational engine: glmnet
```

We create a rid_fit model by using the fit function with the arguments:

- rid_final which is the final workflow containing 4 preprocessing steps and the linear ridge model with best penalty value.
- train_ames which is the whole training data with 2197 rows.

Then, we use the following functions on the rid_fit model:

- The extract_fit_parsnip function to get the model specifications.
- The tidy function to see the model results in a data frame.
- The arrange function to arrange the estimate or regression coefficients

with the desc and abs functions so that the predictors are arranged according to their absolute regression coefficients in descending order.

```
rid_fit <- fit(rid_final, data = train_ames)
rid_fit %>% extract_fit_parsnip() %>%
broom::tidy() %>% arrange(desc(abs(estimate))) %>%
flextable(cwidth = 1.5) %>% theme_box() %>%
set_caption(caption = "Ridge model results of applying best penalty value on the ames training data")
```

Ridge model results of applying best penalty value on the ames training data:

term	estimate	penalty
(Intercept)	180,466.578516	0.0000000001
Gr_Liv_Area	15,135.962090	0.0000000001
Second_Flr_SF	10,929.722112	0.0000000001
Neighborhood_Northridge_Heights	8,381.533808	0.0000000001
Total_Bsmt_SF	7,790.700938	0.0000000001
First_Flr_SF	7,456.221657	0.0000000001
Mas_Vnr_Area	7,438.120917	0.0000000001
Garage_Cars	6,959.879510	0.0000000001
Year_Remod_Add	6,306.032219	0.0000000001
Fireplaces	6,196.871527	0.0000000001
Bsmt_Exposure_Gd	5,114.181282	0.0000000001
House_Style_One_Story	4,411.662236	0.0000000001
BsmtFin_Type_1_GLQ	4,279.260379	0.0000000001
Functional_Typ	4,244.615539	0.0000000001
Neighborhood_Gilbert	–4,242.767183	0.0000000001
Neighborhood_Somerset	4,138.185553	0.0000000001
Year_Built	4,034.624810	0.0000000001
Bsmt_Exposure_No	–3,996.794619	0.0000000001
Garage_Area	3,909.426093	0.0000000001
Neighborhood_Edwards	–3,818.302390	0.0000000001
Roof_Style_Hip	3,810.169760	0.0000000001
Overall_Cond_Good	3,628.517191	0.0000000001
Sale_Type_New	3,438.431412	0.0000000001

Garage_Finish_RFn	–3,433.115624	0.0000000001
MS_Zoning_Residential_Low_Density	3,418.953590	0.0000000001
Lot_Config_CulDSac	3,331.742709	0.0000000001
Bsmt_Full_Bath	3,301.169052	0.0000000001
Mas_Vnr_Type_None	3,234.767255	0.0000000001
Heating_QC_Typical	–3,198.453753	0.0000000001
Sale_Condition_Normal	3,065.880581	0.0000000001
Bedroom_AbvGr	–3,037.204343	0.0000000001
Garage_Finish_Unf	–3,031.387385	0.0000000001
Full_Bath	2,943.440975	0.0000000001
Foundation_PConc	2,808.121342	0.0000000001
Foundation_CBlock	–2,736.063435	0.0000000001
Sale_Condition_Partial	2,735.940167	0.0000000001
Condition_1_Norm	2,362.186784	0.0000000001
MS_SubClass_One_and_Half_Story_Finished_All_Ages	2,172.670615	0.0000000001
Overall_Cond_Above_Average	2,139.244560	0.0000000001
Lot_Shape_Slightly_Irregular	2,130.257178	0.0000000001
Exterior_1st_Wd.Sdng	–2,127.626630	0.0000000001
Overall_Cond_Very_Good	2,062.074733	0.0000000001
Condition_1_Feedr	–2,003.349053	0.0000000001
Neighborhood_College_Creek	–1,997.205791	0.0000000001
MS_SubClass_Two_Story_1946_and_Newer	1,981.094522	0.0000000001
Exterior_1st_VinylSd	–1,973.890844	0.0000000001
Bldg_Type_TwnhsE	–1,909.633458	0.0000000001
Wood_Deck_SF	1,854.237991	0.0000000001
Lot_Area	1,818.103977	0.0000000001
Year_Sold	–1,780.520664	0.0000000001
Exterior_1st_Plywood	–1,763.899726	0.0000000001
Half_Bath	1,671.985053	0.0000000001
Exterior_2nd_Plywood	–1,582.386613	0.0000000001
Bsmt_Exposure_Mn	–1,559.445461	0.0000000001
Garage_Type_Detchd	–1,455.861456	0.0000000001
Exterior_2nd_Wd.Sdng	1,451.424118	0.0000000001

Exterior_2nd_HdBoard	–1,395.057248	0.0000000001
Exterior_1st_MetalSd	–1,388.943174	0.0000000001
House_Style_Two_Story	–1,329.636763	0.0000000001
Exterior_1st_HdBoard	–1,257.715622	0.0000000001
Heating_QC_Good	–1,255.763327	0.0000000001
MS_SubClass_One_Story_ PUD_1946_and_Newer	–1,245.511027	0.0000000001
Garage_Cond_Typical	1,225.149715	0.0000000001
BsmtFin_SF_1	–1,161.511030	0.0000000001
Exter_Cond_Good	1,151.799872	0.0000000001
Overall_Cond_Average	1,026.552368	0.0000000001
Central_Air_Y	1,005.358617	0.0000000001
Exter_Cond_Typical	1,000.737182	0.0000000001
Bsmt_Unf_SF	–978.699857	0.0000000001
Bsmt_Cond_Typical	953.766254	0.0000000001
TotRms_AbvGrd	949.710989	0.0000000001
Open_Porch_SF	–909.217437	0.0000000001
Neighborhood_Old_Town	–892.653245	0.0000000001
Fence_Minimum_Privacy	859.124299	0.0000000001
Land_Contour_Lvl	–832.143111	0.0000000001
Lot_Config_Inside	804.701241	0.0000000001
Lot_Frontage	798.373463	0.0000000001
Bsmt_Half_Bath	–688.235204	0.0000000001
Mas_Vnr_Type_Stone	660.680070	0.0000000001
Fence_No_Fence	–523.328160	0.0000000001
Alley_No_Alley_Access	481.481239	0.0000000001
BsmtFin_Type_1_Rec	391.043800	0.0000000001
BsmtFin_Type_1_Unf	324.319482	0.0000000001
MS_Zoning_Residential_Medium_ Density	–322.128573	0.0000000001
Sale_Type_WD.	–295.578059	0.0000000001
Paved_Drive_Paved	277.563404	0.0000000001
Mo_Sold	–272.668322	0.0000000001
BsmtFin_Type_2_Unf	270.882613	0.0000000001
Exterior_2nd_MetalSd	268.716635	0.0000000001
Garage_Type_BuiltIn	200.546286	0.0000000001

BsmtFin_Type_1_LwQ	–190.061234	0.0000000001
Garage_Finish_No_Garage	139.117168	0.0000000001
Exterior_2nd_VinylSd	–134.425834	0.0000000001
Garage_Cond_No_Garage	116.823002	0.0000000001
Mas_Vnr_Type_BrkFace	71.603223	0.0000000001
Garage_Type_No_Garage	50.948983	0.0000000001
Roof_Style_Gable	–31.340203	0.0000000001
BsmtFin_Type_1_BLQ	–14.308888	0.0000000001
Electrical_SBrkr	–8.846982	0.0000000001

- The result is 99 rows with a regression coefficient for each 98 predictors and the intercept.
- All 98 predictors were kept in the ridge model but some have low absolute cofficients indicating their low importance in the model.
- The most important predictor is Gr_Liv_Area (the above grade living area square feet) with the highest coefficient = 15135.96. The positive coefficient means that as the Gr_Liv_Area increases, the price increases too.
- The most important predictor with negative impact on price is Neighborhood_Gilbert. This means that Gilbert neighborhood is associated with lower price than other neighborhoods.
- The least important predictor is Electrical_SBrkr (or the SBrkr electrical system) with the lowest absolute coefficient = –8.85. The negative coefficient means that as the the SBrkr electrical system is associated with lower price than other electrical systems.

3.4.9. Model Performance on Testing Data

To get the RMSE on the testing data, we use the following functions on the rid_fit model:

- The predict function with the argument new_data = test_ames to get the predicted price (.pred column) for each row of the testing data after being preprocessed using the rid_fit model.
- The mutate function with the argument truth = test_ames$Sale_Price to add a truth column containing the actual price for each row in the testing data.
- The rmse function with the arguments truth = truth, estimate = .pred to get the RMSE of applying this ridge model on the testing data.

```
rid_fit %>% predict(new_data = test_ames) %>%
mutate(truth = test_ames$Sale_Price) %>%
rmse(truth = truth, estimate = .pred)
## # A tibble: 1 × 3
## .metric .estimator .estimate
## <chr> <chr> <dbl>
## 1 rmse standard 29747.
```

- The RMSE of the ridge model on testing data = 29747.

3.5. LASSO REGRESSION

In lasso regression, we will use the same steps of ridge regression till defining the machine learning (ML) model.

3.5.1. Define Machine Learning (ML) Model

We define a linear lasso regression model by using the functions:

- The linear_reg function to define the linear regression model type with the following arguments:
  - mixture = 1 to indicate a lasso regression model.
  - penalty = tune() to tune the penalty term on the different resamples of training data.
- The set_engine function with the argument "glmnet" to define the engine that will use the glmnet function from the glmnet package.
- The set_mode function with the argument "regression" to define the mode of learning. We use regression because we have a numerical outcome (price).
- All the three functions are applied in sequence using the piping "%>%" operator and the resulting object is called "lasso_model."

```
lasso_model <- linear_reg(mixture = 1, penalty = tune()) %>%
set_engine("glmnet") %>%
set_mode("regression")
lasso_model
## Linear Regression Model Specification (regression)
##
## Main Arguments:
```

```
## penalty = tune()
## mixture = 1
##
## Computational engine: glmnet
```

The only difference of the lasso model is that the mixture argument = 1, instead of 0 for the ridge model, in the linear_reg function.

3.5.2. Generate Workflow

We create the "wflow2" object by using the following functions:

- The workflow function to create a workflow.
- The add_recipe function with the argument "rec" to add the above created recipe with 4 preprocessing steps.
- The add_model function with the argument lasso_model to add the above created lasso model.

```
wflow2 <- workflow() %>%
add_recipe(rec) %>%
add_model(lasso_model)
wflow2
## ══ Workflow ═══════════════════════════════════════════════════════
═══════════════════════════════════════════════════
## Preprocessor: Recipe
## Model: linear_reg()
##
## ── Preprocessor ───────────────────────────────────────────────────
─────────────────────────────────────────────────
## 4 Recipe Steps
##
## • step_rm()
## • step_dummy()
## • step_nzv()
## • step_normalize()
##
## ── Model ──────────────────────────────────────────────────────────
───────────────────────────────
```

```
## Linear Regression Model Specification (regression)
##
## Main Arguments:
## penalty = tune()
## mixture = 1
##
## Computational engine: glmnet
```

3.5.3. Fit Model on Different Resamples with Tuning

We will use the same my_grid with 50 different penalty values. To try these 50 different penalties on the 50 resamples of the training data using the lasso model, we use the tune_grid function with the arguments:

- wflow2 which is the workflow containing 4 preprocessing steps and the linear lasso model.
- folds which are the 50 resamples of training data created above.
- metrics = metrics_set(rmse) to get the RMSE of the linear lasso model on each resample using the 50 penalty values.
- grid = my_grid to use the 50 penalty values in the my_grid data in tuning.

We also use the set.seed function before using these functions for reproducibility.

```
set.seed(123)
lasso_res <- tune_grid(wflow2, folds,
metrics = metric_set(rmse),
grid = my_grid)
lasso_res
## # Tuning results
## # 10-fold cross-validation repeated 5 times using stratification
## # A tibble: 50 × 5
## splits id id2 .metrics .notes
## <list> <chr> <chr> <list> <list>
## 1 <split [1976/221]> Repeat1 Fold01 <tibble [50 × 5]> <tibble [0 × 3]>
## 2 <split [1976/221]> Repeat1 Fold02 <tibble [50 × 5]> <tibble [0 × 3]>
## 3 <split [1976/221]> Repeat1 Fold03 <tibble [50 × 5]> <tibble [0 × 3]>
## 4 <split [1976/221]> Repeat1 Fold04 <tibble [50 × 5]> <tibble [0 × 3]>
```

```
## 5 <split [1977/220]> Repeat1 Fold05 <tibble [50 × 5]> <tibble [0 × 3]>
## 6 <split [1977/220]> Repeat1 Fold06 <tibble [50 × 5]> <tibble [0 × 3]>
## 7 <split [1978/219]> Repeat1 Fold07 <tibble [50 × 5]> <tibble [0 × 3]>
## 8 <split [1978/219]> Repeat1 Fold08 <tibble [50 × 5]> <tibble [0 × 3]>
## 9 <split [1979/218]> Repeat1 Fold09 <tibble [50 × 5]> <tibble [0 × 3]>
## 10 <split [1980/217]> Repeat1 Fold10 <tibble [50 × 5]> <tibble [0 × 3]>
## # i 40 more rows
```

The resulting object "lasso_res" contains 50 rows (for 50 resamples) and 5 columns:

- The splits column is a list of each combination of analysis and assessment data withing each resample. The sum is 2197, which are total rows of training data.
- The id column is an id column for the repeat number from 1 to 5.
- The id2 column is an id column for the fold number from 1 to 10 so we have 50 resamples because 5 × 10 = 50.
- The .metrics column is a list of performance metric (RMSE) of applying the lasso model to the corresponding assessment data (221,220,219,218, or 217 rows) within each resample. Each performance metric is saved in 50 rows and 5 columns [50 × 5] tibble or data frame. The 50 rows are for the RMSE of applying the 50 penalty values in the assessment data within each resample.
- The .notes column is a list of notes or warnings when applying the lasso model to each analysis data (1976, 1977, 1978, 1979, or 1980 rows) within each resample. Each note is saved in 0 rows and 3 columns [0 × 3] tibble or data frame meaning that there are no rows or no notes when applying this model to each analysis data.

3.5.4. The Model Performance on 50 Resamples of the Training Data

To get the performance metric (RMSE) on the 50 resamples of training data using the 50 penalty values, we will use the unnest function with the ".metrics" argument to expand the .metrics list column of the lasso_res object into rows and columns.

```
lasso_res %>% unnest(.metrics)
## # A tibble: 2,500 × 9
## splits id id2 penalty .metric .estimator .estimate .config
```

```
## <list> <chr> <chr> <dbl> <chr> <chr> <dbl> <chr>
## 1 <split [1976/221]> Repea… Fold… 1e-10 rmse standard 27609. Prepro…
## 2 <split [1976/221]> Repea… Fold… 1.60e-10 rmse standard 27609. Prepro…
## 3 <split [1976/221]> Repea… Fold… 2.56e-10 rmse standard 27609. Prepro…
## 4 <split [1976/221]> Repea… Fold… 4.09e-10 rmse standard 27609. Prepro…
## 5 <split [1976/221]> Repea… Fold… 6.55e-10 rmse standard 27609. Prepro…
## 6 <split [1976/221]> Repea… Fold… 1.05e-9 rmse standard 27609. Prepro…
## 7 <split [1976/221]> Repea… Fold… 1.68e-9 rmse standard 27609. Prepro…
## 8 <split [1976/221]> Repea… Fold… 2.68e-9 rmse standard 27609. Prepro…
## 9 <split [1976/221]> Repea… Fold… 4.29e-9 rmse standard 27609. Prepro…
## 10 <split [1976/221]> Repea… Fold… 6.87e-9 rmse standard 27609. Prepro…
## # i 2,490 more rows
## # i 1 more variable: .notes <list>
```

- The result is 2500 rows because we have applied the 50 penalties to 50 resamples of the training data so we have 50 × 50 = 2500 rows. Each row contains the RMSE of the lasso model on 1 resample using 1 penalty.

  To get the mean RMSE of each penalty value on the 50 resamples of the training data, we use the following functions on the "lasso_res" object:
- The collect_metrics function to get the mean for each penalty across the 50 resamples of the training data.
- The arrange function with a mean argument to arrange by mean RMSE value in ascending order.
- The flextable, theme_box, and set_caption functions are described previously.

```
lasso_res %>% collect_metrics() %>%
arrange(mean) %>%
flextable(cwidth = 1) %>% theme_box() %>%
set_caption(caption = "The mean RMSE of applying 50 penalties on 50 resamples of ames training data when using lasso regression model")
```

The mean RMSE of applying 50 penalties on 50 resamples of ames training data when using lasso regression model:

penalty	.metric	.estimator	mean	n	std_err	.config
0.0000000001000000	rmse	standard	34,502.98	50	1,046.925	Preprocessor1_Model01
0.0000000001599859	rmse	standard	34,502.98	50	1,046.925	Preprocessor1_Model02
0.0000000002559548	rmse	standard	34,502.98	50	1,046.925	Preprocessor1_Model03
0.0000000004094915	rmse	standard	34,502.98	50	1,046.925	Preprocessor1_Model04
0.0000000006551286	rmse	standard	34,502.98	50	1,046.925	Preprocessor1_Model05
0.0000000010481131	rmse	standard	34,502.98	50	1,046.925	Preprocessor1_Model06
0.0000000016768329	rmse	standard	34,502.98	50	1,046.925	Preprocessor1_Model07
0.0000000026826958	rmse	standard	34,502.98	50	1,046.925	Preprocessor1_Model08
0.0000000042919343	rmse	standard	34,502.98	50	1,046.925	Preprocessor1_Model09
0.0000000068664885	rmse	standard	34,502.98	50	1,046.925	Preprocessor1_Model10
0.0000000109854114	rmse	standard	34,502.98	50	1,046.925	Preprocessor1_Model11
0.0000000175751062	rmse	standard	34,502.98	50	1,046.925	Preprocessor1_Model12
0.0000000281176870	rmse	standard	34,502.98	50	1,046.925	Preprocessor1_Model13

0.0000000449843267	rmse	stan-dard	34,502.98	50	1,046.925	Preproces-sor1_Mod-el14
0.0000000719685673	rmse	stan-dard	34,502.98	50	1,046.925	Preproces-sor1_Mod-el15
0.0000001151395399	rmse	stan-dard	34,502.98	50	1,046.925	Preproces-sor1_Mod-el16
0.0000001842069969	rmse	stan-dard	34,502.98	50	1,046.925	Preproces-sor1_Mod-el17
0.0000002947051703	rmse	stan-dard	34,502.98	50	1,046.925	Preproces-sor1_Mod-el18
0.0000004714866363	rmse	stan-dard	34,502.98	50	1,046.925	Preproces-sor1_Mod-el19
0.0000007543120063	rmse	stan-dard	34,502.98	50	1,046.925	Preproces-sor1_Mod-el20
0.0000012067926406	rmse	stan-dard	34,502.98	50	1,046.925	Preproces-sor1_Mod-el21
0.0000019306977289	rmse	stan-dard	34,502.98	50	1,046.925	Preproces-sor1_Mod-el22
0.0000030888435965	rmse	stan-dard	34,502.98	50	1,046.925	Preproces-sor1_Mod-el23
0.0000049417133613	rmse	stan-dard	34,502.98	50	1,046.925	Preproces-sor1_Mod-el24
0.0000079060432109	rmse	stan-dard	34,502.98	50	1,046.925	Preproces-sor1_Mod-el25
0.0000126485521686	rmse	stan-dard	34,502.98	50	1,046.925	Preproces-sor1_Mod-el26
0.0000202358964773	rmse	stan-dard	34,502.98	50	1,046.925	Preproces-sor1_Mod-el27
0.0000323745754282	rmse	stan-dard	34,502.98	50	1,046.925	Preproces-sor1_Mod-el28

0.0000517947467923	rmse	standard	34,502.98	50	1,046.925	Preprocessor1_Model29
0.0000828642772855	rmse	standard	34,502.98	50	1,046.925	Preprocessor1_Model30
0.0001325711365590	rmse	standard	34,502.98	50	1,046.925	Preprocessor1_Model31
0.0002120950887920	rmse	standard	34,502.98	50	1,046.925	Preprocessor1_Model32
0.0003393221771895	rmse	standard	34,502.98	50	1,046.925	Preprocessor1_Model33
0.0005428675439324	rmse	standard	34,502.98	50	1,046.925	Preprocessor1_Model34
0.0008685113737514	rmse	standard	34,502.98	50	1,046.925	Preprocessor1_Model35
0.0013894954943731	rmse	standard	34,502.98	50	1,046.925	Preprocessor1_Model36
0.0022229964825262	rmse	standard	34,502.98	50	1,046.925	Preprocessor1_Model37
0.0035564803062231	rmse	standard	34,502.98	50	1,046.925	Preprocessor1_Model38
0.0056898660290183	rmse	standard	34,502.98	50	1,046.925	Preprocessor1_Model39
0.0091029817799152	rmse	standard	34,502.98	50	1,046.925	Preprocessor1_Model40
0.0145634847750124	rmse	standard	34,502.98	50	1,046.925	Preprocessor1_Model41
0.0232995181051537	rmse	standard	34,502.98	50	1,046.925	Preprocessor1_Model42
0.0372759372031494	rmse	standard	34,502.98	50	1,046.925	Preprocessor1_Model43

0.0596362331659464	rmse	standard	34,502.98	50	1,046.925	Preprocessor1_Model44
0.0954095476349996	rmse	standard	34,502.98	50	1,046.925	Preprocessor1_Model45
0.1526417967175236	rmse	standard	34,502.98	50	1,046.925	Preprocessor1_Model46
0.2442053094548655	rmse	standard	34,502.98	50	1,046.925	Preprocessor1_Model47
0.3906939937054621	rmse	standard	34,502.98	50	1,046.925	Preprocessor1_Model48
0.6250551925273976	rmse	standard	34,502.98	50	1,046.925	Preprocessor1_Model49
1.0000000000000000	rmse	standard	34,502.98	50	1,046.925	Preprocessor1_Model50

- The result is 50 rows with 1 mean RMSE value for each penalty across the 50 resamples (n = 50).
- All penalties have the same mean RMSE value (34502.98) across the 50 resamples with the same standard error (1046.925).
- The ridge model has attained a lower RMSE value (34206.08) on 50 resamples of training data than the lasso model (34502.98).

We can use the select_best function to create an object "best_pen2" that contains the best penalty value for the best lasso model.

best_pen2<-lasso_res **%>% select_best**()

best_pen2

A tibble: 1 × 2

penalty .config

<dbl> <chr>

1 0.0000000001 Preprocessor1_Model01

- Because all penalties are the same, so the function selects the 1st tried penalty = 0.0000000001.

To get the final workflow with the best penalty, we use the finalize_workflow function with the arguments:

- wflow2 which is the original workflow with tuned penalty.
- best_pen2 which is the data of 1 row containing the best penalty value for the lasso model.

The resulting workflow "lasso_final" is the final workflow containing the best penalty.

```
lasso_final <- finalize_workflow(wflow2, best_pen2)
lasso_final
## ══ Workflow ════════════════════════════════════════════════════════════
## Preprocessor: Recipe
## Model: linear_reg()
##
## ── Preprocessor ────────────────────────────────────────────────────────
## 4 Recipe Steps
##
## • step_rm()
## • step_dummy()
## • step_nzv()
## • step_normalize()
##
## ── Model ───────────────────────────────────────────────────────────────
## Linear Regression Model Specification (regression)
##
## Main Arguments:
## penalty = 1e-10
## mixture = 1
##
## Computational engine: glmnet
```

Finally, we create a lasso_fit model by using the fit function with the arguments:

- lasso_final which is the final workflow containing 4 preprocessing steps and the linear lasso model with best penalty value.

- train_ames which is the whole training data with 2197 rows.

Then, we use the following functions on the lasso_fit model:

- The extract_fit_parsnip function to get the model specifications.
- The tidy function to see the model results in a data frame.
- The arrange function to arrange the estimate or regression coefficients with the desc and abs functions so that the predictors are arranged according to their absolute regression coefficients in descending order.

```
lasso_fit <- fit(lasso_final, data = train_ames)
lasso_fit %>% extract_fit_parsnip() %>%
broom::tidy() %>% arrange(desc(abs(estimate))) %>%
flextable(cwidth = 1.5) %>% theme_box() %>%
set_caption(caption = "Lasso model results of applying best penalty value on the ames training data")
```

Lasso model results of applying best penalty value on the ames training data:

term	estimate	penalty
(Intercept)	180,466.578516	0.0000000001
Gr_Liv_Area	26,463.859315	0.0000000001
Second_Flr_SF	10,434.594131	0.0000000001
Mas_Vnr_Type_None	9,827.969223	0.0000000001
Neighborhood_North-ridge_Heights	9,402.824096	0.0000000001
BsmtFin_Type_1_Unf	9,296.254507	0.0000000001
Garage_Cars	8,902.016452	0.0000000001
House_Style_One_Story	8,184.086708	0.0000000001
BsmtFin_SF_1	–7,854.734029	0.0000000001
Mas_Vnr_Area	7,750.768873	0.0000000001
Exterior_1st_VinylSd	–7,228.805036	0.0000000001
BsmtFin_Type_1_GLQ	7,165.635053	0.0000000001
Total_Bsmt_SF	6,438.310873	0.0000000001
Roof_Style_Hip	6,402.724455	0.0000000001
Year_Remod_Add	6,261.161587	0.0000000001
Year_Built	5,919.766296	0.0000000001
Fireplaces	5,689.577593	0.0000000001

MS_Zoning_Residential_Low_Density	5,664.915639	0.0000000001
Mas_Vnr_Type_BrkFace	5,568.885919	0.0000000001
Neighborhood_Somerset	5,457.630689	0.0000000001
Bsmt_Exposure_No	–5,440.634155	0.0000000001
Overall_Cond_Good	4,886.654990	0.0000000001
Bsmt_Exposure_Gd	4,856.504352	0.0000000001
BsmtFin_Type_1_Rec	4,806.895581	0.0000000001
Sale_Type_New	4,743.094813	0.0000000001
Functional_Typ	4,493.083463	0.0000000001
Neighborhood_Gilbert	–4,436.344897	0.0000000001
Exterior_2nd_VinylSd	4,409.538191	0.0000000001
Neighborhood_Edwards	–4,046.924536	0.0000000001
Exterior_1st_MetalSd	–4,015.583972	0.0000000001
Bedroom_AbvGr	–4,011.926489	0.0000000001
Mas_Vnr_Type_Stone	3,907.044201	0.0000000001
Garage_Finish_RFn	–3,688.369764	0.0000000001
Exterior_1st_Wd.Sdng	–3,634.405991	0.0000000001
Overall_Cond_Above_Average	3,585.821747	0.0000000001
Lot_Config_CulDSac	3,443.813158	0.0000000001
Sale_Condition_Normal	3,421.156655	0.0000000001
Garage_Finish_Unf	–3,257.045052	0.0000000001
Heating_QC_Typical	–3,147.281184	0.0000000001
Bsmt_Full_Bath	3,137.484939	0.0000000001
Overall_Cond_Very_Good	3,040.821921	0.0000000001
Foundation_CBlock	–2,942.762614	0.0000000001
Roof_Style_Gable	2,713.884155	0.0000000001
House_Style_Two_Story	–2,707.450225	0.0000000001
Exterior_2nd_Wd.Sdng	2,674.427304	0.0000000001
Condition_1_Norm	2,650.156257	0.0000000001
Bsmt_Exposure_Mn	–2,538.014294	0.0000000001
Exterior_2nd_MetalSd	2,464.244955	0.0000000001
Overall_Cond_Average	2,457.082826	0.0000000001

MS_SubClass_One_and_Half_Story_Finished_All_Ages	2,455.530594	0.0000000001
Exterior_1st_HdBoard	–2,306.263622	0.0000000001
First_Flr_SF	2,299.376017	0.0000000001
Bldg_Type_TwnhsE	–2,213.192500	0.0000000001
Neighborhood_College_Creek	–2,199.940157	0.0000000001
Exterior_1st_Plywood	–2,191.327546	0.0000000001
MS_SubClass_One_Story_PUD_1946_and_Newer	–2,074.721508	0.0000000001
Foundation_PConc	1,999.248963	0.0000000001
Lot_Shape_Slightly_Irregular	1,916.928834	0.0000000001
Year_Sold	–1,862.993352	0.0000000001
Condition_1_Feedr	–1,794.915012	0.0000000001
Bsmt_Unf_SF	–1,753.516178	0.0000000001
Lot_Area	1,734.933806	0.0000000001
Garage_Area	1,688.766899	0.0000000001
Sale_Condition_Partial	1,657.064863	0.0000000001
Full_Bath	1,656.682299	0.0000000001
BsmtFin_Type_1_LwQ	1,643.471383	0.0000000001
MS_SubClass_Two_Story_1946_and_Newer	1,461.318397	0.0000000001
Garage_Type_Detchd	–1,426.540333	0.0000000001
Open_Porch_SF	–1,384.526307	0.0000000001
Heating_QC_Good	–1,323.804072	0.0000000001
MS_Zoning_Residential_Medium_Density	1,314.699908	0.0000000001
Wood_Deck_SF	1,247.183448	0.0000000001
Garage_Cond_Typical	1,134.201304	0.0000000001
Neighborhood_Old_Town	–1,109.787291	0.0000000001
Exterior_2nd_Plywood	–1,107.245237	0.0000000001
Exter_Cond_Good	1,076.919083	0.0000000001
TotRms_AbvGrd	–1,012.330463	0.0000000001
Fence_Minimum_Privacy	1,004.911802	0.0000000001

Lot_Config_Inside	959.655731	0.0000000001
Exter_Cond_Typical	901.642399	0.0000000001
BsmtFin_Type_1_BLQ	884.548877	0.0000000001
Half_Bath	730.874179	0.0000000001
Garage_Type_BuiltIn	–722.855109	0.0000000001
Bsmt_Cond_Typical	608.102437	0.0000000001
Land_Contour_Lvl	–584.611730	0.0000000001
Exterior_2nd_HdBoard	–556.622772	0.0000000001
Alley_No_Alley_Access	525.601329	0.0000000001
Fence_No_Fence	–517.395159	0.0000000001
Central_Air_Y	482.110822	0.0000000001
Bsmt_Half_Bath	–459.944343	0.0000000001
Garage_Finish_No_Garage	409.386396	0.0000000001
Lot_Frontage	277.078259	0.0000000001
Mo_Sold	–233.794997	0.0000000001
Sale_Type_WD.	–215.279260	0.0000000001
Paved_Drive_Paved	–138.048919	0.0000000001
Garage_Cond_No_Garage	1.339945	0.0000000001
BsmtFin_Type_2_Unf	0.000000	0.0000000001
Electrical_SBrkr	0.000000	0.0000000001
Garage_Type_No_Garage	0.000000	0.0000000001

- The result is 99 rows with a regression coefficient for each 98 predictors and the intercept.
- Only three predictors are removed from the lasso model with a coefficient of 0.000 which are BsmtFin_Type_2_Unf, Electrical_SBrkr, and Garage_Type_No_Garage.
- The most important predictor is Gr_Liv_Area (as in the ridge model) with the highest absolute coefficient = 26463.859315. The positive coefficient means that as the Gr_Liv_Area increases, the price increases too.
- The most important predictor with negative impact on price is BsmtFin_SF_1. This means that as BsmtFin_SF_1 increases, the property price decreases and vice versa.
- The least important predictor is Garage_Cond_No_Garage with the lowest absolute coefficient = 1.33.

3.5.5. Model Performance on Testing Data

To get the RMSE on the testing data, we use the same above functions on the lasso_fit model.

```
lasso_fit %>% predict(new_data = test_ames) %>%
mutate(truth = test_ames$Sale_Price) %>%
rmse(truth = truth, estimate = .pred)
## # A tibble: 1 × 3
## .metric .estimator .estimate
## <chr> <chr> <dbl>
## 1 rmse standard 29421.
```

- The RMSE of the lasso model on testing data = 29421 which is lower than that of the ridge model (29747).

3.6. ELASTIC NET REGRESSION

In elastic net regression, we will use the same steps of ridge regression till defining the ML model.

3.6.1. Define Machine Learning (ML) Model

We define a linear elastic net regression model by using the functions:

- The linear_reg function to define the linear regression model type with the following arguments:
  - mixture = tune() to indicate an elastic net regression model. The elastic net is mixture of lasso (with 1 mixture) and ridge regression (with 0 mixture).
  - penalty = tune() to tune the penalty term on the different resamples of training data.
- The set_engine function with the argument "glmnet" to define the engine that will use the glmnet function from the glmnet package.
- The set_mode function with the argument "regression" to define the mode of learning. We use regression because we have a numerical outcome (price).
- All the three functions are applied in sequence using the piping "%>%" operator and the resulting object is called "elastic_model."

```
elastic_model <- linear_reg(mixture = tune(), penalty = tune()) %>%
set_engine("glmnet") %>%
```

```
set_mode("regression")
elastic_model
## Linear Regression Model Specification (regression)
##
## Main Arguments:
## penalty = tune()
## mixture = tune()
##
## Computational engine: glmnet
```

The difference of the elastic net model is that both the mixture and penalty arguments are now fine-tuned.

3.6.2. Generate Workflow

We create the "wflow3" object by using the following functions:

- The workflow function to create a workflow.
- The add_recipe function with the argument "rec" to add the above created recipe with 4 preprocessing steps.
- The add_model function with the argument elastic_model to add the above created elastic model.

```
wflow3 <- workflow() %>%
add_recipe(rec) %>%
add_model(elastic_model)
wflow3
## ══ Workflow ════════════════════════════════════════════
═══════════════════════════════════
## Preprocessor: Recipe
## Model: linear_reg()
##
## ── Preprocessor ────────────────────────────────────────
───────────────────────────────────
## 4 Recipe Steps
##
## • step_rm()
## • step_dummy()
```

```
## • step_nzv()
## • step_normalize()
##
## ── Model ──────────────────────────────────────────
##
## Linear Regression Model Specification (regression)
##
## Main Arguments:
## penalty = tune()
## mixture = tune()
##
## Computational engine: glmnet
```

3.6.3. Fit Model on Different Resamples with Tuning

Again, we can use the grid_regular function to chooses sensible values for the penalty and mixture terms.

We create a grid of penalty and mixture values "my_grid2" by using the grid_regular function with the arguments:

- penalty() to choose sensible values for the penalty term.
- mixture() to choose sensible values for the mixture term.
- levels = 10 to choose 10 different penalty and mixture values. The result is 10 × 10 = 100 or 100 different combinations of penalty and mixture values.

```
my_grid2 <- grid_regular(penalty(), mixture(), levels = 10)
my_grid2 %>% flextable(cwidth = 1.5) %>% theme_box() %>%
set_caption(caption = "The different 100 combinations of penalty and mixture values chosen by using the grid_regular function")
```

The different 100 combinations of penalty and mixture values chosen by using the grid_regular function:

penalty	mixture
0.00000000010000	0.0000000
0.00000000129155	0.0000000
0.00000001668101	0.0000000
0.00000021544347	0.0000000

0.00000278255940	0.0000000
0.00003593813664	0.0000000
0.00046415888336	0.0000000
0.00599484250319	0.0000000
0.07742636826811	0.0000000
1.00000000000000	0.0000000
0.00000000010000	0.1111111
0.00000000129155	0.1111111
0.00000001668101	0.1111111
0.00000021544347	0.1111111
0.00000278255940	0.1111111
0.00003593813664	0.1111111
0.00046415888336	0.1111111
0.00599484250319	0.1111111
0.07742636826811	0.1111111
1.00000000000000	0.1111111
0.00000000010000	0.2222222
0.00000000129155	0.2222222
0.00000001668101	0.2222222
0.00000021544347	0.2222222
0.00000278255940	0.2222222
0.00003593813664	0.2222222
0.00046415888336	0.2222222
0.00599484250319	0.2222222
0.07742636826811	0.2222222
1.00000000000000	0.2222222
0.00000000010000	0.3333333
0.00000000129155	0.3333333
0.00000001668101	0.3333333
0.00000021544347	0.3333333
0.00000278255940	0.3333333
0.00003593813664	0.3333333
0.00046415888336	0.3333333
0.00599484250319	0.3333333
0.07742636826811	0.3333333

1.00000000000000	0.3333333
0.00000000010000	0.4444444
0.00000000129155	0.4444444
0.00000001668101	0.4444444
0.00000021544347	0.4444444
0.00000278255940	0.4444444
0.00003593813664	0.4444444
0.00046415888336	0.4444444
0.00599484250319	0.4444444
0.07742636826811	0.4444444
1.00000000000000	0.4444444
0.00000000010000	0.5555556
0.00000000129155	0.5555556
0.00000001668101	0.5555556
0.00000021544347	0.5555556
0.00000278255940	0.5555556
0.00003593813664	0.5555556
0.00046415888336	0.5555556
0.00599484250319	0.5555556
0.07742636826811	0.5555556
1.00000000000000	0.5555556
0.00000000010000	0.6666667
0.00000000129155	0.6666667
0.00000001668101	0.6666667
0.00000021544347	0.6666667
0.00000278255940	0.6666667
0.00003593813664	0.6666667
0.00046415888336	0.6666667
0.00599484250319	0.6666667
0.07742636826811	0.6666667
1.00000000000000	0.6666667
0.00000000010000	0.7777778
0.00000000129155	0.7777778
0.00000001668101	0.7777778
0.00000021544347	0.7777778

0.00000278255940	0.7777778
0.00003593813664	0.7777778
0.00046415888336	0.7777778
0.00599484250319	0.7777778
0.07742636826811	0.7777778
1.00000000000000	0.7777778
0.00000000010000	0.8888889
0.00000000129155	0.8888889
0.00000001668101	0.8888889
0.00000021544347	0.8888889
0.00000278255940	0.8888889
0.00003593813664	0.8888889
0.00046415888336	0.8888889
0.00599484250319	0.8888889
0.07742636826811	0.8888889
1.00000000000000	0.8888889
0.00000000010000	1.0000000
0.00000000129155	1.0000000
0.00000001668101	1.0000000
0.00000021544347	1.0000000
0.00000278255940	1.0000000
0.00003593813664	1.0000000
0.00046415888336	1.0000000
0.00599484250319	1.0000000
0.07742636826811	1.0000000
1.00000000000000	1.0000000

To try these 100 combinations on the 50 resamples of the training data using the elastic net model, we use the tune_grid function with the arguments:

- wflow3 which is the workflow containing 4 preprocessing steps and the linear elastic net model.
- folds which are the 50 resamples of training data created above.
- metrics = metrics_set(rmse) to get the RMSE of the linear elastic model on each resample using the 100 different penalty and mixture combinations. So, we will try 100 combinations × 50 resamples = 5000 different elastic net models.

- grid = my_grid2 to use the 100 combinations in the my_grid2 data in tuning.

We also use the set.seed function before using these functions for reproducibility.

```
set.seed(123)
elastic_res <- tune_grid(wflow3, folds,
metrics = metric_set(rmse),
grid = my_grid2)
elastic_res
## # Tuning results
## # 10-fold cross-validation repeated 5 times using stratification
## # A tibble: 50 × 5
## splits id id2 .metrics .notes
## <list> <chr> <chr> <list> <list>
## 1 <split [1976/221]> Repeat1 Fold01 <tibble [100 × 6]> <tibble [0 × 3]>
## 2 <split [1976/221]> Repeat1 Fold02 <tibble [100 × 6]> <tibble [0 × 3]>
## 3 <split [1976/221]> Repeat1 Fold03 <tibble [100 × 6]> <tibble [0 × 3]>
## 4 <split [1976/221]> Repeat1 Fold04 <tibble [100 × 6]> <tibble [0 × 3]>
## 5 <split [1977/220]> Repeat1 Fold05 <tibble [100 × 6]> <tibble [0 × 3]>
## 6 <split [1977/220]> Repeat1 Fold06 <tibble [100 × 6]> <tibble [0 × 3]>
## 7 <split [1978/219]> Repeat1 Fold07 <tibble [100 × 6]> <tibble [0 × 3]>
## 8 <split [1978/219]> Repeat1 Fold08 <tibble [100 × 6]> <tibble [0 × 3]>
## 9 <split [1979/218]> Repeat1 Fold09 <tibble [100 × 6]> <tibble [0 × 3]>
## 10 <split [1980/217]> Repeat1 Fold10 <tibble [100 × 6]> <tibble [0 × 3]>
## # i 40 more rows
```

The resulting object "elastic_res" contains 50 rows (for 50 resamples) and 5 columns:

- The splits column is a list of each combination of analysis and assessment data withing each resample. The sum is 2197, which are total rows of training data.
- The id column is an id column for the repeat number from 1 to 5.
- The id2 column is an id column for the fold number from 1 to 10 so we have 50 resamples because 5 × 10 = 50.

- The .metrics column is a list of performance metric (RMSE) of applying the elastic model to the corresponding assessment data (221,220,219,218, or 217 rows) within each resample. Each performance metric is saved in 100 rows and 6 columns [100 × 6] tibble or data frame. The 100 rows are for the RMSE of applying the 100 different penalty and mixture combinations of the elastic model on the assessment data within each resample.
- The .notes column is a list of notes or warnings when applying the elastic model to each analysis data (1976, 1977, 1978, 1979, or 1980 rows) within each resample. Each note is saved in 0 rows and 3 columns [0 × 3] tibble or data frame meaning that there are no rows or no notes when applying this model to each analysis data.

3.6.4. The Model Performance on 50 Resamples of the Training Data

To get the performance metric (RMSE) on the 50 resamples of training data using the 100 different combinations, we will use the unnest function with the ".metrics" argument to expand the .metrics list column of the elastic_res object into rows and columns.

```
elastic_res %>% unnest(.metrics)
## # A tibble: 5,000 × 10
## splits id id2 penalty mixture .metric .estimator .estimate
## <list> <chr> <chr> <dbl> <dbl> <chr> <chr> <dbl>
## 1 <split [1976/221]> Repea… Fold… 1 e-10 0 rmse standard 28216.
## 2 <split [1976/221]> Repea… Fold… 1.29e-9 0 rmse standard 28216.
## 3 <split [1976/221]> Repea… Fold… 1.67e-8 0 rmse standard 28216.
## 4 <split [1976/221]> Repea… Fold… 2.15e-7 0 rmse standard 28216.
## 5 <split [1976/221]> Repea… Fold… 2.78e-6 0 rmse standard 28216.
## 6 <split [1976/221]> Repea… Fold… 3.59e-5 0 rmse standard 28216.
## 7 <split [1976/221]> Repea… Fold… 4.64e-4 0 rmse standard 28216.
## 8 <split [1976/221]> Repea… Fold… 5.99e-3 0 rmse standard 28216.
## 9 <split [1976/221]> Repea… Fold… 7.74e-2 0 rmse standard 28216.
## 10 <split [1976/221]> Repea… Fold… 1 e+ 0 0 rmse standard 28216.
## # i 4,990 more rows
## # i 2 more variables: .config <chr>, .notes <list>
```

- The result is 5000 rows because we have applied the 100 different combinations to 50 resamples of the training data so we have 100 × 50 = 5000 rows. Each row contains the RMSE of the elastic model on 1 resample using 1 penalty and mixture combination.
- To get the mean RMSE of each combination on the 50 resamples of the training data, we use the following functions on the "elastic_res" object:
- The collect_metrics function to get the mean for each combination across the 50 resamples of the training data.
- The arrange function with a mean argument to arrange by mean RMSE value in ascending order.
- The flextable, theme_box, and set_caption functions are described previously.

elastic_res **%>% collect_metrics**() **%>%**

arrange(mean) **%>%**

flextable() **%>% theme_box**() **%>%**

set_caption(caption = "The mean RMSE of applying 100 penalty and mixture combinations on 50 resamples of ames training data when using elastic net regression model")

The mean RMSE of applying 100 penalty and mixture combinations on 50 resamples of ames training data when using elastic net regression model:

penalty	**mixture**	**.metric**	**.estimator**	**mean**	**n**	**std_err**	**.config**
0.00000000010000	0.0000000	rmse	standard	34,206.08	50	986.5667	Preprocessor1_Model001
0.00000000129155	0.0000000	rmse	standard	34,206.08	50	986.5667	Preprocessor1_Model002
0.00000001668101	0.0000000	rmse	standard	34,206.08	50	986.5667	Preprocessor1_Model003
0.00000021544347	0.0000000	rmse	standard	34,206.08	50	986.5667	Preprocessor1_Model004
0.00000278255940	0.0000000	rmse	standard	34,206.08	50	986.5667	Preprocessor1_Model005
0.00003593813664	0.0000000	rmse	standard	34,206.08	50	986.5667	Preprocessor1_Model006

0.00046415888336	0.0000000	rmse	standard	34,206.08	50	986.5667	Prepro-cessor1_Model007
0.00599484250319	0.0000000	rmse	standard	34,206.08	50	986.5667	Prepro-cessor1_Model008
0.07742636826811	0.0000000	rmse	standard	34,206.08	50	986.5667	Prepro-cessor1_Model009
1.00000000000000	0.0000000	rmse	standard	34,206.08	50	986.5667	Prepro-cessor1_Model010
0.00000000010000	0.1111111	rmse	standard	34,491.21	50	1,046.7207	Prepro-cessor1_Model011
0.00000000129155	0.1111111	rmse	standard	34,491.21	50	1,046.7207	Prepro-cessor1_Model012
0.00000001668101	0.1111111	rmse	standard	34,491.21	50	1,046.7207	Prepro-cessor1_Model013
0.00000021544347	0.1111111	rmse	standard	34,491.21	50	1,046.7207	Prepro-cessor1_Model014
0.00000278255940	0.1111111	rmse	standard	34,491.21	50	1,046.7207	Prepro-cessor1_Model015
0.00003593813664	0.1111111	rmse	standard	34,491.21	50	1,046.7207	Prepro-cessor1_Model016
0.00046415888336	0.1111111	rmse	standard	34,491.21	50	1,046.7207	Prepro-cessor1_Model017
0.00599484250319	0.1111111	rmse	standard	34,491.21	50	1,046.7207	Prepro-cessor1_Model018
0.07742636826811	0.1111111	rmse	standard	34,491.21	50	1,046.7207	Prepro-cessor1_Model019
1.00000000000000	0.1111111	rmse	standard	34,491.21	50	1,046.7207	Prepro-cessor1_Model020
0.00000000010000	0.2222222	rmse	standard	34,498.37	50	1,046.6611	Prepro-cessor1_Model021
0.00000000129155	0.2222222	rmse	standard	34,498.37	50	1,046.6611	Prepro-cessor1_Model022

0.00000001668101	0.2222222	rmse	standard	34,498.37	50	1,046.6611	Prepro-cessor1_Model023
0.00000021544347	0.2222222	rmse	standard	34,498.37	50	1,046.6611	Prepro-cessor1_Model024
0.00000278255940	0.2222222	rmse	standard	34,498.37	50	1,046.6611	Prepro-cessor1_Model025
0.00003593813664	0.2222222	rmse	standard	34,498.37	50	1,046.6611	Prepro-cessor1_Model026
0.00046415888336	0.2222222	rmse	standard	34,498.37	50	1,046.6611	Prepro-cessor1_Model027
0.00599484250319	0.2222222	rmse	standard	34,498.37	50	1,046.6611	Prepro-cessor1_Model028
0.07742636826811	0.2222222	rmse	standard	34,498.37	50	1,046.6611	Prepro-cessor1_Model029
1.00000000000000	0.2222222	rmse	standard	34,498.37	50	1,046.6611	Prepro-cessor1_Model030
0.00000000010000	0.5555556	rmse	standard	34,502.32	50	1,046.7936	Prepro-cessor1_Model051
0.00000000129155	0.5555556	rmse	standard	34,502.32	50	1,046.7936	Prepro-cessor1_Model052
0.00000001668101	0.5555556	rmse	standard	34,502.32	50	1,046.7936	Prepro-cessor1_Model053
0.00000021544347	0.5555556	rmse	standard	34,502.32	50	1,046.7936	Prepro-cessor1_Model054
0.00000278255940	0.5555556	rmse	standard	34,502.32	50	1,046.7936	Prepro-cessor1_Model055
0.00003593813664	0.5555556	rmse	standard	34,502.32	50	1,046.7936	Prepro-cessor1_Model056
0.00046415888336	0.5555556	rmse	standard	34,502.32	50	1,046.7936	Prepro-cessor1_Model057
0.00599484250319	0.5555556	rmse	standard	34,502.32	50	1,046.7936	Prepro-cessor1_Model058

0.07742636826811	0.5555556	rmse	standard	34,502.32	50	1,046.7936	Prepro-cessor1_ Model059
1.00000000000000	0.5555556	rmse	standard	34,502.32	50	1,046.7936	Prepro-cessor1_ Model060
0.00000000010000	0.4444444	rmse	standard	34,502.56	50	1,046.6562	Prepro-cessor1_ Model041
0.00000000129155	0.4444444	rmse	standard	34,502.56	50	1,046.6562	Prepro-cessor1_ Model042
0.00000001668101	0.4444444	rmse	standard	34,502.56	50	1,046.6562	Prepro-cessor1_ Model043
0.00000021544347	0.4444444	rmse	standard	34,502.56	50	1,046.6562	Prepro-cessor1_ Model044
0.00000278255940	0.4444444	rmse	standard	34,502.56	50	1,046.6562	Prepro-cessor1_ Model045
0.00003593813664	0.4444444	rmse	standard	34,502.56	50	1,046.6562	Prepro-cessor1_ Model046
0.00046415888336	0.4444444	rmse	standard	34,502.56	50	1,046.6562	Prepro-cessor1_ Model047
0.00599484250319	0.4444444	rmse	standard	34,502.56	50	1,046.6562	Prepro-cessor1_ Model048
0.07742636826811	0.4444444	rmse	standard	34,502.56	50	1,046.6562	Prepro-cessor1_ Model049
1.00000000000000	0.4444444	rmse	standard	34,502.56	50	1,046.6562	Prepro-cessor1_ Model050
0.00000000010000	0.7777778	rmse	standard	34,502.71	50	1,047.1045	Prepro-cessor1_ Model071
0.00000000129155	0.7777778	rmse	standard	34,502.71	50	1,047.1045	Prepro-cessor1_ Model072
0.00000001668101	0.7777778	rmse	standard	34,502.71	50	1,047.1045	Prepro-cessor1_ Model073
0.00000021544347	0.7777778	rmse	standard	34,502.71	50	1,047.1045	Prepro-cessor1_ Model074

0.00000278255940	0.7777778	rmse	standard	34,502.71	50	1,047.1045	Prepro-cessor1_Model075
0.00003593813664	0.7777778	rmse	standard	34,502.71	50	1,047.1045	Prepro-cessor1_Model076
0.00046415888336	0.7777778	rmse	standard	34,502.71	50	1,047.1045	Prepro-cessor1_Model077
0.00599484250319	0.7777778	rmse	standard	34,502.71	50	1,047.1045	Prepro-cessor1_Model078
0.07742636826811	0.7777778	rmse	standard	34,502.71	50	1,047.1045	Prepro-cessor1_Model079
1.00000000000000	0.7777778	rmse	standard	34,502.71	50	1,047.1045	Prepro-cessor1_Model080
0.00000000010000	0.3333333	rmse	standard	34,502.87	50	1,046.4644	Prepro-cessor1_Model031
0.00000000129155	0.3333333	rmse	standard	34,502.87	50	1,046.4644	Prepro-cessor1_Model032
0.00000001668101	0.3333333	rmse	standard	34,502.87	50	1,046.4644	Prepro-cessor1_Model033
0.00000021544347	0.3333333	rmse	standard	34,502.87	50	1,046.4644	Prepro-cessor1_Model034
0.00000278255940	0.3333333	rmse	standard	34,502.87	50	1,046.4644	Prepro-cessor1_Model035
0.00003593813664	0.3333333	rmse	standard	34,502.87	50	1,046.4644	Prepro-cessor1_Model036
0.00046415888336	0.3333333	rmse	standard	34,502.87	50	1,046.4644	Prepro-cessor1_Model037
0.00599484250319	0.3333333	rmse	standard	34,502.87	50	1,046.4644	Prepro-cessor1_Model038
0.07742636826811	0.3333333	rmse	standard	34,502.87	50	1,046.4644	Prepro-cessor1_Model039
1.00000000000000	0.3333333	rmse	standard	34,502.87	50	1,046.4644	Prepro-cessor1_Model040

0.00000000010000	0.8888889	rmse	standard	34,502.92	50	1,046.8866	Preprocessor1_Model081
0.00000000129155	0.8888889	rmse	standard	34,502.92	50	1,046.8866	Preprocessor1_Model082
0.00000001668101	0.8888889	rmse	standard	34,502.92	50	1,046.8866	Preprocessor1_Model083
0.00000021544347	0.8888889	rmse	standard	34,502.92	50	1,046.8866	Preprocessor1_Model084
0.00000278255940	0.8888889	rmse	standard	34,502.92	50	1,046.8866	Preprocessor1_Model085
0.00003593813664	0.8888889	rmse	standard	34,502.92	50	1,046.8866	Preprocessor1_Model086
0.00046415888336	0.8888889	rmse	standard	34,502.92	50	1,046.8866	Preprocessor1_Model087
0.00599484250319	0.8888889	rmse	standard	34,502.92	50	1,046.8866	Preprocessor1_Model088
0.07742636826811	0.8888889	rmse	standard	34,502.92	50	1,046.8866	Preprocessor1_Model089
1.00000000000000	0.8888889	rmse	standard	34,502.92	50	1,046.8866	Preprocessor1_Model090
0.00000000010000	1.0000000	rmse	standard	34,502.98	50	1,046.9252	Preprocessor1_Model091
0.00000000129155	1.0000000	rmse	standard	34,502.98	50	1,046.9252	Preprocessor1_Model092
0.00000001668101	1.0000000	rmse	standard	34,502.98	50	1,046.9252	Preprocessor1_Model093
0.00000021544347	1.0000000	rmse	standard	34,502.98	50	1,046.9252	Preprocessor1_Model094
0.00000278255940	1.0000000	rmse	standard	34,502.98	50	1,046.9252	Preprocessor1_Model095
0.00003593813664	1.0000000	rmse	standard	34,502.98	50	1,046.9252	Preprocessor1_Model096

0.00046415888336	1.0000000	rmse	standard	34,502.98	50	1,046.9252	Prepro-cessor1_Model097
0.00599484250319	1.0000000	rmse	standard	34,502.98	50	1,046.9252	Prepro-cessor1_Model098
0.07742636826811	1.0000000	rmse	standard	34,502.98	50	1,046.9252	Prepro-cessor1_Model099
1.00000000000000	1.0000000	rmse	standard	34,502.98	50	1,046.9252	Prepro-cessor1_Model100
0.00000000010000	0.6666667	rmse	standard	34,503.38	50	1,046.9017	Prepro-cessor1_Model061
0.00000000129155	0.6666667	rmse	standard	34,503.38	50	1,046.9017	Prepro-cessor1_Model062
0.00000001668101	0.6666667	rmse	standard	34,503.38	50	1,046.9017	Prepro-cessor1_Model063
0.00000021544347	0.6666667	rmse	standard	34,503.38	50	1,046.9017	Prepro-cessor1_Model064
0.00000278255940	0.6666667	rmse	standard	34,503.38	50	1,046.9017	Prepro-cessor1_Model065
0.00003593813664	0.6666667	rmse	standard	34,503.38	50	1,046.9017	Prepro-cessor1_Model066
0.00046415888336	0.6666667	rmse	standard	34,503.38	50	1,046.9017	Prepro-cessor1_Model067
0.00599484250319	0.6666667	rmse	standard	34,503.38	50	1,046.9017	Prepro-cessor1_Model068
0.07742636826811	0.6666667	rmse	standard	34,503.38	50	1,046.9017	Prepro-cessor1_Model069
1.00000000000000	0.6666667	rmse	standard	34,503.38	50	1,046.9017	Prepro-cessor1_Model070

- The result is 100 rows with 1 mean RMSE value for each penalty and mixture combination across the 50 resamples (n = 50).
- The lowest mean RMSE value (34206.08) was attained when using the 0 mixture value with 10 penalty values or a ridge regression.

We can plot the 100 mean RMSE values from the 100 combinations by using the following functions after the arrange function:

- The mutate function with the arguments:

  ++ penalty = scientific(penalty) to convert the penalty values to scientific notations (e.g., 1e05 or 100000, 1.5e-02 or 0.015).

  ++ mixture = scientific(mixture) to convert the mixture values to scientific notations. The scientific function is from the scales package.
- The mutate function with the argument comb = paste(penalty, mixture, sep = " ") to create a new"comb" column that holds the pasted penalty and mixture values with a " " separator.
- The mutate function with the argument "comb = fct_inorder(comb)" to convert the comb column to a factor column with levels according to their appearance in the data. Since the data are arranged by the mean value so the levels of comb column will be plotted according to their mean RMSE value.
- The ggplot function with the argument "aes(x = mean, y = comb)" to plot the mean RMSE value on the x-axis, and the "comb" combination on the y-axis.
- The geom_point function to plot a scatter plot.
- The labs function with the argument title to add a plot title, *x* to add an *x*-axis title, y to add a y-axis title.
- The theme_classic function as described in previous chapters. We use a lower base size to avoid crowding of text on the y-axis.

```
library(scales)
elastic_res %>% collect_metrics() %>%
arrange(mean) %>%
mutate(penalty = scientific(penalty), mixture = scientific(mixture)) %>%
mutate(comb = paste(penalty, mixture, sep = " ")) %>%
mutate(comb = fct_inorder(comb)) %>%
ggplot(aes(x = mean, y = comb))+ geom_point()+
labs(title = "The mean RMSE of 100 different combinations across 50 resamples of training data \nwhen using the elastic net regression model",
x = "mean RMSE", y = "Penalty_mixture combination")+
theme_classic(base_size = 7)
```

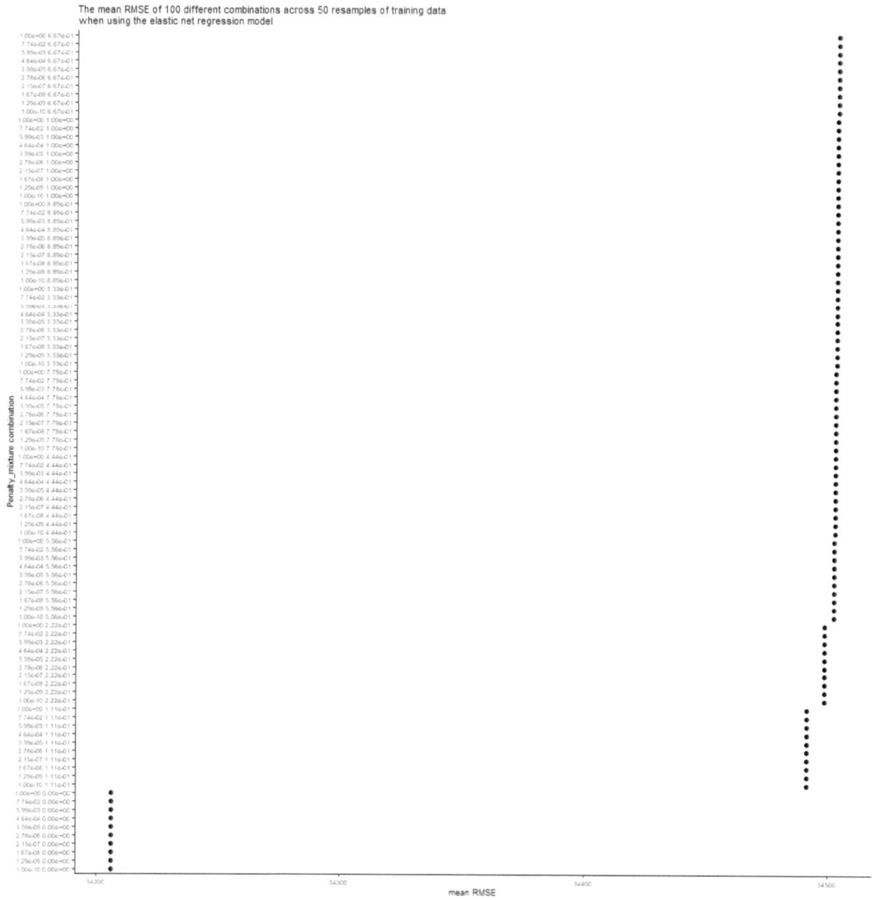

- All penalties with 0 mixture have the lowest RMSE value.

As before, we can use the select_best function to create an object "best_pen3" that contains the best penalty and mixture value for the best elastic net model from the elastic_res object.

```
best_pen3<-elastic_res %>% select_best()
best_pen3
## # A tibble: 1 × 3
## penalty mixture .config
## <dbl> <dbl> <chr>
## 1 0.0000000001 0 Preprocessor1_Model001
```

- Because all penalties with the 0 mixture have the same mean RMSE, so the function selects the 1st tried penalty = 0.0000000001 and mixture = 0.

To get the final workflow with the best penalty, we use the finalize_workflow function with the arguments:

- wflow3 which is the original workflow with tuned penalty and mixture.
- best_pen3 which is the data of 1 row containing the best penalty and mixture values for the elastic net model.

The resulting workflow "elastic_final" is the final workflow containing the best penalty and mixture values.

```
elastic_final <- finalize_workflow(wflow3, best_pen3)
elastic_final
## ══ Workflow ════════════════════════════════════════════
## Preprocessor: Recipe
## Model: linear_reg()
##
## ── Preprocessor ────────────────────────────────────────
## 4 Recipe Steps
##
## • step_rm()
## • step_dummy()
## • step_nzv()
## • step_normalize()
##
## ── Model ───────────────────────────────────────────────
## Linear Regression Model Specification (regression)
##
## Main Arguments:
## penalty = 1e-10
## mixture = 0
##
## Computational engine: glmnet
```

Finally, we create an elastic_fit model by using the fit function with the arguments:

- elastic_final which is the final workflow containing 4 preprocessing steps and the linear elastic net model with best penalty and mixture values.
- train_ames which is the whole training data with 2197 rows.

Then, we use the following functions on the elastic_fit model:

- The extract_fit_parsnip function to get the model specifications.
- The tidy function to see the model results in a data frame.
- The arrange function to arrange the estimate or regression coefficients with the desc and abs functions so that the predictors are arranged according to their absolute regression coefficients in descending order.

```
elastic_fit <- fit(elastic_final, data = train_ames)
elastic_fit %>% extract_fit_parsnip() %>%
broom::tidy() %>% arrange(desc(abs(estimate))) %>%
flextable(cwidth = 1.5) %>% theme_box() %>%
set_caption(caption = "Elastic net model results of applying best penalty and mixture values on the ames training data")
```

Elastic net model results of applying best penalty and mixture values on the ames training data:

term	estimate	penalty
(Intercept)	180,466.578516	0.0000000001
Gr_Liv_Area	15,135.962090	0.0000000001
Second_Flr_SF	10,929.722112	0.0000000001
Neighborhood_Northridge_Heights	8,381.533808	0.0000000001
Total_Bsmt_SF	7,790.700938	0.0000000001
First_Flr_SF	7,456.221657	0.0000000001
Mas_Vnr_Area	7,438.120917	0.0000000001
Garage_Cars	6,959.879510	0.0000000001
Year_Remod_Add	6,306.032219	0.0000000001
Fireplaces	6,196.871527	0.0000000001
Bsmt_Exposure_Gd	5,114.181282	0.0000000001
House_Style_One_Story	4,411.662236	0.0000000001
BsmtFin_Type_1_GLQ	4,279.260379	0.0000000001

Functional_Typ	4,244.615539	0.0000000001
Neighborhood_Gilbert	–4,242.767183	0.0000000001
Neighborhood_Somerset	4,138.185553	0.0000000001
Year_Built	4,034.624810	0.0000000001
Bsmt_Exposure_No	–3,996.794619	0.0000000001
Garage_Area	3,909.426093	0.0000000001
Neighborhood_Edwards	–3,818.302390	0.0000000001
Roof_Style_Hip	3,810.169760	0.0000000001
Overall_Cond_Good	3,628.517191	0.0000000001
Sale_Type_New	3,438.431412	0.0000000001
Garage_Finish_RFn	–3,433.115624	0.0000000001
MS_Zoning_Residential_Low_Density	3,418.953590	0.0000000001
Lot_Config_CulDSac	3,331.742709	0.0000000001
Bsmt_Full_Bath	3,301.169052	0.0000000001
Mas_Vnr_Type_None	3,234.767255	0.0000000001
Heating_QC_Typical	–3,198.453753	0.0000000001
Sale_Condition_Normal	3,065.880581	0.0000000001
Bedroom_AbvGr	–3,037.204343	0.0000000001
Garage_Finish_Unf	–3,031.387385	0.0000000001
Full_Bath	2,943.440975	0.0000000001
Foundation_PConc	2,808.121342	0.0000000001
Foundation_CBlock	–2,736.063435	0.0000000001
Sale_Condition_Partial	2,735.940167	0.0000000001
Condition_1_Norm	2,362.186784	0.0000000001
MS_SubClass_One_and_Half_Story_Finished_All_Ages	2,172.670615	0.0000000001
Overall_Cond_Above_Average	2,139.244560	0.0000000001
Lot_Shape_Slightly_Irregular	2,130.257178	0.0000000001
Exterior_1st_Wd.Sdng	–2,127.626630	0.0000000001
Overall_Cond_Very_Good	2,062.074733	0.0000000001
Condition_1_Feedr	–2,003.349053	0.0000000001
Neighborhood_College_Creek	–1,997.205791	0.0000000001
MS_SubClass_Two_Story_1946_and_Newer	1,981.094522	0.0000000001
Exterior_1st_VinylSd	–1,973.890844	0.0000000001
Bldg_Type_TwnhsE	–1,909.633458	0.0000000001
Wood_Deck_SF	1,854.237991	0.0000000001

Lot_Area	1,818.103977	0.0000000001
Year_Sold	–1,780.520664	0.0000000001
Exterior_1st_Plywood	–1,763.899726	0.0000000001
Half_Bath	1,671.985053	0.0000000001
Exterior_2nd_Plywood	–1,582.386613	0.0000000001
Bsmt_Exposure_Mn	–1,559.445461	0.0000000001
Garage_Type_Detchd	–1,455.861456	0.0000000001
Exterior_2nd_Wd.Sdng	1,451.424118	0.0000000001
Exterior_2nd_HdBoard	–1,395.057248	0.0000000001
Exterior_1st_MetalSd	–1,388.943174	0.0000000001
House_Style_Two_Story	–1,329.636763	0.0000000001
Exterior_1st_HdBoard	–1,257.715622	0.0000000001
Heating_QC_Good	–1,255.763327	0.0000000001
MS_SubClass_One_Story_PUD_1946_and_Newer	–1,245.511027	0.0000000001
Garage_Cond_Typical	1,225.149715	0.0000000001
BsmtFin_SF_1	–1,161.511030	0.0000000001
Exter_Cond_Good	1,151.799872	0.0000000001
Overall_Cond_Average	1,026.552368	0.0000000001
Central_Air_Y	1,005.358617	0.0000000001
Exter_Cond_Typical	1,000.737182	0.0000000001
Bsmt_Unf_SF	–978.699857	0.0000000001
Bsmt_Cond_Typical	953.766254	0.0000000001
TotRms_AbvGrd	949.710989	0.0000000001
Open_Porch_SF	–909.217437	0.0000000001
Neighborhood_Old_Town	–892.653245	0.0000000001
Fence_Minimum_Privacy	859.124299	0.0000000001
Land_Contour_Lvl	–832.143111	0.0000000001
Lot_Config_Inside	804.701241	0.0000000001
Lot_Frontage	798.373463	0.0000000001
Bsmt_Half_Bath	–688.235204	0.0000000001
Mas_Vnr_Type_Stone	660.680070	0.0000000001
Fence_No_Fence	–523.328160	0.0000000001
Alley_No_Alley_Access	481.481239	0.0000000001
BsmtFin_Type_1_Rec	391.043800	0.0000000001
BsmtFin_Type_1_Unf	324.319482	0.0000000001
MS_Zoning_Residential_Medium_Density	–322.128573	0.0000000001

Sale_Type_WD.	–295.578059	0.0000000001
Paved_Drive_Paved	277.563404	0.0000000001
Mo_Sold	–272.668322	0.0000000001
BsmtFin_Type_2_Unf	270.882613	0.0000000001
Exterior_2nd_MetalSd	268.716635	0.0000000001
Garage_Type_BuiltIn	200.546286	0.0000000001
BsmtFin_Type_1_LwQ	–190.061234	0.0000000001
Garage_Finish_No_Garage	139.117168	0.0000000001
Exterior_2nd_VinylSd	–134.425834	0.0000000001
Garage_Cond_No_Garage	116.823002	0.0000000001
Mas_Vnr_Type_BrkFace	71.603223	0.0000000001
Garage_Type_No_Garage	50.948983	0.0000000001
Roof_Style_Gable	–31.340203	0.0000000001
BsmtFin_Type_1_BLQ	–14.308888	0.0000000001
Electrical_SBrkr	–8.846982	0.0000000001

- We get the same regression coefficients as that of the ridge model discussed in Section 3.4.8.

3.6.5. Model Performance on Testing Data

To get the RMSE on the testing data, we use the same above functions on the elastic_fit model.

elastic_fit **%>% predict**(new_data = test_ames) **%>%**

mutate(truth = test_ames$Sale_Price) **%>%**

rmse(truth = truth, estimate = .pred)

A tibble: 1 × 3

.metric .estimator .estimate

<chr> <chr> <dbl>

1 rmse standard 29747.

- The RMSE of the elastic net model on testing data = 29747 which is the same as that of using the ridge model.

3.7. CONCLUSION

We have tried 3 penalized regression models on the ames data (ridge, lasso, and elastic net) and the best model was the lasso model because it has the lowest RMSE on testing data.

CHAPTER 4

PENALIZED CLASSIFICATION MODELING

Contents

4.1. Data Used in This Chapter 221
4.2. Data Exploration 226
4.3. Ridge Classification 230
4.4. Lasso Classification 278
4.5. Elastic Net Classification 297
4.6. Conclusion 316

4.1. DATA USED IN THIS CHAPTER

4.1.1. Leaf Identification Data of Flavia Species

This data contains 1907 leaf images' characteristics of 32 different Flavia species.

The data is part of the modeldata package under the name "leaf_id_flavia." The modeldata package is part of tidymodels package which is a collection of different packages for data modeling.

First, we load the tidymodels package using the library function then we load the leaf_id_flavia data using the data function.

We also load the tidyverse and flextable packages for the reasons described above.

```
library(tidymodels)
data("leaf_id_flavia")
library(tidyverse)
library(flextable)
```

Then, to see the data structure, we use the glimpse function.

```
glimpse(leaf_id_flavia)
## Rows: 1,907
## Columns: 59
## $ species <fct> chinese_redbud, chinese_redbud, chinese_red…
## $ apex <fct> none, none, none, none, none, none, none, n…
## $ base <fct> none, none, none, none, none, none, none, n…
## $ shape <fct> heart_shape, heart_shape, heart_shape, hear…
## $ denate_edge <fct> no, no, no, no, no, no, no, no, no, no, no,…
## $ lobed_edge <fct> no, no, no, no, no, no, no, no, no, no, no,…
## $ smooth_edge <fct> yes, yes, yes, yes, yes, yes, yes, yes, yes…
## $ toothed_edge <fct> no, no, no, no, no, no, no, no, no, no, no,…
## $ undulate_edge <fct> no, no, no, no, no, no, no, no, no, no, no,…
## $ outlying_polar <dbl> 0, 0, 0, 0, 0, 0, 0, 0, 0, 0, 0, 0, 0, 0…
## $ skewed_polar <dbl> 0.4610066, 0.4747877, 0.5356883, 0.4771338,…
## $ clumpy_polar <dbl> 0.006479784, 0.011100482, 0.017317486, 0.01…
## $ sparse_polar <dbl> 0.01449941, 0.01451566, 0.02953578, 0.01425…
## $ striated_polar <dbl> 0.9788360, 0.9797980, 0.6758621, 0.9896373,…
## $ convex_polar <dbl> 0.000899987, 0.000152532, 0.035230741, 0.00…
## $ skinny_polar <dbl> 0.1177954, 0.5440493, 0.7764908, 0.7067394,…
## $ stringy_polar <dbl> 1.0000000, 1.0000000, 0.8544140, 1.0000000,…
## $ monotonic_polar <dbl> 0.026807610, 0.005554220, 0.068481538, 0.09…
## $ outlying_contour <dbl> 0, 0, 0, 0, 0, 0, 0, 0, 0, 0, 0, 0, 0, 0…
## $ skewed_contour <dbl> 0.4954035, 0.5321818, 0.5451171, 0.4675013,…
## $ clumpy_contour <dbl> 0.007898114, 0.010846498, 0.020271493, 0.01…
## $ sparse_contour <dbl> 0.01449941, 0.01436114, 0.02903878, 0.01451…
```

$ striated_contour <dbl> 0.9744898, 0.9811321, 0.6766917, 0.9784946,...

$ convex_contour <dbl> 0.000479470, 0.000000000, 0.035908221, 0.00...

$ skinny_contour <dbl> 0.1810093, 1.0000000, 0.7806988, 0.1348225,...

$ stringy_contour <dbl> 1.0000000, 1.0000000, 0.8864787, 1.0000000,...

$ monotonic_contour <dbl> 0.000816260, 0.000008740, 0.001253195, 0.32...

$ num_max_ponits <dbl> 1, 3, 4, 1, 1, 1, 1, 1, 1, 1, 1, 1, 1, 6, 1...

$ num_min_points <dbl> 2, 4, 7, 1, 1, 1, 1, 1, 1, 1, 1, 2, 2, 8, 2...

$ diameter <dbl> 1255.830, 1227.826, 1113.228, 1219.185, 118...

$ area <dbl> 936626.5, 917300.5, 855376.5, 901303.0, 885...

$ perimeter <dbl> 3830.534, 3781.445, 3695.646, 3678.409, 383...

$ physiological_length <dbl> 1253, 1218, 1098, 1205, 1153, 1179, 1188, 1...

$ physiological_width <dbl> 1088, 1091, 1083, 1053, 1078, 1073, 1054, 1...

$ aspect_ratio <dbl> 0.8683160, 0.8957307, 0.9863388, 0.8738589,...

$ rectangularity <dbl> 0.6870470, 0.6903027, 0.7193273, 0.7103222,...

$ circularity <dbl> 0.8021540, 0.8061315, 0.7870211, 0.8370680,...

$ compactness <dbl> 15.66578, 15.58849, 15.96701, 15.01237, 16...

$ narrow_factor <dbl> 1.154255, 1.125413, 1.027912, 1.157821, 1.1...

$ perimeter_ratio_diameter <dbl> 3.050202, 3.079790, 3.319756, 3.017104, 3.2...

$ perimeter_ratio_length <dbl> 3.520711, 3.466036, 3.412416, 3.493266, 3.5...

$ perimeter_ratio_lw <dbl> 1.636281, 1.637698, 1.694473, 1.629056, 1.7...

$ num_convex_points <dbl> 125, 128, 114, 138, 125, 125, 121, 112, 115...

$ perimeter_convexity <dbl> 0.9404967, 0.9393550, 0.9232549, 0.9502414,...

$ area_convexity <dbl> 0.02359372, 0.03175513, 0.03932713, 0.01740...

$ area_ratio_convexity <dbl> 0.9769501, 0.9692222, 0.9621610, 0.9828892,...

$ equivalent_diameter <dbl> 1092.0393, 1080.7142, 1043.5992, 1071.2491,...

$ eccentriciry <dbl> 0.44400376, 0.26866788, 0.31952502, 0.44811...

$ contrast <dbl> 38.69163, 32.73154, 23.20849, 30.14546, 23...

$ correlation_texture <dbl> 0.9959609, 0.9967740, 0.9975354, 0.9968981,...

$ inverse_difference_moments <dbl> 0.5951133, 0.6022763, 0.6363508, 0.6135506,...

$ entropy <dbl> 6.291552, 6.273267, 5.764995, 6.203471, 5.9...

$ mean_red_val <dbl> 38.02429, 34.55425, 30.92509, 33.44151, 33...

$ mean_green_val <dbl> 72.38449, 69.89448, 69.22250, 71.32743, 70...

$ mean_blue_val <dbl> 42.78902, 42.93044, 40.80089, 40.73282, 42...

$ std_red_val <dbl> 41.66486, 40.48649, 38.55110, 39.09408, 40...

$ std_green_val <dbl> 74.26665, 73.05275, 76.77596, 75.85529, 75...

$ std_blue_val <dbl> 46.36232, 48.04195, 48.09177, 46.57170, 48...

$ correlation <dbl> –0.027629688, –0.003103965, –0.036341630, 0...

The data contains 1907 rows (leaf images) and 59 columns:

1. **species:** a factor column with 32 levels or species. This is our outcome categorical column.
2. **apex:** a factor or categorical column with 9 levels or categories.
3. **base:** a factor column with 6 levels.
4. **shape:** a factor column with 5 levels.
5. **denate_edge:** a factor column with 2 levels: 'no' and 'yes.'
6. **lobed_edge:** a factor column with 2 levels: 'no' and 'yes.'
7. **smooth_edge:** a factor column with 2 levels: 'no' and 'yes.'
8. **toothed_edge:** a factor column with 2 levels: 'no' and 'yes.'
9. **undulate_edge:** a factor column with 2 levels: 'no' and 'yes.'
10. **outlying_polar:** a numeric or double column.
11. **skewed_polar:** a numeric column.
12. **clumpy_polar:** a numeric column.
13. **sparse_polar:** a numeric column.
14. **striated_polar:** a numeric column.
15. **convex_polar:** a numeric column.
16. **skinny_polar:** a numeric column.
17. **stringy_polar:** a numeric column.
18. **monotonic_polar:** a numeric column.
19. **outlying_contour:** a numeric column.
20. **skewed_contour:** a numeric column.
21. **clumpy_contour:** a numeric column.

22. **sparse_contour:** a numeric column.
23. **striated_contour:** a numeric column.
24. **convex_contour:** a numeric column.
25. **skinny_contour:** a numeric column.
26. **stringy_contour:** a numeric column.
27. **monotonic_contour:** a numeric column.
28. **num_max_ponits:** a numeric column.
29. **num_min_points:** a numeric column.
30. **diameter:** a numeric column.
31. **area:** a numeric column.
32. **perimeter:** a numeric column.
33. **physiological_length:** a numeric column.
34. **physiological_width:** a numeric column.
35. **aspect_ratio:** a numeric column.
36. **rectangularity:** a numeric column.
37. **circularity:** a numeric column.
38. **compactness:** a numeric column.
39. **narrow_factor:** a numeric column.
40. **perimeter_ratio_diameter:** a numeric column.
41. **perimeter_ratio_length:** a numeric column.
42. **perimeter_ratio_lw:** a numeric column.
43. **num_convex_points:** a numeric column.
44. **perimeter_convexity:** a numeric column.
45. **area_convexity:** a numeric column.
46. **area_ratio_convexity:** a numeric column.
47. **equivalent_diameter:** a numeric column.
48. **eccentriciry:** a numeric column.
49. **contrast:** a numeric column.
50. **correlation_texture:** a numeric column.
51. **inverse_difference_moments:** a numeric column.
52. **entropy:** a numeric column.
53. **mean_red_val:** a numeric column.
54. **mean_green_val:** a numeric column.
55. **mean_blue_val:** a numeric column.

56. **std_red_val:** a numeric column.
57. **std_green_val:** a numeric column.
58. **std_blue_val:** a numeric column.
59. **correlation:** a numeric column.

The reference Lakshika et al. (2021) has detailed information on all columns of this data.

4.2. DATA EXPLORATION

4.2.1. Categorical Columns

To examine all factor categorical columns at once, we use the following functions on the leaf_id_flavia data:

- The skim function that produces information about all data columns.
- The yank function with "factor" argument to get only the information related to factor or categorical columns.

Then, we convert the result to a table as explained in previous chapters using functions from the flextable package. To use functions from the skimr package, we should first load the skimr package first using the library function.

library(skimr)

leaf_id_flavia **%>% skim**() **%>% yank**("factor") **%>%**

flextable(cwidth = 1) **%>% theme_box**() **%>%**

set_caption(caption = "The information gained from skim function on the categorical columns of the Flavia leaf data")

The information gained from skim function on the categorical columns of the Flavia leaf data:

skim_variable	**n_missing**	**complete_rate**	**ordered**	**n_unique**	**top_counts**
species	0	1	FALSE	32	deo: 77, tru: 73, chi: 72, ole: 66
apex	0	1	FALSE	9	non: 510, acu: 356, api: 344, acu: 283
base	0	1	FALSE	6	non: 1333, acu: 235, acu: 180, cor: 56

shape	0	1	FALSE	5	sim: 852, dia: 725, hea: 136, rou: 117
denate_edge	0	1	FALSE	2	no: 1842, yes: 65
lobed_edge	0	1	FALSE	2	no: 1637, yes: 270
smooth_ edge	0	1	FALSE	2	yes: 1256, no: 651
toothed_ edge	0	1	FALSE	2	no: 1492, yes: 415
undulate_ edge	0	1	FALSE	2	no: 1845, yes: 62

We have 6 columns:

1. The skim_variable is the factor or categorical column name. We have 9 different factor columns including the species outcome column.
2. The n_missing is the number of missing values. All factor columns have zero or no missing values.
3. The complete_rate is the proportion of present values in each column. All factor columns have a complete rate of 1 or 100%.
4. The ordered column denotes if the factor column is an ordered factor. All factor columns are unordered and so have a FALSE value.
5. The n_unique is the number of unique values in each factor column.
6. The top_counts is the number of rows for the most frequent categories in the factor columns. Some categories have exceptionally low frequency and so should be removed in the preprocessing steps because of low variability after dummification.

4.2.2. Numerical Columns

We use the same above functions but use the yank function with the "numeric" argument to get useful information about numeric columns in the leaf_id_flavia data.

leaf_id_flavia **%>% skim**() **%>% yank**("numeric") **%>%**

flextable() **%>% theme_box**() **%>%**

set_caption(caption = "The information gained from skim function on numerical columns from the Flavia leaf data")

The information gained from skim function on numerical columns from the Flavia leaf data:

skim_variable	n_missing	complete_rate	mean	sd	p0	p25	p50	p75	p100	hist
outlying_polar	0	1	0.002609061	0.022722289	0.000000000000	0.0000000000	0.000000000	0.000000000	0.37558582	
skewed_polar	0	1	0.501225233	0.036797563	0.386699004000	0.4776570545	0.496498747	0.515735241	0.77525128	
clumpy_polar	0	1	0.011524124	0.011044254	0.000496269000	0.0054169195	0.008834356	0.014001386	0.18035841	
sparse_polar	0	1	0.015348359	0.003304238	0.013847258000	0.0144905230	0.014524374	0.014755712	0.03019082	
striated_polar	0	1	0.936603274	0.067909152	0.565789474000	0.9306930690	0.957894737	0.973262032	0.99052133	
convex_polar	0	1	0.003525218	0.007394379	0.000000000000	0.0005134210	0.001466576	0.003164854	0.04903111	
skinny_polar	0	1	0.584902588	0.336569696	–11.657181510000	0.4708767305	0.602555299	0.721174581	1.00000000	
stringy_polar	0	1	0.983683739	0.028258767	0.766699614000	0.9841272830	0.987069127	1.000000000	1.00000000	
monotonic_polar	0	1	0.140834312	0.156184438	0.000001130000	0.0248810750	0.085875237	0.198606271	0.80573215	
outlying_contour	0	1	0.000000000	0.000000000	0.000000000000	0.0000000000	0.000000000	0.000000000	0.00000000	
skewed_contour	0	1	0.502233459	0.033808950	0.418815481000	0.4794857575	0.497453838	0.518585256	0.66184375	
clumpy_contour	0	1	0.014687431	0.011400698	0.003429275000	0.0108406525	0.013083760	0.015674559	0.36065578	
sparse_contour	0	1	0.014986177	0.002691397	0.013967128000	0.0144343980	0.014491622	0.014516170	0.02962879	
striated_contour	0	1	0.952429355	0.059978368	0.582089552000	0.9545454550	0.968468468	0.979166667	0.99118943	
convex_contour	0	1	0.019905867	0.090640153	0.000000000000	0.0001862265	0.000870190	0.002335544	0.67657828	
skinny_contour	0	1	0.572760860	0.217495861	–0.358802122000	0.4154412210	0.585470664	0.733974122	1.00000000	
stringy_contour	0	1	0.992271738	0.025557469	0.793832241000	1.0000000000	1.000000000	1.000000000	1.00000000	
monotonic_contour	0	1	0.265459547	0.308514812	0.000000000215	0.0016319185	0.151176961	0.460791283	0.99436518	
num_max_ponits	0	1	2.014682748	1.848908371	0.000000000000	1.0000000000	1.000000000	2.000000000	14.00000000	
num_min_points	0	1	2.3340 32512	2.103589758	0.000000000000	1.0000000000	1.000000000	3.000000000	16.00000000	
diameter	0	1	1,471.5 18927292	246.609892467	701.28524 8700000	1,282.158 7855000	1,513.277899000	1,680.496041500	1,893.56304400	
area	0	1	612,828. 343471421	252,675.58 8291081	47,207.5000 00000000	425,484.25 00000000	636,895.500 000000	820,479.500000000	1,211,202.5 0000000	
perimeter	0	1	3,775.5 28135387	581.043821816	1,865.716 943000000	3,512.295 9170000	3,811.403567000	4,082.954259000	6,104.72859700	
physiological_length	0	1	1,448.351949264	255.127910737	700.392334000000	1,247.000 0000000	1,480.000000000	1,670.310058500	1,893.54370100	

physiological_width	0	1	666.515457436	291.483965962	41.233367920000	452.0670471000	676.000000000	922.413726800	1,198.77734400	
aspect_ratio	0	1	0.490998032	0.263692594	0.022893104000	0.3114716620	0.440519559	0.668043040	1.22022472	
rectangularity	0	1	0.665366264	0.087040031	0.338200421000	0.6392648790	0.678197439	0.710876088	0.88514455	
circularity	0	1	0.538428842	0.189049863	0.050383113000	0.4252426465	0.578615620	0.671891866	0.87380232	
compactness	0	1	32.947061564	37.885107265	14.381251150000	18.7029658700	21.717936560	29.551059295	249.41631860	
narrow_factor	0	1	3.794763227	5.820788644	1.000246716000	1.5818667935	2.288552632	3.227078531	43.68189999	
perimeter_ratio_diameter	0	1	2.617784394	0.537390081	2.092964463000	2.2780318310	2.419876449	2.736675149	5.12767797	
perimeter_ratio_length	0	1	8.876488336	12.175858226	3.201990879000	4.4911049710	5.574307946	7.347528883	92.53440654	
perimeter_ratio_lw	0	1	1.790048147	0.168610367	1.598303545000	1.6886535855	1.737296800	1.833015200	2.78050641	
num_convex_points	0	1	86.850026219	30.733197642	17.000000000000	64.0000000000	86.000000000	107.500000000	184.00000000	
perimeter_convexity	0	1	0.918951050	0.064089624	0.591923499000	0.9250844465	0.942712595	0.947149358	0.96976636	
area_convexity	0	1	0.093716338	0.183491601	0.001836473000	0.0123445425	0.025100089	0.067288302	1.17991275	
area_ratio_convexity	0	1	0.931831003	0.106223536	0.458733957000	0.9369539590	0.975514499	0.987805988	0.99816689	
equivalent_diameter	0	1	858.687459495	207.257456309	245.166180000000	736.032 1745000	900.511263900	1,022.089485500	1,241.83369200	
eccentriciry	0	1	0.810339481	0.208156915	0.072246449000	0.7764668360	0.892169572	0.946639003	0.99986519	
contrast	0	1	26.891657568	25.593338427	2.122061581000	10.6093135200	19.782002590	32.369154335	205.07577570	
correlation_texture	0	1	0.996962564	0.001889760	0.986782515000	0.9960116110	0.997323356	0.998320500	0.99968121	
inverse_difference_moments	0	1	0.743901720	0.101006012	0.513156090000	0.6605112510	0.737906904	0.818146076	0.97195715	
entropy	0	1	4.442424601	1.616770508	0.612923107000	3.2671051050	4.685763714	5.700188586	8.10881550	
mean_red_val	0	1	28.096283085	37.356487176	0.995642188000	11.0602549500	17.724205730	26.643597920	193.44200830	
mean_green_val	0	1	60.937937582	45.541138058	4.896819792000	34.5895901050	51.838146350	71.626111980	228.54077920	
mean_blue_val	0	1	36.935456091	39.030569338	3.069502604000	17.9154856800	27.039338540	39.800269790	194.51516300	
std_red_val	0	1	38.051639083	20.371097432	13.320071060000	28.3718018700	33.499864170	38.797948155	126.04660290	
std_green_val	0	1	69.538660953	17.466064987	14.452639520000	58.3518475550	70.847588480	81.678510140	118.96222180	
std_blue_val	0	1	46.035566930	16.380684506	14.763071120000	38.0139575000	44.273370230	50.330392115	120.81649650	
correlation	0	1	0.273293358	0.438667366	–0.946553513000	–0.0113475820	0.116045354	0.667952113	0.99723653	

We have 11 columns:

1. skim_variable is the column name. There are 50 numeric columns.
2. n_missing is the number of missings in each column. All numeric columns have 0 or no missings.
3. complete_rate is the proportion of present values in each column. All numeric columns have no missings and 1 or 100% complete rate.
4. mean is the mean or average value for each column.
5. sd is the standard deviation for each column.
6. p0 is the 0% percentile or the minimum value for each column.
7. p25 is the 25% percentile or the 1st quartile for each column.
8. p50 is the 50% percentile, the median, or the 2nd quartile for each column.
9. p75 is the 75% percentile or the 3rd quartile for each column.
10. p100 is the 100% percentile or the maximum value for each column.
11. hist is the histogram plot for each column.

4.3. RIDGE CLASSIFICATION

4.3.1. Split the Data

we first do a stratified splitting of the data using the categorical outcome (species). This ensures that both the resulting training and testing data have the same species distribution as the original Flavia leaf data.

We create an object called "split_leaf" by using the initial_split function with the arguments:

- data = leaf_id_flavia which is the data we want to split.
- strata = species to make a stratified splitting using the species outcome column.

To make the splitting reproducible, we use the set.seed function with any number before using the initial_split function.

```
set.seed(123)
split_leaf <- initial_split(data = leaf_id_flavia,
strata = species)
split_leaf
## <Training/Testing/Total>
## <1430/477/1907>
```

The training data has 1430 rows and the testing data has 477 rows with a total of 1907 which is the total rows of original data.

The warning message "Too little data to stratify. Resampling will be unstratified" means that the species proportions will not be exactly the same in training and testing data because of low frequent species and can be ignored for now.

To get the actual training and testing data, we use the training and testing functions, respectively, on the split_leaf object. The resulting data is called train_leaf for the training data and test_leaf for the testing data. Finally, we use the dim function to see the data dimensions.

train_leaf<-**training**(split_leaf)

test_leaf<-**testing**(split_leaf)

dim(train_lcaf)

[1] 1430 59

dim(test_leaf)
[1] 477 59

The training data has 1430 rows (1st number) and the testing data has 477 rows (1st number) with the same 59 columns (2nd number) of the original data.

4.3.2. Generate the Recipe

We create an object "rec" by applying the following functions on the train_leaf data using the "%>%" operator:

- The recipe function with the argument species ~ . meaning define the species column as an outcome and all other columns as predictors.
- The step_dummy with the arguments:

++ all_nominal_predictors() to convert all categorical or factor predictors into numerical columns containing 1 and 0 values.

++ one_hot = FALSE to convert any categorical predictor with n categories into n–1 columns so the resulting numerical columns will not be perfectly correlated and can be used in linear models.

- The step_nzv function with the argument all_predictors() to remove near zero variance predictors or predictors with low variability.
- The step_normalize function with the argument all_predictors to convert all (now numeric) predictors into columns having 0 mean and 1 standard deviation so all predictors will have a common scale.

rec <- train_leaf **%>%**

```
recipe(species ~ .) %>%
step_dummy(all_nominal_predictors(), one_hot = FALSE) %>%
step_nzv(all_predictors()) %>%
step_normalize(all_predictors())
rec
##
## ── Recipe ────────────────────────────────────────────────────────────
##
## ── Inputs
## Number of variables by role
## outcome: 1
## predictor: 58
##
## ── Operations
## • Dummy variables from: all_nominal_predictors()
## • Sparse, unbalanced variable filter on: all_predictors()
## • Centering and scaling for: all_predictors()
```

- The recipe object "rec":

++ Defines the variables by role: 1 outcome and 58 predictors.

++ Contains 3 preprocessing operations of dummification for all categorical predictors, removing predictors with low variability, and normalizing all (numeric) predictors.

4.3.3. Look at Preprocessed Data

First, we prepare the recipe using the prep function on the "rec" recipe. The resulting object is called "prep_rec."

```
prep_rec <- prep(rec)
prep_rec
##
## ── Recipe ────────────────────────────────────────────────────────────
##
## ── Inputs
```

```
## Number of variables by role
## outcome: 1
## predictor: 58
##
## ── Training information
## Training data contained 1430 data points and no incomplete rows.
##
## ── Operations
## • Dummy variables from: apex, base, shape, denate_edge, ... | Trained
## • Sparse, unbalanced variable filter removed: outlying_polar, ... | Trained
## • Centering and scaling for: skewed_polar and clumpy_polar, ... | Trained
```

Second, to get the preprocessed training data, we use the bake function with the arguments:

- prep_rec which is the prepared recipe.
- new_data = NULL to apply the prepared recipe to training data contained in the original recipe.

The resulting data is called "train_leaf2" and we use the glimpse function to see the data structure.

```
train_leaf2 <- bake(prep_rec, new_data = NULL)
glimpse(train_leaf2)
## Rows: 1,430
## Columns: 61
## $ skewed_polar <dbl> –1.1095609, –0.7273162, –0.6622416, –0.2642...
## $ clumpy_polar <dbl> –0.51055976, –0.04090137, 0.17930831, –0.03...
## $ sparse_polar <dbl> –0.2571258, –0.2522472, –0.3296512, –0.3616...
## $ striated_polar <dbl> 0.62286940, 0.63713173, 0.78300662, 0.48509...
## $ convex_polar <dbl> –0.3616544, –0.4655237, –0.4863645, –0.4742...
## $ skinny_polar <dbl> –2.46727932, –0.21984863, 0.63793790, 0.273...
## $ stringy_polar <dbl> 0.58067387, 0.58067387, 0.58067387, 0.58067...
## $ monotonic_polar <dbl> –0.7278037, –0.8616801, –0.2952760, –0.8361...
## $ skewed_contour <dbl> –0.20769160, 0.87039452, –1.02559187, –0.03...
## $ clumpy_contour <dbl> –0.79711040, –0.43102840, –0.42464726, –0.7...
## $ sparse_contour <dbl> –0.18050632, –0.23213913, –0.17414543, –0.1...
```

```
## $ striated_contour <dbl> 0.37654932, 0.48927124, 0.44451273, 0.46313…
## $ convex_contour <dbl> –0.2068659, –0.2121550, –0.2017972, –0.2075…
## $ skinny_contour <dbl> –1.8280168, 1.9816653, –2.0428629, –0.58012…
## $ monotonic_contour <dbl> –0.85843099, –0.86108803, 0.19945216, 0.063…
## $ num_max_ponits <dbl> –0.5463698, 0.5202634, –0.5463698, –0.54636…
## $ num_min_points <dbl> –0.1616652, 0.7857990, –0.6353973, –0.63539…
## $ diameter <dbl> –0.8839601, –0.9966802, –1.0314589, –1.1619…
## $ area <dbl> 1.28076828, 1.20420437, 1.14082699, 1.07897…
## $ perimeter <dbl> 0.093737377, 0.008826190, –0.169402763, 0.0…
## $ physiological_length <dbl> –0.7733647, –0.9096579, –0.9602811, –1.1627…
## $ physiological_width <dbl> 1.4588999, 1.4692485, 1.3381659, 1.4244045,…
## $ aspect_ratio <dbl> 1.452820, 1.557742, 1.474034, 1.707853, 1.6…
## $ rectangularity <dbl> 0.2516609, 0.2896249, 0.5230681, 0.5494059,…
## $ circularity <dbl> 1.403533, 1.424698, 1.589317, 1.165017, 1.3…
## $ compactness <dbl> –0.4526129, –0.4546485, –0.4698215, –0.4281…
## $ narrow_factor <dbl> –0.4552078, –0.4601900, –0.4545918, –0.4644…
## $ perimeter_ratio_diameter <dbl> 0.8248470, 0.8804440, 0.7626549, 1.1632007,…
## $ perimeter_ratio_length <dbl> –0.4407329, –0.4452482, –0.4429995, –0.4378…
## $ perimeter_ratio_lw <dbl> –0.9157585, –0.9072598, –0.9590794, –0.4238…
## $ num_convex_points <dbl> 1.2309312, 1.3281834, 1.6523572, 1.2309312,…
## $ perimeter_convexity <dbl> 0.33333088, 0.31530350, 0.48720988, –0.0989…
## $ area_convexity <dbl> –0.3811637, –0.3356644, –0.4156448, –0.2369…
## $ area_ratio_convexity <dbl> 0.4229555, 0.3491191, 0.4797005, 0.1928839,…
## $ equivalent_diameter <dbl> 1.126194294, 1.071419319, 1.025640147, 0.98…
```

$ eccentriciry <dbl> –1.8083109, –2.6663233, –1.7882052, –2.8829…

$ contrast <dbl> 0.46475963, 0.22981691, 0.12787530, –0.1214…

$ correlation_texture <dbl> –0.53672899, –0.10168123, –0.03531575, 0.29…

$ inverse_difference_moments <dbl> –1.47337076, –1.40233174, –1.29051965, –1.2…

$ entropy <dbl> 1.143007768, 1.131684911, 1.088464637, 0.93…

$ mean_red_val <dbl> 0.25453781, 0.16271689, 0.13327250, 0.14269…

$ mean_green_val <dbl> 0.24164611, 0.18752592, 0.21867098, 0.20400…

$ mean_blue_val <dbl> 0.140770519, 0.144349188, 0.088736695, 0.13…

$ std_red_val <dbl> 0.16855007, 0.11121799, 0.04347290, 0.12299…

$ std_green_val <dbl> 0.271913803, 0.202653499, 0.362555014, 0.35…

$ std_blue_val <dbl> 0.0160315100, 0.1185616100, 0.0288125871, 0…

$ correlation <dbl> –0.6689144, –0.6130460, 0.6888409, 0.603839…

$ species <fct> chinese_redbud, chinese_redbud, chinese_red…

$ apex_acute <dbl> –0.4296817, –0.4296817, –0.4296817, –0.4296…

$ apex_apiculate <dbl> –0.4601263, –0.4601263, –0.4601263, –0.4601…

$ apex_none <dbl> 1.641099, 1.641099, 1.641099, 1.641099, 1.6…

$ apex_obtuse <dbl> –0.2497268, –0.2497268, –0.2497268, –0.2497…

$ apex_round <dbl> –0.2590699, –0.2590699, –0.2590699, –0.2590…

$ base_acute <dbl> –0.3757156, –0.3757156, –0.3757156, –0.3757…

$ base_none <dbl> 0.6522462, 0.6522462, 0.6522462, 0.6522462,…

$ shape_heart_shape <dbl> 3.626185, 3.626185, 3.626185, 3.626185, 3.6…

$ shape_round <dbl> –0.2559842, –0.2559842, –0.2559842, –0.2559…

$ shape_simple_round <dbl> –0.8946773, –0.8946773, –0.8946773, –0.8946…

$ lobed_edge_yes <dbl> –0.406606, –0.406606, –0.406606, –0.406606,…

$ smooth_edge_yes <dbl> 0.7139153, 0.7139153, 0.7139153, 0.7139153,…

$ toothed_edge_yes <dbl> –0.5259203, –0.5259203, –0.5259203, –0.5259…

- The training data has the same 1430 rows of the original training data but 61 columns (60 predictors + 1 outcome) because of dummification.
- All columns have negative values because of normalization.

We can use the skim function again with the yank function with the "numeric" argument on the train_leaf2 data to get useful information about numeric columns in the Flavia leaf training data after normalization.

train_leaf2 **%>% skim() %>% yank**("numeric") **%>%**

flextable() %>% theme_box() %>%

set_caption(caption = "The information gained from skim function on all columns from the Flavia leaf training data after normalization")

The information gained from skim function on all columns from the Flavia leaf training data after normalization:

skim_ variable	**n_miss- ing**	**com- plete_ rate**	**mean**	**sd**	**p0**	**p25**	**p50**	**p75**	**p100**	**hist**
skewed_ polar	0	1	–0.000 000000 0000008 758573339	1	–3.1706276	–0.64946654	–0.11509817	0.43666055	7.0766559	
clumpy_ polar	0	1	–0.000 0000000 0000001 20972701	1	–1.0959492	–0.61881398	–0.25728767	0.27217802	10.3005833	
sparse_po- lar	0	1	0.0000 000000 0000001 06059993	1	–0.3905765	–0.25979689	–0.25029412	–0.18207866	4.4563824	
striated_ polar	0	1	–0.000 0000000 00000622 0790791	1	–5.5008337	–0.09241194	0.31240085	0.54390499	0.7961128	

convex_ polar	0	1	0.000 000000 0000000 119173058	1	−0.4867202	−0.41083495	−0.28228326	−0.04563404	6.3268386	
skinny_ polar	0	1	0.000 000000 00000016 22827746	1	−9.1450896	−0.63135210	0.07374286	0.70548067	2.1841597	
stringy_ polar	0	1	−0.000 0000000 000000985 026485	1	−7.7484283	0.01098482	0.11701915	0.58067387	0.5806739	
monoton-ic_polar	0	1	−0.00 00000000 0000007749 27058	1	−0.8966594	−0.73549756	−0.34770476	0.34899832	4.1786907	
skewed_ contour	0	1	0.00 0000000 00000056 43513789	1	−2.4270809	−0.67375913	−0.14039516	0.50498589	4.6711939	
clumpy_ contour	0	1	−0.000 00000000 000000057 24853	1	−1.3519776	−0.44565578	−0.16555090	0.15518812	21.6493451	
sparse_ contour	0	1	0.000 0000000 000001877 554650	1	−0.3792630	−0.20455868	−0.1834[illegible]624	−0.17404060	5.4688199	
striated_ contour	0	1	−0.000 000000000 00088256 58017	1	−6.0258206	0.03179991	0.27396283	0.45591754	0.6572663	

convex_ contour	0	1	−0.000 0000000 00000013 9649410	1	−0.2121550	−0.20991015	−0.20262026	−0.18754290	7.2512108	
skinny_ contour	0	1	−0.000 0000000 0000023 24258028	1	−2.0870220	−0.71937774	0.04855506	0.75557251	1.9816653	
monoton-ic_contour	0	1	−0.000 000000 0000000 669102103	1	−0.8611168	−0.85601813	−0.38073290	0.65050081	2.4107126	
num_ max_po-nits	0	1	−0.00000 0000000 00006578 26400	1	−0.5463698	−0.54636981	−0.54636981	−0.01305320	6.3867460	
num_min_ points	0	1	−0.000000 000000000 0506551386	1	−1.1091294	−0.63539731	−0.63539731	0.31206687	6.4705841	
diameter	0	1	−0.000 0000000000 003545870 316	1	−3.1160889	−0.74593994	0.17223258	0.85282773	1.6817892	
area	0	1	−0.000 00000000 000010661 33147	1	−2.2219336	−0.75859760	0.09353840	0.81840165	2.3685574	
perimeter	0	1	0.000 0000000 000001972 333585	1	−3.3049314	−0.44476032	0.06803419	0.53468315	3.7178793	

physiolog-ical_length	0	1	–0.000 0000000 00000244 9497785	1	–2.9252699	–0.78107207	0.12547491	0.87035587	1.7128377	
physiolog-ical_width	0	1	0.0000 0000000 000009124 15266	1	–2.1519665	–0.73393196	0.02891490	0.86299137	1.8410311	
aspect_ra-tio	0	1	–0.00000 000000000 003943 38747	1	–1.7828125	–0.67572025	–0.19703551	0.64512047	2.7996573	
rectangu-larity	0	1	–0.00 000000 0000000 1119513140	1	–3.8050172	–0.31359659	0.14573233	0.52788352	2.2760959	
circularity	0	1	–0.0000 0000000 00000943 641805	1	–2.5967903	–0.60114613	0.21159996	0.70198662	1.7107974	
compact-ness	0	1	0.000 000000 00000001 95168522	1	–0.4803183	–0.37146490	–0.29276550	–0.08724775	5.7035399	
narrow_ factor	0	1	–0.0000 0000000 00000086 049070	1	–0.4818113	–0.38046428	–0.25705166	–0.09912004	6.8910467	
perimeter_ ratio_di-ameter	0	1	–0.000 00000000 000026596 96865	1	–0.9738268	–0.62677959	–0.36014259	0.21501024	4.7284797	

perimeter_ratio_length	0	1	0.000000000000000323958661	1	–0.4638195	–0.36003429	–0.27001266	–0.12726821	6.9103533	
perimeter_ratio_lw	0	1	–0.00000000000000126501990	1	–1.1434763	–0.59616416	–0.32288175	0.25698815	5.9451924	
num_convex_points	0	1	0.0000000000000002037681288	1	–2.2701464	–0.71411193	–0.03334683	0.64741826	3.0787222	
perimeter_convexity	0	1	0.0000000000000007435721115	1	–5.1710118	0.08341580	0.37075672	0.43737270	0.7955306	
area_convexity	0	1	0.000000000000000217152048	1	–0.5024587	–0.44409274	–0.37275038	–0.13463797	5.9194590	
area_ratio_convexity	0	1	0.0000000000000001280052443	1	–4.4751416	0.03640282	0.40921372	0.52703891	0.6256717	
equivalent_diameter	0	1	–0.0000000000000001218610640	1	–2.9052530	–0.61087911	0.20003515	0.78618129	1.8506904	
eccentriciry	0	1	–0.000000000000000186379661	1	–3.6275186	–0.16243557	0.39045680	0.64727140	0.9118168	

contrast	0	1	−0.0000000000000000064550687	1	−0.9712857	−0.64271241	−0.27392811	0.22602924	7.0235063	
correlation_texture	0	1	0.000000000000007895001002	1	−5.4470460	−0.51542075	0.18454951	0.71603077	1.4437281	
inverse_difference_moments	0	1	0.0000000000000000199556887	1	−2.2861775	−0.82624501	−0.06107247	0.75586576	2.2639613	
entropy	0	1	0.0000000000000001867441195	1	−2.3733922	−0.73941222	0.15780198	0.77470939	2.2683187	
mean_red_val	0	1	0.0000000000000000057551802	1	−0.7252798	−0.45590716	−0.28290974	−0.04691089	4.1590184	
mean_green_val	0	1	0.0000000000000000716975315	1	−1.2251895	−0.57516110	−0.20915042	0.22560193	3.6356822	
mean_blue_val	0	1	−0.000000000000000791772755	1	−0.8551304	−0.48646803	−0.25887906	0.06951496	3.9803150	
std_red_val	0	1	0.0000000000000001685765303	1	−1.2105197	−0.47170153	−0.22746448	0.02118545	4.0057354	

std_green_val	0	1	–0.000 000000 00000023 71127406	1	–3.1408326	–0.63622992	0.06460824	0.67503269	2.8220627	
std_blue_val	0	1	–0.00 000000 00000001 087786 863	1	–1.8264976	–0.49162360	–0.11718881	0.26558162	4.0791941	
correlation	0	1	–0.000 000000 0000000 084146 978	1	–2.7590827	–0.63151478	–0.35317917	0.90164311	1.6656778	
apex_acute	0	1	–0.000 0000000 000000233001491	1	–0.4296817	–0.42968173	–0.42968173	–0.42968173	2.3256765	
apex_apiculate	0	1	0.0000 0000 00000000109264454	1	–0.4601263	–0.46012634	–0.46012634	–0.46012634	2.1717963	
apex_none	0	1	–0.00 000000 0000000 0533119646	1	–0.6089217	–0.60892166	–0.60892166	1.64109895	1.6410989	
apex_obtuse	0	1	0.00000 00000000 000051080328	1	–0.2497268	–0.24972683	–0.24972683	–0.24972683	4.0015752	
apex_round	0	1	–0.00000 0000000 0000036912914	1	–0.2590699	–0.25906990	–0.25906990	–0.25906990	3.8572629	

base_acute	0	1	–0.000 00000000 00000202 847403	1	–0.3757156	–0.37571557	–0.37571557	–0.37571557	2.6597266	
base_none	0	1	–0.000 0000000 00000068 9872535	1	–1.5320912	–1.53209122	0.65224621	0.65224621	0.6522462	
shape_ heart_ shape	0	1	–0.0000 0000000 00000264 886513	1	–0.2755791	–0.27557911	–0.27557911	–0.27557911	3.6261845	
shape_ round	0	1	–0.0000 0000000 00000328 262679	1	–0.2559842	–0.25598421	–0.25598421	–0.25598421	3.9037592	
shape_ simple_ round	0	1	–0.0000 00000000 00000481 96957	1	–0.8946773	–0.89467727	–0.89467727	1.11693986	1.1169399	
lobed_ edge_yes	0	1	–0.0000 00000 00000 00190974252	1	–0.4066060	–0.40660605	–0.40660605	–0.40660605	2.4576632	
smooth_ edge_yes	0	1	0.000 0000000 000000961650934	1	–1.3997469	–1.39974692	0.71391527	0.71391527	0.7139153	
toothed_ edge_yes	0	1	0.0000 0000 000000 00958 095054	1	–0.5259203	–0.52592030	–0.52592030	–0.52592030	1.9000991	

- The mean of all 60 predictors is extremely low and nearly equals zero.
- The standard deviation of all 60 predictors = 1. So, all 60 predictors are now on a comparable scale.

Finally, to get the preprocessed testing data, we use the bake function with the arguments:

- prep_rec which is the prepared recipe.
- new_data = test_leaf to apply the prepared recipe to the testing data.

The resulting data is called "test_leaf2" and we use the glimpse function to see the data structure.

```
test_leaf2 <- bake(prep_rec, new_data = test_leaf)
glimpse(test_leaf2)
## Rows: 477
## Columns: 61
## $ skewed_polar <dbl> 0.9618806, –0.7374110, 3.6081591, –1.896125…
## $ clumpy_polar <dbl> 0.5910092, –0.5879351, 0.6583238, –0.555953…
## $ sparse_polar <dbl> 4.2596176, –0.2587176, –0.2557690, –0.25640…
## $ striated_polar <dbl> –3.8689306, 0.4016929, 0.4376990, 0.3932906…
## $ convex_polar <dbl> 4.4090841, –0.4720085, –0.2958469, –0.26020…
## $ skinny_polar <dbl> 1.0057034, 0.9960537, –1.4699662, –1.875974…
## $ stringy_polar <dbl> –4.61692012, 0.58067387, 0.06327339, 0.0169…
## $ monotonic_polar <dbl> –0.46529702, –0.87555896, –0.19388700, –0.4…
## $ skewed_contour <dbl> 1.24957088, –0.26999737, –1.35804990, –0.46…
## $ clumpy_contour <dbl> 0.73921298, –0.51568687, –0.15419893, 0.603…
## $ sparse_contour <dbl> 5.2485120, –0.1824850, –0.1788197, –0.17960…
## $ striated_contour <dbl> –4.6771938, 0.4577494, 0.2952133, 0.4559175…
## $ convex_contour <dbl> 0.1839502, –0.2008938, –0.2023101, –0.20746…
## $ skinny_contour <dbl> 0.9615467, –2.0496970, –1.5261510, –1.10684…
## $ monotonic_contour <dbl> –0.85699332, 0.04956683, –0.27843183, –0.38…
## $ num_max_ponits <dbl> 1.0535800, –0.5463698, –0.5463698, –0.54636…
## $ num_min_points <dbl> 2.2069952, –0.6353973, –0.1616652, –0.16166…
## $ diameter <dbl> –1.4579534, –1.1239155, –1.3570016, –0.8200…
```

$ area <dbl> 0.9588797, 1.0103007, 0.8706229, 1.2240664,…

$ perimeter <dbl> –0.13958581, –0.21531790, –0.23226782, 0.07…

$ physiological_length <dbl> –1.3769490, –1.0264807, –1.4314663, –0.8006…

$ physiological_width <dbl> 1.4416522, 1.3416154, 1.3657622, 1.3588632,…

$ aspect_ratio <dbl> 1.904521, 1.525114, 1.875600, 1.382413, 1.9…

$ rectangularity <dbl> 0.6280742, 0.3268013, 0.6867111, 0.3908097,…

$ circularity <dbl> 1.323008, 1.489107, 1.334833, 1.362526, 1.4…

$ compactness <dbl> –0.4446797, –0.4607217, –0.4458638, –0.4486…

$ narrow_factor <dbl> –0.4770325, –0.4585461, –0.4692674, –0.4471…

$ perimeter_ratio_diameter <dbl> 1.3313472, 0.8298192, 1.1054614, 0.7370663,…

$ perimeter_ratio_length <dbl> –0.4496764, –0.4453530, –0.4480035, –0.4336…

$ perimeter_ratio_lw <dbl> –0.5668279, –0.9603612, –0.5460851, –0.7911…

$ num_convex_points <dbl> 0.8743400, 1.1012617, 1.1660964, 1.6199398,…

$ perimeter_convexity <dbl> 0.06106482, 0.35413590, 0.14606290, 0.27444…

$ area_convexity <dbl> –0.2934511, –0.3859450, –0.3130172, –0.3547…

$ area_ratio_convexity <dbl> 0.2816523, 0.4307831, 0.3128008, 0.3799994,…

$ equivalent_diameter <dbl> 0.8919083, 0.9300594, 0.8257462, 1.0856839,…

$ eccentriciry <dbl> –2.4174521, –1.9657406, –2.9069857, –1.6710…

$ contrast <dbl> –0.145575202, 0.508490698, –0.005751413, 0…

$ correlation_texture <dbl> 0.305618217, –0.920062501, 0.197142630, –0…

$ inverse_difference_moments <dbl> –1.0643991, –1.2522364, –1.0500345, –1.3932…

$ entropy <dbl> 0.8169454, 1.0260017, 0.8300911, 1.0815395,…

$ mean_red_val <dbl> 0.06668540, 0.18477056, –0.01073393, 0.1884…

$ mean_green_val <dbl> 0.17292064, 0.26955872, 0.12110779, 0.22263…

```
## $ mean_blue_val <dbl> 0.090459305, 0.123866776, –0.007658802, 0.0…
## $ std_red_val <dbl> 0.017054871, 0.180032774, –0.022218413, 0.0…
## $ std_green_val <dbl> 0.41508459, 0.66555483, 0.35911608, 0.28894…
## $ std_blue_val <dbl> 0.12160322, 0.17078885, 0.02719857, –0.0456…
## $ correlation <dbl> –0.6887597, 0.5943164, 0.3557083, 0.2602059…
## $ species <fct> chinese_redbud, chinese_redbud, chinese_red…
## $ apex_acute <dbl> –0.4296817, –0.4296817, –0.4296817, –0.4296…
## $ apex_apiculate <dbl> –0.4601263, –0.4601263, –0.4601263, –0.4601…
## $ apex_none <dbl> 1.6410989, 1.6410989, 1.6410989, 1.6410989,…
## $ apex_obtuse <dbl> –0.2497268, –0.2497268, –0.2497268, –0.2497…
## $ apex_round <dbl> –0.2590699, –0.2590699, –0.2590699, –0.2590…
## $ base_acute <dbl> –0.3757156, –0.3757156, –0.3757156, –0.3757…
## $ base_none <dbl> 0.6522462, 0.6522462, 0.6522462, 0.6522462,…
## $ shape_heart_shape <dbl> 3.6261845, 3.6261845, 3.6261845, 3.6261845,…
## $ shape_round <dbl> –0.2559842, –0.2559842, –0.2559842, –0.2559…
## $ shape_simple_round <dbl> –0.8946773, –0.8946773, –0.8946773, –0.8946…
## $ lobed_edge_yes <dbl> –0.406606, –0.406606, –0.406606, –0.406606,…
## $ smooth_edge_yes <dbl> 0.7139153, 0.7139153, 0.7139153, 0.7139153,…
## $ toothed_edge_yes <dbl> –0.5259203, –0.5259203, –0.5259203, –0.5259…
```

- The testing data has the same 477 rows as the original testing data but 61 columns (60 predictors + 1 outcome) as that of the preprocessed training data.

4.3.4. Generate Different Resamples of Training Data

We split the train_leaf data using the vfold_cv function with the arguments:

- v = 10 to split the data into 10 folds.
- repeats = 5 to repeat this process 5 times.
- strata = species to make stratified resampling using the species column.

The result is 50 different resamples of train_leaf data contained in folds data frame.

- We also use the set.seed function before splitting to make the splitting reproducible.

```
set.seed(123)
folds<-vfold_cv(train_leaf, v = 10, repeats = 5, strata = species)
folds
## # 10-fold cross-validation repeated 5 times using stratification
## # A tibble: 50 × 3
## splits id id2
## <list> <chr> <chr>
## 1 <split [1287/143]> Repeat1 Fold01
## 2 <split [1287/143]> Repeat1 Fold02
## 3 <split [1287/143]> Repeat1 Fold03
## 4 <split [1287/143]> Repeat1 Fold04
## 5 <split [1287/143]> Repeat1 Fold05
## 6 <split [1287/143]> Repeat1 Fold06
## 7 <split [1287/143]> Repeat1 Fold07
## 8 <split [1287/143]> Repeat1 Fold08
## 9 <split [1287/143]> Repeat1 Fold09
## 10 <split [1287/143]> Repeat1 Fold10
## # ℹ 40 more rows
```

- There are 50 different rows. Each row corresponds to 1 resample of train_leaf data. Each resample has 1 analysis (training) data, with 1287 rows, for model building, and 1 assessment (testing) data with 143 rows, for model testing.
- Each resample has 2 id values. id for the repeat number from 1 to 5 and id2 for the resample number from 1 to 10 within that repeat.
- Each resample has a total rows of 1430 which is the number of rows in original train_leaf data. 1287 + 143 = 1430.

4.3.5. Define Machine Learning (ML) Model

We define a multinomial classification model, to predict the different classes or species, by using the functions:

- The multinom_reg function to define the multinomial classification model type with the following arguments:
- mixture = 0 to indicate a ridge classification models.
- penalty = tune() to tune the penalty term on the different resamples of training data.

- The set_engine function with the argument "glmnet" to define the engine that will use the glmnet function from the glmnet package.
- The set_mode function with the argument "classification" to define the mode of learning. We use classification because we have a categorical outcome (species).

All the three functions are applied in sequence using the piping "%>%" operator and the resulting object is called "rid_model."

```
rid_model <- multinom_reg(mixture = 0, penalty = tune()) %>%
set_engine("glmnet") %>%
set_mode("classification")
rid_model
## Multinomial Regression Model Specification (classification)
##
## Main Arguments:
## penalty = tune()
## mixture = 0
##
## Computational engine: glmnet
```

4.3.6. Generate Workflow

We create the "wflow" object by using the following functions:

- The workflow function to create a workflow.
- The add_recipe function with the argument "rec" to add the above created recipe with three preprocessing steps.
- The add_model function with the argument rid_model to add the above created ridge model.

```
wflow <- workflow() %>%
add_recipe(rec) %>%
add_model(rid_model)
wflow
## ══ Workflow ══════════════════════════════════════════
══════════════════════════════════════
## Preprocessor: Recipe
## Model: multinom_reg()
```

```
##
## ── Preprocessor ────────────────────────────────────────
##
## 3 Recipe Steps
##
## • step_dummy()
## • step_nzv()
## • step_normalize()
##
## ── Model ──────────────────────────────────────────────
##
## Multinomial Regression Model Specification (classification)
##
## Main Arguments:
## penalty = tune()
## mixture = 0
##
## Computational engine: glmnet
```

- The "wflow" object contains three preprocessing steps and the multinomial classification model with 0 mixture and tuned penalty (ridge classification).

4.3.7. Fit Model on Different Resamples with Tuning

We can use the grid_regular function to chooses sensible values for the penalty term.

We create a grid of penalty values "my_grid" by using the grid_regular function with the arguments:

- penalty() to choose sensible values for the penalty term.
- levels = 50 to choose 50 different penalty values.

```
my_grid <- grid_regular(penalty(), levels = 50)
my_grid %>% flextable(cwidth = 2) %>% theme_box() %>%
set_caption(caption = "The different 50 penalty values chosen by using the grid_regular function")
```

The different 50 penalty values chosen by using the grid_regular function:

penalty
0.0000000001000000
0.0000000001599859
0.0000000002559548
0.0000000004094915
0.0000000006551286
0.0000000010481131
0.0000000016768329
0.0000000026826958
0.0000000042919343
0.0000000068664885
0.0000000109854114
0.0000000175751062
0.0000000281176870
0.0000000449843267
0.0000000719685673
0.0000001151395399
0.0000001842069969
0.0000002947051703
0.0000004714866363
0.0000007543120063
0.0000012067926406
0.0000019306977289
0.0000030888435965
0.0000049417133613
0.0000079060432109
0.0000126485521686
0.0000202358964773
0.0000323745754282
0.0000517947467923
0.0000828642772855
0.0001325711365590
0.0002120950887920
0.0003393221771895

0.0005428675439324
0.0008685113737514
0.0013894954943731
0.0022229964825262
0.0035564803062231
0.0056898660290183
0.0091029817799152
0.0145634847750124
0.0232995181051537
0.0372759372031494
0.0596362331659464
0.0954095476349996
0.1526417967175236
0.2442053094548655
0.3906939937054621
0.6250551925273976
1.0000000000000000

- The penalty values range from 0.0000000001 (1e-10) to 1.00.

To try all these 50 different penalties on the 50 resamples of the training data, we use the tune_grid function with the arguments:

- wflow which is the workflow containing three preprocessing steps and the linear ridge model.
- folds which are the 50 resamples of training data created above.
- metrics = metrics_set(accuracy) to get the accuracy of the linear ridge model on each resample using the 50 penalty values.
- grid = my_grid to use the 50 penalty values in the my_grid data in tuning.
- control = control_grid(verbose = TRUE) to monitor the training process.

```
set.seed(123)
rid_res <- tune_grid(wflow, folds,
metrics = metric_set(accuracy),
grid = my_grid,
control = control_grid(verbose = TRUE))
## i Fold01, Repeat1: preprocessor 1/1
```

```
## ✓ Fold01, Repeat1: preprocessor 1/1
## i Fold01, Repeat1: preprocessor 1/1, model 1/1
## ✓ Fold01, Repeat1: preprocessor 1/1, model 1/1
## i Fold01, Repeat1: preprocessor 1/1, model 1/1 (extracts)
## i Fold01, Repeat1: preprocessor 1/1, model 1/1 (predictions)
## i Fold02, Repeat1: preprocessor 1/1
## ✓ Fold02, Repeat1: preprocessor 1/1
## i Fold02, Repeat1: preprocessor 1/1, model 1/1
## ✓ Fold02, Repeat1: preprocessor 1/1, model 1/1
## i Fold02, Repeat1: preprocessor 1/1, model 1/1 (extracts)
## i Fold02, Repeat1: preprocessor 1/1, model 1/1 (predictions)
## i Fold03, Repeat1: preprocessor 1/1
## ✓ Fold03, Repeat1: preprocessor 1/1
## i Fold03, Repeat1: preprocessor 1/1, model 1/1
## ✓ Fold03, Repeat1: preprocessor 1/1, model 1/1
## i Fold03, Repeat1: preprocessor 1/1, model 1/1 (extracts)
## i Fold03, Repeat1: preprocessor 1/1, model 1/1 (predictions)
## i Fold04, Repeat1: preprocessor 1/1
## ✓ Fold04, Repeat1: preprocessor 1/1
## i Fold04, Repeat1: preprocessor 1/1, model 1/1
## ✓ Fold04, Repeat1: preprocessor 1/1, model 1/1
## i Fold04, Repeat1: preprocessor 1/1, model 1/1 (extracts)
## i Fold04, Repeat1: preprocessor 1/1, model 1/1 (predictions)
## i Fold05, Repeat1: preprocessor 1/1
## ✓ Fold05, Repeat1: preprocessor 1/1
## i Fold05, Repeat1: preprocessor 1/1, model 1/1
## ✓ Fold05, Repeat1: preprocessor 1/1, model 1/1
## i Fold05, Repeat1: preprocessor 1/1, model 1/1 (extracts)
## i Fold05, Repeat1: preprocessor 1/1, model 1/1 (predictions)
## i Fold06, Repeat1: preprocessor 1/1
## ✓ Fold06, Repeat1: preprocessor 1/1
## i Fold06, Repeat1: preprocessor 1/1, model 1/1
```

```
## ✓ Fold06, Repeat1: preprocessor 1/1, model 1/1
## i Fold06, Repeat1: preprocessor 1/1, model 1/1 (extracts)
## i Fold06, Repeat1: preprocessor 1/1, model 1/1 (predictions)
## i Fold07, Repeat1: preprocessor 1/1
## ✓ Fold07, Repeat1: preprocessor 1/1
## i Fold07, Repeat1: preprocessor 1/1, model 1/1
## ✓ Fold07, Repeat1: preprocessor 1/1, model 1/1
## i Fold07, Repeat1: preprocessor 1/1, model 1/1 (extracts)
## i Fold07, Repeat1: preprocessor 1/1, model 1/1 (predictions)
## i Fold08, Repeat1: preprocessor 1/1
## ✓ Fold08, Repeat1: preprocessor 1/1
## i Fold08, Repeat1: preprocessor 1/1, model 1/1
## ✓ Fold08, Repeat1: preprocessor 1/1, model 1/1
## i Fold08, Repeat1: preprocessor 1/1, model 1/1 (extracts)
## i Fold08, Repeat1: preprocessor 1/1, model 1/1 (predictions)
## i Fold09, Repeat1: preprocessor 1/1
## ✓ Fold09, Repeat1: preprocessor 1/1
## i Fold09, Repeat1: preprocessor 1/1, model 1/1
## ✓ Fold09, Repeat1: preprocessor 1/1, model 1/1
## i Fold09, Repeat1: preprocessor 1/1, model 1/1 (extracts)
## i Fold09, Repeat1: preprocessor 1/1, model 1/1 (predictions)
## i Fold10, Repeat1: preprocessor 1/1
## ✓ Fold10, Repeat1: preprocessor 1/1
## i Fold10, Repeat1: preprocessor 1/1, model 1/1
## ✓ Fold10, Repeat1: preprocessor 1/1, model 1/1
## i Fold10, Repeat1: preprocessor 1/1, model 1/1 (extracts)
## i Fold10, Repeat1: preprocessor 1/1, model 1/1 (predictions)
## i Fold01, Repeat2: preprocessor 1/1
## ✓ Fold01, Repeat2: preprocessor 1/1
## i Fold01, Repeat2: preprocessor 1/1, model 1/1
## ✓ Fold01, Repeat2: preprocessor 1/1, model 1/1
## i Fold01, Repeat2: preprocessor 1/1, model 1/1 (extracts)
```

i Fold01, Repeat2: preprocessor 1/1, model 1/1 (predictions)
i Fold02, Repeat2: preprocessor 1/1
✓ Fold02, Repeat2: preprocessor 1/1
i Fold02, Repeat2: preprocessor 1/1, model 1/1
✓ Fold02, Repeat2: preprocessor 1/1, model 1/1
i Fold02, Repeat2: preprocessor 1/1, model 1/1 (extracts)
i Fold02, Repeat2: preprocessor 1/1, model 1/1 (predictions)
i Fold03, Repeat2: preprocessor 1/1
✓ Fold03, Repeat2: preprocessor 1/1
i Fold03, Repeat2: preprocessor 1/1, model 1/1
✓ Fold03, Repeat2: preprocessor 1/1, model 1/1
i Fold03, Repeat2: preprocessor 1/1, model 1/1 (extracts)
i Fold03, Repeat2: preprocessor 1/1, model 1/1 (predictions)
i Fold04, Repeat2: preprocessor 1/1
✓ Fold04, Repeat2: preprocessor 1/1
i Fold04, Repeat2: preprocessor 1/1, model 1/1
✓ Fold04, Repeat2: preprocessor 1/1, model 1/1
i Fold04, Repeat2: preprocessor 1/1, model 1/1 (extracts)
i Fold04, Repeat2: preprocessor 1/1, model 1/1 (predictions)
i Fold05, Repeat2: preprocessor 1/1
✓ Fold05, Repeat2: preprocessor 1/1
i Fold05, Repeat2: preprocessor 1/1, model 1/1
✓ Fold05, Repeat2: preprocessor 1/1, model 1/1
i Fold05, Repeat2: preprocessor 1/1, model 1/1 (extracts)
i Fold05, Repeat2: preprocessor 1/1, model 1/1 (predictions)
i Fold06, Repeat2: preprocessor 1/1
✓ Fold06, Repeat2: preprocessor 1/1
i Fold06, Repeat2: preprocessor 1/1, model 1/1
✓ Fold06, Repeat2: preprocessor 1/1, model 1/1
i Fold06, Repeat2: preprocessor 1/1, model 1/1 (extracts)
i Fold06, Repeat2: preprocessor 1/1, model 1/1 (predictions)
i Fold07, Repeat2: preprocessor 1/1

```
## ✓ Fold07, Repeat2: preprocessor 1/1
## i Fold07, Repeat2: preprocessor 1/1, model 1/1
## ✓ Fold07, Repeat2: preprocessor 1/1, model 1/1
## i Fold07, Repeat2: preprocessor 1/1, model 1/1 (extracts)
## i Fold07, Repeat2: preprocessor 1/1, model 1/1 (predictions)
## i Fold08, Repeat2: preprocessor 1/1
## ✓ Fold08, Repeat2: preprocessor 1/1
## i Fold08, Repeat2: preprocessor 1/1, model 1/1
## ✓ Fold08, Repeat2: preprocessor 1/1, model 1/1
## i Fold08, Repeat2: preprocessor 1/1, model 1/1 (extracts)
## i Fold08, Repeat2: preprocessor 1/1, model 1/1 (predictions)
## i Fold09, Repeat2: preprocessor 1/1
## ✓ Fold09, Repeat2: preprocessor 1/1
## i Fold09, Repeat2: preprocessor 1/1, model 1/1
## ✓ Fold09, Repeat2: preprocessor 1/1, model 1/1
## i Fold09, Repeat2: preprocessor 1/1, model 1/1 (extracts)
## i Fold09, Repeat2: preprocessor 1/1, model 1/1 (predictions)
## i Fold10, Repeat2: preprocessor 1/1
## ✓ Fold10, Repeat2: preprocessor 1/1
## i Fold10, Repeat2: preprocessor 1/1, model 1/1
## ✓ Fold10, Repeat2: preprocessor 1/1, model 1/1
## i Fold10, Repeat2: preprocessor 1/1, model 1/1 (extracts)
## i Fold10, Repeat2: preprocessor 1/1, model 1/1 (predictions)
## i Fold01, Repeat3: preprocessor 1/1
## ✓ Fold01, Repeat3: preprocessor 1/1
## i Fold01, Repeat3: preprocessor 1/1, model 1/1
## ✓ Fold01, Repeat3: preprocessor 1/1, model 1/1
## i Fold01, Repeat3: preprocessor 1/1, model 1/1 (extracts)
## i Fold01, Repeat3: preprocessor 1/1, model 1/1 (predictions)
## i Fold02, Repeat3: preprocessor 1/1
## ✓ Fold02, Repeat3: preprocessor 1/1
## i Fold02, Repeat3: preprocessor 1/1, model 1/1
```

```
## ✓ Fold02, Repeat3: preprocessor 1/1, model 1/1
## i Fold02, Repeat3: preprocessor 1/1, model 1/1 (extracts)
## i Fold02, Repeat3: preprocessor 1/1, model 1/1 (predictions)
## i Fold03, Repeat3: preprocessor 1/1
## ✓ Fold03, Repeat3: preprocessor 1/1
## i Fold03, Repeat3: preprocessor 1/1, model 1/1
## ✓ Fold03, Repeat3: preprocessor 1/1, model 1/1
## i Fold03, Repeat3: preprocessor 1/1, model 1/1 (extracts)
## i Fold03, Repeat3: preprocessor 1/1, model 1/1 (predictions)
## i Fold04, Repeat3: preprocessor 1/1
## ✓ Fold04, Repeat3: preprocessor 1/1
## i Fold04, Repeat3: preprocessor 1/1, model 1/1
## ✓ Fold04, Repeat3: preprocessor 1/1, model 1/1
## i Fold04, Repeat3: preprocessor 1/1, model 1/1 (extracts)
## i Fold04, Repeat3: preprocessor 1/1, model 1/1 (predictions)
## i Fold05, Repeat3: preprocessor 1/1
## ✓ Fold05, Repeat3: preprocessor 1/1
## i Fold05, Repeat3: preprocessor 1/1, model 1/1
## ✓ Fold05, Repeat3: preprocessor 1/1, model 1/1
## i Fold05, Repeat3: preprocessor 1/1, model 1/1 (extracts)
## i Fold05, Repeat3: preprocessor 1/1, model 1/1 (predictions)
## i Fold06, Repeat3: preprocessor 1/1
## ✓ Fold06, Repeat3: preprocessor 1/1
## i Fold06, Repeat3: preprocessor 1/1, model 1/1
## ✓ Fold06, Repeat3: preprocessor 1/1, model 1/1
## i Fold06, Repeat3: preprocessor 1/1, model 1/1 (extracts)
## i Fold06, Repeat3: preprocessor 1/1, model 1/1 (predictions)
## i Fold07, Repeat3: preprocessor 1/1
## ✓ Fold07, Repeat3: preprocessor 1/1
## i Fold07, Repeat3: preprocessor 1/1, model 1/1
## ✓ Fold07, Repeat3: preprocessor 1/1, model 1/1
## i Fold07, Repeat3: preprocessor 1/1, model 1/1 (extracts)
```

```
## i Fold07, Repeat3: preprocessor 1/1, model 1/1 (predictions)
## i Fold08, Repeat3: preprocessor 1/1
## ✓ Fold08, Repeat3: preprocessor 1/1
## i Fold08, Repeat3: preprocessor 1/1, model 1/1
## ✓ Fold08, Repeat3: preprocessor 1/1, model 1/1
## i Fold08, Repeat3: preprocessor 1/1, model 1/1 (extracts)
## i Fold08, Repeat3: preprocessor 1/1, model 1/1 (predictions)
## i Fold09, Repeat3: preprocessor 1/1
## ✓ Fold09, Repeat3: preprocessor 1/1
## i Fold09, Repeat3: preprocessor 1/1, model 1/1
## ✓ Fold09, Repeat3: preprocessor 1/1, model 1/1
## i Fold09, Repeat3: preprocessor 1/1, model 1/1 (extracts)
## i Fold09, Repeat3: preprocessor 1/1, model 1/1 (predictions)
## i Fold10, Repeat3: preprocessor 1/1
## ✓ Fold10, Repeat3: preprocessor 1/1
## i Fold10, Repeat3: preprocessor 1/1, model 1/1
## ✓ Fold10, Repeat3: preprocessor 1/1, model 1/1
## i Fold10, Repeat3: preprocessor 1/1, model 1/1 (extracts)
## i Fold10, Repeat3: preprocessor 1/1, model 1/1 (predictions)
## i Fold01, Repeat4: preprocessor 1/1
## ✓ Fold01, Repeat4: preprocessor 1/1
## i Fold01, Repeat4: preprocessor 1/1, model 1/1
## ✓ Fold01, Repeat4: preprocessor 1/1, model 1/1
## i Fold01, Repeat4: preprocessor 1/1, model 1/1 (extracts)
## i Fold01, Repeat4: preprocessor 1/1, model 1/1 (predictions)
## i Fold02, Repeat4: preprocessor 1/1
## ✓ Fold02, Repeat4: preprocessor 1/1
## i Fold02, Repeat4: preprocessor 1/1, model 1/1
## ✓ Fold02, Repeat4: preprocessor 1/1, model 1/1
## i Fold02, Repeat4: preprocessor 1/1, model 1/1 (extracts)
## i Fold02, Repeat4: preprocessor 1/1, model 1/1 (predictions)
## i Fold03, Repeat4: preprocessor 1/1
```

```
## ✓ Fold03, Repeat4: preprocessor 1/1
## i Fold03, Repeat4: preprocessor 1/1, model 1/1
## ✓ Fold03, Repeat4: preprocessor 1/1, model 1/1
## i Fold03, Repeat4: preprocessor 1/1, model 1/1 (extracts)
## i Fold03, Repeat4: preprocessor 1/1, model 1/1 (predictions)
## i Fold04, Repeat4: preprocessor 1/1
## ✓ Fold04, Repeat4: preprocessor 1/1
## i Fold04, Repeat4: preprocessor 1/1, model 1/1
## ✓ Fold04, Repeat4: preprocessor 1/1, model 1/1
## i Fold04, Repeat4: preprocessor 1/1, model 1/1 (extracts)
## i Fold04, Repeat4: preprocessor 1/1, model 1/1 (predictions)
## i Fold05, Repeat4: preprocessor 1/1
## ✓ Fold05, Repeat4: preprocessor 1/1
## i Fold05, Repeat4: preprocessor 1/1, model 1/1
## ✓ Fold05, Repeat4: preprocessor 1/1, model 1/1
## i Fold05, Repeat4: preprocessor 1/1, model 1/1 (extracts)
## i Fold05, Repeat4: preprocessor 1/1, model 1/1 (predictions)
## i Fold06, Repeat4: preprocessor 1/1
## ✓ Fold06, Repeat4: preprocessor 1/1
## i Fold06, Repeat4: preprocessor 1/1, model 1/1
## ✓ Fold06, Repeat4: preprocessor 1/1, model 1/1
## i Fold06, Repeat4: preprocessor 1/1, model 1/1 (extracts)
## i Fold06, Repeat4: preprocessor 1/1, model 1/1 (predictions)
## i Fold07, Repeat4: preprocessor 1/1
## ✓ Fold07, Repeat4: preprocessor 1/1
## i Fold07, Repeat4: preprocessor 1/1, model 1/1
## ✓ Fold07, Repeat4: preprocessor 1/1, model 1/1
## i Fold07, Repeat4: preprocessor 1/1, model 1/1 (extracts)
## i Fold07, Repeat4: preprocessor 1/1, model 1/1 (predictions)
## i Fold08, Repeat4: preprocessor 1/1
## ✓ Fold08, Repeat4: preprocessor 1/1
## i Fold08, Repeat4: preprocessor 1/1, model 1/1
```

```
## ✓ Fold08, Repeat4: preprocessor 1/1, model 1/1
## i Fold08, Repeat4: preprocessor 1/1, model 1/1 (extracts)
## i Fold08, Repeat4: preprocessor 1/1, model 1/1 (predictions)
## i Fold09, Repeat4: preprocessor 1/1
## ✓ Fold09, Repeat4: preprocessor 1/1
## i Fold09, Repeat4: preprocessor 1/1, model 1/1
## ✓ Fold09, Repeat4: preprocessor 1/1, model 1/1
## i Fold09, Repeat4: preprocessor 1/1, model 1/1 (extracts)
## i Fold09, Repeat4: preprocessor 1/1, model 1/1 (predictions)
## i Fold10, Repeat4: preprocessor 1/1
## ✓ Fold10, Repeat4: preprocessor 1/1
## i Fold10, Repeat4: preprocessor 1/1, model 1/1
## ✓ Fold10, Repeat4: preprocessor 1/1, model 1/1
## i Fold10, Repeat4: preprocessor 1/1, model 1/1 (extracts)
## i Fold10, Repeat4: preprocessor 1/1, model 1/1 (predictions)
## i Fold01, Repeat5: preprocessor 1/1
## ✓ Fold01, Repeat5: preprocessor 1/1
## i Fold01, Repeat5: preprocessor 1/1, model 1/1
## ✓ Fold01, Repeat5: preprocessor 1/1, model 1/1
## i Fold01, Repeat5: preprocessor 1/1, model 1/1 (extracts)
## i Fold01, Repeat5: preprocessor 1/1, model 1/1 (predictions)
## i Fold02, Repeat5: preprocessor 1/1
## ✓ Fold02, Repeat5: preprocessor 1/1
## i Fold02, Repeat5: preprocessor 1/1, model 1/1
## ✓ Fold02, Repeat5: preprocessor 1/1, model 1/1
## i Fold02, Repeat5: preprocessor 1/1, model 1/1 (extracts)
## i Fold02, Repeat5: preprocessor 1/1, model 1/1 (predictions)
## i Fold03, Repeat5: preprocessor 1/1
## ✓ Fold03, Repeat5: preprocessor 1/1
## i Fold03, Repeat5: preprocessor 1/1, model 1/1
## ✓ Fold03, Repeat5: preprocessor 1/1, model 1/1
## i Fold03, Repeat5: preprocessor 1/1, model 1/1 (extracts)
```

```
## i Fold03, Repeat5: preprocessor 1/1, model 1/1 (predictions)
## i Fold04, Repeat5: preprocessor 1/1
## ✓ Fold04, Repeat5: preprocessor 1/1
## i Fold04, Repeat5: preprocessor 1/1, model 1/1
## ✓ Fold04, Repeat5: preprocessor 1/1, model 1/1
## i Fold04, Repeat5: preprocessor 1/1, model 1/1 (extracts)
## i Fold04, Repeat5: preprocessor 1/1, model 1/1 (predictions)
## i Fold05, Repeat5: preprocessor 1/1
## ✓ Fold05, Repeat5: preprocessor 1/1
## i Fold05, Repeat5: preprocessor 1/1, model 1/1
## ✓ Fold05, Repeat5: preprocessor 1/1, model 1/1
## i Fold05, Repeat5: preprocessor 1/1, model 1/1 (extracts)
## i Fold05, Repeat5: preprocessor 1/1, model 1/1 (predictions)
## i Fold06, Repeat5: preprocessor 1/1
## ✓ Fold06, Repeat5: preprocessor 1/1
## i Fold06, Repeat5: preprocessor 1/1, model 1/1
## ✓ Fold06, Repeat5: preprocessor 1/1, model 1/1
## i Fold06, Repeat5: preprocessor 1/1, model 1/1 (extracts)
## i Fold06, Repeat5: preprocessor 1/1, model 1/1 (predictions)
## i Fold07, Repeat5: preprocessor 1/1
## ✓ Fold07, Repeat5: preprocessor 1/1
## i Fold07, Repeat5: preprocessor 1/1, model 1/1
## ✓ Fold07, Repeat5: preprocessor 1/1, model 1/1
## i Fold07, Repeat5: preprocessor 1/1, model 1/1 (extracts)
## i Fold07, Repeat5: preprocessor 1/1, model 1/1 (predictions)
## i Fold08, Repeat5: preprocessor 1/1
## ✓ Fold08, Repeat5: preprocessor 1/1
## i Fold08, Repeat5: preprocessor 1/1, model 1/1
## ✓ Fold08, Repeat5: preprocessor 1/1, model 1/1
## i Fold08, Repeat5: preprocessor 1/1, model 1/1 (extracts)
## i Fold08, Repeat5: preprocessor 1/1, model 1/1 (predictions)
## i Fold09, Repeat5: preprocessor 1/1
```

```
## ✓ Fold09, Repeat5: preprocessor 1/1
## i Fold09, Repeat5: preprocessor 1/1, model 1/1
## ✓ Fold09, Repeat5: preprocessor 1/1, model 1/1
## i Fold09, Repeat5: preprocessor 1/1, model 1/1 (extracts)
## i Fold09, Repeat5: preprocessor 1/1, model 1/1 (predictions)
## i Fold10, Repeat5: preprocessor 1/1
## ✓ Fold10, Repeat5: preprocessor 1/1
## i Fold10, Repeat5: preprocessor 1/1, model 1/1
## ✓ Fold10, Repeat5: preprocessor 1/1, model 1/1
## i Fold10, Repeat5: preprocessor 1/1, model 1/1 (extracts)
## i Fold10, Repeat5: preprocessor 1/1, model 1/1 (predictions)
rid_res
## # Tuning results
## # 10-fold cross-validation repeated 5 times using stratification
## # A tibble: 50 × 5
## splits id id2 .metrics .notes
## <list> <chr> <chr> <list> <list>
## 1 <split [1287/143]> Repeat1 Fold01 <tibble [50 × 5]> <tibble [0 × 3]>
## 2 <split [1287/143]> Repeat1 Fold02 <tibble [50 × 5]> <tibble [0 × 3]>
## 3 <split [1287/143]> Repeat1 Fold03 <tibble [50 × 5]> <tibble [0 × 3]>
## 4 <split [1287/143]> Repeat1 Fold04 <tibble [50 × 5]> <tibble [0 × 3]>
## 5 <split [1287/143]> Repeat1 Fold05 <tibble [50 × 5]> <tibble [0 × 3]>
## 6 <split [1287/143]> Repeat1 Fold06 <tibble [50 × 5]> <tibble [0 × 3]>
## 7 <split [1287/143]> Repeat1 Fold07 <tibble [50 × 5]> <tibble [0 × 3]>
## 8 <split [1287/143]> Repeat1 Fold08 <tibble [50 × 5]> <tibble [0 × 3]>
## 9 <split [1287/143]> Repeat1 Fold09 <tibble [50 × 5]> <tibble [0 × 3]>
## 10 <split [1287/143]> Repeat1 Fold10 <tibble [50 × 5]> <tibble [0 × 3]>
## # ℹ 40 more rows
```

- For every fold within each repeat or every resample is monitored during model fitting on it.

The resulting object "rid_res" contains 50 rows (for 50 resamples) and 5 columns:

- The splits column is a list of each combination of analysis and assessment data withing each resample. The sum is 1430, which are total rows of training data.
- The id column is an id column for the repeat number from 1 to 5.
- The id2 column is an id column for the fold number from 1 to 10 so we have 50 resamples because 5 × 10 = 50.
- The .metrics column is a list of performance metric (accuracy) of applying the ridge model to the corresponding assessment data (143 rows) within each resample. Each performance metric is saved in 50 rows and 5 columns [50 × 5] tibble or data frame. The 50 rows are for the accuracy of applying the 50 penalty values in the ridge model to the corresponding assessment data within each resample.
- The .notes column is a list of notes or warnings when applying the ridge model to each analysis data (1287 rows) within each resample. Each note is saved in 0 rows and 3 columns [0 × 3] tibble or data frame meaning that there are no rows or no notes when applying this model to each analysis data.

4.3.8. The Model Performance on 50 Resamples of the Training Data

To get the performance metric (accuracy) on the 50 resamples of training data using the 50 penalty values, we will use the unnest function with the ".metrics" argument to expand the .metrics list column of the rid_res object into rows and columns.

```
rid_res %>% unnest(.metrics)
## # A tibble: 2,500 × 9
## splits id id2 penalty .metric .estimator .estimate .config
## <list> <chr> <chr> <dbl> <chr> <chr> <dbl> <chr>
## 1 <split [1287/143]> Repea… Fold… 1 e-10 accura… multiclass 0.993
Prepro…
## 2 <split [1287/143]> Repea… Fold… 1.60e-10 accura… multiclass 0.993
Prepro…
## 3 <split [1287/143]> Repea… Fold… 2.56e-10 accura… multiclass 0.993
Prepro…
## 4 <split [1287/143]> Repea… Fold… 4.09e-10 accura… multiclass 0.993
Prepro…
```

5 <split [1287/143]> Repea... Fold... 6.55e-10 accura... multiclass 0.993 Prepro...

6 <split [1287/143]> Repea... Fold... 1.05e-9 accura... multiclass 0.993 Prepro...

7 <split [1287/143]> Repea... Fold... 1.68e-9 accura... multiclass 0.993 Prepro...

8 <split [1287/143]> Repea... Fold... 2.68e-9 accura... multiclass 0.993 Prepro...

9 <split [1287/143]> Repea... Fold... 4.29e-9 accura... multiclass 0.993 Prepro...

10 <split [1287/143]> Repea... Fold... 6.87e-9 accura... multiclass 0.993 Prepro...

i 2,490 more rows

i 1 more variable: .notes <list>

- The result is 2500 rows because we have applied the 50 penalties to 50 resamples of the training data so we have 50 × 50 = 2500 rows. Each row contains the accuracy of the ridge model on 1 resample using 1 penalty value. To get the mean accuracy of each penalty value on the 50 resamples of the training data, we use the following functions on the "rid_res" object:
- The collect_metrics function to get the mean accuracy for each penalty across the 50 resamples of the training data.
- The arrange function with mean argument to arrange by mean accuracy value in ascending order.
- The flextable, theme_box, and set_caption functions are described previously.

rid_res %>% **collect_metrics**() %>%

arrange(mean) %>%

flextable() %>% **theme_box**() %>%

set_caption(caption = "The mean accuracy of applying 50 penalties on 50 resamples of Flavia leaf training data when using ridge classification model")

The mean accuracy of applying 50 penalties on 50 resamples of Flavia leaf training data when using ridge classification model:

penalty	.metric	.estimator	mean	n	std_err	.config
1.0000000000000000	accuracy	multiclass	0.7127273	50	0.005615203	Preprocessor1_Model50
0.6250551925273976	accuracy	multiclass	0.8026573	50	0.005024051	Preprocessor1_Model49
0.3906939937054621	accuracy	multiclass	0.8654545	50	0.004523434	Preprocessor1_Model48
0.2442053094548655	accuracy	multiclass	0.9121678	50	0.004080818	Preprocessor1_Model47
0.1526417967175236	accuracy	multiclass	0.9363636	50	0.003438944	Preprocessor1_Model46
0.0954095476349996	accuracy	multiclass	0.9509091	50	0.002299786	Preprocessor1_Model45
0.0596362331659464	accuracy	multiclass	0.9622378	50	0.002372496	Preprocessor1_Model44
0.0372759372031494	accuracy	multiclass	0.9718881	50	0.002012832	Preprocessor1_Model43
0.0232995181051537	accuracy	multiclass	0.9783217	50	0.001898102	Preprocessor1_Model42
0.0000000001000000	accuracy	multiclass	0.9802797	50	0.001783602	Preprocessor1_Model01
0.0000000001599859	accuracy	multiclass	0.9802797	50	0.001783602	Preprocessor1_Model02
0.0000000002559548	accuracy	multiclass	0.9802797	50	0.001783602	Preprocessor1_Model03
0.0000000004094915	accuracy	multiclass	0.9802797	50	0.001783602	Preprocessor1_Model04
0.0000000006551286	accuracy	multiclass	0.9802797	50	0.001783602	Preprocessor1_Model05

0.0000000010481131	accu-racy	multi-class	0.9802797	50	0.001783602	Prepro-cessor1_Model06
0.0000000016768329	accu-racy	multi-class	0.9802797	50	0.001783602	Prepro-cessor1_Model07
0.0000000026826958	accu-racy	multi-class	0.9802797	50	0.001783602	Prepro-cessor1_Model08
0.0000000042919343	accu-racy	multi-class	0.9802797	50	0.001783602	Prepro-cessor1_Model09
0.0000000068664885	accu-racy	multi-class	0.9802797	50	0.001783602	Prepro-cessor1_Model10
0.0000000109854114	accu-racy	multi-class	0.9802797	50	0.001783602	Prepro-cessor1_Model11
0.0000000175751062	accu-racy	multi-class	0.9802797	50	0.001783602	Prepro-cessor1_Model12
0.0000000281176870	accu-racy	multi-class	0.9802797	50	0.001783602	Prepro-cessor1_Model13
0.0000000449843267	accu-racy	multi-class	0.9802797	50	0.001783602	Prepro-cessor1_Model14
0.0000000719685673	accu-racy	multi-class	0.9802797	50	0.001783602	Prepro-cessor1_Model15
0.0000001151395399	accu-racy	multi-class	0.9802797	50	0.001783602	Prepro-cessor1_Model16
0.0000001842069969	accu-racy	multi-class	0.9802797	50	0.001783602	Prepro-cessor1_Model17
0.0000002947051703	accu-racy	multi-class	0.9802797	50	0.001783602	Prepro-cessor1_Model18
0.0000004714866363	accu-racy	multi-class	0.9802797	50	0.001783602	Prepro-cessor1_Model19
0.0000007543120063	accu-racy	multi-class	0.9802797	50	0.001783602	Prepro-cessor1_Model20

0.0000012067926406	accu-racy	multi-class	0.9802797	50	0.001783602	Prepro-cessor1_Model21
0.0000019306977289	accu-racy	multi-class	0.9802797	50	0.001783602	Prepro-cessor1_Model22
0.0000030888435965	accu-racy	multi-class	0.9802797	50	0.001783602	Prepro-cessor1_Model23
0.0000049417133613	accu-racy	multi-class	0.9802797	50	0.001783602	Prepro-cessor1_Model24
0.0000079060432109	accu-racy	multi-class	0.9802797	50	0.001783602	Prepro-cessor1_Model25
0.0000126485521686	accu-racy	multi-class	0.9802797	50	0.001783602	Prepro-cessor1_Model26
0.0000202358964773	accu-racy	multi-class	0.9802797	50	0.001783602	Prepro-cessor1_Model27
0.0000323745754282	accu-racy	multi-class	0.9802797	50	0.001783602	Prepro-cessor1_Model28
0.0000517947467923	accu-racy	multi-class	0.9802797	50	0.001783602	Prepro-cessor1_Model29
0.0000828642772855	accu-racy	multi-class	0.9802797	50	0.001783602	Prepro-cessor1_Model30
0.0001325711365590	accu-racy	multi-class	0.9802797	50	0.001783602	Prepro-cessor1_Model31
0.0002120950887920	accu-racy	multi-class	0.9802797	50	0.001783602	Prepro-cessor1_Model32
0.0003393221771895	accu-racy	multi-class	0.9802797	50	0.001783602	Prepro-cessor1_Model33
0.0005428675439324	accu-racy	multi-class	0.9802797	50	0.001783602	Prepro-cessor1_Model34
0.0008685113737514	accu-racy	multi-class	0.9802797	50	0.001783602	Prepro-cessor1_Model35

0.0013894954943731	accuracy	multiclass	0.9802797	50	0.001783602	Preprocessor1_Model36
0.0022229964825262	accuracy	multiclass	0.9802797	50	0.001783602	Preprocessor1_Model37
0.0035564803062231	accuracy	multiclass	0.9802797	50	0.001783602	Preprocessor1_Model38
0.0056898660290183	accuracy	multiclass	0.9802797	50	0.001783602	Preprocessor1_Model39
0.0091029817799152	accuracy	multiclass	0.9802797	50	0.001783602	Preprocessor1_Model40
0.0145634847750124	accuracy	multiclass	0.9802797	50	0.001783602	Preprocessor1_Model41

- The result is 50 rows with 1 mean accuracy value for each penalty across the 50 resamples (n = 50).
- The lowest accuracy (0.71) was achieved when using 1.00 penalty with the highest standard error (0.0056) indicating high variability between the 50 resamples in the accuracy value.
- The highest accuracy (0.98) was achieved when using many penalty values (0.0000000001, 0.00000000016, etc.) with the lowest standard error (0.0018) indicating low variability between the 50 resamples in the accuracy value.

We can plot the 50 mean accuracy values from the 50 penalties by using the following functions after the collect_metrics function:

- The ggplot function with the argument aes(x = penalty, y = mean) to plot the penalty on the x-axis and the mean accuracy value on the y-axis.
- The geom_errorbar function with the argument aes(ymin = mean–std_err, ymax = mean + std_err) to plot an error bar that represents mean–standard error at the lower end and the mean+ standard error at the upper end.
- The geom_line function to connect the 50 mean values by a line.
- The scale_x_log10() to plot the x-axis values after being log transformed with the base 10.

1. The labs function with title = "…" argument to add a plot title. We use the "\n" inside the title to make it into 2 lines. Also, we use the y argument to add a y-axis title.
   - The theme_classic function as explained before.

rid_res **%>% collect_metrics**() **%>%**

ggplot(**aes**(x = penalty, y = mean)) +

geom_errorbar(**aes**(ymin = mean–std_err, ymax = mean + std_err)) +

geom_line() + **scale_x_log10**()+

labs(title = "The mean accuracy ± standard error of 50 penalties across 50 resamples of Flavia leaf**\n** training data when using the ridge classification model", y = "mean accuracy")+

theme_classic()

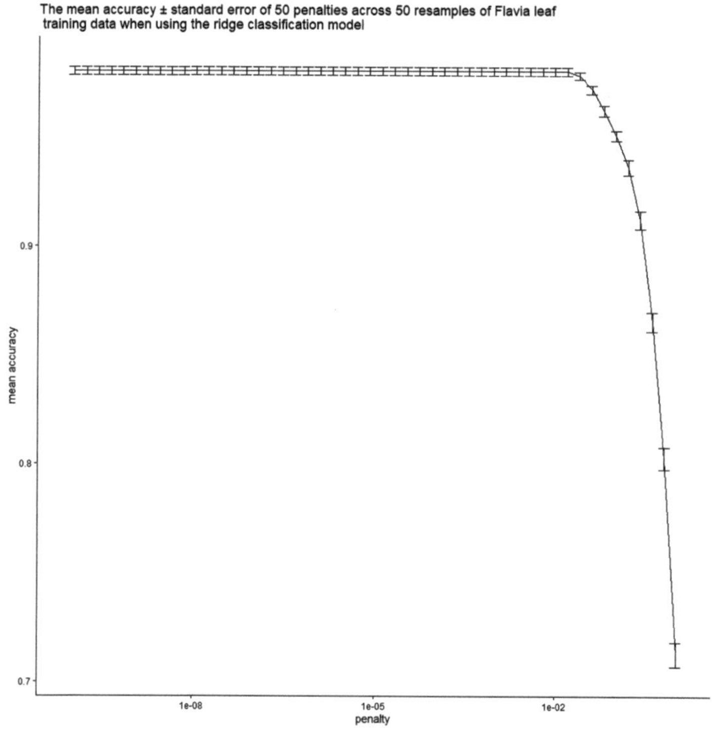

- As we have seen before, some penalties have the highest accuracy of 0.98 or 98% with the lowest standard error.

We can use the select_best function to create an object "best_pen" that contains the best penalty value for the best ridge model.

```
best_pen<-rid_res %>% select_best()
best_pen
## # A tibble: 1 × 2
## penalty .config
## <dbl> <chr>
## 1 0.0000000001 Preprocessor1_Model01
```

- Because many penalties have the same highest accuracy, the function selects the 1st penalty of these penalties = 0.0000000001.

To get the final workflow with the best penalty, we use the finalize_workflow function with the arguments:

- wflow which is the original workflow with tuned penalty.
- best_pen which is the data of 1 row containing the best penalty value.

The resulting workflow "rid_final" is the final workflow containing the best penalty.

```
rid_final <- finalize_workflow(wflow, best_pen)
rid_final
## ══ Workflow ═════════════════════════════════════════════════
## Preprocessor: Recipe
## Model: multinom_reg()
##
## ── Preprocessor ─────────────────────────────────────────────
## 3 Recipe Steps
##
## • step_dummy()
## • step_nzv()
## • step_normalize()
##
## ── Model ────────────────────────────────────────────────────
## Multinomial Regression Model Specification (classification)
```

```
##
## Main Arguments:
## penalty = 1e-10
## mixture = 0
##
## Computational engine: glmnet
```

- The rid_final workflow contains the best penalty of 0.0000000001 or 1e-10.

Then, we create the final rid_fit model by using the fit function with the arguments:

- rid_final which is the final workflow containing 3 preprocessing steps and the linear ridge model with best penalty value.
- train_leaf which is the whole training data with 1430 rows.

```
rid_fit <- fit(rid_final, data = train_leaf)
```

To see some model results, we use the following functions on rid_fit model:

- The extract_fit_parsnip function to extract the model specifications.
- The tidy function to convert the result to a data frame.

```
rid_fit %>% extract_fit_parsnip() %>%
tidy()
## # A tibble: 1,952 × 4
## class term estimate penalty
## <chr> <chr> <dbl> <dbl>
## 1 anhui_barberry (Intercept) 0.116 0.0000000001
## 2 anhui_barberry skewed_polar –0.00303 0.0000000001
## 3 anhui_barberry clumpy_polar –0.0251 0.0000000001
## 4 anhui_barberry sparse_polar –0.0506 0.0000000001
## 5 anhui_barberry striated_polar –0.0599 0.0000000001
## 6 anhui_barberry convex_polar –0.0211 0.0000000001
## 7 anhui_barberry skinny_polar 0.103 0.0000000001
## 8 anhui_barberry stringy_polar –0.104 0.0000000001
## 9 anhui_barberry monotonic_polar –0.0750 0.0000000001
## 10 anhui_barberry skewed_contour 0.0605 0.0000000001
## # i 1,942 more rows
```

- We have an estimate for 60 predictors (after preprocessing) with the intercept for every class or species of 32 species so we have 61 × 32 = 1952 rows.

To get the most important predictor for every species, we use the following functions:

- The filter function with the argument !term=="(Intercept)" to remove rows containing the intercept in the term column.
- The group_by function with the class argument to split the result to 32 data each containing a single class or species.
- The slice_max function with the arguments abs(estimate) and n = 1 to select the highest row of absolute estimate for each species.
- The arrange function with the argument term to arrange the result by the term (predictor) column so we see which predictor is important for most species.

```
rid_fit %>% extract_fit_parsnip() %>%
broom::tidy() %>% filter(!term=="(Intercept)") %>%
group_by(class) %>% slice_max(abs(estimate), n = 1) %>%
arrange(term) %>%
flextable(cwidth = 1.5) %>% theme_box() %>%
set_caption(caption = "The most important predictor for every species in the Flavia leaf training data when using ridge classification")
```

The most important predictor for every species in the Flavia leaf training data when using ridge classification:

class	term	estimate	penalty
castor_aralia	apex_acute	0.3632637	0.0000000001
japanese_viburnum	apex_acute	0.6787414	0.0000000001
nanmu	apex_acute	0.9948983	0.0000000001
trident_maple	apex_acute	0.3397143	0.0000000001
big_fruited_holly	apex_apicu-late	0.4321472	0.0000000001
chinese_cinnamon	apex_apicu-late	0.8527706	0.0000000001
chinese_horse_chest-nut	apex_apicu-late	0.6980017	0.0000000001
anhui_barberry	apex_none	0.5600081	0.0000000001
goldenrain_tree	apex_none	0.4998168	0.0000000001

glossy_privet	apex_obtuse	0.7950226	0.0000000001
southern_magnolia	apex_obtuse	0.7398142	0.0000000001
crape_myrtle	apex_round	0.7375426	0.0000000001
japanese_cheesewood	apex_round	0.8484348	0.0000000001
camphortree	base_acute	0.5189905	0.0000000001
japanese_flower-ing_cherry	base_acute	0.6370884	0.0000000001
pubescent_bamboo	base_acute	0.9189620	0.0000000001
sweet_osmanthus	base_acute	0.5097132	0.0000000001
oleander	base_none	–0.4939111	0.0000000001
peach	base_none	–0.5819253	0.0000000001
yew_plum_pine	base_none	–0.4320230	0.0000000001
deodar	compactness	0.4386025	0.0000000001
chinese_tulip_tree	lobed_edge_yes	0.4437856	0.0000000001
tangerine	lobed_edge_yes	0.5731864	0.0000000001
japanese_maple	perimeter_ra-tio_lw	0.4258527	0.0000000001
true_indigo	rectangular-ity	0.3872608	0.0000000001
canadian_poplar	shape_heart_shape	0.5754220	0.0000000001
chinese_redbud	shape_heart_shape	0.5727531	0.0000000001
beale_s_barberry	shape_round	0.7147374	0.0000000001
ginkgo_maidenhair_tree	shape_round	0.6731494	0.0000000001
ford_woodlotus	shape_sim-ple_round	0.5663693	0.0000000001
wintersweet	shape_sim-ple_round	0.3983877	0.0000000001
chinese_toon	toothed_edge_yes	0.6465181	0.0000000001

- The apex categorical predictor is most important for many species:

1. castor_aralia, japanese_viburnum, nanmu, trident_maple where the apex_acute is the most important.

2. big_fruited_holly, chinese_cinnamon, chinese_horse_chestnut where the apex_apiculate is the most important.
3. anhui_barberry, goldenrain_tree where apex_none is the most important.
4. glossy_privet, southern_magnolia where apex_obtuse is the most important.
5. crape_myrtle, japanese_cheesewood where apex_round is the most important.

To get the least important predictor for every species, we use the same above functions except using slice_min instead of using slice_max with the same arguments.

rid_fit **%>% extract_fit_parsnip**() **%>%**

broom**::tidy**() **%>% filter**(**!**term==“(Intercept)”) **%>%**

group_by(class) **%>% slice_min**(**abs**(estimate), n = 1) **%>%**

arrange(term) **%>%**

flextable(cwidth = 1.5) **%>% theme_box**() **%>%**

set_caption(caption = “The least important predictor for every species in the Flavia leaf training data when using ridge classification”)

The least important predictor for every species in the Flavia leaf training data when using ridge classification:

class	term	estimate	penalty
japanese_maple	apex_obtuse	–0.0008922743	0.0000000001
chinese_cinnamon	clumpy_contour	–0.0040257604	0.0000000001
ford_woodlotus	compactness	0.0021231230	0.0000000001
trident_maple	contrast	–0.0015898768	0.0000000001
castor_aralia	convex_contour	–0.0025360943	0.0000000001
chinese_toon	convex_contour	0.0005375024	0.0000000001
deodar	convex_contour	–0.0015064881	0.0000000001
beale_s_barberry	eccentriciry	–0.0038156088	0.0000000001

camphortree	inverse_difference_moments	–0.0062050210	0.0000000001
wintersweet	mean_green_val	0.0058262470	0.0000000001
chinese_redbud	mean_red_val	0.0003356853	0.0000000001
nanmu	mean_red_val	0.0018833584	0.0000000001
big_fruited_holly	monotonic_polar	0.0012813613	0.0000000001
chinese_horse_chestnut	narrow_factor	–0.0036362478	0.0000000001
sweet_osmanthus	narrow_factor	–0.0006390836	0.0000000001
goldenrain_tree	perimeter_ratio_diameter	0.0015241621	0.0000000001
japanese_viburnum	physiological_width	–0.0001561155	0.0000000001
tangerine	physiological_width	–0.0002666446	0.0000000001
oleander	shape_heart_shape	–0.0052252024	0.0000000001
pubescent_bamboo	shape_heart_shape	–0.0019259186	0.0000000001
yew_plum_pine	shape_heart_shape	–0.0004021329	0.0000000001
anhui_barberry	skewed_polar	–0.0030325892	0.0000000001
crape_myrtle	skewed_polar	0.0032290094	0.0000000001
japanese_flowering_cherry	skewed_polar	–0.0001690952	0.0000000001
canadian_poplar	skinny_polar	0.0041769030	0.0000000001
japanese_cheesewood	striated_contour	0.0011691561	0.0000000001

chinese_tu-lip_tree	striated_po-lar	0.0043767930	0.0000000001
ginkgo_maidenhair_tree	striated_po-lar	0.0011061585	0.0000000001
glossy_privet	striated_po-lar	0.0050732601	0.0000000001
southern_magnolia	striated_po-lar	–0.0003532701	0.0000000001
peach	stringy_polar	0.0005528518	0.0000000001
true_indigo	stringy_polar	–0.0018864780	0.0000000001

To see the model accuracy on the whole training data, we use the following functions on the rid_fit model:

- The predict function with the argument new_data = train_leaf to get the predicted leaf species (.pred_class column) for each row of the training data after being preprocessed using the rid_fit model.
- The mutate function with the argument truth = train_leaf$species to add a truth column containing the actual species for each row in the training data.
- The accuracy function with the arguments truth = truth, estimate = .pred_class to get the accuracy of applying this ridge model on the training data using the actual and predicted species columns.

```
rid_fit %>% predict(new_data = train_leaf) %>%
mutate(truth = train_leaf$species) %>%
accuracy(truth = truth, estimate = .pred_class)
## # A tibble: 1 × 3
## .metric .estimator .estimate
## <chr> <chr> <dbl>
## 1 accuracy multiclass 0.988
```

- The accuracy of the ridge model on training data = 0.988 or 98.8%.

4.3.9. Model Performance on Testing Data

To get the model accuracy on the testing data, we use the same above functions on the rid_fit model but using the test_leaf data.

```
rid_fit %>% predict(new_data = test_leaf) %>%
mutate(truth = test_leaf$species) %>%
```

```
accuracy(truth = truth, estimate = .pred_class)
## # A tibble: 1 × 3
## .metric .estimator .estimate
## <chr> <chr> <dbl>
## 1 accuracy multiclass 0.981
```

- The accuracy of the ridge model on testing data = 0.981 or 98.1%. To see how many actual species are predicted correctly, we create a confusion matrix by using the conf_mat function instead of the accuracy function with the same arguments.
- The result will be 32 true species in columns and the predicted 32 species are in rows, so we use the autoplot function with the argument "heatmap" to plot it as a heatmap. We add a plot title using the labs function.
- We also use the theme function with the argument axis.text.x = element_text(angle = 60, hjust = 1) to plot the x-axis text at an angle of 60 with 1 horizontal justification.

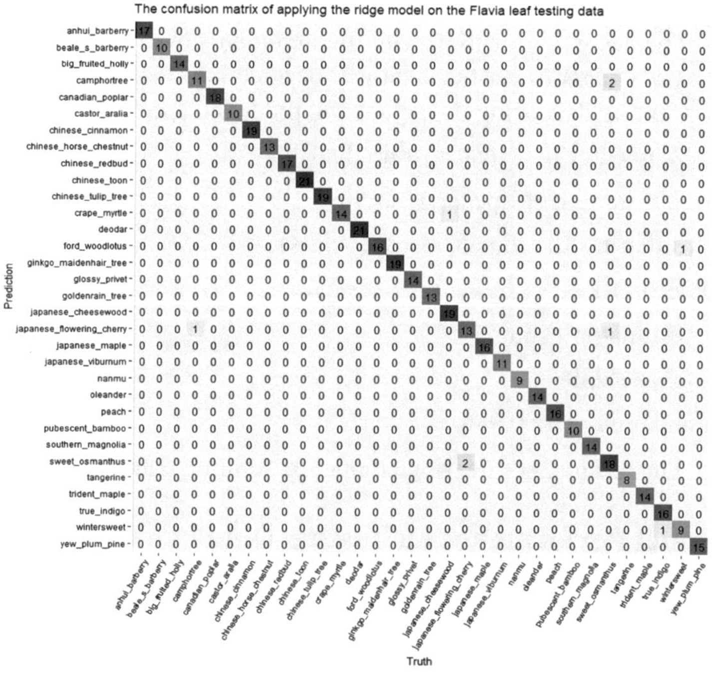


```
rid_fit %>% predict(new_data = test_leaf) %>%
```

mutate(truth = test_leaf$species) %>%

conf_mat(truth = truth, estimate = .pred_class) %>%

autoplot(type = "heatmap")+

labs(title = "The confusion matrix of applying the ridge model on the Flavia leaf testing data")+

theme(axis.text.x = **element_text**(angle = 60, hjust = 1))

- Most species are predicted correctly:
- There are 17 anhui_barberry rows that are predicted correctly.
- There are 10 beale_s_barberry rows that are predicted correctly.
- There are 14 big_fruited_holly rows that are predicted correctly.
- There are 11 camphortree rows that are predicted correctly and 1 camphortree row that is predicted incorrectly as japanese_flowering_cherry.
- There are 18 canadian_poplar rows that are predicted correctly.
- There are 10 castor_aralia rows that are predicted correctly.
- There are 19 chinese_cinnamon rows that are predicted correctly.
- There are 13 chinese_horse_chestnut rows that are predicted correctly.
- There are 17 chinese_redbud rows that are predicted correctly.
- There are 21 chinese_toon rows that are predicted correctly.
- There are 19 chinese_tulip_tree rows that are predicted correctly.
- There are 14 crape_myrtle rows that are predicted correctly.
- There are 21 deodar rows that are predicted correctly.
- There are 16 ford_woodlotus rows that are predicted correctly.
- There are 19 ginkgo_maidenhair_tree rows that are predicted correctly.
- There are 14 glossy_privet rows that are predicted correctly.
- There are 13 goldenrain_tree rows that are predicted correctly.
- There are 19 japanese_cheesewood rows that are predicted correctly and 1 row predicted incorrectly as crape_myrtle.

- There are 13 japanese_flowering_cherry rows that are predicted correctly and 2 rows predicted incorrectly as sweet_osmanthus.
- There are 16 japanese_maple rows that are predicted correctly.
- There are 11 japanese_viburnum rows that are predicted correctly.
- There are 9 nanmu rows that are predicted correctly.
- There are 14 oleander rows that are predicted correctly.
- There are 16 peach rows that are predicted correctly.
- There are 10 pubescent_bamboo rows that are predicted correctly.
- There are 14 southern_magnolia rows that are predicted correctly.
- There are 18 sweet_osmanthus rows that are predicted correctly, 2 rows predicted incorrectly as camphortree, and 1 row predicted incorrectly as japanese_flowering_cherry.
- There are 8 tangerine rows that are predicted correctly.
- There are 14 trident_maple rows that are predicted correctly.
- There are 16 true_indigo rows that are predicted correctly and 1 row predicted incorrectly as wintersweet.
- There are 9 wintersweet rows that are predicted correctly and 1 row predicted incorrectly as ford_woodlotus.
- There are 15 yew_plum_pine rows that are predicted correctly.

4.4. LASSO CLASSIFICATION

We will use the same steps and outputs of ridge classification till defining the machine learning (ML) model.

4.4.1. Define Machine Learning (ML) Model

We define a multinomial classification model by using the functions:

- The multinom_reg function to define the multinomial classification model type with the following arguments:
  - mixture = 1 to indicate a lasso classification model.
  - penalty = tune() to tune the penalty term on the different resamples of training data.

- The set_engine function with the argument "glmnet" to define the engine that will use the glmnet function from the glmnet package.
- The set_mode function with the argument "classification" to define the mode of learning. We use classification because we have a categorical outcome (species).
- All the 3 functions are applied in sequence using the piping "%>%" operator and the resulting object is called "lasso_model."

```
lasso_model <- multinom_reg(mixture = 1, penalty = tune()) %>%
set_engine("glmnet") %>%
set_mode("classification")
lasso_model
## Multinomial Regression Model Specification (classification)
##
## Main Arguments:
## penalty = tune()
## mixture = 1
##
## Computational engine: glmnet
```

4.4.2. Generate Workflow

We create the "wflow2" object by using the following functions:

- The workflow function to create a workflow.
- The add_recipe function with the argument "rec" to add the above created recipe with 3 preprocessing steps.
- The add_model function with the argument lasso_model to add the above created lasso model.

```
wflow2 <- workflow() %>%
add_recipe(rec) %>%
add_model(lasso_model)
wflow2
## ══ Workflow ════════════════════════════════════════════════
════════════════════════════════════════

## Preprocessor: Recipe
## Model: multinom_reg()
```

```
##
## —— Preprocessor ————————————————————————————————
## 3 Recipe Steps
##
## • step_dummy()
## • step_nzv()
## • step_normalize()
##
## —— Model ————————————————————————————————
## Multinomial Regression Model Specification (classification)
##
## Main Arguments:
## penalty = tune()
## mixture = 1
##
## Computational engine: glmnet
```

- The "wflow2" object contains 3 preprocessing steps and the multinomial classification model with 1 mixture and tuned penalty (lasso model).

4.4.3. Fit Model on Different Resamples with Tuning

We use the "my_grid" created above that contains 50 different penalty values.

Then we use the tune_grid function with the arguments:

- wflow2 which is the workflow containing 3 preprocessing steps and the linear lasso model.
- folds which are the 50 resamples of training data created above.
- metrics = metrics_set(accuracy) to get the accuracy of the linear lasso model on each resample using the 50 penalty values.
- grid = my_grid to use the 50 penalty values in the my_grid data in tuning.

```
set.seed(123)
lasso_res <- tune_grid(wflow2, folds,
```

```
metrics = metric_set(accuracy),
grid = my_grid)
lasso_res
## # Tuning results
## # 10-fold cross-validation repeated 5 times using stratification
## # A tibble: 50 × 5
## splits id id2 .metrics .notes
## <list> <chr> <chr> <list> <list>
## 1 <split [1287/143]> Repeat1 Fold01 <tibble [50 × 5]> <tibble [0 × 3]>
## 2 <split [1287/143]> Repeat1 Fold02 <tibble [50 × 5]> <tibble [0 × 3]>
## 3 <split [1287/143]> Repeat1 Fold03 <tibble [50 × 5]> <tibble [0 × 3]>
## 4 <split [1287/143]> Repeat1 Fold04 <tibble [50 × 5]> <tibble [0 × 3]>
## 5 <split [1287/143]> Repeat1 Fold05 <tibble [50 × 5]> <tibble [0 × 3]>
## 6 <split [1287/143]> Repeat1 Fold06 <tibble [50 × 5]> <tibble [0 × 3]>
## 7 <split [1287/143]> Repeat1 Fold07 <tibble [50 × 5]> <tibble [0 × 3]>
## 8 <split [1287/143]> Repeat1 Fold08 <tibble [50 × 5]> <tibble [0 × 3]>
## 9 <split [1287/143]> Repeat1 Fold09 <tibble [50 × 5]> <tibble [0 × 3]>
## 10 <split [1287/143]> Repeat1 Fold10 <tibble [50 × 5]> <tibble [0 × 3]>
## # ℹ 40 more rows
```

The resulting object "lasso_res" contains 50 rows (for 50 resamples) and 5 columns:

- The splits column is a list of each combination of analysis and assessment data withing each resample. The sum is 1430, which are total rows of training data.
- The id column is an id column for the repeat number from 1 to 5.
- The id2 column is an id column for the fold number from 1 to 10 so we have 50 resamples because 5 × 10 = 50.
- The .metrics column is a list of performance metric (accuracy) of applying the lasso model to the corresponding assessment data (143 rows) within each resample. Each performance metric is saved in 50 rows and 5 columns [50 × 5] tibble or data frame. The 50 rows are for the accuracy of applying the 50 penalty values in the lasso model to the corresponding assessment data within each resample.
- The .notes column is a list of notes or warnings when applying the lasso model to each analysis data (1287 rows) within each resample.

Each note is saved in 0 rows and 3 columns [0 × 3] tibble or data frame meaning that there are no rows or no notes when applying this model to each analysis data.

4.4.4. The Model Performance on 50 Resamples of the Training Data

To get the performance metric (accuracy) on the 50 resamples of training data using the 50 penalty values, we will use the unnest function with the ".metrics" argument to expand the .metrics list column of the lasso_res object into rows and columns.

lasso_res **%>%** **unnest**(.metrics)

A tibble: 2,500 × 9

splits id id2 penalty .metric .estimator .estimate .config

<list> <chr> <chr> <dbl> <chr> <chr> <dbl> <chr>

1 <split [1287/143]> Repea... Fold... 1 e-10 accura... multiclass 0.993 Prepro...

2 <split [1287/143]> Repea... Fold... 1.60e-10 accura... multiclass 0.993 Prepro...

3 <split [1287/143]> Repea... Fold... 2.56e-10 accura... multiclass 0.993 Prepro...

4 <split [1287/143]> Repea... Fold... 4.09e-10 accura... multiclass 0.993 Prepro...

5 <split [1287/143]> Repea... Fold... 6.55e-10 accura... multiclass 0.993 Prepro...

6 <split [1287/143]> Repea... Fold... 1.05e-9 accura... multiclass 0.993 Prepro...

7 <split [1287/143]> Repea... Fold... 1.68e-9 accura... multiclass 0.993 Prepro...

8 <split [1287/143]> Repea... Fold... 2.68e-9 accura... multiclass 0.993 Prepro...

9 <split [1287/143]> Repea... Fold... 4.29e-9 accura... multiclass 0.993 Prepro...

10 <split [1287/143]> Repea... Fold... 6.87e-9 accura... multiclass 0.993 Prepro...

i 2,490 more rows

i 1 more variable: .notes <list>

- The result is 2500 rows because we have applied the 50 penalties to 50 resamples of the training data so we have 50 × 50 = 2500 rows. Each row contains the accuracy of the lasso model on 1 resample using 1 penalty value.

To get the mean accuracy of each penalty value on the 50 resamples of the training data, we use the following functions on the "lasso_res" object:

- The collect_metrics function to get the mean accuracy for each penalty across the 50 resamples of the training data.
- The arrange function with mean argument to arrange by mean accuracy value in ascending order.
- The flextable, theme_box, and set_caption functions are described previously.

lasso_res **%>% collect_metrics() %>%**

arrange(mean) **%>%**

flextable() %>% theme_box() %>%

set_caption(caption = "The mean accuracy of applying 50 penalties on 50 resamples of Flavia leaf training data when using lasso classification model")

The mean accuracy of applying 50 penalties on 50 resamples of Flavia leaf training data when using lasso classification model:

penalty	.metric	.estimator	mean	n	std_err	.config
0.2442053094548655	accuracy	multiclass	0.02181818	50	0.001289292	Preprocessor1_Model47
0.3906939937054621	accuracy	multiclass	0.02181818	50	0.001289292	Preprocessor1_Model48
0.6250551925273976	accuracy	multiclass	0.02181818	50	0.001289292	Preprocessor1_Model49
1.0000000000000000	accuracy	multiclass	0.02181818	50	0.001289292	Preprocessor1_Model50
0.1526417967175236	accuracy	multiclass	0.06433566	50	0.002312855	Preprocessor1_Model46
0.0954095476349996	accuracy	multiclass	0.25664336	50	0.005863549	Preprocessor1_Model45
0.0596362331659464	accuracy	multiclass	0.47090909	50	0.006580103	Preprocessor1_Model44
0.0372759372031494	accuracy	multiclass	0.79762238	50	0.004992647	Preprocessor1_Model43
0.0232995181051537	accuracy	multiclass	0.87734266	50	0.003241508	Preprocessor1_Model42
0.0145634847750124	accuracy	multiclass	0.94685315	50	0.002495504	Preprocessor1_Model41
0.0091029817799152	accuracy	multiclass	0.96000000	50	0.002381229	Preprocessor1_Model40
0.0056898660290183	accuracy	multiclass	0.97286713	50	0.002024204	Preprocessor1_Model39
0.0035564803062231	accuracy	multiclass	0.98167832	50	0.001717468	Preprocessor1_Model38
0.0022229964825262	accuracy	multiclass	0.98475524	50	0.001726741	Preprocessor1_Model37
0.0013894954943731	accuracy	multiclass	0.98727273	50	0.001655933	Preprocessor1_Model36

0.000 86851 13737514	accu-racy	multi-class	0.98881119	50	0.0015 85865	Preprocessor1_ Model35
0.000 542867 5439324	accu-racy	multi-class	0.99076923	50	0.001 446862	Preprocessor1_ Model34
0.0003 3932217 71895	accu-racy	multi-class	0.99146853	50	0.0013 14588	Preprocessor1_ Model33
0.000 21209508 87920	accu-racy	multi-class	0.99202797	50	0.001 263805	Preprocessor1_ Model32
0.0001 3257113 65590	accu-racy	multi-class	0.99230769	50	0.001 202957	Preprocessor1_ Model31
0.0000 828642 772855	accu-racy	multi-class	0.99244755	50	0.0012 12707	Preprocessor1_ Model30
0.00 0000 000100 0000	accu-racy	multi-class	0.99272727	50	0.0012 31003	Preprocessor1_ Model01
0.00 000 00001 599859	accu-racy	multi-class	0.99272727	50	0.0012 31003	Preprocessor1_ Model02
0.0 00000 000255 9548	accu-racy	multi-class	0.99272727	50	0.00123 1003	Preprocessor1_ Model03
0.000 000000 4094915	accu-racy	multi-class	0.99272727	50	0.001 231003	Preprocessor1_ Model04
0.00 00000 006551 286	accu-racy	multi-class	0.99272727	50	0.001 231003	Preprocessor1_ Model05
0.00 0000001 0481131	accu-racy	multi-class	0.99272727	50	0.00123 1003	Preprocessor1_ Model06

0.00000000016768329	accuracy	multiclass	0.99272727	50	0.001231003	Preprocessor1_Model07
0.00000000026826958	accuracy	multiclass	0.99272727	50	0.001231003	Preprocessor1_Model08
0.000000042919343	accuracy	multiclass	0.99272727	50	0.001231003	Preprocessor1_Model09
0.0000000068664885	accuracy	multiclass	0.99272727	50	0.001231003	Preprocessor1_Model10
0.0000000109854114	accuracy	multiclass	0.99272727	50	0.001231003	Preprocessor1_Model11
0.0000000175751062	accuracy	multiclass	0.99272727	50	0.001231003	Preprocessor1_Model12
0.0000000281176870	accuracy	multiclass	0.99272727	50	0.001231003	Preprocessor1_Model13
0.0000000449843267	accuracy	multiclass	0.99272727	50	0.001231003	Preprocessor1_Model14
0.0000000719685673	accuracy	multiclass	0.99272727	50	0.001231003	Preprocessor1_Model15
0.0000001151395399	accuracy	multiclass	0.99272727	50	0.001231003	Preprocessor1_Model16
0.0000001842069969	accuracy	multiclass	0.99272727	50	0.001231003	Preprocessor1_Model17

0.000 0002 94705 1703	accu-racy	multi-class	0.99272727	50	0.001 231003	Preprocessor1_ Model18
0.000 00047 148663 63	accu-racy	multi-class	0.99272727	50	0.001 231003	Preprocessor1_ Model19
0.000 000754 3120063	accu-racy	multi-class	0.99272727	50	0.0012 31003	Preprocessor1_ Model20
0.00 000120 67926406	accu-racy	multi-class	0.99272727	50	0.001 231003	Preprocessor1_ Model21
0.00 000193 06977289	accu-racy	multi-class	0.99272727	50	0.0012 31003	Preprocessor1_ Model22
0.0000 030888 435965	accu-racy	multi-class	0.99272727	50	0.001 231003	Preprocessor1_ Model23
0.000 004941 7133613	accu-racy	multi-class	0.99272727	50	0.0012 31003	Preprocessor1_ Model24
0.00 00079 060432109	accu-racy	multi-class	0.99272727	50	0.001 231003	Preprocessor1_ Model25
0.0000 126485 521686	accu-racy	multi-class	0.99272727	50	0.0012 31003	Preprocessor1_ Model26
0.000 0202358 964773	accu-racy	multi-class	0.99272727	50	0.0012 31003	Preprocessor1_ Model27
0.00 003237 45754282	accu-racy	multi-class	0.99272727	50	0.0012 31003	Preprocessor1_ Model28
0.000 0517947 467923	accu-racy	multi-class	0.99272727	50	0.00 1231003	Preprocessor1_ Model29

- The result is 50 rows with 1 mean accuracy value for each penalty across the 50 resamples (n = 50).

- The lowest accuracy (0.022) was achieved when using 0.24, 0.39, 0.63, or 1.00 penalties.
- The highest accuracy (0.993) was achieved when using many penalty values (0.0000000001, 0.00000000016, etc.).

We can plot the 50 mean accuracy values from the 50 penalties by using the same functions described in the ridge classification.

lasso_res **%>% collect_metrics**() **%>%**

ggplot(**aes**(x = penalty, y = mean)) +

geom_errorbar(**aes**(ymin = mean–std_err, ymax = mean + std_err)) +

geom_line() + **scale_x_log10**()+

labs(title = "The mean accuracy ± standard error of 50 penalties across 50 resamples of Flavia leaf**n** training data when using the lasso classification model", y = "mean accuracy")+

theme_classic()

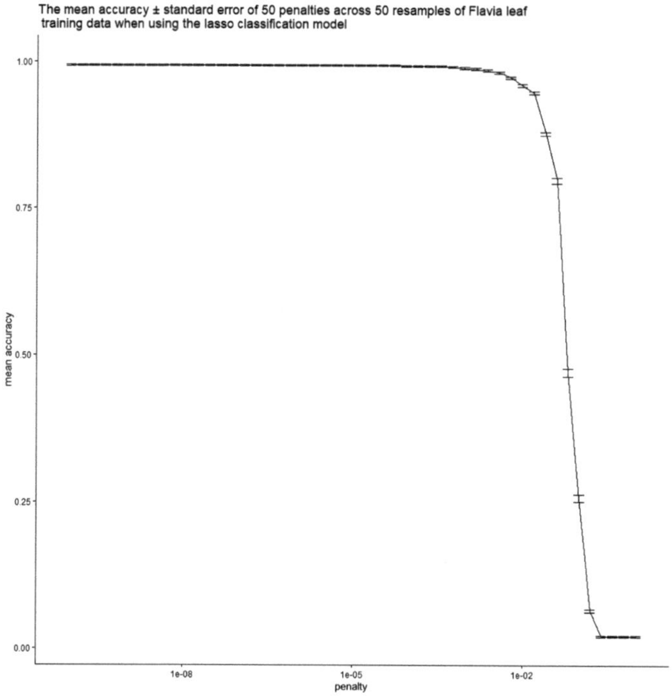

- As we have seen before, some penalties have the highest accuracy of 0.993 or 99.3%.

We can use the select_best function to create an object "best_pen2" that contains the best penalty value for the best lasso model.

```
best_pen2<-lasso_res %>% select_best()
best_pen2
## # A tibble: 1 × 2
## penalty .config
## <dbl> <chr>
## 1 0.0000000001 Preprocessor1_Model01
```

- Because many penalties have the same highest accuracy, so the function selects the 1st penalty of these penalties = 0.0000000001.

To get the final workflow with the best penalty, we use the finalize_workflow function with the arguments:

- wflow2 which is the original workflow with tuned penalty.
- best_pen2 which is the data of 1 row containing the best penalty value.

The resulting workflow "lasso_final" is the final workflow containing the best penalty.

```
lasso_final <- finalize_workflow(wflow2, best_pen2)
lasso_final
## ══ Workflow ════════════════════════════════════════
════════════════════════════════════
## Preprocessor: Recipe
## Model: multinom_reg()
##
## ── Preprocessor ────────────────────────────────────
──────────────────────────────────
## 3 Recipe Steps
##
## • step_dummy()
## • step_nzv()
## • step_normalize()
##
## ── Model ───────────────────────────────────────────
────────────────────────
```

```
## Multinomial Regression Model Specification (classification)
##
## Main Arguments:
## penalty = 1e-10
## mixture = 1
##
## Computational engine: glmnet
```

- The lasso_final workflow contains the best penalty of 0.0000000001 or 1e-10.

Then, we create the final lasso_fit model by using the fit function with the arguments:

- lasso_final which is the final workflow containing 3 preprocessing steps and the linear lasso model with best penalty value.
- train_leaf which is the whole training data with 1430 rows.

```
lasso_fit <- fit(lasso_final, data = train_leaf)
```

To see some model results, we use the following functions on lasso_fit model:

- The extract_fit_parsnip function to extract the model specifications.
- The tidy function to convert the result to a data frame.

```
lasso_fit %>% extract_fit_parsnip() %>%
tidy()
## # A tibble: 1,952 × 4
## class term estimate penalty
## <chr> <chr> <dbl> <dbl>
## 1 anhui_barberry (Intercept) 2.07 0.0000000001
## 2 anhui_barberry skewed_polar 0 0.0000000001
## 3 anhui_barberry clumpy_polar 0 0.0000000001
## 4 anhui_barberry sparse_polar 0 0.0000000001
## 5 anhui_barberry striated_polar 0 0.0000000001
## 6 anhui_barberry convex_polar 0 0.0000000001
## 7 anhui_barberry skinny_polar 0 0.0000000001
## 8 anhui_barberry stringy_polar 0 0.0000000001
## 9 anhui_barberry monotonic_polar 0 0.0000000001
## 10 anhui_barberry skewed_contour 0 0.0000000001
```

i 1,942 more rows

- We have an estimate for 60 predictors (after preprocessing) with the intercept for every class or species of 32 species so we have 61 × 32 = 1952 rows.

To get the most important predictor for every species, we use the same functions described under ridge classification model.

lasso_fit **%>% extract_fit_parsnip() %>%**

broom::**tidy**() **%>% filter**(!term==“(Intercept)”) **%>%**

filter(**abs**(estimate) > 0) **%>%**

group_by(class) **%>% slice_max**(**abs**(estimate), n = 1) **%>%**

arrange(term) **%>%**

flextable(cwidth = 1) **%>% theme box**() **%>%**

set_caption(caption = “The most important predictor for every species in the Flavia leaf training data when using lasso classification”)

The most important predictor for every species in the Flavia leaf training data when using lasso classification:

class	**term**	**estimate**	**penalty**
japanese_viburnum	apex_acute	3.039483	0.0000000001
nanmu	apex_acute	3.915360	0.0000000001
chinese_cinnamon	apex_apicu-late	2.819016	0.0000000001
anhui_barberry	apex_none	2.637283	0.0000000001
goldenrain_tree	apex_none	2.841917	0.0000000001
glossy_privet	apex_obtuse	2.973384	0.0000000001
southern_magnolia	apex_obtuse	2.366174	0.0000000001
japanese_cheesewood	apex_round	2.673669	0.0000000001
camphortree	base_acute	4.401263	0.0000000001
pubescent_bamboo	base_acute	5.471762	0.0000000001
big_fruited_holly	base_none	–2.062510	0.0000000001
oleander	base_none	–2.496108	0.0000000001
peach	base_none	–3.103082	0.0000000001
japanese_flowering_cherry	correlation	4.626521	0.0000000001

wintersweet	inverse_difference_moments	−1.780032	0.0000000001
chinese_tulip_tree	lobed_edge_yes	2.079413	0.0000000001
tangerine	lobed_edge_yes	2.649723	0.0000000001
deodar	perimeter_ratio_length	5.414170	0.0000000001
japanese_maple	perimeter_ratio_lw	2.725362	0.0000000001
yew_plum_pine	perimeter_ratio_lw	6.153108	0.0000000001
sweet_osmanthus	rectangularity	6.978005	0.0000000001
true_indigo	rectangularity	3.514714	0.0000000001
chinese_redbud	shape_heart_shape	4.158261	0.0000000001
ginkgo_maidenhair_tree	shape_round	3.581065	0.0000000001
crape_myrtle	shape_simple_round	3.618502	0.0000000001
ford_woodlotus	shape_simple_round	3.354400	0.0000000001
castor_aralia	smooth_edge_yes	2.464145	0.0000000001
beale_s_barberry	toothed_edge_yes	3.924205	0.0000000001
canadian_poplar	toothed_edge_yes	3.501331	0.0000000001
chinese_horse_chestnut	toothed_edge_yes	5.536451	0.0000000001
chinese_toon	toothed_edge_yes	3.931030	0.0000000001
trident_maple	toothed_edge_yes	1.821495	0.0000000001

- The apex categorical predictor is most important for many species followed by the base categorical predictor.

To get the least important predictor (predictors with 0 estimate), we use the following functions after the tidy function:

- The filter function with the argument "estimate==0" to get only predictors with 0 estimate.

```
lasso_fit %>% extract_fit_parsnip() %>%
broom::tidy() %>%
filter(estimate==0)
## # A tibble: 1,683 × 4
## class term estimate penalty
## <chr> <chr> <dbl> <dbl>
## 1 anhui_barberry skewed_polar 0 0.0000000001
## 2 anhui_barberry clumpy_polar 0 0.0000000001
## 3 anhui_barberry sparse_polar 0 0.0000000001
## 4 anhui_barberry striated_polar 0 0.0000000001
## 5 anhui_barberry convex_polar 0 0.0000000001
## 6 anhui_barberry skinny_polar 0 0.0000000001
## 7 anhui_barberry stringy_polar 0 0.0000000001
## 8 anhui_barberry monotonic_polar 0 0.0000000001
## 9 anhui_barberry skewed_contour 0 0.0000000001
## 10 anhui_barberry clumpy_contour 0 0.0000000001
## # i 1,673 more rows
```

- The count function with the arguments:
  - term to give the number of species in which each predictor has an estimate of 0.
  - sort = TRUE to arrange the predictors in descending order.

```
lasso_fit %>% extract_fit_parsnip() %>%
broom::tidy() %>%
filter(estimate==0) %>%
count(term, sort = TRUE) %>%
flextable(cwidth = 1.5) %>% theme_box() %>%
set_caption(caption = "The predictors with 0 estimate in the Flavia leaf training
data when using lasso classification")
```

The predictors with 0 estimate in the Flavia leaf training data when using lasso classification:

term	n
mean_blue_val	32
striated_polar	32
area_convexity	31
area_ratio_convexity	31
compactness	31
eccentriciry	31
equivalent_diameter	31
mean_green_val	31
narrow_factor	31
perimeter_ratio_length	31
std_red_val	31
stringy_polar	31
apex_obtuse	30
aspect_ratio	30
clumpy_contour	30
convex_contour	30
convex_polar	30
perimeter_convexity	30
perimeter_ratio_diameter	30
shape_heart_shape	30
shape_round	30
std_blue_val	30
apex_round	29
area	29
clumpy_polar	29
inverse_difference_moments	29
mean_red_val	29
perimeter	29
physiological_length	29
physiological_width	29
skinny_contour	29
striated_contour	29

apex_none	28
diameter	28
entropy	28
num_max_ponits	28
perimeter_ratio_lw	28
skewed_contour	28
smooth_edge_yes	28
sparse_polar	28
std_green_val	28
lobed_edge_yes	27
num_min_points	27
skewed_polar	27
sparse_contour	27
apex_acute	26
base_acute	26
contrast	26
correlation	26
monotonic_contour	26
skinny_polar	26
circularity	25
correlation_texture	25
apex_apiculate	24
monotonic_polar	24
rectangularity	24
base_none	23
toothed_edge_yes	22
num_convex_points	21
shape_simple_round	15

- The mean_blue_val and striated_polar predictors have 0 estimate in 32 species or all species in our data.
- The shape_simple_round has 0 estimate in 15 species only.

To see the model accuracy on the whole training data, we use the same functions described above on the lasso_fit model.

lasso_fit **%>%** **predict**(new_data = train_leaf) **%>%**

mutate(truth = train_leaf$species) **%>%**

```
accuracy(truth = truth, estimate = .pred_class)
## # A tibble: 1 × 3
## .metric .estimator .estimate
## <chr> <chr> <dbl>
## 1 accuracy multiclass 1
```

- The accuracy of the lasso model on training data = 1 or 100% which is perfect.

4.4.5. Model Performance on Testing Data

To get the model accuracy on the testing data, we use the same above functions on the lasso_fit model but using the test_leaf data.

```
lasso_fit %>% predict(new_data = test_leaf) %>%
mutate(truth = test_leaf$species) %>%
accuracy(truth = truth, estimate = .pred_class)
## # A tibble: 1 × 3
## .metric .estimator .estimate
## <chr> <chr> <dbl>
## 1 accuracy multiclass 0.992
```

- The accuracy of the lasso model on testing data = 0.992 or 99.2% which is higher than that of the ridge model (0.981 or 98.1%).

To see how many actual species are predicted correctly, we create a confusion matrix by using the conf_mat function instead of the accuracy function with the same arguments. Then, we plot it as a heatmap using the autoplot function.

```
lasso_fit %>% predict(new_data = test_leaf) %>%
mutate(truth = test_leaf$species) %>%
conf_mat(truth = truth, estimate = .pred_class) %>%
autoplot(type = "heatmap")+
theme(axis.text.x = element_text(angle = 60, hjust = 1))+
labs(title = "The confusion matrix of applying the lasso model on the Flavia leaf testing data")
```

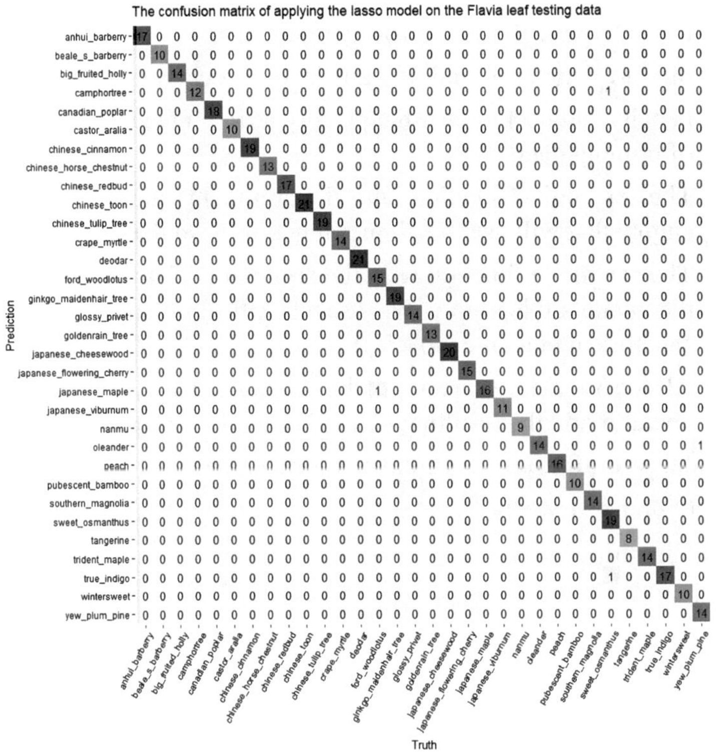

- All species are predicted correctly except:
  - There is 1 sweet_osmanthus row that is predicted incorrectly as camphortree and another 1 sweet_osmanthus row that is predicted incorrectly as true_indigo.
  - There is 1 ford_woodlotus row that is predicted incorrectly as japanese_maple.
  - There is 1 yew_plum_pine row that is predicted incorrectly as oleander.

4.5. ELASTIC NET CLASSIFICATION

We will use the same steps and outputs of ridge classification till defining the ML model.

4.5.1. Define Machine Learning (ML) Model

We define a multinomial classification model by using the functions:

- The multinom_reg function to define the multinomial classification model type with the following arguments:
  - mixture = tune() to indicate an elastic net classification model.
  - penalty = tune() to tune the penalty term on the different resamples of training data.
- The set_engine function with the argument "glmnet" to define the engine that will use the glmnet function from the glmnet package.
- The set_mode function with the argument "classification" to define the mode of learning. We use classification because we have a categorical outcome (species).
- All the 3 functions are applied in sequence using the piping "%>%" operator and the resulting object is called "elastic_model."

```
elastic_model <- multinom_reg(mixture = tune(), penalty = tune()) %>%
set_engine("glmnet") %>%
set_mode("classification")
elastic_model
## Multinomial Regression Model Specification (classification)
##
## Main Arguments:
## penalty = tune()
## mixture = tune()
##
## Computational engine: glmnet
```

4.5.2. Generate Workflow

We create the "wflow3" object by using the following functions:

- The workflow function to create a workflow.
- The add_recipe function with the argument "rec" to add the above created recipe with 3 preprocessing steps.
- The add_model function with the argument elastic_model to add the above created elastic model.

```
wflow3 <- workflow() %>%
add_recipe(rec) %>%
add_model(elastic_model)
wflow3
```

```
## ══ Workflow ════════════════════════════════════════════════════════════════
## Preprocessor: Recipe
## Model: multinom_reg()
##
## ── Preprocessor ────────────────────────────────────────────────────────────
## 3 Recipe Steps
##
## • step_dummy()
## • step_nzv()
## • step_normalize()
##
## ── Model ───────────────────────────────────────────────────────────────────
## Multinomial Regression Model Specification (classification)
##
## Main Arguments:
## penalty = tune()
## mixture = tune()
##
## Computational engine: glmnet
```

- The "wflow3" object contains 3 preprocessing steps and the multinomial classification model with tuned mixture and penalty (elastic net model).

4.5.3. Fit Model on Different Resamples with Tuning

Again, we can use the grid_regular function to chooses sensible values for the penalty and mixture terms.

We create a grid of penalty and mixture values "my_grid2" by using the grid_regular function with the arguments:

- penalty() to choose sensible values for the penalty term.
- mixture() to choose sensible values for the mixture term.

- levels = 10 to choose 10 different penalty and mixture values. The result is 10 × 10 = 100 or 100 different combinations of penalty and mixture values.

```
my_grid2 <- grid_regular(penalty(), mixture(), levels = 10)
my_grid2
## # A tibble: 100 × 2
## penalty mixture
## <dbl> <dbl>
## 1 0.0000000001 0
## 2 0.00000000129 0
## 3 0.0000000167 0
## 4 0.000000215 0
## 5 0.00000278 0
## 6 0.0000359 0
## 7 0.000464 0
## 8 0.00599 0
## 9 0.0774 0
## 10 1 0
## # i 90 more rows
```

To try these 100 combinations on the 50 resamples of the training data using the elastic net model, we use the tune_grid function with the arguments:

- wflow3 which is the workflow containing 3 preprocessing steps and the linear elastic net model.
- folds which are the 50 resamples of training data created above.
- metrics = metrics_set(accuracy) to get the accuracy of the elastic net model on each resample using the 100 different combinations of penalty and mixture values.
- grid = my_grid2 to use the 100 penalty and mixture combinations in the my_grid2 data in tuning.

```
set.seed(123)
elastic_res <- tune_grid(wflow3, folds,
metrics = metric_set(accuracy),
grid = my_grid2)
elastic_res
```

```
## # Tuning results
## # 10-fold cross-validation repeated 5 times using stratification
## # A tibble: 50 × 5
## splits id id2 .metrics .notes
## <list> <chr> <chr> <list> <list>
## 1 <split [1287/143]> Repeat1 Fold01 <tibble [100 × 6]> <tibble [0 × 3]>
## 2 <split [1287/143]> Repeat1 Fold02 <tibble [100 × 6]> <tibble [0 × 3]>
## 3 <split [1287/143]> Repeat1 Fold03 <tibble [100 × 6]> <tibble [0 × 3]>
## 4 <split [1287/143]> Repeat1 Fold04 <tibble [100 × 6]> <tibble [0 × 3]>
## 5 <split [1287/143]> Repeat1 Fold05 <tibble [100 × 6]> <tibble [0 × 3]>
## 6 <split [1287/143]> Repeat1 Fold06 <tibble [100 × 6]> <tibble [0 × 3]>
## 7 <split [1287/143]> Repeat1 Fold07 <tibble [100 × 6]> <tibble [0 × 3]>
## 8 <split [1287/143]> Repeat1 Fold08 <tibble [100 × 6]> <tibble [0 × 3]>
## 9 <split [1287/143]> Repeat1 Fold09 <tibble [100 × 6]> <tibble [0 × 3]>
## 10 <split [1287/143]> Repeat1 Fold10 <tibble [100 × 6]> <tibble [0 × 3]>
## # ℹ 40 more rows
```

The resulting object "elastic_res" contains 50 rows (for 50 resamples) and 5 columns:

- The splits column is a list of each combination of analysis and assessment data withing each resample. The sum is 1430, which are total rows of training data.
- The id column is an id column for the repeat number from 1 to 5.
- The id2 column is an id column for the fold number from 1 to 10 so we have 50 resamples because 5 × 10 = 50.
- The .metrics column is a list of performance metric (accuracy) of applying the elastic net model to the corresponding assessment data (143 rows) within each resample. Each performance metric is saved in 100 rows and 6 columns [100 × 6] tibble or data frame. The 100 rows are for the accuracy of applying the 100 penalty and mixture combinations in the elastic net model to the corresponding assessment data within each resample.
- The .notes column is a list of notes or warnings when applying the elastic net model to each analysis data (1287 rows) within each resample. Each note is saved in 0 rows and 3 columns [0 × 3] tibble or data frame meaning that there are no rows or no notes when applying this model to each analysis data.

4.5.4. The Model Performance on 50 Resamples of the Training Data

To get the performance metric (accuracy) on the 50 resamples of training data using the 100 penalty and mixture combinations, we will use the unnest function with the ".metrics" argument to expand the .metrics list column of the elastic_res object into rows and columns.

```
elastic_res %>% unnest(.metrics)
## # A tibble: 5,000 × 10
## splits id id2 penalty mixture .metric .estimator .estimate
## <list> <chr> <chr> <dbl> <dbl> <chr> <chr> <dbl>
## 1 <split [1287/143]> Repea… Fold… 1 e-10 0 accura… multiclass 0.993
## 2 <split [1287/143]> Repea… Fold… 1.29e-9 0 accura… multiclass 0.993
## 3 <split [1287/143]> Repea… Fold… 1.67e-8 0 accura… multiclass 0.993
## 4 <split [1287/143]> Repea… Fold… 2.15e-7 0 accura… multiclass 0.993
## 5 <split [1287/143]> Repea… Fold… 2.78e-6 0 accura… multiclass 0.993
## 6 <split [1287/143]> Repea… Fold… 3.59e-5 0 accura… multiclass 0.993
## 7 <split [1287/143]> Repea… Fold… 4.64e-4 0 accura… multiclass 0.993
## 8 <split [1287/143]> Repea… Fold… 5.99e-3 0 accura… multiclass 0.993
## 9 <split [1287/143]> Repea… Fold… 7.74e-2 0 accura… multiclass 0.979
## 10 <split [1287/143]> Repea… Fold… 1 e + 0 0 accura… multiclass 0.685
## # i 4,990 more rows
## # i 2 more variables: .config <chr>, .notes <list>
```

- The result is 5000 rows because we have applied the 100 penalty and mixture combinations to 50 resamples of the training data so we have 100 × 50 = 5000 rows. Each row contains the accuracy of the elastic net model on 1 resample using 1 combination of penalty and mixture values.

To get the mean accuracy of each penalty and mixture combination on the 50 resamples of the training data, we use the following functions on the "elastic_res" object:

- The collect_metrics function to get the mean accuracy for each penalty and mixture combination across the 50 resamples of the training data.
- The arrange function with mean argument to arrange by mean accuracy value in ascending order.

- The flextable, theme_box, and set_caption functions are described previously.

elastic_res **%>% collect_metrics()** %>%

arrange(mean) %>%

flextable() %>% **theme_box()** %>%

set_caption(caption = "The mean accuracy of applying 100 penalty and mixture combinations on 50 resamples of Flavia leaf training data when using the elastic net classification model")

The mean accuracy of applying 100 penalty and mixture combinations on 50 resamples of Flavia leaf training data when using the elastic net classification model:

penalty	mixture	.metric	.estimator	mean	n	std_err	.config
1.00000000000000	0.2222222	accuracy	multiclass	0.02181818	50	0.001289292	Preprocessor1_Model030
1.00000000000000	0.3333333	accuracy	multiclass	0.02181818	50	0.001289292	Preprocessor1_Model040
1.00000000000000	0.4444444	accuracy	multiclass	0.02181818	50	0.001289292	Preprocessor1_Model050
1.00000000000000	0.5555556	accuracy	multiclass	0.02181818	50	0.001289292	Preprocessor1_Model060
1.00000000000000	0.6666667	accuracy	multiclass	0.02181818	50	0.001289292	Preprocessor1_Model070
1.00000000000000	0.7777778	accuracy	multiclass	0.02181818	50	0.001289292	Preprocessor1_Model080
1.00000000000000	0.8888889	accuracy	multiclass	0.02181818	50	0.001289292	Preprocessor1_Model090
1.00000000000000	1.0000000	accuracy	multiclass	0.02181818	50	0.001289292	Preprocessor1_Model100

1.00000000000000	0.1111111	accuracy	multi-class	0.08629371	50	0.004097658	Preprocessor1_Model020
0.07742636826811	1.0000000	accuracy	multi-class	0.38181818	50	0.005957263	Preprocessor1_Model099
0.07742636826811	0.8888889	accuracy	multi-class	0.43244755	50	0.005877523	Preprocessor1_Model089
0.07742636826811	0.7777778	accuracy	multi-class	0.46419580	50	0.006535299	Preprocessor1_Model079
0.07742636826811	0.6666667	accuracy	multi-class	0.52811189	50	0.006675360	Preprocessor1_Model069
0.07742636826811	0.5555556	accuracy	multi-class	0.62153846	50	0.006279069	Preprocessor1_Model059
1.00000000000000	0.0000000	accuracy	multi-class	0.71272727	50	0.005615203	Preprocessor1_Model010
0.07742636826811	0.4444444	accuracy	multi-class	0.73762238	50	0.006444106	Preprocessor1_Model049
0.07742636826811	0.3333333	accuracy	multi-class	0.82965035	50	0.005367751	Preprocessor1_Model039
0.07742636826811	0.2222222	accuracy	multi-class	0.88349650	50	0.004236565	Preprocessor1_Model029
0.07742636826811	0.1111111	accuracy	multi-class	0.93804196	50	0.002550956	Preprocessor1_Model019
0.07742636826811	0.0000000	accuracy	multi-class	0.95580420	50	0.002308017	Preprocessor1_Model009

0.00599484250319	1.0000000	accuracy	multi-class	0.97146853	50	0.002093998	Prepro-cessor1_Mod-el098
0.00599484250319	0.8888889	accuracy	multi-class	0.97328671	50	0.001954471	Prepro-cessor1_Mod-el088
0.00599484250319	0.7777778	accuracy	multi-class	0.97552448	50	0.001929391	Prepro-cessor1_Mod-el078
0.00599484250319	0.6666667	accuracy	multi-class	0.97650350	50	0.001955186	Prepro-cessor1_Mod-el068
0.00599484250319	0.5555556	accuracy	multi-class	0.97888112	50	0.001825632	Prepro-cessor1_Mod-el058
0.00000000010000	0.0000000	accuracy	multi-class	0.98027972	50	0.001783602	Prepro-cessor1_Mod-el001
0.00000000129155	0.0000000	accuracy	multi-class	0.98027972	50	0.001783602	Prepro-cessor1_Mod-el002
0.00000001668101	0.0000000	accuracy	multi-class	0.98027972	50	0.001783602	Prepro-cessor1_Mod-el003
0.00000021544347	0.0000000	accuracy	multi-class	0.98027972	50	0.001783602	Prepro-cessor1_Mod-el004
0.00000278255940	0.0000000	accuracy	multi-class	0.98027972	50	0.001783602	Prepro-cessor1_Mod-el005
0.00003593813664	0.0000000	accuracy	multi-class	0.98027972	50	0.001783602	Prepro-cessor1_Mod-el006
0.00046415888336	0.0000000	accuracy	multi-class	0.98027972	50	0.001783602	Prepro-cessor1_Mod-el007

0.00599484250319	0.0000000	accuracy	multi-class	0.98027972	50	0.001783602	Preprocessor1_Model008
0.00599484250319	0.4444444	accuracy	multi-class	0.98097902	50	0.001765040	Preprocessor1_Model048
0.00599484250319	0.3333333	accuracy	multi-class	0.98279720	50	0.001686034	Preprocessor1_Model038
0.00599484250319	0.1111111	accuracy	multi-class	0.98419580	50	0.001465640	Preprocessor1_Model018
0.00599484250319	0.2222222	accuracy	multi-class	0.98461538	50	0.001598402	Preprocessor1_Model028
0.00046415888336	0.6666667	accuracy	multi-class	0.99062937	50	0.001407280	Preprocessor1_Model067
0.00046415888336	0.7777778	accuracy	multi-class	0.99090909	50	0.001402165	Preprocessor1_Model077
0.00046415888336	0.8888889	accuracy	multi-class	0.99090909	50	0.001402165	Preprocessor1_Model087
0.00046415888336	1.0000000	accuracy	multi-class	0.99118881	50	0.001337468	Preprocessor1_Model097
0.00046415888336	0.1111111	accuracy	multi-class	0.99160839	50	0.001310178	Preprocessor1_Model017
0.00046415888336	0.4444444	accuracy	multi-class	0.99160839	50	0.001412801	Preprocessor1_Model047
0.00046415888336	0.2222222	accuracy	multi-class	0.99174825	50	0.001290066	Preprocessor1_Model027

0.00046415888336	0.3333333	accuracy	multi-class	0.99174825	50	0.001305446	Preprocessor1_Model037
0.00046415888336	0.5555556	accuracy	multi-class	0.99188811	50	0.001360403	Preprocessor1_Model057
0.00000000010000	0.5555556	accuracy	multi-class	0.99216783	50	0.001273716	Preprocessor1_Model051
0.00000000129155	0.5555556	accuracy	multi-class	0.99216783	50	0.001273716	Preprocessor1_Model052
0.00000001668101	0.5555556	accuracy	multi-class	0.99216783	50	0.001273716	Preprocessor1_Model053
0.00000021544347	0.5555556	accuracy	multi-class	0.99216783	50	0.001273716	Preprocessor1_Model054
0.00000278255940	0.5555556	accuracy	multi-class	0.99216783	50	0.001273716	Preprocessor1_Model055
0.00003593813664	0.5555556	accuracy	multi-class	0.99216783	50	0.001273716	Preprocessor1_Model056
0.00000000010000	0.4444444	accuracy	multi-class	0.99230769	50	0.001283240	Preprocessor1_Model041
0.00000000129155	0.4444444	accuracy	multi-class	0.99230769	50	0.001283240	Preprocessor1_Model042
0.00000001668101	0.4444444	accuracy	multi-class	0.99230769	50	0.001283240	Preprocessor1_Model043
0.00000021544347	0.4444444	accuracy	multi-class	0.99230769	50	0.001283240	Preprocessor1_Model044

0.00000278255940	0.4444444	accuracy	multi-class	0.99230769	50	0.001283240	Prepro-cessor1_Mod-el045
0.00003593813664	0.4444444	accuracy	multi-class	0.99230769	50	0.001283240	Prepro-cessor1_Mod-el046
0.00000000010000	0.6666667	accuracy	multi-class	0.99230769	50	0.001267590	Prepro-cessor1_Mod-el061
0.00000000129155	0.6666667	accuracy	multi-class	0.99230769	50	0.001267590	Prepro-cessor1_Mod-el062
0.00000001668101	0.6666667	accuracy	multi-class	0.99230769	50	0.001267590	Prepro-cessor1_Mod-el063
0.00000021544347	0.6666667	accuracy	multi-class	0.99230769	50	0.001267590	Prepro-cessor1_Mod-el064
0.00000278255940	0.6666667	accuracy	multi-class	0.99230769	50	0.001267590	Prepro-cessor1_Mod-el065
0.00003593813664	0.6666667	accuracy	multi-class	0.99230769	50	0.001267590	Prepro-cessor1_Mod-el066
0.00000000010000	0.1111111	accuracy	multi-class	0.99244755	50	0.001292385	Prepro-cessor1_Mod-el011
0.00000000129155	0.1111111	accuracy	multi-class	0.99244755	50	0.001292385	Prepro-cessor1_Mod-el012
0.00000001668101	0.1111111	accuracy	multi-class	0.99244755	50	0.001292385	Prepro-cessor1_Mod-el013
0.00000021544347	0.1111111	accuracy	multi-class	0.99244755	50	0.001292385	Prepro-cessor1_Mod-el014

0.00000278255940	0.1111111	accuracy	multi-class	0.99244755	50	0.001292385	Preprocessor1_Model015
0.00003593813664	0.1111111	accuracy	multi-class	0.99244755	50	0.001292385	Preprocessor1_Model016
0.00000000010000	0.2222222	accuracy	multi-class	0.99258741	50	0.001270107	Preprocessor1_Model021
0.00000000129155	0.2222222	accuracy	multi-class	0.99258741	50	0.001270107	Preprocessor1_Model022
0.00000001668101	0.2222222	accuracy	multi-class	0.99258741	50	0.001270107	Preprocessor1_Model023
0.00000021544347	0.2222222	accuracy	multi-class	0.99258741	50	0.001270107	Preprocessor1_Model024
0.00000278255940	0.2222222	accuracy	multi-class	0.99258741	50	0.001270107	Preprocessor1_Model025
0.00003593813664	0.2222222	accuracy	multi-class	0.99258741	50	0.001270107	Preprocessor1_Model026
0.00000000010000	0.3333333	accuracy	multi-class	0.99258741	50	0.001285726	Preprocessor1_Model031
0.00000000129155	0.3333333	accuracy	multi-class	0.99258741	50	0.001285726	Preprocessor1_Model032
0.00000001668101	0.3333333	accuracy	multi-class	0.99258741	50	0.001285726	Preprocessor1_Model033
0.00000021544347	0.3333333	accuracy	multi-class	0.99258741	50	0.001285726	Preprocessor1_Model034

0.00000278255940	0.3333333	accuracy	multi-class	0.99258741	50	0.001285726	Preprocessor1_Model035
0.00003593813664	0.3333333	accuracy	multi-class	0.99258741	50	0.001285726	Preprocessor1_Model036
0.00000000010000	0.7777778	accuracy	multi-class	0.99258741	50	0.001188937	Preprocessor1_Model071
0.00000000129155	0.7777778	accuracy	multi-class	0.99258741	50	0.001188937	Preprocessor1_Model072
0.00000001668101	0.7777778	accuracy	multi-class	0.99258741	50	0.001188937	Preprocessor1_Model073
0.00000021544347	0.7777778	accuracy	multi-class	0.99258741	50	0.001188937	Preprocessor1_Model074
0.00000278255940	0.7777778	accuracy	multi-class	0.99258741	50	0.001188937	Preprocessor1_Model075
0.00003593813664	0.7777778	accuracy	multi-class	0.99258741	50	0.001188937	Preprocessor1_Model076
0.00000000010000	0.8888889	accuracy	multi-class	0.99258741	50	0.001205608	Preprocessor1_Model081
0.00000000129155	0.8888889	accuracy	multi-class	0.99258741	50	0.001205608	Preprocessor1_Model082
0.00000001668101	0.8888889	accuracy	multi-class	0.99258741	50	0.001205608	Preprocessor1_Model083
0.00000021544347	0.8888889	accuracy	multi-class	0.99258741	50	0.001205608	Preprocessor1_Model084

0.00000278255940	0.8888889	accuracy	multi-class	0.99258741	50	0.001205608	Preprocessor1_Model085
0.00003593813664	0.8888889	accuracy	multi-class	0.99258741	50	0.001205608	Preprocessor1_Model086
0.00000000010000	1.0000000	accuracy	multi-class	0.99272727	50	0.001231003	Preprocessor1_Model091
0.00000000129155	1.0000000	accuracy	multi-class	0.99272727	50	0.001231003	Preprocessor1_Model092
0.00000001668101	1.0000000	accuracy	multi-class	0.99272727	50	0.001231003	Preprocessor1_Model093
0.00000021544347	1.0000000	accuracy	multi-class	0.99272727	50	0.001231003	Preprocessor1_Model094
0.00000278255940	1.0000000	accuracy	multi-class	0.99272727	50	0.001231003	Preprocessor1_Model095
0.00003593813664	1.0000000	accuracy	multi-class	0.99272727	50	0.001231003	Preprocessor1_Model096

- The result is 100 rows with 1 mean accuracy value for each penalty and mixture combination across the 50 resamples (n = 50).
- The lowest accuracy (0.022) was achieved when using 0.22, 0.33, 0.44, 0.56, 0.67, 0.78, 0.89, or 1.00 mixture with 1.00 penalty.
- The highest accuracy (0.993) was achieved when using many penalty values (0.0000000001, 0.0000000013, etc.) with 1.00 mixture or lasso model.

We can plot the 100 mean accuracy values from the 100 combinations by using the following functions after the arrange function:

- The mutate function with the arguments:

++ penalty = scientific(penalty) to convert the penalty values to scientific notations (e.g., 1e05 or 100000, 1.5e-02 or 0.015).

++ mixture = scientific(mixture) to convert the mixture values to scientific notations. The scientific function is from the scales package.

- The mutate function with the argument "comb = paste(penalty, mixture, sep =" ")" to create a new "comb" column that holds the pasted penalty and mixture values with a " " separator.
- The mutate function with the argument "comb = fct_inorder(comb)" to convert the comb column to a factor column with levels according to their appearance in the data. Since the data are arranged by the mean value so the levels of comb column will be plotted according to their mean accuracy value.
- The ggplot function with the argument "aes(x = mean, y = comb)" to plot the mean accuracy value on the x-axis, and the "comb" combination on the y-axis.
- The geom_point function to plot a scatter plot.
- The labs function with the argument title to add a plot title, *x* to add an *x*-axis title, y to add a y-axis title.
- The theme_classic function as described in previous chapters. We use a lower base size to avoid crowding of text on the y-axis.

```
library(scales)
elastic_res %>% collect_metrics() %>%
arrange(mean) %>%
mutate(penalty = scientific(penalty), mixture = scientific(mixture)) %>%
mutate(comb = paste(penalty, mixture, sep = " ")) %>%
mutate(comb = fct_inorder(comb)) %>%
ggplot(aes(x = mean, y = comb))+ geom_point()+
labs(title = "The mean accuracy of 100 different combinations across 50 resamples of Flavia leaf training data \nwhen using the elastic net classification model",
x = "mean accuracy", y = "Penalty_mixture combination")+
theme_classic(base_size = 7)
```

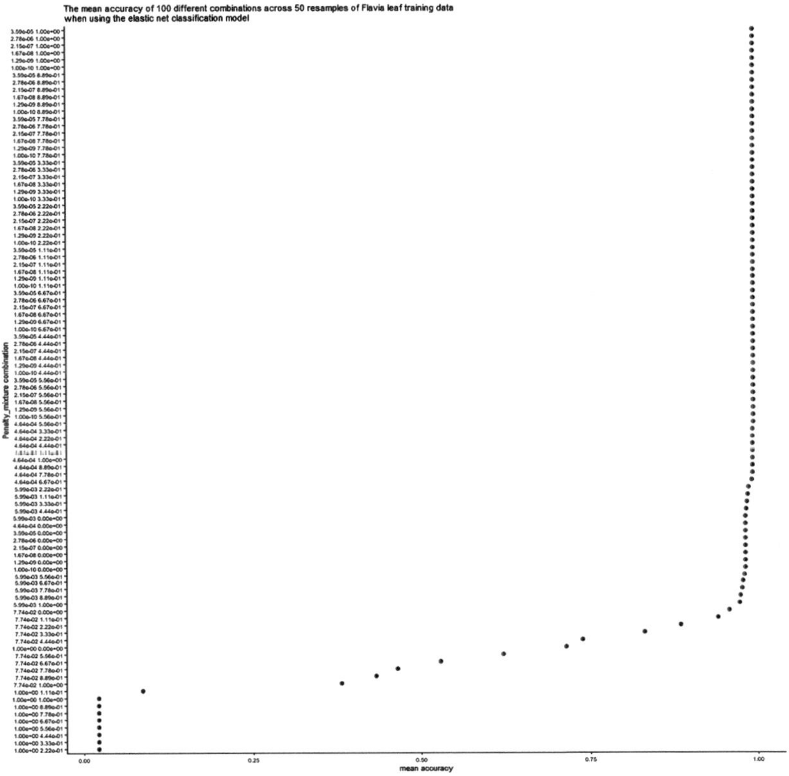

- All penalties with 1 mixture (lasso model) have the highest accuracy value.

We can use the select_best function to create an object "best_pen3" that contains the best penalty value and mixture value for the best elastic net model.

best_pen3<-elastic_res **%>% select_best**()

best_pen3

A tibble: 1 × 3

penalty mixture .config

<dbl> <dbl> <chr>

1 0.0000000001 1 Preprocessor1_Model091

- Because many penalties have the same highest accuracy, so the function selects the 1st penalty of these penalties = 0.0000000001 and mixture = 1 which is the same as that selected in the lasso model.

To get the final workflow with the best penalty, we use the finalize_workflow function with the arguments:

- wflow3 which is the original workflow with tuned penalty and mixture values.
- best_pen3 which is the data of 1 row containing the best penalty and mixture values.

The resulting workflow "elastic_final" is the final workflow containing the best penalty and mixture values.

```
elastic_final <- finalize_workflow(wflow3, best_pen3)
elastic_final
## ══ Workflow ════════════════════════════════════════════════════
## Preprocessor: Recipe
## Model: multinom_reg()
##
## ── Preprocessor ────────────────────────────────────────────────
## 3 Recipe Steps
##
## • step_dummy()
## • step_nzv()
## • step_normalize()
##
## ── Model ───────────────────────────────────────────────────────
## Multinomial Regression Model Specification (classification)
##
## Main Arguments:
## penalty = 1e-10
## mixture = 1
##
## Computational engine: glmnet
```

- The elastic_final workflow contains the best penalty of 0.0000000001 or 1e-10 and the best mixture or 1.

Then, we create the final elastic_fit model by using the fit function with the arguments:

- elastic_final which is the final workflow containing 3 preprocessing steps and the linear elastic model with best penalty and mixture value.
- train_leaf which is the whole training data with 1430 rows.

```
elastic_fit <- fit(elastic_final, data = train_leaf)
```

To see some model results, we use the following functions on elastic_fit model:

- The extract_fit_parsnip function to extract the model specifications.
- The tidy function to convert the result to a data frame.

```
elastic_fit %>% extract_fit_parsnip() %>%
tidy()
## # A tibble: 1,952 × 4
## class term estimate penalty
## <chr> <chr> <dbl> <dbl>
## 1 anhui_barberry (Intercept) 2.07 0.0000000001
## 2 anhui_barberry skewed_polar 0 0.0000000001
## 3 anhui_barberry clumpy_polar 0 0.0000000001
## 4 anhui_barberry sparse_polar 0 0.0000000001
## 5 anhui_barberry striated_polar 0 0.0000000001
## 6 anhui_barberry convex_polar 0 0.0000000001
## 7 anhui_barberry skinny_polar 0 0.0000000001
## 8 anhui_barberry stringy_polar 0 0.0000000001
## 9 anhui_barberry monotonic_polar 0 0.0000000001
## 10 anhui_barberry skewed_contour 0 0.0000000001
## # i 1,942 more rows
```

- We have an estimate for 60 predictors (after preprocessing) with the intercept for every class or species of 32 species so we have 61 × 32 = 1952 rows.

The elastic_fit model is the same as the lasso_fit model as can be seen by using the identical function.

```
identical(elastic_fit %>% extract_fit_parsnip() %>%
tidy(), lasso_fit %>% extract_fit_parsnip() %>% tidy())
## [1] TRUE
```

So, the elastic_fit model will have:

- The same accuracy as the lasso model on training data = 1 or 100% which is perfect.
- The same accuracy as the lasso model on testing data = 0.992 or 99.2% which is higher than that of the ridge model (0.981 or 98.1%).

4.6. CONCLUSION

We have tried 3 penalized regression models on the Flavia leaf data (ridge, lasso, and elastic net) and the best model was the lasso model because it has the highest accuracy of 99.2% on testing data.

CHAPTER 5

K-NEAREST NEIGHBORS (KNN) REGRESSION

Contents

5.1. Data Used in This Chapter 317
5.2. Data Exploration 319
5.3. knn Model 320
5.4. knn Regression 321
5.5. Comparison Between Different Models 345

5.1. DATA USED IN THIS CHAPTER

5.1.1. Concrete Data

This data contains 1030 different concrete mixtures and their compressive strength. There are 9 columns in the data which are 7 different ingredients, the concrete mixture age, and the compressive strength outcome. The data is part of the modeldata package under the name "concrete." The modeldata package is part of tidymodels package which is a collection of different packages for data modeling. First, we load the tidymodels package using the library function then, we load the concrete data using the data function. We also load the tidyverse and flextable packages for the reasons described above.

```
library(tidymodels)
data("concrete")
library(tidyverse)
library(flextable)
```

Then, to see the data structure, we use the glimpse function.

```
glimpse(concrete)
## Rows: 1,030
## Columns: 9
## $ cement <dbl> 540.0, 540.0, 332.5, 332.5, 198.6, 266.0, 380.0, …
## $ blast_furnace_slag <dbl> 0.0, 0.0, 142.5, 142.5, 132.4, 114.0, 95.0, 95.0,…
## $ fly_ash <dbl> 0, 0, 0, 0, 0, 0, 0, 0, 0, 0, 0, 0, 0, 0, 0, 0…
## $ water <dbl> 162, 162, 228, 228, 192, 228, 228, 228, 228, 228,…
## $ superplasticizer <dbl> 2.5, 2.5, 0.0, 0.0, 0.0, 0.0, 0.0, 0.0, 0.0, 0.0,…
## $ coarse_aggregate <dbl> 1040.0, 1055.0, 932.0, 932.0, 978.4, 932.0, 932.0…
## $ fine_aggregate <dbl> 676.0, 676.0, 594.0, 594.0, 825.5, 670.0, 594.0, …
## $ age <int> 28, 28, 270, 365, 360, 90, 365, 28, 28, 28, 90, 2…
## $ compressive_strength <dbl> 79.99, 61.89, 40.27, 41.05, 44.30, 47.03, 43.70, …
```

The data has 1030 rows (concrete mixtures) and 9 columns:

1. **cement:** A numeric column for the cement ingredient.
2. **blast_furnace_slag:** A numeric column for the blast furnace slag ingredient.
3. **fly_ash:** A numeric column for the fly ash ingredient.
4. **water:** A numeric column for the water ingredient.
5. **superplasticizer:** A numeric column for the superplasticizer ingredient.
6. **coarse_aggregate:** A numeric column for the coarse aggregate ingredient.
7. **fine_aggregate:** A numeric column for the fine aggregate ingredient.
8. **age:** An integer column for the concrete mixture age.
9. **compressive_strength:** A numeric column for the concrete mixture compressive strength. This is the numeric outcome that will be modeled using the next regression models described in further

sections.

5.2. DATA EXPLORATION

The first step in any data modeling is exploring the data using the functions from the skimr package as described in previous chapters.

To examine all numeric columns at once, we use the following functions on the concrete data:

- The skim function that produces information about all data columns.
- The yank function with "numeric" argument to get only the information related to numeric columns.

Then, we convert the result to a table as explained in previous chapters using functions from the flextable package. To use functions from the skimr package, we should first load the skimr package first using the library function.

library(skimr)

concrete **%>% skim() %>% yank**("numeric") **%>%**

flextable() %>% theme_box() %>%

set_caption(caption = "The information gained from skim function on numeric columns from the concrete data")

The information gained from skim function on numeric columns from the concrete data:

skim_variable	n_missing	complete_rate	mean	sd	p0	p25	p50	p75	p100	hist
cement	0	1	281.16786	104.506364	102.00	192.375	272.900	350.000	540.0	
blast_furnace_slag	0	1	73.89583	86.279342	0.00	0.000	22.000	142.950	359.4	
fly_ash	0	1	54.18835	63.997004	0.00	0.000	0.000	118.300	200.1	
water	0	1	181.56728	21.354219	121.80	164.900	185.000	192.000	247.0	
superplasticizer	0	1	6.20466	5.973841	0.00	0.000	6.400	10.200	32.2	
coarse_aggregate	0	1	972.91893	77.753954	801.00	932.000	968.000	1,029.400	1,145.0	
fine_aggregate	0	1	773.58049	80.175980	594.00	730.950	779.500	824.000	992.6	
age	0	1	45.66214	63.169912	1.00	7.000	28.000	56.000	365.0	
compressive_strength	0	1	35.81796	16.705742	2.33	23.710	34.445	46.135	82.6	

We have 11 columns:

1. skim_variable is the column name. There are 9 numeric columns which are all columns in our data.
2. n_missing is the number of missings in each column. All numeric columns have 0 or no missings.
3. complete_rate is the proportion of present values in each column. All numeric columns have no missings and 1 or 100% complete rate.
4. mean is the mean or average value for each column.
5. sd is the standard deviation for each column.
6. p0 is the 0% percentile or the minimum value for each column.
7. p25 is the 25% percentile or the 1st quartile for each column.
8. p50 is the 50% percentile, the median, or the 2nd quartile for each column.
9. p75 is the 75% percentile or the 3rd quartile for each column.
10. p100 is the 100% percentile or the maximum value for each column.
11. hist is the histogram plot for each column.

5.3. KNN MODEL

The knn model predicts the outcome of a data row by comparing it to k similar rows in the training data where k is defined by the analyst or determined by cross-validation.

For regression modeling with numerical outcome, the knn model computes the average outcome value of the k training rows that are the most similar to the desired data row and returns this average as predicted outcome value of the desired data row.

The knn model has three tuning parameters:

1. **neighbors:** Which are an integer number of nearest neighbors used to determine the outcome value and can be determined using the neighbors function.

neighbors()

Nearest Neighbors (quantitative)

Range: [1, 10]

- The default range is from 1 to 10.

2. **weight_func:** Which are the kernel functions for distance weighting and determined using the weight_func function. There are 10 values that can be seen using the values_weight_func function.

values_weight_func

[1] "rectangular" "triangular" "epanechnikov" "biweight" "triweight"

[6] "cos" "inv" "gaussian" "rank" "optimal"

3. **dist_power:** Which is the Minkowski distance order used to determine the similarity between the different rows. This can be determined using the dist_power function.

dist_power()

Minkowski Distance Order (quantitative)

Range: [1, 2]

The default range is from 1 (corresponding to Manhattan distance) to 2 (corresponding to Euclidean distance).

The distance measurement is very sensitive to the scale on which predictor variable measurements are made. So, it is recommended to normalize the predictor variables for making their scales comparable.

5.4. KNN REGRESSION

5.4.1. Split the Data

We first do a stratified splitting of the data using the numerical outcome (compressive_strength). This ensures that both the resulting training and testing data have the same compressive strength distribution as the original concrete data.

We create an object called "split_con" by using the initial_split function with the arguments:

- data = concrete which is the data we want to split.
- strata = compressive_strength to make a stratified splitting using the compressive strength outcome column.

To make the splitting reproducible, we use the set.seed function with any number before using the initial_split function.

set.seed(123)

split_con <- **initial_split**(data = concrete,

strata = compressive_strength)

split_con

<Training/Testing/Total>

<770/260/1030>

The training data has 770 rows and the testing data has 260 rows with a total of 1030 which is the total rows of original data.

To get the actual training and testing data, we use the training and testing functions, respectively, on the split_con object. The resulting data is called train_con for the training data and test_con for the testing data. Finally, we use the dim function to see the data dimensions.

```
train_con<-training(split_con)
test_con<-testing(split_con)
dim(train_con)
## [1] 770 9
dim(test_con)
## [1] 260 9
```

- The training data has 770 rows (1st number) and the same 9 columns of the concrete data (2nd number), while the testing data has 260 rows (1st number) and the same 9 columns of the concrete data (2nd number).

5.4.2. Generate the Recipe

We create an object "rec" by applying the following functions on the train_con data using the "%>%" operator:

- The recipe function with the argument compressive_strength ~ . meaning define the compressive_strength column as an outcome and all 8 other columns as predictors.
- The step_normalize function with the argument all_predictors to convert all numeric predictors into columns having 0 mean and 1 standard deviation so all predictors will have a common scale.

```
rec <- train_con %>%
recipe(compressive_strength ~ .) %>%
step_normalize(all_predictors())
rec
##
## ── Recipe ──────────────────────────────────────────────────────────────
##
## ── Inputs
```

```
## Number of variables by role
## outcome: 1
## predictor: 8
##
## — Operations
## • Centering and scaling for: all_predictors()
```

- The recipe object "rec":

++ Defines the variables by role: 1 outcome and 8 predictors.

++ Contains 1 preprocessing operation of normalizing all predictors.

5.4.3. Look at Preprocessed Data

First, wc prcparc thc rccipc using thc prcp function on thc "rcc" rccipc. Thc resulting object is called "prep_rec."

```
prep_rec <- prep(rec)
prep_rec
##
## — Recipe ——————————————————————————————————————————————
##
## — Inputs
## Number of variables by role
## outcome: 1
## predictor: 8
##
## — Training information
## Training data contained 770 data points and no incomplete rows.
##
## — Operations
## • Centering and scaling for: cement and blast_furnace_slag, ... | Trained
```

Second, to get the preprocessed training data, we use the bake function with the arguments:

- prep_rec which is the prepared recipe.
- new_data = NULL to apply the prepared recipe to training data contained in the original recipe.

The resulting data is called "train_con2" and we use the glimpse function to see the data structure.

```
train_con2 <- bake(prep_rec, new_data = NULL)
glimpse(train_con2)
## Rows: 770
## Columns: 9
## $ cement <dbl> –1.3501358, –0.7766140, –0.7766140, 0.3062730, 0…
## $ blast_furnace_slag <dbl> 1.5529565, 0.6588581, 0.6588581, –0.8785267, 1.31…
## $ fly_ash <dbl> –0.8528307, –0.8528307, –0.8528307, –0.8528307, –…
## $ water <dbl> 0.489779796, 0.489779796, 0.489779796, 0.48977979…
## $ superplasticizer <dbl> –1.02637194, –1.02637194, –1.02637194, –1.0263719…
## $ coarse_aggregate <dbl> 0.979750207, 0.092272664, 0.092272664, –0.0034610…
## $ fine_aggregate <dbl> 0.38758933, 0.61864451, 0.61864451, 0.93044478, –…
## $ age <dbl> –0.6700327, –0.6083358, –0.6700327, –0.6700327, –…
## $ compressive_strength <dbl> 8.06, 14.64, 9.13, 9.87, 22.90, 11.58, 10.38, 22…
```

- The training data has the same 770 rows and 9 columns of the original training data but all columns, except for the outcome, have negative values because of normalization.

We can use the skim and yank functions again on the train_con2 data to get useful information about all columns in the concrete training data after normalization.

```
train_con2 %>% skim() %>% yank("numeric") %>%
flextable() %>% theme_box() %>%
set_caption(caption = "The information gained from skim function on all columns from the concrete training data after normalization")
```

The information gained from skim function on all columns from the concrete training data after normalization:

skim_ variable	n_ miss- ing	compl ete_ rate	mean	sd	p0	p25	p50	p75	p100	hist
cement	0	1	–0.0000 0000000 0000060 592796	1.00 000	–1.715 6345	–0.853 4076	–0.1214 3817	0.685 3807	2.542 036	
blast_fur- nace_slag	0	1	–0.00000 0000000 0000082 57678	1.00 000	–0.878 5267	–0.878 5267	–0.5998 4669	0.801 6816	3.294 707	
fly_ash	0	1	0.0000 00000000 0000338 66463	1.00 000	–0.852 8307	–0.852 8307	–0.8528 3073	1.004 4717	2.288 727	
water	0	1	0.00000 00000000 0040396 2254	1.00 000	–2.825 8810	–0.790 1975	0.1355 4253	0.489 7798	3.087 520	
superplas- ticizer	0	1	–0.0000000 00000000 010289 853	1.00 000	–1.026 3719	–1.026 3719	0.0327 0701	0.658 1473	4.344 076	
coarse_ aggregate	0	1	0.00000 0000000 0006092 30097	1.00 000	–2.202 7494	–0.508 0037	–0.0539 1533	0.739 1222	2.109 149	
fine_ag- gregate	0	1	0.00000 000000 00006126 02424	1.00 000	–2.257 1229	–0.510 2339	0.0546 7112	0.630 7563	2.694 414	
age	0	1	–0.000 00000000 00000180 05289	1.00 000	–0.700 8812	–0.608 3358	–0.2844 2687	0.147 4517	4.913 540	
compres- sive_ strength	0	1	35.6281 0389610 3894498 992304	16.6 86 45	2.330 0000	23.710 0000	34.3650 0000	46. 125 0000	82.600 000	

- The mean of all 8 predictors is extremely low and nearly equals zero while the mean of the compressive strength outcome has not been changed.
- The standard deviation of all 8 predictors = 1 while the standard deviation of the outcome column has not been changed. So, all 8 predictors are now on a comparable scale.

Finally, to get the preprocessed testing data, we use the bake function with the arguments:

- prep_rec which is the prepared recipe.
- new_data = test_con to apply the prepared recipe to the testing data.

The resulting data is called "test_con2" and we use the glimpse function to see the data structure.

```
test_con2 <- bake(prep_rec, new_data = test_con)
glimpse(test_con2)
## Rows: 260
## Columns: 9
## $ cement <dbl> 2.5420362, –0.7766140, –0.1214382, 0.9867227, –0…
## $ blast_furnace_slag <dbl> –0.878526722, 0.658858095, 0.445203408, 0.2245817…
## $ fly_ash <dbl> –0.8528307, –0.8528307, –0.8528307, –0.8528307, –…
## $ water <dbl> –0.92716928, 0.48977980, 2.19011869, 2.19011869, …
## $ superplasticizer <dbl> –0.6094117, –1.0263719, –1.0263719, –1.0263719, –…
## $ coarse_aggregate <dbl> 0.88919127, 0.09227266, –0.50800369, –0.50800369,…
## $ fine_aggregate <dbl> –1.23849253, 0.61864451, –1.31302646, –2.25712289…
## $ age <dbl> –0.2844269, 4.8364187, 0.6718756, 4.9135398, –0.2…
## $ compressive_strength <dbl> 79.99, 44.30, 47.03, 43.70, 28.02, 43.01, 52.91, …
```

- The testing data has the same 260 rows and 9 columns of the original testing data but all columns, except the outcome, have negative values because of normalization.

5.4.4. Generate Different Resamples of Training Data

We split the train_con data using the vfold_cv function with the arguments:

- v = 10 to split the data into 10 folds.
- repeats = 5 to repeat this process 5 times.
- strata = compressive_strength to make stratified resampling using the compressive strength column.

The result is 50 different resamples of train_con data contained in folds data frame.

We also use the set.seed function before splitting to make the splitting reproducible.

```
set.seed(123)
folds<-vfold_cv(train_con, v = 10, repeats = 5,
```

```
strata = compressive_strength)
folds
## # 10-fold cross-validation repeated 5 times using stratification
## # A tibble: 50 × 3
## splits id id2
## <list> <chr> <chr>
## 1 <split [690/80]> Repeat1 Fold01
## 2 <split [690/80]> Repeat1 Fold02
## 3 <split [692/78]> Repeat1 Fold03
## 4 <split [694/76]> Repeat1 Fold04
## 5 <split [694/76]> Repeat1 Fold05
## 6 <split [694/76]> Repeat1 Fold06
## 7 <split [694/76]> Repeat1 Fold07
## 8 <split [694/76]> Repeat1 Fold08
## 9 <split [694/76]> Repeat1 Fold09
## 10 <split [694/76]> Repeat1 Fold10
## # i 40 more rows
```

- There are 50 different rows. Each row corresponds to 1 resample of train_con data. Each resample has 1 analysis (training) data, with 690, 692, or 694 rows and 1 assessment (testing) data with 80, 78, or 76 rows.
- Each resample has 2 id values. id for the repeat number from 1 to 5 and id2 for the resample number from 1 to 10 within that repeat.
- Each resample has a total rows of 770 which is the number of rows in the original train_con data. 690 + 80 = 692 + 78 = 694 + 76 = 770.

5.4.5. Define Machine Learning (ML) Model

We define a knn regression model by using the functions:

- The nearest_neighbor function to define the k-nearest neighbor (knn) regression model type with the following arguments:
  - neighbors = tune() to tune the neighbors number on the different resamples of training data.
  - weight_func = tune() to tune the weight function on the different resamples of training data.

  - dist_power = tune() to tune the distance power on the different resamples of the training data.
- The set_engine function with the argument "kknn" to define the engine that will use the train.kknn function from the kknn package.
- The set_mode function with the argument "regression" to define the mode of learning. We use regression because we have a numerical outcome (compressive strength).
- All the 3 functions are applied in sequence using the piping "%>%" operator and the resulting object is called "knn_model."

```
knn_model <- nearest_neighbor(neighbors = tune(), weight_func = tune(),
dist_power = tune()) %>%
set_engine("kknn") %>%
set_mode("regression")
knn_model
## K-Nearest Neighbor Model Specification (regression)
##
## Main Arguments:
## neighbors = tune()
## weight_func = tune()
## dist_power = tune()
##
## Computational engine: kknn
```

5.4.6. Generate Workflow

We create the "wflow" object by using the following functions:

- The workflow function to create a workflow.
- The add_recipe function with the argument "rec" to add the above created recipe with 1 preprocessing step.
- The add_model function with the argument knn_model to add the above created knn model.

```
wflow <- workflow() %>%
add_recipe(rec) %>%
add_model(knn_model)
wflow
```

```
## ══ Workflow ════════════════════════════════════════
## Preprocessor: Recipe
## Model: nearest_neighbor()
##
## ── Preprocessor ────────────────────────────────────
## 1 Recipe Step
##
## • step_normalize()
##
## ── Model ───────────────────────────────────────────
## K-Nearest Neighbor Model Specification (regression)
##
## Main Arguments:
## neighbors = tune()
## weight_func = tune()
## dist_power = tune()
##
## Computational engine: kknn
```

- The “wflow” object contains 1 preprocessing step (normalization) and the knn regression model with tuned neighbors, distance weighting, and Minkowski distance.

5.4.7. Fit Model on Different Resamples with Tuning

We can train many models using 50 resamples of training data in the folds data fame and see which models turn out best. We can use the grid_regular function to chooses sensible values for the neighbors, distance weighting, and Minkowski distance terms.

However, if we choose 10 levels for each of the 3 parameters, this means that we will have $10 \times 10 \times 10 = 1000$ different combinations. Instead, we use the grid_random function to choose 100 different combinations of these 3 parameters.

We create a grid of neighbors, distance weighting, and Minkowski distance values “my_grid” by using the grid_random function with the arguments:

- neighbors with the argument range = c(1,40) to choose different neighbors (k) from 1 to 40.
- weight_func to choose from 10 different distance weighting functions.
- dist_power to choose different values of the Minkowski distance from 1 to 2.
- size = 100 to choose 100 different combinations.

For reproducibility, we use the set.seed function with any number before using the grid_random function.

set.seed(123)

my_grid <- **grid_random**(**neighbors**(range = **c**(1,40)), **weight_func**(), **dist_power**(), size = 100)

my_grid **%>% flextable**(cwidth = 1) **%>% theme_box**() **%>% set_caption**(caption = "The different 100 combinations of neighbors, distance weighting, and Minkowski distance values chosen by using the grid_random function")

The different 100 combinations of neighbors, distance weighting, and Minkowski distance values chosen by using the grid_random function:

neighbors	**weight_func**	**dist_power**
31	rectangular	1.492293
15	inv	1.389587
14	inv	1.464666
3	inv	1.713279
37	optimal	1.055302
14	cos	1.354783
25	inv	1.802812
26	optimal	1.835709
27	triweight	1.237749
5	cos	1.353986
27	gaussian	1.856885
28	triweight	1.853763
9	inv	1.295895
29	biweight	1.147048
35	epanechnikov	1.703992
8	rank	1.103807

26	inv	1.033728
7	cos	1.999405
9	optimal	1.034875
19	rank	1.338391
36	inv	1.915064
14	triangular	1.617235
17	epanechnikov	1.286285
39	gaussian	1.737797
12	biweight	1.834054
15	inv	1.314271
32	biweight	1.492567
7	rectangular	1.697374
9	gaussian	1.641462
10	biweight	1.643923
23	rank	1.977853
27	gaussian	1.414735
7	cos	1.119405
27	biweight	1.526030
32	gaussian	1.225073
38	epanechnikov	1.486412
25	biweight	1.370215
34	biweight	1.983350
29	cos	1.388319
5	rectangular	1.229245
8	optimal	1.623298
12	biweight	1.136540
13	rank	1.967469
18	inv	1.515072
33	gaussian	1.163070
27	triweight	1.621902
25	triangular	1.985954
38	cos	1.668772
21	rank	1.418916
15	gaussian	1.323345
26	optimal	1.835255
31	biweight	1.143817

16	triweight	1.192816
30	inv	1.896739
6	rectangular	1.308120
8	gaussian	1.363301
22	gaussian	1.783946
22	optimal	1.193379
39	rank	1.017766
31	gaussian	1.406608
17	triangular	1.483168
34	triweight	1.421845
4	rank	1.342809
13	inv	1.866483
5	inv	1.455108
25	optimal	1.533765
22	optimal	1.963843
25	gaussian	1.774592
32	cos	1.208876
25	inv	1.308787
23	optimal	1.971342
35	rectangular	1.584900
40	rank	1.760824
30	epanechnikov	1.372709
12	optimal	1.769194
31	triweight	1.537677
30	cos	1.913995
35	rank	1.185296
14	biweight	1.282218
29	optimal	1.094962
32	inv	1.210487
7	rank	1.977099
3	inv	1.296302
23	optimal	1.725983
15	biweight	1.785688
21	gaussian	1.105418
37	rank	1.239595
8	rank	1.270545

10	rank	1.101058
34	triweight	1.117914
10	inv	1.991237
22	cos	1.986054
12	rectangular	1.137067
20	optimal	1.905310
17	optimal	1.576302
35	rectangular	1.395449
40	optimal	1.449802
30	rectangular	1.706502
15	optimal	1.082503
24	triweight	1.339313

- The neighbors values range from 1 to 40, the weight_func has 10 different values, and the dist_power ranges from 1 to 2.

To try all these 100 different combinations on the 50 resamples of the training data, we use the tune_grid function with the arguments:

- wflow which is the workflow containing 1 preprocessing step and the knn model.
- folds which are the 50 resamples of training data created above.
- metrics = metrics_set(rmse) to get the RMSE of the knn model on each resample using the 100 different combinations.
- grid = my_grid to use the 100 combinations in the my_grid data in tuning.

```
set.seed(123)
knn_res <- tune_grid(wflow, folds,
metrics = metric_set(rmse),
grid = my_grid)
knn_res
## # Tuning results
## # 10-fold cross-validation repeated 5 times using stratification
## # A tibble: 50 × 5
## splits id id2 .metrics .notes
## <list> <chr> <chr> <list> <list>
## 1 <split [690/80]> Repeat1 Fold01 <tibble [100 × 7]> <tibble [0 × 3]>
```

```
## 2 <split [690/80]> Repeat1 Fold02 <tibble [100 × 7]> <tibble [0 × 3]>
## 3 <split [692/78]> Repeat1 Fold03 <tibble [100 × 7]> <tibble [0 × 3]>
## 4 <split [694/76]> Repeat1 Fold04 <tibble [100 × 7]> <tibble [0 × 3]>
## 5 <split [694/76]> Repeat1 Fold05 <tibble [100 × 7]> <tibble [0 × 3]>
## 6 <split [694/76]> Repeat1 Fold06 <tibble [100 × 7]> <tibble [0 × 3]>
## 7 <split [694/76]> Repeat1 Fold07 <tibble [100 × 7]> <tibble [0 × 3]>
## 8 <split [694/76]> Repeat1 Fold08 <tibble [100 × 7]> <tibble [0 × 3]>
## 9 <split [694/76]> Repeat1 Fold09 <tibble [100 × 7]> <tibble [0 × 3]>
## 10 <split [694/76]> Repeat1 Fold10 <tibble [100 × 7]> <tibble [0 × 3]>
## # ℹ 40 more rows
```

The resulting object "knn_res" contains 50 rows (for 50 resamples) and 5 columns:

- The splits column is a list of each combination of analysis and assessment data withing each resample. The sum is 770, which are total rows of training data.
- The id column is an id column for the repeat number from 1 to 5.
- The id2 column is an id column for the fold number from 1 to 10 so we have 50 resamples because 5 × 10 = 50.
- The .metrics column is a list of performance metric (RMSE) of applying the knn model to the corresponding assessment data (80, 78, or 76 rows) within each resample. Each performance metric is saved in 100 rows and 7 columns [100 × 7] tibble or data frame. The 100 rows are for the RMSE of applying the 100 different combinations of neighbors, distance weighting, and Minkowski distance on the assessment data within each resample.
- The .notes column is a list of notes or warnings when applying the knn model to each analysis data (690, 692, or 694 rows) within each resample. Each note is saved in 0 rows and 3 columns [0 × 3] tibble or data frame meaning that there are no rows or no notes when applying this model to each analysis data.

5.4.8. The Model Performance on 50 Resamples of the Training Data

To get the performance metric (RMSE) on the 50 resamples of training data using the 100 different combinations, we will use the unnest function with the ".metrics" argument to expand the .metrics list column of the knn_res object into rows and columns.

```
knn_res %>% unnest(.metrics)
## # A tibble: 5,000 × 11
## splits id id2 neighbors weight_func dist_power .metric
## <list> <chr> <chr> <int> <chr> <dbl> <chr>
## 1 <split [690/80]> Repeat1 Fold01 12 biweight 1.14 rmse
## 2 <split [690/80]> Repeat1 Fold01 31 biweight 1.14 rmse
## 3 <split [690/80]> Repeat1 Fold01 29 biweight 1.15 rmse
## 4 <split [690/80]> Repeat1 Fold01 14 biweight 1.28 rmse
## 5 <split [690/80]> Repeat1 Fold01 25 biweight 1.37 rmse
## 6 <split [690/80]> Repeat1 Fold01 32 biweight 1.49 rmse
## 7 <split [690/80]> Repeat1 Fold01 27 biweight 1.53 rmse
## 8 <split [690/80]> Repeat1 Fold01 10 biweight 1.64 rmse
## 9 <split [690/80]> Repeat1 Fold01 15 biweight 1.79 rmse
## 10 <split [690/80]> Repeat1 Fold01 12 biweight 1.83 rmse
## # i 4,990 more rows
## # i 4 more variables: .estimator <chr>, .estimate <dbl>, .config <chr>,
## # .notes <list>
```

- The result is 5000 rows because we have applied the 100 combinations to 50 resamples of the training data so we have 100 × 50 or 5000 models or rows. Each row contains the RMSE of the knn model on 1 resample using 1 combination.

To get the mean RMSE of each combination on the 50 resamples of the training data, we use the following functions on the "knn_res" object:

- The collect_metrics function to get the mean RMSE for each combination across the 50 resamples of the training data.
- The arrange function with a mean argument to arrange by mean RMSE value in ascending order.
- The flextable, theme_box, and set_caption functions are described previously.

```
knn_res %>% collect_metrics() %>%
arrange(mean) %>%
flextable() %>% theme_box() %>%
set_caption(caption = "The mean RMSE of applying 100 combinations of neighbors, distance weighting, and Minkowski distance on 50 resamples of concrete training data when using knn regression model")
```

The mean RMSE of applying 100 combinations of neighbors, distance weighting, and Minkowski distance on 50 resamples of concrete training data when using knn regression model:

neighbors	weight_func	dist_power	.metric	.estimator	mean	n	std_err	.config
5	inv	1.455108	rmse	standard	8.240025	50	0.1143685	Preprocessor1_Model044
10	inv	1.991237	rmse	standard	8.294512	50	0.1180590	Preprocessor1_Model052
9	inv	1.295895	rmse	standard	8.333614	50	0.1163781	Preprocessor1_Model039
3	inv	1.713279	rmse	standard	8.376390	50	0.1377613	Preprocessor1_Model047
13	inv	1.866483	rmse	standard	8.418252	50	0.1153480	Preprocessor1_Model049
14	inv	1.464666	rmse	standard	8.487205	50	0.1198994	Preprocessor1_Model045
8	optimal	1.623298	rmse	standard	8.490700	50	0.1161440	Preprocessor1_Model061
15	inv	1.389587	rmse	standard	8.532688	50	0.1182126	Preprocessor1_Model043
15	inv	1.314271	rmse	standard	8.539658	50	0.1171107	Preprocessor1_Model042
18	inv	1.515072	rmse	standard	8.612530	50	0.1170792	Preprocessor1_Model046
3	inv	1.296302	rmse	standard	8.649340	50	0.1392353	Preprocessor1_Model040
7	rank	1.977099	rmse	standard	8.679758	50	0.1196328	Preprocessor1_Model080
12	optimal	1.769194	rmse	standard	8.695365	50	0.1161600	Preprocessor1_Model063
4	rank	1.342809	rmse	standard	8.789242	50	0.1245501	Preprocessor1_Model076

9	optimal	1.034875	rmse	standard	8.791882	50	0.1163654	Preprocessor1_Model053
25	inv	1.308787	rmse	standard	8.839203	50	0.1187242	Preprocessor1_Model041
8	rank	1.270545	rmse	standard	8.853766	50	0.1117753	Preprocessor1_Model074
8	rank	1.103807	rmse	standard	8.888816	50	0.1118390	Preprocessor1_Model071
26	inv	1.033728	rmse	standard	8.889115	50	0.1181473	Preprocessor1_Model037
25	inv	1.802812	rmse	standard	8.906400	50	0.1203330	Preprocessor1_Model048
7	cos	1.999405	rmse	standard	8.918690	50	0.1284865	Preprocessor1_Model020
17	optimal	1.576302	rmse	standard	8.974439	50	0.1173026	Preprocessor1_Model060
15	optimal	1.082503	rmse	standard	8.986757	50	0.1173082	Preprocessor1_Model055
10	rank	1.101058	rmse	standard	8.989134	50	0.1141915	Preprocessor1_Model070
9	gaussian	1.641462	rmse	standard	8.999250	50	0.1179868	Preprocessor1_Model032
8	gaussian	1.363301	rmse	standard	9.003418	50	0.1166055	Preprocessor1_Model029
12	biweight	1.834054	rmse	standard	9.004482	50	0.1228873	Preprocessor1_Model010
32	inv	1.210487	rmse	standard	9.025108	50	0.1186681	Preprocessor1_Model038
10	biweight	1.643923	rmse	standard	9.051531	50	0.1316164	Preprocessor1_Model008
30	inv	1.896739	rmse	standard	9.081139	50	0.1211355	Preprocessor1_Model050

15	biweight	1.785688	rmse	stan-dard	9.124532	50	0.1224735	Preproces-sor1_Mod-el009
14	triangular	1.617235	rmse	stan-dard	9.125487	50	0.1184345	Preproces-sor1_Mod-el091
7	rectangu-lar	1.697374	rmse	stan-dard	9.127016	50	0.1150563	Preproces-sor1_Mod-el088
13	rank	1.967469	rmse	stan-dard	9.129691	50	0.1192939	Preproces-sor1_Mod-el079
5	cos	1.353986	rmse	stan-dard	9.134584	50	0.1349931	Preproces-sor1_Mod-el014
20	optimal	1.905310	rmse	stan-dard	9.143645	50	0.1192420	Preproces-sor1_Mod-el066
6	rectangu-lar	1.308120	rmse	stan-dard	9.163832	50	0.1151732	Preproces-sor1_Mod-el084
5	rectangu-lar	1.229245	rmse	stan-dard	9.184775	50	0.1109466	Preproces-sor1_Mod-el083
22	optimal	1.963843	rmse	stan-dard	9.251936	50	0.1204179	Preproces-sor1_Mod-el067
36	inv	1.915064	rmse	stan-dard	9.274773	50	0.1256145	Preproces-sor1_Mod-el051
17	triangular	1.483168	rmse	stan-dard	9.276283	50	0.1219762	Preproces-sor1_Mod-el090
22	optimal	1.193379	rmse	stan-dard	9.277117	50	0.1215479	Preproces-sor1_Mod-el057
7	cos	1.119405	rmse	stan-dard	9.281102	50	0.1285533	Preproces-sor1_Mod-el012
28	triweight	1.853763	rmse	stan-dard	9.282608	50	0.1256712	Preproces-sor1_Mod-el100
23	optimal	1.725983	rmse	stan-dard	9.285658	50	0.1216158	Preproces-sor1_Mod-el062
23	optimal	1.971342	rmse	stan-dard	9.302552	50	0.1210720	Preproces-sor1_Mod-el068

14	cos	1.354783	rmse	standard	9.363790	50	0.1209161	Preprocessor1_Model015
27	triweight	1.621902	rmse	standard	9.372296	50	0.1287278	Preprocessor1_Model099
25	optimal	1.533765	rmse	standard	9.394763	50	0.1227586	Preprocessor1_Model059
14	biweight	1.282218	rmse	standard	9.399801	50	0.1274609	Preprocessor1_Model004
26	optimal	1.835255	rmse	standard	9.437678	50	0.1233328	Preprocessor1_Model064
26	optimal	1.835709	rmse	standard	9.437743	50	0.1233648	Preprocessor1_Model065
15	gaussian	1.323345	rmse	standard	9.447010	50	0.1242730	Preprocessor1_Model028
31	triweight	1.537677	rmse	standard	9.472018	50	0.1287663	Preprocessor1_Model098
24	triweight	1.339313	rmse	standard	9.508588	50	0.1338706	Preprocessor1_Model096
19	rank	1.338391	rmse	standard	9.509507	50	0.1246896	Preprocessor1_Model075
17	epanechnikov	1.286285	rmse	standard	9.522015	50	0.1246813	Preprocessor1_Model021
12	biweight	1.136540	rmse	standard	9.528859	50	0.1313011	Preprocessor1_Model001
16	triweight	1.192816	rmse	standard	9.558485	50	0.1379970	Preprocessor1_Model094
25	triangular	1.985954	rmse	standard	9.559253	50	0.1247972	Preprocessor1_Model092
29	optimal	1.094962	rmse	standard	9.561549	50	0.1249680	Preprocessor1_Model056
34	triweight	1.421845	rmse	standard	9.562908	50	0.1288511	Preprocessor1_Model097

27	biweight	1.526030	rmse	standard	9.596426	50	0.1276684	Preprocessor1_Model007
22	cos	1.986054	rmse	standard	9.601687	50	0.1240859	Preprocessor1_Model019
25	biweight	1.370215	rmse	standard	9.616963	50	0.1302856	Preprocessor1_Model005
21	rank	1.418916	rmse	standard	9.622278	50	0.1260174	Preprocessor1_Model077
34	biweight	1.983350	rmse	standard	9.632992	50	0.1252656	Preprocessor1_Model011
27	triweight	1.237749	rmse	standard	9.643014	50	0.1337703	Preprocessor1_Model095
22	gaussian	1.783946	rmse	standard	9.675838	50	0.1279485	Preprocessor1_Model035
32	biweight	1.492567	rmse	standard	9.706589	50	0.1273545	Preprocessor1_Model006
12	rectangular	1.137067	rmse	standard	9.748755	50	0.1312554	Preprocessor1_Model082
23	rank	1.977853	rmse	standard	9.754449	50	0.1261740	Preprocessor1_Model081
34	triweight	1.117914	rmse	standard	9.772657	50	0.1306886	Preprocessor1_Model093
21	gaussian	1.105418	rmse	standard	9.778909	50	0.1316998	Preprocessor1_Model025
29	biweight	1.147048	rmse	standard	9.802028	50	0.1297605	Preprocessor1_Model003
37	optimal	1.055302	rmse	standard	9.804410	50	0.1258920	Preprocessor1_Model054
25	gaussian	1.774592	rmse	standard	9.810570	50	0.1289929	Preprocessor1_Model034
31	biweight	1.143817	rmse	standard	9.828625	50	0.1297827	Preprocessor1_Model002

27	gaussian	1.856885	rmse	standard	9.863844	50	0.1279823	Preprocessor1_Model036
27	gaussian	1.414735	rmse	standard	9.921043	50	0.1295900	Preprocessor1_Model031
40	optimal	1.449802	rmse	standard	9.922480	50	0.1242076	Preprocessor1_Model058
30	cos	1.913995	rmse	standard	9.948436	50	0.1272716	Preprocessor1_Model018
29	cos	1.388319	rmse	standard	9.967518	50	0.1300413	Preprocessor1_Model016
31	gaussian	1.406608	rmse	standard	9.995681	50	0.1293383	Preprocessor1_Model030
32	gaussian	1.225073	rmse	standard	10.023544	50	0.1291201	Preprocessor1_Model027
32	cos	1.208876	rmse	standard	10.043475	50	0.1293860	Preprocessor1_Model013
30	epanechnikov	1.372709	rmse	standard	10.051047	50	0.1299292	Preprocessor1_Model022
33	gaussian	1.163070	rmse	standard	10.051329	50	0.1295293	Preprocessor1_Model026
39	gaussian	1.737797	rmse	standard	10.146734	50	0.1285825	Preprocessor1_Model033
35	rank	1.185296	rmse	standard	10.155972	50	0.1274874	Preprocessor1_Model072
35	epanechnikov	1.703992	rmse	standard	10.189177	50	0.1277566	Preprocessor1_Model024
38	cos	1.668772	rmse	standard	10.192632	50	0.1268160	Preprocessor1_Model017
37	rank	1.239595	rmse	standard	10.223684	50	0.1273513	Preprocessor1_Model073
39	rank	1.017766	rmse	standard	10.238720	50	0.1284393	Preprocessor1_Model069

38	epanech-nikov	1.486412	rmse	stan-dard	10.259029	50	0.1272165	Preproces-sor1_Mod-el023
40	rank	1.760824	rmse	stan-dard	10.432020	50	0.1280170	Preproces-sor1_Mod-el078
31	rectangu-lar	1.492293	rmse	stan-dard	10.783950	50	0.1269571	Preproces-sor1_Mod-el086
30	rectangu-lar	1.706502	rmse	stan-dard	10.834404	50	0.1283305	Preproces-sor1_Mod-el089
35	rectangu-lar	1.395449	rmse	stan-dard	10.837144	50	0.1269830	Preproces-sor1_Mod-el085
35	rectangu-lar	1.584900	rmse	stan-dard	10.914676	50	0.1274756	Preproces-sor1_Mod-el087

- The result is 100 rows with 1 mean RMSE value for each combination across the 50 resamples (n = 50).
- The lowest mean RMSE value (8.24) was achieved when using 5 neighbors, inv weighting function, and 1.455108 Minkowski distance.
- The highest mean RMSE value (10.91) was achieved when using 35 neighbors, rectangular weighting function, and 1.584900 Minkowski distance.

We can use the select_best function to create an object "best_pen" that contains the best combination value for the best knn model.

```
best_pen<-knn_res %>% select_best()
best_pen
## # A tibble: 1 × 4
## neighbors weight_func dist_power .config
## <int> <chr> <dbl> <chr>
## 1 5 inv 1.46 Preprocessor1_Model044
```

- The best combination with the lowest mean RMSE value (8.24) was using 5 neighbors, inv weighting function, and 1.46 Minkowski distance.

To get the final workflow with the best penalty, we use the finalize_workflow function with the arguments:

- wflow which is the original workflow with tuned 3 parameters.
- best_pen which is the data of 1 row containing the best combination of 3 parameters.

The resulting workflow "knn_final" is the final workflow containing the best combination of 3 parameters.

```
knn_final <- finalize_workflow(wflow, best_pen)
knn_final
## ══ Workflow ════════════════════════════════════════════════════
## Preprocessor: Recipe
## Model: nearest_neighbor()
##
## ── Preprocessor ────────────────────────────────────────────────
## 1 Recipe Step
##
## • step_normalize()
##
## ── Model ───────────────────────────────────────────────────────
## K-Nearest Neighbor Model Specification (regression)
##
## Main Arguments:
## neighbors = 5
## weight_func = inv
## dist_power = 1.45510805095546
##
## Computational engine: kknn
```

Finally, we create a knn_fit model by using the fit function with the arguments:

- knn_final which is the final workflow containing 1 preprocessing step (normalization) and the knn model with best combinations of 3 parameters.
- train_con which is the whole training data with 770 rows.

```
knn_fit <- fit(knn_final, data = train_con)
```

Then to see the RMSE on the whole training data, we use the following functions on the knn_fit model:

- The predict function with the argument new_data = train_con to get the predicted compressive strength (.pred) column for each row of the training data after being preprocessed using the knn_fit model.
- The mutate function with the argument truth = train_con$compressive_strength to add a truth column containing the actual compressive strength for each row in the training data.
- The rmse function with the arguments truth = truth, estimate = .pred to get the RMSE of applying this knn model on the training data.

```
knn_fit <- fit(knn_final, data = train_con)
knn_fit %>% predict(new_data = train_con) %>%
mutate(truth = train_con$compressive_strength) %>%
rmse(truth = truth, estimate = .pred)
## # A tibble: 1 × 3
## .metric .estimator .estimate
## <chr> <chr> <dbl>
## 1 rmse standard 1.08
```

- The RMSE of this knn model on whole training data = 1.08 which is very low compared to that obtained by using cross-validation on 50 resamples (8.24).

5.4.9. Model Performance on Testing Data

To get the RMSE on the testing data, we use the same above functions on the knn_fit model but use the test_con data.

```
knn_fit %>% predict(new_data = test_con) %>%
mutate(truth = test_con$compressive_strength) %>%
rmse(truth = truth, estimate = .pred)
## # A tibble: 1 × 3
## .metric .estimator .estimate
## <chr> <chr> <dbl>
## 1 rmse standard 8.27
```

- The RMSE of the knn model on testing data = 8.27 which is nearer to that obtained on the training when using cross-validation (8.24) with the best 3 parameters.

- This highlights the importance of using cross-validation to determine the model performance on future unseen data.

5.5. COMPARISON BETWEEN DIFFERENT MODELS

We will test the linear regression and the elastic net model in addition to the knn model to see the best performing model on the training data.

5.5.1. Linear Regression Model

The linear regression model has no required preprocessing steps so we create the "lm_rec" by using the recipe function on the train_con data with the argument:

- compressive_strength ~ . meaning define compressive_strength as outcome and all other columns as predictors.

```
lm_rec<-train_con %>%
recipe(compressive_strength ~ .)
lm_rec
##
## — Recipe ——————————————————————————————————
##
## — Inputs
## Number of variables by role
## outcome: 1
## predictor: 8
```

The linear regression model has no tuning parameters so we create "lm_model" by using the functions: linear_reg, set_engine with the argument "lm," and set_mode with "regression" argument.

```
lm_model<-linear_reg() %>% set_engine("lm") %>%
set_mode("regression")
lm_model
## Linear Regression Model Specification (regression)
##
## Computational engine: lm
```

5.5.2. Elastic Net Model

The elastic net model requires normalization of all predictors so we create "elastic_rec" by using the step_normalize function as described before.

elastic_rec<-train_con **%>%**

recipe(compressive_strength ~ .) **%>%**

step_normalize(**all_predictors**())

elastic_rec

##

— Recipe ——————————————————————

##

— Inputs

Number of variables by role

outcome: 1

predictor: 8

##

— Operations

• Centering and scaling for: all_predictors()

The elastic net model has 2 tuning parameters: the mixture and penalty, so we create "elastic_model" by using the linear_reg function with the arguments:

- mixture = tune() to tune the different mixture values on the different resamples.
- penalty = tune() to tune the different penalty values on the different resamples.

elastic_model<-**linear_reg**(mixture = **tune**(), penalty = **tune**()) **%>%**

set_engine("glmnet") **%>%**

set_mode("regression")

elastic_model

Linear Regression Model Specification (regression)

##

Main Arguments:

penalty = tune()

mixture = tune()

```
##
## Computational engine: glmnet
```

Then, we create a grid "my_grid2" of 100 different values of mixture and penalty by using the levels = 10 argument within the grid_regular function.

```
my_grid2<-grid_regular(mixture(), penalty(), levels = 10)
my_grid2
## # A tibble: 100 × 2
## mixture penalty
## <dbl> <dbl>
## 1 0 0.0000000001
## 2 0.111 0.0000000001
## 3 0.222 0.0000000001
## 4 0.333 0.0000000001
## 5 0.444 0.0000000001
## 6 0.556 0.0000000001
## 7 0.667 0.0000000001
## 8 0.778 0.0000000001
## 9 0.889 0.0000000001
## 10 1 0.0000000001
## # i 90 more rows
```

To try all these 100 different combinations on the 50 resamples of the training data, we create a workflow "wflow2" containing the elastic_rec recipe and the elastic_model model.

```
wflow2<-workflow() %>% add_recipe(elastic_rec) %>%
add_model(elastic_model)
wflow2
## ══ Workflow ════════════════════════════════════════════
════════════════════════════════════

## Preprocessor: Recipe
## Model: linear_reg()
##
## ── Preprocessor ────────────────────────────────────────
────────────────────────────────
```

```
## 1 Recipe Step
##
## • step_normalize()
##
## ── Model ───────────────────────────────────────────
##
## Linear Regression Model Specification (regression)
##
## Main Arguments:
## penalty = tune()
## mixture = tune()
##
## Computational engine: glmnet
```

Then, we use the tune_grid function to determine the best tuning mixture and penalty values.

```
set.seed(123)
elastic_res <- tune_grid(wflow2, folds,
metrics = metric_set(rmse),
grid = my_grid2)
elastic_res
## # Tuning results
## # 10-fold cross-validation repeated 5 times using stratification
## # A tibble: 50 × 5
## splits id id2 .metrics .notes
## <list> <chr> <chr> <list> <list>
## 1 <split [690/80]> Repeat1 Fold01 <tibble [100 × 6]> <tibble [0 × 3]>
## 2 <split [690/80]> Repeat1 Fold02 <tibble [100 × 6]> <tibble [0 × 3]>
## 3 <split [692/78]> Repeat1 Fold03 <tibble [100 × 6]> <tibble [0 × 3]>
## 4 <split [694/76]> Repeat1 Fold04 <tibble [100 × 6]> <tibble [0 × 3]>
## 5 <split [694/76]> Repeat1 Fold05 <tibble [100 × 6]> <tibble [0 × 3]>
## 6 <split [694/76]> Repeat1 Fold06 <tibble [100 × 6]> <tibble [0 × 3]>
## 7 <split [694/76]> Repeat1 Fold07 <tibble [100 × 6]> <tibble [0 × 3]>
## 8 <split [694/76]> Repeat1 Fold08 <tibble [100 × 6]> <tibble [0 × 3]>
```

9 <split [694/76]> Repeat1 Fold09 <tibble [100 × 6]> <tibble [0 × 3]>

10 <split [694/76]> Repeat1 Fold10 <tibble [100 × 6]> <tibble [0 × 3]>

i 40 more rows

The resulting object "elastic_res" contains 50 rows (for 50 resamples) and 5 columns. Finally, by using the collect_metrics function, we can see the best mixture and penalty parameters.

elastic_res **%>% collect_metrics**() **%>%**

arrange(mean) **%>%**

flextable() **%>% theme_box**() **%>%**

set_caption(caption = "The mean RMSE of applying 100 combinations of mixture and penalty values on 50 resamples of concrete training data when using elastic net regression model")

The mean RMSE of applying 100 combinations of mixture and penalty values on 50 resamples of concrete training data when using elastic net regression model:

penalty	mixture	.metric	.estimator	mean	n	std_err	.config
0.00000000010000	0.2222222	rmse	standard	10.44122	50	0.1279631	Preprocessor1_Model021
0.00000000129155	0.2222222	rmse	standard	10.44122	50	0.1279631	Preprocessor1_Model022
0.00000001668101	0.2222222	rmse	standard	10.44122	50	0.1279631	Preprocessor1_Model023
0.00000021544347	0.2222222	rmse	standard	10.44122	50	0.1279631	Preprocessor1_Model024
0.00000278255940	0.2222222	rmse	standard	10.44122	50	0.1279631	Preprocessor1_Model025
0.00003593813664	0.2222222	rmse	standard	10.44122	50	0.1279631	Preprocessor1_Model026
0.00046415888336	0.2222222	rmse	standard	10.44122	50	0.1279631	Preprocessor1_Model027
0.00599484250319	0.2222222	rmse	standard	10.44122	50	0.1279631	Preprocessor1_Model028

0.00000000010000	0.4444444	rmse	standard	10.44128	50	0.1279743	Preprocessor1_Model041
0.00000000129155	0.4444444	rmse	standard	10.44128	50	0.1279743	Preprocessor1_Model042
0.00000001668101	0.4444444	rmse	standard	10.44128	50	0.1279743	Preprocessor1_Model043
0.00000021544347	0.4444444	rmse	standard	10.44128	50	0.1279743	Preprocessor1_Model044
0.00000278255940	0.4444444	rmse	standard	10.44128	50	0.1279743	Preprocessor1_Model045
0.00003593813664	0.4444444	rmse	standard	10.44128	50	0.1279743	Preprocessor1_Model046
0.00046415888336	0.4444444	rmse	standard	10.44128	50	0.1279743	Preprocessor1_Model047
0.00599484250319	0.4444444	rmse	standard	10.44128	50	0.1279743	Preprocessor1_Model048
0.00000000010000	0.1111111	rmse	standard	10.44132	50	0.1279604	Preprocessor1_Model011
0.00000000129155	0.1111111	rmse	standard	10.44132	50	0.1279604	Preprocessor1_Model012
0.00000001668101	0.1111111	rmse	standard	10.44132	50	0.1279604	Preprocessor1_Model013
0.00000021544347	0.1111111	rmse	standard	10.44132	50	0.1279604	Preprocessor1_Model014
0.00000278255940	0.1111111	rmse	standard	10.44132	50	0.1279604	Preprocessor1_Model015
0.00003593813664	0.1111111	rmse	standard	10.44132	50	0.1279604	Preprocessor1_Model016
0.00046415888336	0.1111111	rmse	standard	10.44132	50	0.1279604	Preprocessor1_Model017
0.00599484250319	0.1111111	rmse	standard	10.44132	50	0.1279604	Preprocessor1_Model018

0.00000000010000	0.3333333	rmse	standard	10.44137	50	0.1279780	Preprocessor1_Model031
0.00000000129155	0.3333333	rmse	standard	10.44137	50	0.1279780	Preprocessor1_Model032
0.00000001668101	0.3333333	rmse	standard	10.44137	50	0.1279780	Preprocessor1_Model033
0.00000021544347	0.3333333	rmse	standard	10.44137	50	0.1279780	Preprocessor1_Model034
0.00000278255940	0.3333333	rmse	standard	10.44137	50	0.1279780	Preprocessor1_Model035
0.00003593813664	0.3333333	rmse	standard	10.44137	50	0.1279780	Preprocessor1_Model036
0.00046415888336	0.3333333	rmse	standard	10.44137	50	0.1279780	Preprocessor1_Model037
0.00599484250319	0.3333333	rmse	standard	10.44137	50	0.1279780	Preprocessor1_Model038
0.00000000010000	0.5555556	rmse	standard	10.44147	50	0.1279772	Preprocessor1_Model051
0.00000000129155	0.5555556	rmse	standard	10.44147	50	0.1279772	Preprocessor1_Model052
0.00000001668101	0.5555556	rmse	standard	10.44147	50	0.1279772	Preprocessor1_Model053
0.00000021544347	0.5555556	rmse	standard	10.44147	50	0.1279772	Preprocessor1_Model054
0.00000278255940	0.5555556	rmse	standard	10.44147	50	0.1279772	Preprocessor1_Model055
0.00003593813664	0.5555556	rmse	standard	10.44147	50	0.1279772	Preprocessor1_Model056
0.00046415888336	0.5555556	rmse	standard	10.44147	50	0.1279772	Preprocessor1_Model057
0.00599484250319	0.5555556	rmse	standard	10.44147	50	0.1279772	Preprocessor1_Model058

0.00000000010000	0.7777778	rmse	stan-dard	10.44149	50	0.1279876	Preproces-sor1_Mod-el071
0.00000000129155	0.7777778	rmse	stan-dard	10.44149	50	0.1279876	Preproces-sor1_Mod-el072
0.00000001668101	0.7777778	rmse	stan-dard	10.44149	50	0.1279876	Preproces-sor1_Mod-el073
0.00000021544347	0.7777778	rmse	stan-dard	10.44149	50	0.1279876	Preproces-sor1_Mod-el074
0.00000278255940	0.7777778	rmse	stan-dard	10.44149	50	0.1279876	Preproces-sor1_Mod-el075
0.00003593813664	0.7777778	rmse	stan-dard	10.44149	50	0.1279876	Preproces-sor1_Mod-el076
0.00046415888336	0.7777778	rmse	stan-dard	10.44149	50	0.1279876	Preproces-sor1_Mod-el077
0.00599484250319	0.7777778	rmse	stan-dard	10.44149	50	0.1279876	Preproces-sor1_Mod-el078
0.00000000010000	0.8888889	rmse	stan-dard	10.44152	50	0.1279925	Preproces-sor1_Mod-el081
0.00000000129155	0.8888889	rmse	stan-dard	10.44152	50	0.1279925	Preproces-sor1_Mod-el082
0.00000001668101	0.8888889	rmse	stan-dard	10.44152	50	0.1279925	Preproces-sor1_Mod-el083
0.00000021544347	0.8888889	rmse	stan-dard	10.44152	50	0.1279925	Preproces-sor1_Mod-el084
0.00000278255940	0.8888889	rmse	stan-dard	10.44152	50	0.1279925	Preproces-sor1_Mod-el085
0.00003593813664	0.8888889	rmse	stan-dard	10.44152	50	0.1279925	Preproces-sor1_Mod-el086
0.00046415888336	0.8888889	rmse	stan-dard	10.44152	50	0.1279925	Preproces-sor1_Mod-el087
0.00599484250319	0.8888889	rmse	stan-dard	10.44152	50	0.1279925	Preproces-sor1_Mod-el088

0.00000000010000	1.0000000	rmse	standard	10.44156	50	0.1279867	Preprocessor1_Model091
0.00000000129155	1.0000000	rmse	standard	10.44156	50	0.1279867	Preprocessor1_Model092
0.00000001668101	1.0000000	rmse	standard	10.44156	50	0.1279867	Preprocessor1_Model093
0.00000021544347	1.0000000	rmse	standard	10.44156	50	0.1279867	Preprocessor1_Model094
0.00000278255940	1.0000000	rmse	standard	10.44156	50	0.1279867	Preprocessor1_Model095
0.00003593813664	1.0000000	rmse	standard	10.44156	50	0.1279867	Preprocessor1_Model096
0.00046415888336	1.0000000	rmse	standard	10.44156	50	0.1279867	Preprocessor1_Model097
0.00599484250319	1.0000000	rmse	standard	10.44156	50	0.1279867	Preprocessor1_Model098
0.00000000010000	0.6666667	rmse	standard	10.44156	50	0.1279785	Preprocessor1_Model061
0.00000000129155	0.6666667	rmse	standard	10.44156	50	0.1279785	Preprocessor1_Model062
0.00000001668101	0.6666667	rmse	standard	10.44156	50	0.1279785	Preprocessor1_Model063
0.00000021544347	0.6666667	rmse	standard	10.44156	50	0.1279785	Preprocessor1_Model064
0.00000278255940	0.6666667	rmse	standard	10.44156	50	0.1279785	Preprocessor1_Model065
0.00003593813664	0.6666667	rmse	standard	10.44156	50	0.1279785	Preprocessor1_Model066
0.00046415888336	0.6666667	rmse	standard	10.44156	50	0.1279785	Preprocessor1_Model067
0.00599484250319	0.6666667	rmse	standard	10.44156	50	0.1279785	Preprocessor1_Model068

0.07742636826811	0.1111111	rmse	stan-dard	10.44503	50	0.1263054	Preproces-sor1_Mod-el019
0.07742636826811	0.2222222	rmse	stan-dard	10.44726	50	0.1260211	Preproces-sor1_Mod-el029
0.07742636826811	0.3333333	rmse	stan-dard	10.44958	50	0.1257290	Preproces-sor1_Mod-el039
0.07742636826811	1.0000000	rmse	stan-dard	10.45077	50	0.1247936	Preproces-sor1_Mod-el099
0.07742636826811	0.4444444	rmse	stan-dard	10.45187	50	0.1254915	Preproces-sor1_Mod-el049
0.07742636826811	0.8888889	rmse	stan-dard	10.45211	50	0.1248972	Preproces-sor1_Mod-el089
0.07742636826811	0.7777778	rmse	stan-dard	10.45329	50	0.1250166	Preproces-sor1_Mod-el079
0.07742636826811	0.5555556	rmse	stan-dard	10.45329	50	0.1253240	Preproces-sor1_Mod-el059
0.07742636826811	0.6666667	rmse	stan-dard	10.45380	50	0.1251579	Preproces-sor1_Mod-el069
0.00000000010000	0.0000000	rmse	stan-dard	10.54454	50	0.1204583	Preproces-sor1_Mod-el001
0.00000000129155	0.0000000	rmse	stan-dard	10.54454	50	0.1204583	Preproces-sor1_Mod-el002
0.00000001668101	0.0000000	rmse	stan-dard	10.54454	50	0.1204583	Preproces-sor1_Mod-el003
0.00000021544347	0.0000000	rmse	stan-dard	10.54454	50	0.1204583	Preproces-sor1_Mod-el004
0.00000278255940	0.0000000	rmse	stan-dard	10.54454	50	0.1204583	Preproces-sor1_Mod-el005
0.00003593813664	0.0000000	rmse	stan-dard	10.54454	50	0.1204583	Preproces-sor1_Mod-el006
0.00046415888336	0.0000000	rmse	stan-dard	10.54454	50	0.1204583	Preproces-sor1_Mod-el007

0.00599484250319	0.0000000	rmse	standard	10.54454	50	0.1204583	Preprocessor1_Model008
0.07742636826811	0.0000000	rmse	standard	10.54454	50	0.1204583	Preprocessor1_Model009
1.00000000000000	0.0000000	rmse	standard	10.56817	50	0.1198578	Preprocessor1_Model010
1.00000000000000	0.1111111	rmse	standard	10.58911	50	0.1198704	Preprocessor1_Model020
1.00000000000000	0.2222222	rmse	standard	10.61683	50	0.1199696	Preprocessor1_Model030
1.00000000000000	0.3333333	rmse	standard	10.65154	50	0.1201624	Preprocessor1_Model040
1.00000000000000	0.4444444	rmse	standard	10.69369	50	0.1204695	Preprocessor1_Model050
1.00000000000000	0.5555556	rmse	standard	10.74162	50	0.1208086	Preprocessor1_Model060
1.00000000000000	0.6666667	rmse	standard	10.79817	50	0.1212184	Preprocessor1_Model070
1.00000000000000	0.7777778	rmse	standard	10.86867	50	0.1216881	Preprocessor1_Model080
1.00000000000000	0.8888889	rmse	standard	10.95068	50	0.1222894	Preprocessor1_Model090
1.00000000000000	1.0000000	rmse	standard	11.04291	50	0.1229161	Preprocessor1_Model100

The lowest mean RMSE value (10.44) was achieved when using 0.0000000001 penalty and 0.2222222 mixture, so we recreate the elastic_model object using these values.

elastic_model<-**linear_reg**(mixture = 0.2222222, penalty = 0.0000000001) **%>%**

set_engine("glmnet") **%>%**

set_mode("regression")

elastic_model

Linear Regression Model Specification (regression)

```
##
## Main Arguments:
## penalty = 1e-10
## mixture = 0.2222222
##
## Computational engine: glmnet
```

5.5.3. knn Model

We create knn_rec recipe as described above with step_normalize function.

```
knn_rec<-train_con %>%
recipe(compressive_strength ~ .) %>%
step_normalize(all_predictors())
knn_rec
##
## ── Recipe ──────────────────────────────────────────────────────────
##
## ── Inputs
## Number of variables by role
## outcome: 1
## predictor: 8
##
## ── Operations
## • Centering and scaling for: all_predictors()
```

We create knn_model by using the best combination determined by using the tune_grid function in Section 5.4.8.

```
knn_model<-nearest_neighbor(neighbors = 5, weight_func = "inv",
dist_power = 1.455108) %>%
set_engine("kknn") %>%
set_mode("regression")
knn_model
```

```
## K-Nearest Neighbor Model Specification (regression)
##
## Main Arguments:
## neighbors = 5
## weight_func = inv
## dist_power = 1.455108
##
## Computational engine: kknn
```

5.5.4. Comparing the 3 Models

We create a list of preprocessing recipes "preproc" by using the list function with the arguments:

- lm = lm_rec to hold the recipe of the linear regression model.
- elastic = elastic_rec to hold the recipe of elastic net model.

knn = knn_rec to hold the recipe of knn regression model.

```
preproc <- list(lm = lm_rec, elastic = elastic_rec, knn = knn_rec)
preproc
## $lm
##
## ── Recipe ──────────────────────────────────────────────────────────────────
##
## ── Inputs
## Number of variables by role
## outcome: 1
## predictor: 8
##
## $elastic
##
## ── Recipe ──────────────────────────────────────────────────────────────────
##
## ── Inputs
```

```
## Number of variables by role
## outcome: 1
## predictor: 8
##
## ── Operations
## • Centering and scaling for: all_predictors()
##
## $knn
##
## ── Recipe ──────────────────────────────────────────────────────────────────────────────────────
##
## ── Inputs
## Number of variables by role
## outcome: 1
## predictor: 8
##
## ── Operations
## • Centering and scaling for: all_predictors()
```

We have a list of 3 recipes with lm, elastic, and knn names.

We create a list of models "models" by using the list function with the arguments:

- lm = lm_model to hold the linear regression model.
- elastic = elastic_model to hold the elastic net model.
- knn = knn_model to hold the knn regression model.

```
models<-list(lm = lm_model, elastic = elastic_model, knn = knn_model)
models
## $lm
## Linear Regression Model Specification (regression)
##
## Computational engine: lm
##
##
## $elastic
```

```
## Linear Regression Model Specification (regression)
##
## Main Arguments:
## penalty = 1e-10
## mixture = 0.2222222
##
## Computational engine: glmnet
##
##
## $knn
## K-Nearest Neighbor Model Specification (regression)
##
## Main Arguments:
## neighbors = 5
## weight_func = inv
## dist_power = 1.455108
##
## Computational engine: kknn
```

We have a list of three models with lm, elastic, and knn names.

Then, we use the workflow_set functions to create a set of three workflows "reg_models" by using the arguments:

- preproc which is the list of three recipes.
- models which is the list of three models.
- cross = FALSE so every recipe will only be combined with its model.

```
reg_models <- workflow_set(preproc, models, cross = FALSE)
reg_models
## # A workflow set/tibble: 3 × 4
## wflow_id info option result
## <chr> <list> <list> <list>
## 1 lm_lm <tibble [1 × 4]> <opts[0]> <list [0]>
## 2 elastic_elastic <tibble [1 × 4]> <opts[0]> <list [0]>
## 3 knn_knn <tibble [1 × 4]> <opts[0]> <list [0]>
```

The reg_models contains 3 workflows: lm_lm, elastic_elastic, and knn_knn.

To fit all 3 workflows on 50 resamples of training data, we use the workflow_map function on the reg_models with the arguments:

- "fit_resamples" which is the function required to run on each workflow.
- seed = 123 for reproducibility.
- verbose = TRUE to monitor the fitting of 3 workflows.
- resamples = folds which contains the 50 resamples of training data.

```
fit_models <- reg_models %>% workflow_map("fit_resamples",
seed = 123, verbose = TRUE,
resamples = folds,
metrics = metric_set(rmse))
## i 1 of 3 resampling: lm_lm
## ✔ 1 of 3 resampling: lm_lm (1.2s)
## i 2 of 3 resampling: elastic_elastic
## ✔ 2 of 3 resampling: elastic_elastic (1.9s)
## i 3 of 3 resampling: knn_knn
## ✔ 3 of 3 resampling: knn_knn (11.8s)
fit_models
## # A workflow set/tibble: 3 × 4
## wflow_id info option result
## <chr> <list> <list> <list>
## 1 lm_lm <tibble [1 × 4]> <opts[2]> <rsmp[+]>
## 2 elastic_elastic <tibble [1 × 4]> <opts[2]> <rsmp[+]>
## 3 knn_knn <tibble [1 × 4]> <opts[2]> <rsmp[+]>
```

The fit_models contains the results of applying the 3 models on 50 resamples of training data.

By using the collect_metrics function, we get the mean RMSE value for each model across the 50 resamples of training data.

```
fit_models %>% collect_metrics() %>% flextable() %>%
theme_box() %>% set_caption(caption = "The mean RMSE of linear regression, elastic net, and k-nearest neighbors models on 50 resamples of concrete training data")
```

The mean RMSE of linear regression, elastic net, and k-nearest neighbors (knn) models on 50 resamples of concrete training data:

wflow_id	.config	preproc	model	.metric	.estimator	mean	n	std_err
lm_lm	Preprocessor1_Model1	recipe	linear_reg	rmse	standard	10.440997	50	0.1286204
elastic_elastic	Preprocessor1_Model1	recipe	linear_reg	rmse	standard	10.441218	50	0.1279631
knn_knn	Preprocessor1_Model1	recipe	nearest_neighbor	rmse	standard	8.240096	50	0.1143702

- The knn model has the lowest RMSE value = 8.24 that is lower than that of linear and the elastic net models (10.44).

5.5.5. Plotting the Performance on Training Data

We can plot the 3 models' performances on the training data by using the following functions after collect_metrics:

- The ggplot function with the argument "aes(x = wflow_id, y = mean, color = wflow_id" to plot workflow name on x-axis, mean RMSE on y-axis, and a distinct color for each workflow name.
- The geom_point function to plot a scatter plot.
- The geom_errorbar function with the arguments:

+ aes(ymin = mean-std_err, ymax = mean+std_err) to plot an error bar with its minimum at the mean RMSE minus the corresponding standard error and its maximum at the mean RMSE plus the corresponding standard error.

+ width = 0.1 to decrease width of horizontal lines of the error bar to 0.1 its default.

- The labs function with the title argument to add a plot title, *x* argument to add *x*-axis title, y argument to add y-axis title, and color argument to add legend title.
- The theme_classic function as described before.

fit_models **%>% collect_metrics() %>% ggplot(aes(**x = wflow_id, y = mean, color = wflow_id))+

geom_point()+

geom_errorbar(**aes**(ymin = mean-std_err, ymax = mean+std_err), width = 0.1)+

labs(title = "The mean RMSE ± standard error of 3 models on 50 resamples of the concrete training data", x = "Model", y = "Mean RMSE", color = "Model")+

theme_classic()

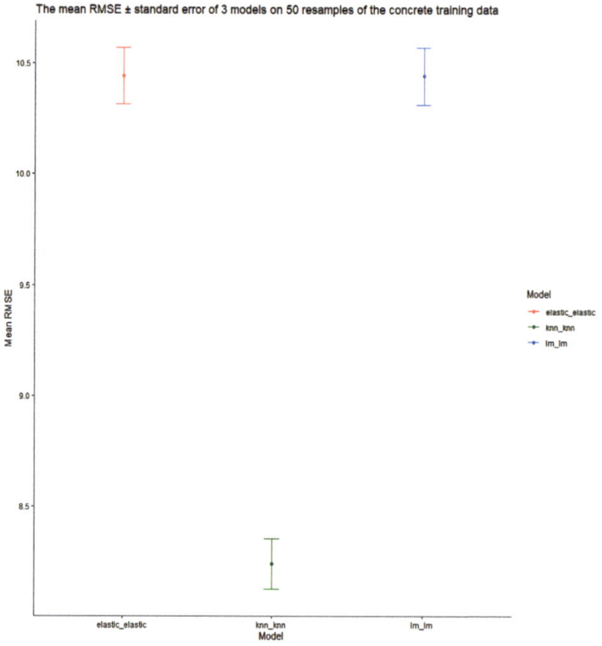

5.5.6. Comparing the Models Statistically

If we use the collect_metrics function with the argument summarize = FALSE, we will get the RMSE value of applying each model on each resample.

```
fit_models %>% collect_metrics(summarize = FALSE)
## # A tibble: 150 × 9
## wflow_id .config preproc model id id2 .metric .estimator .estimate
## <chr> <chr> <chr> <chr> <chr> <chr> <chr> <chr> <dbl>
## 1 lm_lm Preprocessor… recipe line… Repe… Fold… rmse standard 10.6
## 2 lm_lm Preprocessor… recipe line… Repe… Fold… rmse standard 10.6
## 3 lm_lm Preprocessor… recipe line… Repe… Fold… rmse standard 9.75
## 4 lm_lm Preprocessor… recipe line… Repe… Fold… rmse standard 10.2
## 5 lm_lm Preprocessor… recipe line… Repe… Fold… rmse standard 10.9
## 6 lm_lm Preprocessor… recipe line… Repe… Fold… rmse standard 9.94
## 7 lm_lm Preprocessor… recipe line… Repe… Fold… rmse standard 11.0
## 8 lm_lm Preprocessor… recipe line… Repe… Fold… rmse standard 9.21
## 9 lm_lm Preprocessor… recipe line… Repe… Fold… rmse standard 10.5
## 10 lm_lm Preprocessor… recipe line… Repe… Fold… rmse standard 11.7
## # ℹ 140 more rows
```

The result is 150 rows because we have 50 resamples × 3 different models. We can do a t-test to see if the mean RMSE value in the .estimate column is different across the 3 models by using the function t_test with the arguments:

- .estimate ~ wflow_id to see if the mean RMSE value in the .estimate column is different across the 3 models in the wflow_id column.
- paired = TRUE because we are comparing the same 50 resamples across the 3 models.
- p.adjust.method = "fdr" to adjust the p-values for pairwise comparison using the false discovery rate (FDR) method (Benjamini and Hochberg, 1995).

```
library(rstatix)
fit_models %>% collect_metrics(summarize = FALSE) %>%
t_test(.estimate ~ wflow_id, paired = TRUE,
p.adjust.method = "fdr") %>%
flextable() %>% theme_box() %>%
set_caption(caption = "t-test results comparing the RMSE of 3 models on 50 resamples of concrete training data")
```

t-test results comparing the RMSE of 3 models on 50 resamples of concrete training data:

.y.	group1	group2	n1	n2	statistic	df	p	p.adj	p.adj.signif
.estimate	elastic_elastic	knn_knn	50	50	15.9799584	49	0.00000000000000000000455	0.00000000000000000000801	****
.estimate	elastic_elastic	lm_lm	50	50	0.1092109	49	0.9130000000000000033375078	0.9130000000000003375078	ns
.estimate	knn_knn	lm_lm	50	50	–15.9179353	49	0.000000000000000000000534	0.00000000000000000000801	****

- The knn model has significantly lower RMSE than the linear regression and the elastic net models because the adjusted p-value is significant or < 0.05 in both cases.
- The linear regression model has equivalent RMSE value to that of the elastic net model because the adjusted p-value is insignificant (> 0.05) and equals 0.913.

CHAPTER 6

K-NEAREST NEIGHBORS (KNN) CLASSIFICATION

Contents

6.1. Data Used in This Chapter 365
6.2. Data Exploration 368
6.3. knn Model 372
6.4. knn Classification 372
6.5. Comparison Between Different Models 402

6.1. DATA USED IN THIS CHAPTER

6.1.1. Ischemic Stroke Data

This data was gathered from 126 patients with a range of carotid artery blockages. All patients had undergone computed tomography angiography (CTA) to generate a detailed three-dimensional visualization and characterization of the blockage. These images were then analyzed to compute several features related to the disease, including percent stenosis, arterial wall thickness, and tissue characteristics such as lipid-rich necrotic core and calcification.

This group of patients also had follow-up information on whether a stroke occurred at a subsequent point in time (categorical outcome column). The data for each patient also included commonly known risk characteristics for stroke such as whether the patient had atrial fibrillation, coronary artery disease, and a history of smoking. Demographics of gender and age were included as well. The data is part of the modeldata package under the name "ischemic_stroke." The modeldata package is part of tidymodels package which is a collection of different packages for data modeling. First, we load the tidymodels package using the library function then, we load the ischemic stroke data using the data function. We also load the tidyverse and flextable packages for the reasons described above.

```
library(tidymodels)
data("ischemic_stroke")
library(tidyverse)
library(flextable)
```

Then, to see the data structure, we use the glimpse function.

```
glimpse(ischemic_stroke)
## Rows: 126
## Columns: 29
## $ stroke <fct> no, no, no, yes, no, no, no, no, no, no, …
## $ nascet_scale <dbl> 0, 0, 0, 0, 0, 0, 0, 0, 0, 0, 0, 0, 0, 0,…
## $ calc_vol <dbl> 235.252599, 31.433595, 113.404823, 780.82…
## $ calc_vol_prop <dbl> 0.070442702, 0.016164769, 0.038081488, 0…
## $ matx_vol <dbl> 3156.835, 3032.861, 3835.220, 3518.877, 2…
## $ matx_vol_prop <dbl> 0.7599582, 0.8133063, 0.7825256, 0.761089…
## $ lrnc_vol <dbl> 224.87171, 368.56066, 321.15893, 140.5173…
## $ lrnc_vol_prop <dbl> 0.09108513, 0.13398944, 0.08303659, 0.032…
## $ max_calc_area <dbl> 12.350494, 7.130660, 16.286916, 63.350869…
## $ max_calc_area_prop <dbl> 0.36576842, 0.21124686, 0.40881121, 0.576…
## $ max_dilation_by_area <dbl> 520.98259, 91.72005, 270.96930, 2270.4512…
## $ max_matx_area <dbl> 71.24743, 27.21084, 38.12211, 341.12089, …
## $ max_matx_area_prop <dbl> 0.9523705, 0.9455539, 0.9459098, 0.969198…
## $ max_lrnc_area <dbl> 21.686815, 6.434661, 5.705054, 6.046787, …
## $ max_lrnc_area_prop <dbl> 0.42957812, 0.28151013, 0.15477857, 0.187…
```

$ max_max_wall_thickness <dbl> 2.409943, 2.540334, 3.708515, 6.115838, 3…

$ max_remodeling_ratio <dbl> 5.697931, 1.739927, 2.831636, 15.647750, …

$ max_stenosis_by_area <dbl> 18.99554, 30.23761, 33.93906, 34.30985, 3…

$ max_wall_area <dbl> 106.20676, 33.36714, 55.34671, 426.47858,…

$ wall_vol <dbl> 4192.170, 3917.040, 4935.327, 4909.504, 4…

$ max_stenosis_by_diameter <dbl> 10.54411, 18.64620, 19.73511, 20.28832, 4…

$ age <int> 72, 76, 72, 61, 65, 64, 82, 83, 85, 56, 5…

$ male <int> 1, 1, 0, 1, 1, 1, 0, 0, 0, 0, 1, 1, 1, 0,…

$ smoking_history <int> 1, 1, 0, 1, 0, 1, 1, 0, 1, 1, 1, 0, 1, 1,…

$ atrial_fibrillation <int> 0, 0, 0, 0, 0, 0, 0, 1, 0, 0, 0, 0, 0, 0,…

$ coronary_artery_disease <int> 0, 0, 0, 0, 0, 1, 1, 1, 1, 0, 0, 0, 0, 0,…

$ diabetes_history <int> 0, 1, 0, 1, 0, 0, 0, 0, 0, 0, 0, 0, 1, 0,…

$ hypercholesterolemia_history <int> 0, 1, 0, 1, 0, 1, 0, 0, 1, 0, 1, 0, 1, 0,…

$ hypertension_history <int> 1, 1, 0, 1, 1, 1, 1, 1, 1, 0, 1, 0, 1, 0,…

The data has 126 rows (patients) and 29 columns:

1. **stroke:** a factor or categorical column with 2 categories: 'yes' and 'no.' This is our binary outcome column that we want to predict.
2. **nascet_scale:** a numeric column.
3. **calc_vol:** a numeric column.
4. **calc_vol_prop:** a numeric column.
5. **matx_vol:** a numeric column.
6. **matx_vol_prop:** a numeric column.
7. **lrnc_vol:** a numeric column.
8. **lrnc_vol_prop:** a numeric column.
9. **max_calc_area:** a numeric column.
10. **max_calc_area_prop:** a numeric column.
11. **max_dilation_by_area:** a numeric column.
12. **max_matx_area:** a numeric column.
13. **max_matx_area_prop:** a numeric column.
14. **max_lrnc_area:** a numeric column.

15. **max_lrnc_area_prop:** a numeric column.
16. **max_max_wall_thickness:** a numeric column.
17. **max_remodeling_ratio:** a numeric column.
18. **max_stenosis_by_area:** a numeric column.
19. **max_wall_area:** a numeric column.
20. **wall_vol:** a numeric column.
21. **max_stenosis_by_diameter:** a numeric column.
22. **age:** an integer column for the patient age.
23. **male:** an integer column with 1 for males and 0 for females.
24. **smoking_history:** an integer column for the smoking history with 1 for a smoking history and 0 for no such history.
25. **atrial_fibrillation:** an integer column with 1 for a history of atrial fibrillation and 0 for no such history.
26. **coronary_artery_disease:** an integer column with 1 for a history of coronary artery disease and 0 for no such history.
27. **diabetes_history:** an integer column with 1 for a history of diabetes and 0 for no such history.
28. **hypercholesterolemia_history:** an integer column with 1 for a history of hypercholesterolemia and 0 for no such history.

    More information about data columns can be found in Kuhn, Max, and Kjell Johnson (2019).

6.2. DATA EXPLORATION

The first step is exploring the data using the functions from the skimr package as described in previous chapters.

6.2.1. Categorical Columns

To examine all factor categorical columns at once, we use the following functions on the ischemic_stroke data:

- The skim function that produces information about all data columns.
- The yank function with "factor" argument to get only the information related to factor or categorical columns.

Then, we convert the result to a table as explained in previous chapters using functions from the flextable package. To use functions from the skimr package, we should first load the skimr package first using the library function.

library(skimr)

ischemic_stroke **%>% skim**() **%>% yank**("factor") **%>%**

flextable(cwidth = 1) **%>% theme_box**() **%>%**

set_caption(caption = "The information gained from skim function on the categorical columns of ischemic stroke data")

The information gained from skim function on the categorical columns of ischemic stroke data:

skim_variable	**n_missing**	**complete_rate**	**ordered**	**n_unique**	**top_counts**
stroke	0	1	FALSE	2	yes: 64, no: 62

We have 6 columns:

- The skim_variable is the factor or categorical column name. We have only 1 factor column which is the stroke outcome column.
- The n_missing is the number of missing values. The factor column has zero or no missing values.
- The complete_rate is the proportion of present values in each column. Because there are no missings so the complete rate = 1 or 100% for the stroke column.
- The ordered column denotes if the factor column is an ordered factor column like months where January < February < March < … December in order. The stroke factor column is unordered and so has a FALSE value.
- The n_unique is the number of unique values in the stroke column. There are 2 distinct categories in the stroke column.
- The top_counts is the number of rows for the most frequent categories in the stroke column. Since there are only 2 categories, so they are listed with their corresponding count in the table.

The yes has a count or frequency of 64 rows whereas the no category has a count of 62. The total is 126 which is the total rows in the ischemic stroke data.

6.2.2. Numeric Columns

We use the same above functions but use the yank function with the "numeric" argument to get useful information about numeric columns in the ischemic stroke data.

ischemic_stroke **%>% skim**() **%>% yank**("numeric") **%>%**

flextable() %>% theme_box() %>%

set_caption(caption = "The information gained from skim function on numerical columns from the ischemic stroke data")

The information gained from skim function on numerical columns from the ischemic stroke data:

skim_variable	n_missing	complete_rate	mean	sd	p0	p25	p50	p75	p100	hist
nascet_scale	0	1	0.34920635	0.47862236	0.000000000	0.00000000	0.00000000	1.00000000	1.0000000	
calc_vol	0	1	199.45045716	213.49047855	4.017739209	77.12477680	146.76306850	253.94680090	1,517.5389510	
calc_vol_prop	0	1	0.07423037	0.06235605	0.002713823	0.03603747	0.05763555	0.09567606	0.4396187	
matx_vol	0	1	3,074.68369937	738.97770375	939.336039100	2,525.40613525	3,070.48840750	3,596.27138250	4,821.5178190	
matx_vol_prop	0	1	0.77281402	0.05935025	0.475413938	0.74887462	0.77553165	0.81384411	0.8696336	
lrnc_vol	0	1	386.99867229	307.26134182	15.660317410	156.84692478	317.69597275	508.37348923	1,612.4045130	
lrnc_vol_prop	0	1	0.11186740	0.07402087	0.008879142	0.05546328	0.09608974	0.14604675	0.4945902	
max_calc_area	0	1	20.39770007	13.12791751	1.754366264	10.85780908	16.54469444	26.76529178	63.3508686	
max_calc_area_prop	0	1	0.35063052	0.16015591	0.007362896	0.24443064	0.33390687	0.42182693	0.9576435	
max_dilation_by_area	0	1	451.17938856	870.05544333	15.533428930	78.83273055	150.25526390	370.27981822	5,920.6283630	
max_matx_area	0	1	65.49474364	58.05195545	17.189463670	36.63200810	45.72604228	67.47881081	341.1208930	
max_matx_area_prop	0	1	0.95108258	0.09148841	0.828647373	0.93766759	0.94893371	0.95609911	1.9381739	
max_lrnc_area	0	1	17.61834232	17.82694810	1.258604023	6.82121019	12.86887348	20.50635443	134.3389732	
max_lrnc_area_prop	0	1	0.33126296	0.14891817	0.027399294	0.20400891	0.31958882	0.44474619	0.7378211	

max_max_wall_thickness	0	1	5.85908793	9.23325011	1.312794780	3.62006544	4.71839819	5.51171112	83.5625198	
max_remodeling_ratio	0	1	4.74932278	4.47774119	1.209191950	2.31497994	3.22392614	5.34818864	27.8808263	
max_stenosis_by_area	0	1	74.79629136	19.67270612	18.995542000	61.81342945	79.33784772	90.00148911	100.0000000	
max_wall_area	0	1	89.94448665	74.97493232	19.965650290	53.20673249	66.67121762	92.80158127	454.1715504	
wall_vol	0	1	4,156.53154689	1,083.81058824	1,416.747628000	3,464.17100200	4,056.41390850	5,066.84182025	6,306.8082240	
max_stenosis_by_diameter	0	1	63.75862269	22.63866721	10.544113150	47.63252479	63.42333276	78.96934058	100.0000000	
age	0	1	72.09523810	10.83286006	39.000000000	65.00000000	72.00000000	80.00000000	90.0000000	
male	0	1	0.56349206	0.49793223	0.000000000	0.00000000	1.00000000	1.00000000	1.0000000	
smoking_history	0	1	0.57936508	0.49563171	0.000000000	0.00000000	1.00000000	1.00000000	1.0000000	
atrial_fibrillation	0	1	0.11904762	0.32513733	0.000000000	0.00000000	0.00000000	0.00000000	1.0000000	
coronary_artery_disease	0	1	0.27777778	0.44969125	0.000000000	0.00000000	0.00000000	1.00000000	1.0000000	
diabetes_history	0	1	0.22222222	0.41739936	0.000000000	0.00000000	0.00000000	0.00000000	1.0000000	
hypercholesterolemia_history	0	1	0.53174603	0.50098316	0.000000000	0.00000000	1.00000000	1.00000000	1.0000000	
hypertension_history	0	1	0.76984127	0.42261469	0.000000000	1.00000000	1.00000000	1.00000000	1.0000000	□□□□□

We have 11 columns:

1. skim_variable is the column name. We have 28 numeric columns or predictors.
2. n_missing is the number of missings in each column. All columns have no missings.
3. complete_rate is the proportion of present values in each column. All numeric columns have no missings and 1 or 100% complete rate.

4. mean is the mean or average value for each column.
5. sd is the standard deviation for each column.
6. p0 is the 0% percentile or the minimum value for each column.
7. p25 is the 25% percentile or the 1st quartile for each column.
8. p50 is the 50% percentile, the median, or the 2nd quartile for each column.
9. p75 is the 75% percentile or the 3rd quartile for each column.
10. p100 is the 100% percentile or the maximum value for each column.
11. hist is the histogram plot for each column. Many columns show non-normal distribution.

6.3. KNN MODEL

The knn model predicts the outcome of a data row by comparing it to k similar rows in the training data where k is defined by the analyst or determined by cross-validation.

For classification modeling with categorical outcome, the knn model identifies the major category of the k training rows that are the most similar to the desired data row and returns this major category as the predicted category of the desired data row.

The knn model has three tuning parameters: neighbors, weight_func, and dist_power that were explained in the previous chapter.

6.4. KNN CLASSIFICATION

6.4.1. Split the Data

We first do a stratified splitting of the data using the categorical outcome (stroke). This ensures that both the resulting training and testing data have the same stroke proportions as the original ischemic stroke data.

We create an object called "split_st" by using the initial_split function with the arguments:

- data = ischemic_stroke which is the data we want to split.
- strata = stroke to make a stratified splitting using the stroke outcome column.

To make the splitting reproducible, we use the set.seed function with any number before using the initial_split function.

```
set.seed(123)
split_st <- initial_split(data = ischemic_stroke,
strata = stroke)
split_st
## <Training/Testing/Total>
## <94/32/126>
```

The training data has 94 rows and the testing data has 32 rows with a total of 126 which is the total rows of original data.

To get the actual training and testing data, we use the training and testing functions, respectively, on the split_st object. The resulting data is called train_st for the training data and test_st for the testing data. Finally, we use the dim function to see the data dimensions.

```
train_st<-training(split_st)
test_st<-testing(split_st)
dim(train_st)
## [1] 94 29
dim(test_st)
## [1] 32 29
```

- The training data has 94 rows (1st number) and the same 29 columns of the ischemic stroke data (2nd number), while the testing data has 32 rows (1st number) and the same 29 columns of the ischemic stroke data (2nd number).

6.4.2. Generate the Recipe

We create an object "rec" by applying the following functions on the train_st data using the "%>%" operator:

- The recipe function with the argument stroke ~ . meaning define the stroke column as an outcome and all other 28 columns as predictors.
- The step_normalize function with the argument all_predictors to convert all numeric predictors into columns having 0 mean and 1 standard deviation so all predictors will have a common scale.

```
rec <- train_st %>%
recipe(stroke ~ .) %>%
step_normalize(all_predictors())
rec
```

```
##
## ── Recipe ──────────────────────────────────────────────────────────────────

##
## ── Inputs
## Number of variables by role
## outcome: 1
## predictor: 28
##
## ── Operations
## • Centering and scaling for: all_predictors()
```

- The recipe object "rec":

++ Defines the variables by role: 1 outcome and 28 predictors.
++ Contains 1 preprocessing operation of normalizing all predictors.

6.4.3. Look at Preprocessed Data

First, we prepare the recipe using the prep function on the "rec" recipe. The resulting object is called "prep_rec."

```
prep_rec <- prep(rec)
prep_rec
##
## ── Recipe ──────────────────────────────────────────────────────────────────

##
## ── Inputs
## Number of variables by role
## outcome: 1
## predictor: 28
##
## ── Training information
## Training data contained 94 data points and no incomplete rows.
##
## ── Operations
```

• Centering and scaling for: nascet_scale and calc_vol, … | Trained

Second, to get the preprocessed training data, we use the bake function with the arguments:

- prep_rec which is the prepared recipe.
- new_data = NULL to apply the prepared recipe to training data contained in the original recipe.

The resulting data is called "train_st2" and we use the glimpse function to see the data structure.

train_st2 <- **bake**(prep_rec, new_data = NULL)

glimpse(train_st2)

Rows: 94

Columns: 29

$ nascet_scale <dbl> –0.7661002, –0.7661002, –0.7661002, –0.76…

$ calc_vol <dbl> –0.79127189, –0.42752627, –0.90571125, 0…

$ calc_vol_prop <dbl> –0.94945540, –0.60689792, –1.15795633, –0…

$ matx_vol <dbl> –0.12857747, 0.94211488, 0.30706318, 1.75…

$ matx_vol_prop <dbl> 0.62170737, 0.09696132, 1.23498358, 0.122…

$ lrnc_vol <dbl> –0.02699036, –0.19451419, –1.13243675, –0…

$ lrnc_vol_prop <dbl> 0.30830635, –0.36253264, –1.19462836, –0…

$ max_calc_area <dbl> –1.04547355, –0.34950264, –1.37151328, 0…

$ max_calc_area_prop <dbl> –0.874469607, 0.330152197, –1.690911309, …

$ max_dilation_by_area <dbl> –0.38378288, –0.19327205, –0.16409544, –0…

$ max_matx_area <dbl> –0.69707395, –0.48607959, –0.56719993, –0…

$ max_matx_area_prop <dbl> –0.096672317, –0.093261432, 0.053343839, …

$ max_lrnc_area <dbl> –0.6641261, –0.7114852, –0.7835266, –0.47…

$ max_lrnc_area_prop <dbl> –0.29763415, –1.13746163, –0.80248352, 0…

$ max_max_wall_thickness <dbl> –0.35188494, –0.24216845, –0.34798029, –0…

$ max_remodeling_ratio <dbl> –0.645310246, –0.418514590, –0.553539934,…

$ max_stenosis_by_area <dbl> –2.32250007, –2.13590705, –1.81435654, –1…

$ max_wall_area <dbl> –0.81576458, –0.47478214, –0.79357576, –0…

$ wall_vol <dbl> –0.25920397, 0.68362905, –0.21865657, 1.4…

$ max_stenosis_by_diameter <dbl> –1.97212441, –1.92598310, –1.46947352, –1…

$ age <dbl> 0.31498043, –0.06829673, –0.83485104, 0.8…

$ male <dbl> 0.9133278, –1.0832493, 0.9133278, –1.0832…

$ smoking_history <dbl> 0.7487578, –1.3213374, 0.7487578, 0.74875…

$ atrial_fibrillation <dbl> –0.4160989, –0.4160989, –0.4160989, –0.41…

$ coronary_artery_disease <dbl> –0.6478651, –0.6478651, 1.5271106, 1.5271…

$ diabetes_history <dbl> 1.7476031, –0.5661249, –0.5661249, –0.566…

$ hypercholesterolemia_history <dbl> 0.8748459, –1.1308983, 0.8748459, –1.1308…

$ hypertension_history <dbl> 0.5006379, –1.9762022, 0.5006379, 0.50063…

$ stroke <fct> no, no, no, no, no, no, no, no, no, no, n…

- The training data has the same 94 rows and 29 columns as the original training data but all columns have negative values because of normalization.

We can use the skim function again on the train_st2 data to get useful information about all numeric columns (by using the yank function with "numeric" argument) in the stroke training data after normalization.

train_st2 **%>% skim**() **%>% yank**("numeric") **%>%**

flextable() **%>% theme_box**() **%>%**

set_caption(caption = "The information gained from skim function on all columns from the stroke training data after normalization")

The information gained from skim function on all columns from the stroke training data after normalization:

skim_variable	n_missing	complete_rate	mean	sd	p0	p25	p50	p75	p100	hist
nascet_scale	0	1	–0.000000000000000037649497	1	–0.7661002	–0.7661002	–0.76610018	1.291426016	1.2914260	
calc_vol	0	1	–0.000000000000000013595203	1	–0.9129292	–0.5700572	–0.27186681	0.243351573	5.8032898	
calc_vol_prop	0	1	0.000000000000000081279407	1	–1.1596932	–0.6340421	–0.26955316	0.312901061	5.6691137	
matx_vol	0	1	–0.000000000000000266809936	1	–2.9222396	–0.7850782	–0.04311921	0.810875252	2.2582600	
matx_vol_prop	0	1	–0.000000000000000110822763	1	–5.1386358	–0.4767152	–0.01250663	0.848124046	1.5819667	
lrnc_vol	0	1	0.000000000000000111059211	1	–1.2741856	–0.7602155	–0.16783308	0.451289927	3.9882930	
lrnc_vol_prop	0	1	0.00000000000000062450045	1	–1.3388806	–0.7520582	–0.19067651	0.398295511	5.0559320	
max_calc_area	0	1	–0.000000000000000115108822	1	–1.4541279	–0.6857760	–0.30676785	0.525189451	2.9126846	
max_calc_area_prop	0	1	0.000000000000000066759316	1	–2.1176243	–0.6881103	–0.08793143	0.527874495	3.6765824	
max_dilation_by_area	0	1	0.000000000000000010070969	1	–0.4647560	–0.3974799	–0.32212903	–0.098554217	5.8113345	
max_matx_area	0	1	0.000000000000000019346377	1	–0.8908600	–0.5148942	–0.34582270	0.110023372	5.0953746	
max_matx_area_prop	0	1	0.00000000000000003161366	1	–0.8181586	–0.1544617	–0.05765659	0.005670339	9.4176850	
max_lrnc_area	0	1	0.000000000000000031802158	1	–1.0001064	–0.6390350	–0.28502162	0.200212171	6.0696998	
max_lrnc_area_prop	0	1	–0.000000000000000080664642	1	–1.9815814	–0.7955884	–0.11229144	0.765524328	2.7262575	

max_max_wall_thickness	0	1	−0.000000000000000007203024	1	−0.4671765	−0.2636324	−0.16272040	−0.058727839	7.2577852	
max_remodeling_ratio	0	1	0.000000000000000050995565	1	−0.7555672	−0.5420329	−0.33240489	0.103105668	4.7852986	
max_stenosis_by_area	0	1	0.000000000000000324008052	1	−2.3225001	−0.7546450	0.29274985	0.878769418	1.1942815	
max_wall_area	0	1	0.000000000000000097646823	1	−1.0236701	−0.5186936	−0.26383503	0.080072896	5.7124300	
wall_vol	0	1	0.000000000000000051763157	1	−2.5742258	−0.6594726	−0.08142224	0.805398256	1.9534838	
max_stenosis_by_diameter	0	1	−0.00000000000000000207975352	1	−1.9721244	−0.8718099	−0.06645416	0.836001084	1.4751267	
age	0	1	0.000000000000000280924857	1	−2.7512368	−0.7150769	−0.02038708	0.698257584	1.6564505	
male	0	1	0.000000000000000061348542	1	−1.0832493	−1.0832493	0.91332782	0.913327822	0.9133278	
smoking_history	0	1	−0.000000000000000037805784	1	−1.3213374	−1.3213374	0.74875784	0.748757837	0.7487578	
atrial_fibrillation	0	1	0.000000000000000028344390	1	−0.4160989	−0.4160989	−0.41609890	−0.416098904	2.3777080	
coronary_artery_disease	0	1	−0.000000000000000007140740	1	−0.6478651	−0.6478651	−0.64786511	1.527110628	1.5271106	
diabetes_history	0	1	0.000000000000000042537634	1	−0.5661249	−0.5661249	−0.56612494	−0.566124945	1.7476031	
hypercholesterolemia_history	0	1	0.000000000000000036637383	1	−1.1308983	−1.1308983	0.87484586	0.874845860	0.8748459	
hypertension_history	0	1	−0.000000000000000007110175	1	−1.9762022	0.5006379	0.50063789	0.500637891	0.5006379	

- The mean of all 28 predictors is extremely low and nearly equals zero.
- The standard deviation of all 28 predictors = 1 so all 28 predictors are now on a comparable scale.

Finally, to get the preprocessed testing data, we use the bake function with the arguments:

- prep_rec which is the prepared recipe.
- new_data = test_st to apply the prepared recipe to the testing data.

The resulting data is called "test_st2" and we use the glimpse function to see the data structure.

```
test_st2 <- bake(prep_rec, new_data = test_st)
glimpse(test_st2)
## Rows: 32
## Columns: 29
## $ nascet_scale <dbl> –0.7661002, –0.7661002, –0.7661002, –0.76…
## $ calc_vol <dbl> 0.11317071, 2.53413154, –0.55776206, –0.8…
## $ calc_vol_prop <dbl> –0.101093381, 2.133824846, –0.555282254, …
## $ matx_vol <dbl> 0.03685701, 0.51997703, –0.18540754, 0.63…
## $ matx_vol_prop <dbl> –0.28776386, –0.26847773, –0.45976172, –2…
## $ lrnc_vol <dbl> –0.5348056, –0.8329248, –0.2930775, 4.368…
## $ lrnc_vol_prop <dbl> –0.2565666, –1.0336137, –0.4631076, 2.537…
## $ max_calc_area <dbl> –0.6487117, 3.2278486, –0.2509441, –1.138…
## $ max_calc_area_prop <dbl> 0.06770462, 1.35081759, –0.20217430, –1.3…
## $ max_dilation_by_area <dbl> 0.07244866, 1.93183001, –0.38013207, –0.4…
## $ max_matx_area <dbl> 0.154473734, 5.373090379, –0.129259509, –…
## $ max_matx_area_prop <dbl> –0.03133456, 0.12996658, –0.32895940, –1…
## $ max_lrnc_area <dbl> 0.32589874, –0.68930317, –0.61357441, 1.0…
## $ max_lrnc_area_prop <dbl> 0.68358605, –0.92329623, –0.72561984, 1.7…
## $ max_max_wall_thickness <dbl> –0.36413143, –0.01607068, –0.21712416, –0…
```

$ max_remodeling_ratio <dbl> 0.17694042, 2.24395327, –0.60954876, –0.6…

$ max_stenosis_by_area <dbl> –2.88922254, –2.11721505, –2.00178969, –1…

$ max_wall_area <dbl> 0.31424063, 5.28281209, –0.40527739, –0.3…

$ wall_vol <dbl> –0.004460489, 0.659718921, –0.140676271, …

$ max_stenosis_by_diameter <dbl> –2.31543862, –1.90254190, –0.67333835, –1…

$ age <dbl> –0.06829673, –1.12230890, –0.73903175, –1…

$ male <dbl> 0.9133278, 0.9133278, 0.9133278, 0.913327…

$ smoking_history <dbl> 0.7487578, 0.7487578, –1.3213374, –1.3213…

$ atrial_fibrillation <dbl> –0.4160989, –0.4160989, –0.4160989, –0.41…

$ coronary_artery_disease <dbl> –0.6478651, –0.6478651, –0.6478651, –0.64…

$ diabetes_history <dbl> –0.5661249, 1.7476031, –0.5661249, –0.566…

$ hypercholesterolemia_history <dbl> –1.1308983, 0.8748459, –1.1308983, –1.130…

$ hypertension_history <dbl> 0.5006379, 0.5006379, 0.5006379, –1.97620…

$ stroke <fct> no, yes, no, no, yes, no, no, yes, no, ye…

- The testing data has the same 32 rows and 29 columns of the original testing data but all numeric columns have negative values because of normalization.

6.4.4. Generate Different Resamples of Training Data

We split the train_st data using the vfold_cv function with the arguments:

- v = 10 to split the data into 10 folds.
- repeats = 5 to repeat this process 5 times.
- strata = stroke to make stratified resampling using the stroke outcome column.

The result is 50 different resamples of train_st data contained in folds data frame.

We also use the set.seed function before splitting to make the splitting reproducible.

```
set.seed(123)
folds<-vfold_cv(train_st, v = 10, repeats = 5,
```

```
strata = stroke)
folds
## # 10-fold cross-validation repeated 5 times using stratification
## # A tibble: 50 × 3
## splits id id2
## <list> <chr> <chr>
## 1 <split [84/10]> Repeat1 Fold01
## 2 <split [84/10]> Repeat1 Fold02
## 3 <split [84/10]> Repeat1 Fold03
## 4 <split [84/10]> Repeat1 Fold04
## 5 <split [84/10]> Repeat1 Fold05
## 6 <split [84/10]> Repeat1 Fold06
## 7 <split [85/9]> Repeat1 Fold07
## 8 <split [85/9]> Repeat1 Fold08
## 9 <split [86/8]> Repeat1 Fold09
## 10 <split [86/8]> Repeat1 Fold10
## # ℹ 40 more rows
```

- There are 50 different rows. Each row corresponds to 1 resample of train_st data. Each resample has 1 analysis (training) data, with 84, 85, or 86 rows and 1 assessment (testing) data with 10, 9, or 8 rows.
- Each resample has 2 id values. id for the repeat number from 1 to 5 and id2 for the resample number from 1 to 10 within that repeat.
- Each resample has a total rows of 94 which is the number of rows in original train_st data. 84 + 10 = 85 + 9 = 86 + 8 = 94.

6.4.5. Define Machine Learning (ML) Model

We define a knn classification model by using the functions:

- The nearest_neighbor function to define the k-nearest neighbor (knn) classification model type with the following arguments:
- neighbors = tune() to tune the neighbors number on the different resamples of training data.
- weight_func = tune() to tune the weight function on the different resamples of training data.

- dist_power = tune() to tune the distance power on the different resamples of the training data.
- The set_engine function with the argument "kknn" to define the engine that will use the train.kknn function from the kknn package.
- The set_mode function with the argument "classification" to define the mode of learning. We use classification because we have a categorical binary outcome (stroke).
- All the 3 functions are applied in sequence using the piping "%>%" operator and the resulting object is called "knn_model."

```
knn_model <- nearest_neighbor(neighbors = tune(), weight_func = tune(),
dist_power = tune()) %>%
set_engine("kknn") %>%
set_mode("classification")
knn_model
## K-Nearest Neighbor Model Specification (classification)
##
## Main Arguments:
## neighbors = tune()
## weight_func = tune()
## dist_power = tune()
##
## Computational engine: kknn
```

6.4.6. Generate Workflow

We create the "wflow" object by using the following functions:

- The workflow function to create a workflow.
- The add_recipe function with the argument "rec" to add the above created recipe with 1 preprocessing step.
- The add_model function with the argument knn_model to add the above created knn model.

```
wflow <- workflow() %>%
add_recipe(rec) %>%
add_model(knn_model)
wflow
```

```
## ══ Workflow ════════════════════════════════════════════
## Preprocessor: Recipe
## Model: nearest_neighbor()
##
## ── Preprocessor ────────────────────────────────────────
## 1 Recipe Step
##
## • step_normalize()
##
## ── Model ───────────────────────────────────────────────
## K-Nearest Neighbor Model Specification (classification)
##
## Main Arguments:
## neighbors = tune()
## weight_func = tune()
## dist_power = tune()
##
## Computational engine: kknn
```

- The "wflow" object contains 1 preprocessing step (normalization) and the knn classification model with tuned neighbors, distance weighting, and Minkowski distance.

6.4.7. Fit Model on Different Resamples with Tuning

We can train many models using 50 resamples of training data in the folds data fame and see which models turn out best. We create a grid of neighbors, distance weighting, and Minkowski distance values "my_grid" by using the grid_random function with the arguments:

- neighbors with the argument range = c(1,20) to choose different neighbors (k) values from 1 to 20.
- weight_func to choose from 10 different distance weighting functions.

- dist_power to choose different values of the Minkowski distance from 1 to 2 (default values).
- size = 100 to choose 100 different combinations.

For reproducibility, we use the set.seed function with any number before using the grid_random function.

set.seed(123)

my_grid <- **grid_random**(**neighbors**(range = **c**(1,20)), **weight_func**(),

dist_power(), size = 100)

my_grid **%>% flextable**(cwidth = 1) **%>% theme_box**() **%>%**

set_caption(caption = "The different 100 combinations of neighbors from 1 to 20, distance weighting, and Minkowski distance values chosen by using the grid_random function")

The different 100 combinations of neighbors from 1 to 20, distance weighting, and Minkowski distance values chosen by using the grid_random function:

neighbors	**weight_func**	**dist_power**
15	cos	1.703992
19	gaussian	1.103807
14	triweight	1.033728
3	inv	1.999405
10	biweight	1.034875
18	epanechnikov	1.338391
11	rank	1.915064
5	inv	1.617235
20	cos	1.286285
14	optimal	1.737797
5	rank	1.834054
19	inv	1.314271
9	triangular	1.492567
3	epanechnikov	1.697374
8	gaussian	1.641462
7	biweight	1.643923
10	inv	1.977853
9	biweight	1.414735
19	rectangular	1.119405
4	gaussian	1.526030

14	biweight	1.225073
17	rank	1.486412
11	gaussian	1.370215
7	cos	1.983350
12	biweight	1.388319
15	gaussian	1.229245
10	epanechnikov	1.623298
13	biweight	1.136540
7	biweight	1.967469
9	cos	1.515072
9	rectangular	1.163070
10	optimal	1.621902
7	biweight	1.985954
6	rank	1.668772
2	inv	1.418916
5	gaussian	1.323345
8	triweight	1.835255
12	triangular	1.143817
13	cos	1.192816
18	rank	1.896739
1	gaussian	1.308120
6	optimal	1.363301
15	biweight	1.783946
9	triweight	1.193379
15	inv	1.017766
16	rectangular	1.406608
20	gaussian	1.483168
6	gaussian	1.421845
11	optimal	1.342809
8	rank	1.866483
7	gaussian	1.455108
16	triangular	1.533765
17	triweight	1.963843
18	rank	1.774592
17	inv	1.208876
2	inv	1.308787

4	optimal	1.971342
13	optimal	1.584900
5	gaussian	1.760824
19	cos	1.372709
20	inv	1.769194
14	optimal	1.537677
3	rectangular	1.913995
8	rank	1.185296
16	epanechnikov	1.282218
12	optimal	1.094962
14	triweight	1.210487
3	cos	1.977099
14	rank	1.296302
7	biweight	1.725983
3	optimal	1.785688
15	inv	1.105418
5	rank	1.239595
8	inv	1.270545
19	optimal	1.101058
10	biweight	1.117914
18	gaussian	1.991237
10	rank	1.986054
12	rank	1.137067
2	rank	1.905310
10	triweight	1.576302
12	inv	1.395449
20	cos	1.449802
14	rectangular	1.706502
17	optimal	1.082503
14	optimal	1.339313
3	rectangular	1.680788
8	optimal	1.316949
14	rectangular	1.831569
19	optimal	1.215172
15	triweight	1.497949
17	inv	1.276050

11	triweight	1.192023
7	optimal	1.950621
15	rank	1.321726
6	biweight	1.478456
14	cos	1.027993
7	triangular	1.547459
10	rectangular	1.644240
5	triweight	1.596264

- The neighbors values range from 1 to 20, the weight_func has 10 different values, and the dist_power ranges from 1 to 2.

To try all these 100 different combinations on the 50 resamples of the training data, we use the tune_grid function with the arguments:

- wflow which is the workflow containing 1 preprocessing step and the knn model.
- folds which are the 50 resamples of training data created above.
- metrics = metrics_set(accuracy) to get the accuracy of the knn model on each resample using the 100 different combinations.
- grid = my_grid to use the 100 combinations in the my_grid data in tuning.

```
set.seed(123)
knn_res <- tune_grid(wflow, folds,
metrics = metric_set(accuracy),
grid = my_grid)
knn_res
## # Tuning results
## # 10-fold cross-validation repeated 5 times using stratification
## # A tibble: 50 × 5
## splits id id2 .metrics .notes
## <list> <chr> <chr> <list> <list>
## 1 <split [84/10]> Repeat1 Fold01 <tibble [100 × 7]> <tibble [0 × 3]>
## 2 <split [84/10]> Repeat1 Fold02 <tibble [100 × 7]> <tibble [0 × 3]>
## 3 <split [84/10]> Repeat1 Fold03 <tibble [100 × 7]> <tibble [0 × 3]>
## 4 <split [84/10]> Repeat1 Fold04 <tibble [100 × 7]> <tibble [0 × 3]>
## 5 <split [84/10]> Repeat1 Fold05 <tibble [100 × 7]> <tibble [0 × 3]>
```

```
## 6 <split [84/10]> Repeat1 Fold06 <tibble [100 × 7]> <tibble [0 × 3]>
## 7 <split [85/9]> Repeat1 Fold07 <tibble [100 × 7]> <tibble [0 × 3]>
## 8 <split [85/9]> Repeat1 Fold08 <tibble [100 × 7]> <tibble [0 × 3]>
## 9 <split [86/8]> Repeat1 Fold09 <tibble [100 × 7]> <tibble [0 × 3]>
## 10 <split [86/8]> Repeat1 Fold10 <tibble [100 × 7]> <tibble [0 × 3]>
## # i 40 more rows
```

The resulting object "knn_res" contains 50 rows (for 50 resamples) and 5 columns:

- The splits column is a list of each combination of analysis and assessment data withing each resample. The sum is 94 which are total rows of training data.
- The id column is an id column for the repeat number from 1 to 5.
- The id2 column is an id column for the fold number from 1 to 10 so we have 50 resamples because 5 × 10 = 50.
- The .metrics column is a list of performance metric (accuracy) of applying the knn model to the corresponding assessment data (10, 9, or 8 rows) within each resample. Each performance metric is saved in 100 rows and 7 columns [100 × 7] tibble or data frame. The 100 rows are for the accuracy of applying the 100 different combinations of neighbors, distance weighting, and Minkowski distance on the assessment data within each resample.
- The .notes column is a list of notes or warnings when applying the knn model to each analysis data (84, 85, or 86 rows) within each resample. Each note is saved in 0 rows and 3 columns [0 × 3] tibble or data frame meaning that there are no rows or no notes when applying this model to each analysis data.

6.4.8. The Model Performance on 50 Resamples of the Training Data

To get the performance metric (accuracy) on the 50 resamples of training data using the 100 different combinations, we will use the unnest function with the ".metrics" argument to expand the .metrics list column of the knn_res object into rows and columns.

```
knn_res %>% unnest(.metrics)
## # A tibble: 5,000 × 11
## splits id id2 neighbors weight_func dist_power .metric
```

```
## <list> <chr> <chr> <int> <chr> <dbl> <chr>
## 1 <split [84/10]> Repeat1 Fold01 10 biweight 1.03 accuracy
## 2 <split [84/10]> Repeat1 Fold01 10 biweight 1.12 accuracy
## 3 <split [84/10]> Repeat1 Fold01 13 biweight 1.14 accuracy
## 4 <split [84/10]> Repeat1 Fold01 14 biweight 1.23 accuracy
## 5 <split [84/10]> Repeat1 Fold01 12 biweight 1.39 accuracy
## 6 <split [84/10]> Repeat1 Fold01 9 biweight 1.41 accuracy
## 7 <split [84/10]> Repeat1 Fold01 6 biweight 1.48 accuracy
## 8 <split [84/10]> Repeat1 Fold01 7 biweight 1.64 accuracy
## 9 <split [84/10]> Repeat1 Fold01 7 biweight 1.73 accuracy
## 10 <split [84/10]> Repeat1 Fold01 15 biweight 1.78 accuracy
## # i 4,990 more rows
## # i 4 more variables: .estimator <chr>, .estimate <dbl>, .config <chr>,
## # .notes <list>
```

- The result is 5000 rows because we have applied the 100 combinations to 50 resamples of the training data so we have 100 × 50 or 5000 models or rows. Each row contains the accuracy of the knn model on 1 resample using 1 combination.

To get the mean accuracy of each combination on the 50 resamples of the training data, we use the following functions on the "knn_res" object:

- The collect_metrics function to get the mean accuracy for each combination across the 50 resamples of the training data.
- The arrange function with mean argument to arrange by mean accuracy value in ascending order.
- The flextable, theme_box, and set_caption functions are described previously.

```
knn_res %>% collect_metrics() %>%
arrange(mean) %>%
flextable() %>% theme_box() %>%
set_caption(caption = "The mean accuracy of applying 100 combinations of neighbors, distance weighting, and Minkowski distance on 50 resamples of stroke training data when using knn classification model")
```

The mean accuracy of applying 100 combinations of neighbors, distance weighting, and Minkowski distance on 50 resamples of stroke training data when using knn classification model:

neighbors	weight_func	dist_power	.metric	.estimator	mean	n	std_err	.config
4	optimal	1.971342	accuracy	binary	0.5074444	50	0.02219208	Preprocessor1_Model065
3	cos	1.977099	accuracy	binary	0.5126111	50	0.02479383	Preprocessor1_Model020
2	rank	1.905310	accuracy	binary	0.5144444	50	0.02260066	Preprocessor1_Model077
17	triweight	1.963843	accuracy	binary	0.5144444	50	0.02520475	Preprocessor1_Model100
3	optimal	1.785688	accuracy	binary	0.5166667	50	0.02155767	Preprocessor1_Model063
7	optimal	1.950621	accuracy	binary	0.5174444	50	0.02213219	Preprocessor1_Model064
1	gaussian	1.308120	accuracy	binary	0.5183333	50	0.02318466	Preprocessor1_Model028
2	inv	1.308787	accuracy	binary	0.5183333	50	0.02318466	Preprocessor1_Model043
7	biweight	1.967469	accuracy	binary	0.5183889	50	0.02469171	Preprocessor1_Model011
7	biweight	1.985954	accuracy	binary	0.5183889	50	0.02469171	Preprocessor1_Model012
8	triweight	1.835255	accuracy	binary	0.5193889	50	0.02399996	Preprocessor1_Model099
8	inv	1.270545	accuracy	binary	0.5215556	50	0.02158738	Preprocessor1_Model041
9	rectangular	1.163070	accuracy	binary	0.5229444	50	0.02343230	Preprocessor1_Model081
6	biweight	1.478456	accuracy	binary	0.5236111	50	0.02304271	Preprocessor1_Model007
7	gaussian	1.455108	accuracy	binary	0.5236667	50	0.02162174	Preprocessor1_Model032

3	epanech-nikov	1.697374	accu-racy	bi-nary	0.5253333	50	0.02396400	Preproces-sor1_Mod-el025
10	triweight	1.576302	accu-racy	bi-nary	0.5253333	50	0.02449048	Preproces-sor1_Mod-el097
3	inv	1.999405	accu-racy	bi-nary	0.5264444	50	0.02538755	Preproces-sor1_Mod-el050
14	triweight	1.033728	accu-racy	bi-nary	0.5265000	50	0.02505778	Preproces-sor1_Mod-el092
7	cos	1.983350	accu-racy	bi-nary	0.5271111	50	0.02452979	Preproces-sor1_Mod-el021
2	inv	1.418916	accu-racy	bi-nary	0.5273333	50	0.02272412	Preproces-sor1_Mod-el046
8	gaussian	1.641462	accu-racy	bi-nary	0.5280000	50	0.02206632	Preproces-sor1_Mod-el035
10	epanech-nikov	1.623298	accu-racy	bi-nary	0.5287222	50	0.02280674	Preproces-sor1_Mod-el024
5	triweight	1.596264	accu-racy	bi-nary	0.5301111	50	0.02214262	Preproces-sor1_Mod-el098
15	triweight	1.497949	accu-racy	bi-nary	0.5302778	50	0.02370722	Preproces-sor1_Mod-el096
14	triweight	1.210487	accu-racy	bi-nary	0.5305000	50	0.02369609	Preproces-sor1_Mod-el095
7	biweight	1.643923	accu-racy	bi-nary	0.5311111	50	0.02363388	Preproces-sor1_Mod-el008
7	biweight	1.725983	accu-racy	bi-nary	0.5311111	50	0.02363388	Preproces-sor1_Mod-el009
9	biweight	1.414735	accu-racy	bi-nary	0.5312778	50	0.02382841	Preproces-sor1_Mod-el006
15	biweight	1.783946	accu-racy	bi-nary	0.5316667	50	0.02226781	Preproces-sor1_Mod-el010
10	rectan-gular	1.644240	accu-racy	bi-nary	0.5316667	50	0.02169601	Preproces-sor1_Mod-el083

5	gaussian	1.760824	accu-racy	bi-nary	0.5330000	50	0.02067634	Preproces-sor1_Mod-el036
9	triweight	1.193379	accu-racy	bi-nary	0.5332778	50	0.02389884	Preproces-sor1_Mod-el094
9	cos	1.515072	accu-racy	bi-nary	0.5336667	50	0.02253851	Preproces-sor1_Mod-el018
14	cos	1.027993	accu-racy	bi-nary	0.5337222	50	0.02222903	Preproces-sor1_Mod-el013
11	triweight	1.192023	accu-racy	bi-nary	0.5340000	50	0.02320076	Preproces-sor1_Mod-el093
3	rectan-gular	1.680788	accu-racy	bi-nary	0.5348889	50	0.02401697	Preproces-sor1_Mod-el084
10	inv	1.977853	accu-racy	bi-nary	0.5357222	50	0.02227432	Preproces-sor1_Mod-el049
9	triangular	1.492567	accu-racy	bi-nary	0.5358889	50	0.02291258	Preproces-sor1_Mod-el089
11	rank	1.915064	accu-racy	bi-nary	0.5365000	50	0.02351672	Preproces-sor1_Mod-el078
5	inv	1.617235	accu-racy	bi-nary	0.5367778	50	0.02201441	Preproces-sor1_Mod-el047
3	rectan-gular	1.913995	accu-racy	bi-nary	0.5368889	50	0.02478810	Preproces-sor1_Mod-el087
4	gaussian	1.526030	accu-racy	bi-nary	0.5373333	50	0.02351178	Preproces-sor1_Mod-el034
19	rectan-gular	1.119405	accu-racy	bi-nary	0.5373333	50	0.02481059	Preproces-sor1_Mod-el080
10	rank	1.986054	accu-racy	bi-nary	0.5387222	50	0.02420965	Preproces-sor1_Mod-el079
13	biweight	1.136540	accu-racy	bi-nary	0.5396111	50	0.02327993	Preproces-sor1_Mod-el003
13	optimal	1.584900	accu-racy	bi-nary	0.5403333	50	0.02286751	Preproces-sor1_Mod-el060

13	cos	1.192816	accu-racy	bi-nary	0.5424444	50	0.02258701	Preproces-sor1_Mod-el014
8	optimal	1.316949	accu-racy	bi-nary	0.5432778	50	0.02160744	Preproces-sor1_Mod-el055
8	rank	1.866483	accu-racy	bi-nary	0.5442222	50	0.02256242	Preproces-sor1_Mod-el075
5	rank	1.834054	accu-racy	bi-nary	0.5443333	50	0.02289761	Preproces-sor1_Mod-el074
7	triangular	1.547459	accu-racy	bi-nary	0.5448333	50	0.02370466	Preproces-sor1_Mod-el091
10	biweight	1.117914	accu-racy	bi-nary	0.5455000	50	0.02330969	Preproces-sor1_Mod-el002
14	biweight	1.225073	accu-racy	bi-nary	0.5456111	50	0.02260778	Preproces-sor1_Mod-el004
12	biweight	1.388319	accu-racy	bi-nary	0.5457778	50	0.02364363	Preproces-sor1_Mod-el005
5	rank	1.239595	accu-racy	bi-nary	0.5465556	50	0.02236414	Preproces-sor1_Mod-el068
12	inv	1.395449	accu-racy	bi-nary	0.5487778	50	0.02371770	Preproces-sor1_Mod-el045
20	gaussian	1.483168	accu-racy	bi-nary	0.5491111	50	0.02323899	Preproces-sor1_Mod-el033
16	epanech-nikov	1.282218	accu-racy	bi-nary	0.5494444	50	0.02294859	Preproces-sor1_Mod-el022
15	gaussian	1.229245	accu-racy	bi-nary	0.5495000	50	0.02176481	Preproces-sor1_Mod-el027
6	rank	1.668772	accu-racy	bi-nary	0.5497778	50	0.02249028	Preproces-sor1_Mod-el072
19	inv	1.314271	accu-racy	bi-nary	0.5508333	50	0.02346983	Preproces-sor1_Mod-el044
12	rank	1.137067	accu-racy	bi-nary	0.5519444	50	0.02183899	Preproces-sor1_Mod-el066

11	gaussian	1.370215	accu-racy	bi-nary	0.5522778	50	0.02353528	Preproces-sor1_Mod-el030
17	optimal	1.082503	accu-racy	bi-nary	0.5525556	50	0.02224656	Preproces-sor1_Mod-el051
6	optimal	1.363301	accu-racy	bi-nary	0.5530000	50	0.02118495	Preproces-sor1_Mod-el058
12	triangular	1.143817	accu-racy	bi-nary	0.5531667	50	0.02305648	Preproces-sor1_Mod-el088
10	optimal	1.621902	accu-racy	bi-nary	0.5535000	50	0.02239795	Preproces-sor1_Mod-el061
5	gaussian	1.323345	accu-racy	bi-nary	0.5544444	50	0.02220819	Preproces-sor1_Mod-el029
20	inv	1.769194	accu-racy	bi-nary	0.5548889	50	0.02533917	Preproces-sor1_Mod-el048
12	optimal	1.094962	accu-racy	bi-nary	0.5555556	50	0.02259955	Preproces-sor1_Mod-el052
17	rank	1.486412	accu-racy	bi-nary	0.5557778	50	0.02262195	Preproces-sor1_Mod-el071
14	rank	1.296302	accu-racy	bi-nary	0.5567222	50	0.02279327	Preproces-sor1_Mod-el069
14	optimal	1.339313	accu-racy	bi-nary	0.5568333	50	0.02155083	Preproces-sor1_Mod-el056
19	optimal	1.101058	accu-racy	bi-nary	0.5570556	50	0.02225539	Preproces-sor1_Mod-el053
15	cos	1.703992	accu-racy	bi-nary	0.5572778	50	0.02286030	Preproces-sor1_Mod-el019
16	triangular	1.533765	accu-racy	bi-nary	0.5573333	50	0.02201602	Preproces-sor1_Mod-el090
11	optimal	1.342809	accu-racy	bi-nary	0.5575000	50	0.02321713	Preproces-sor1_Mod-el057
10	biweight	1.034875	accu-racy	bi-nary	0.5585000	50	0.02316610	Preproces-sor1_Mod-el001

17	inv	1.276050	accuracy	binary	0.5586111	50	0.02541570	Preprocessor1_Model042
6	gaussian	1.421845	accuracy	binary	0.5596111	50	0.02168718	Preprocessor1_Model031
20	cos	1.286285	accuracy	binary	0.5599444	50	0.02147322	Preprocessor1_Model015
18	epanechnikov	1.338391	accuracy	binary	0.5601667	50	0.02181437	Preprocessor1_Model023
19	gaussian	1.103807	accuracy	binary	0.5605000	50	0.02391884	Preprocessor1_Model026
15	rank	1.321726	accuracy	binary	0.5610000	50	0.02380727	Preprocessor1_Model070
19	cos	1.372709	accuracy	binary	0.5628889	50	0.02189725	Preprocessor1_Model016
19	optimal	1.215172	accuracy	binary	0.5640556	50	0.02308902	Preprocessor1_Model054
14	optimal	1.537677	accuracy	binary	0.5665556	50	0.02221839	Preprocessor1_Model059
15	inv	1.105418	accuracy	binary	0.5673333	50	0.02338262	Preprocessor1_Model039
20	cos	1.449802	accuracy	binary	0.5676111	50	0.02221366	Preprocessor1_Model017
15	inv	1.017766	accuracy	binary	0.5686111	50	0.02343492	Preprocessor1_Model038
14	optimal	1.737797	accuracy	binary	0.5687778	50	0.02281295	Preprocessor1_Model062
17	inv	1.208876	accuracy	binary	0.5691667	50	0.02642014	Preprocessor1_Model040
18	rank	1.774592	accuracy	binary	0.5709444	50	0.02162902	Preprocessor1_Model073
8	rank	1.185296	accuracy	binary	0.5715556	50	0.02366272	Preprocessor1_Model067

18	gaussian	1.991237	accu-racy	bi-nary	0.5720556	50	0.02274864	Preproces-sor1_Mod-el037
18	rank	1.896739	accu-racy	bi-nary	0.5731667	50	0.02244441	Preproces-sor1_Mod-el076
14	rectan-gular	1.706502	accu-racy	bi-nary	0.5743889	50	0.02465692	Preproces-sor1_Mod-el085
14	rectan-gular	1.831569	accu-racy	bi-nary	0.5748333	50	0.02470708	Preproces-sor1_Mod-el086
16	rectan-gular	1.406608	accu-racy	bi-nary	0.5791111	50	0.02362698	Preproces-sor1_Mod-el082

- The result is 100 rows with 1 mean accurcy value for each combination across the 50 resamples (n = 50).
- The lowest mean accuracy value (0.507 or 50.7%) was achieved when using 4 neighbors, optimal weighting function, and 1.971342 Minkowski distance.
- The highest mean accuracy value (0.579 or 57.9%) was achieved when using 16 neighbors, rectangular weighting function, and 1.406608 Minkowski distance.

We can use the select_best function to create an object "best_pen" that contains the best combination value for the best knn model.

best_pen<-knn_res **%>% select_best**()

best_pen

A tibble: 1 × 4

neighbors weight_func dist_power .config

<int> <chr> <dbl> <chr>

1 16 rectangular 1.41 Preprocessor1_Model082

- The best combination with the highest mean accuracy value (0.579) was using 16 neighbors, rectangular weighting function, and 1.406608 Minkowski distance.

To get the final workflow with the best 3 parameters, we use the finalize_ workflow function with the arguments:

- wflow which is the original workflow with tuned 3 parameters.
- best_pen which is the data of 1 row containing the best combination of 3 parameters.

The resulting workflow "knn_final" is the final workflow containing the best combination of 3 parameters.

```
knn_final <- finalize_workflow(wflow, best_pen)
knn_final
## ══ Workflow ════════════════════════════════════════════════════════════════
## Preprocessor: Recipe
## Model: nearest_neighbor()
##
## ── Preprocessor ────────────────────────────────────────────────────────────
## 1 Recipe Step
##
## • step_normalize()
##
## ── Model ───────────────────────────────────────────────────────────────────
## K-Nearest Neighbor Model Specification (classification)
##
## Main Arguments:
## neighbors = 16
## weight_func = rectangular
## dist_power = 1.40660786628723
##
## Computational engine: kknn
```

Finally, we create a knn_fit model by using the fit function with the arguments:

- knn_final which is the final workflow containing 1 preprocessing step (normalization) and the knn model with best combinations of 3 parameters.
- train_st which is the whole training data with 94 rows.

```
knn_fit <- fit(knn_final, data = train_st)
knn_fit
## ══ Workflow [trained] ══════════════════════════════════════════════════════
```

```
## Preprocessor: Recipe
## Model: nearest_neighbor()
##
## ── Preprocessor ──────────────────────────────────
## 1 Recipe Step
##
## • step_normalize()
##
## ── Model ──────────────────────────────────────────
##
## Call:
## kknn::train.kknn(formula = ..y ~ ., data = data, ks = min_rows(16L, data, 5), distance = ~1.40660786628723, kernel = ~"rectangular")
##
## Type of response variable: nominal
## Minimal misclassification: 0.4148936
## Best kernel: rectangular
## Best k: 16
```

To get the predicted stroke class for every row in the training data, we use the predict function on the knn_fit model with the argument new_data = train_st to get the predicted stroke value (.pred_class) column for each row of the training data after being preprocessed using the knn_fit model.

```
knn_fit %>% predict(new_data = train_st)
## # A tibble: 94 × 1
## .pred_class
## <fct>
## 1 no
## 2 no
## 3 no
```

```
## 4 no
## 5 no
## 6 no
## 7 no
## 8 no
## 9 yes
## 10 yes
## # ℹ 84 more rows
```

The result is 94 rows (same row number as stroke training data) and 1 column ".pred_class."

By using the mutate function, we can add a truth column containing the actual stroke for every row in the training data by using the argument "truth = train_st$stroke."

```
knn_fit %>% predict(new_data = train_st) %>%
mutate(truth = train_st$stroke)
## # A tibble: 94 × 2
## .pred_class truth
## <fct> <fct>
## 1 no no
## 2 no no
## 3 no no
## 4 no no
## 5 no no
## 6 no no
## 7 no no
## 8 no no
## 9 yes no
## 10 yes no
## # ℹ 84 more rows
```

We have 2 columns: ".pred_class" for the predicted stroke and "truth" for the actual stroke. For example, the 9th and 10th rows have an actual stroke value of "no" but their predicted stroke values were reported incorrectly as "yes."To see how many actual stroke values are predicted correctly, we create a confusion matrix by using the conf_mat function with the arguments:

- truth = truth which is the column containing the actual stroke values.
- estimate = .pred_class which is the column containing the predicted stroke values.

knn_fit **%>%** **predict**(new_data = train_st) **%>%**

mutate(truth = train_st$stroke) **%>%**

conf_mat(truth = truth, estimate = .pred_class)

Truth

Prediction yes no

yes 32 16

no 16 30

- The true stroke values are in columns and the predicted stroke values are in rows.
- There are 32 stroke yes rows that are predicted correctly as yes.
- There are 30 stroke no rows that are predicted correctly as no.
- There are 16 stroke yes rows that are predicted incorrectly as no.
- There are 16 stroke no rows that are predicted incorrectly as yes.
- The model accuracy = (32 + 30)/(32 + 30 + 16 + 16) = (32 + 30)/94 = 0.66 or 66%.

The confusion matrix can be plotted directly as a heatmap using the autoplot function with type = "heatmap" argument. Then, we use the labs function to add a plot title.

knn_fit **%>%** **predict**(new_data = train_st) **%>%**

mutate(truth = train_st$stroke) **%>%**

conf_mat(truth = truth, estimate = .pred_class) **%>%**

autoplot(type = "heatmap")+

labs(title = "The confusion matrix of applying the knn model on the ischemic stroke training data")

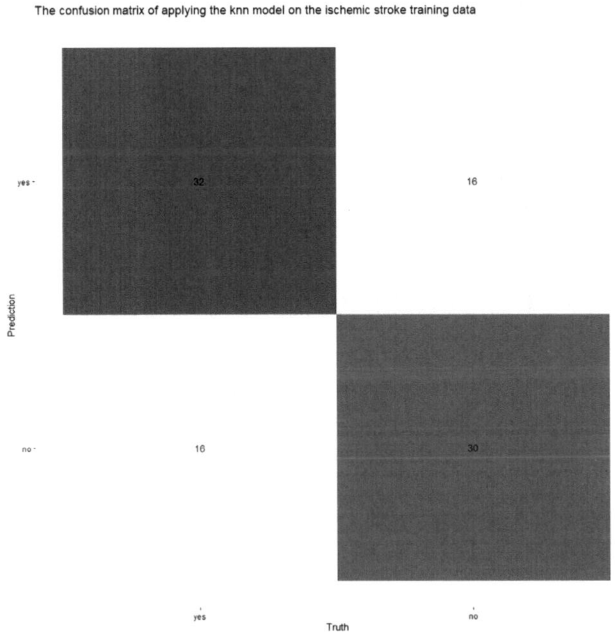

We get the same numbers mentioned above. Alternatively, we can use the accuracy function to get the model accuracy directly with the same arguments as that used with the conf_mat function.

```
knn_fit %>% predict(new_data = train_st) %>%
mutate(truth = train_st$stroke) %>%
accuracy(truth = truth, estimate = .pred_class)
## # A tibble: 1 × 3
## .metric .estimator .estimate
## <chr> <chr> <dbl>
## 1 accuracy binary 0.660
```

The model accuracy on whole training data = 0.66 or 66% as calculated previously.

6.4.9. Model Performance on Testing Data

To get the accuracy on the testing data, we use the same above functions on the knn_fit model but using the test_st data.

```
knn_fit %>% predict(new_data = test_st) %>%
mutate(truth = test_st$stroke) %>%
```

```
accuracy(truth = truth, estimate = .pred_class)
## # A tibble: 1 × 3
## .metric .estimator .estimate
## <chr> <chr> <dbl>
## 1 accuracy binary 0.656
```

The accuracy of the knn model on testing data = 0.656 or 65.6%.

6.5. COMPARISON BETWEEN DIFFERENT MODELS

We will test the linear LDA classification and the elastic net model in addition to the knn model to see the best performing model on the training All 3 models require normalization of all predictors so we use the created recipe "rec" in the 3 models.

6.5.1. Linear Discriminant Analysis (LDA) Model

We define a linear discriminant model by using the functions:

- The discrim_linear function defines the linear discriminant model type. The discrim package is required to fit this model so we must first load this package using the library function.
- The set_engine function with the argument "MASS" to define the engine that will use the lda function from the MASS package.
- The set_mode function with the argument "classification" to define the mode of learning. We use classification because we have a categorical binary outcome (stroke).
- All the 3 functions are applied in sequence using the piping "%>%" operator and the resulting object is called "discrim_model."
- The lda function from the MASS package has no tuning parameters so the model can be created directly.

```
library(discrim)
discrim_model <- discrim_linear() %>%
set_engine("MASS") %>%
set_mode("classification")
discrim_model
## Linear Discriminant Model Specification (classification)
##
## Computational engine: MASS
```

6.5.2. Elastic Net Model

The elastic net model has 2 tuning parameters: the mixture and penalty, so we create "elastic_model" by using the multinom_reg function with the arguments:

- mixture = tune() to tune the different mixture values on the different resamples.
- penalty = tune() to tune the different penalty values on the different resamples.

We also use the set_engine function with "glmnet" argument and set_mode function with "classification" argument.

```
elastic_model<-multinom_reg(mixture = tune(), penalty = tune()) %>%
set_engine("glmnet") %>%
set_mode("classification")
elastic_model
## Multinomial Regression Model Specification (classification)
##
## Main Arguments:
## penalty = tune()
## mixture = tune()
##
## Computational engine: glmnet
```

Then, we create a grid "my_grid2" of 100 different values of mixture and penalty by using the levels = 10 argument within the grid_regular function.

```
my_grid2<-grid_regular(mixture(), penalty(), levels = 10)
my_grid2
## # A tibble: 100 × 2
## mixture penalty
## <dbl> <dbl>
## 1 0 0.0000000001
## 2 0.111 0.0000000001
## 3 0.222 0.0000000001
## 4 0.333 0.0000000001
## 5 0.444 0.0000000001
## 6 0.556 0.0000000001
```

7 0.667 0.0000000001

8 0.778 0.0000000001

9 0.889 0.0000000001

10 1 0.0000000001

i 90 more rows

To try all these 100 different combinations on the 50 resamples of the training data, we create a workflow "wflow2" containing the "rec" recipe and the elastic_model model.

```
wflow2<-workflow() %>% add_recipe(rec) %>%
add_model(elastic_model)
wflow2
## ══ Workflow ════════════════════════════════════════════════════
## Preprocessor: Recipe
## Model: multinom_reg()
##
## ── Preprocessor ────────────────────────────────────────────
## 1 Recipe Step
##
## • step_normalize()
##
## ── Model ───────────────────────────────────────────────
## Multinomial Regression Model Specification (classification)
##
## Main Arguments:
## penalty = tune()
## mixture = tune()
##
## Computational engine: glmnet
```

Then, we use the tune_grid function to determine the best tuning mixture and penalty values.

```
set.seed(123)
elastic_res <- tune_grid(wflow2, folds,
metrics = metric_set(accuracy),
grid = my_grid2)
elastic_res
## # Tuning results
## # 10-fold cross-validation repeated 5 times using stratification
## # A tibble: 50 × 5
## splits id id2 .metrics .notes
## <list> <chr> <chr> <list> <list>
## 1 <split [84/10]> Repeat1 Fold01 <tibble [100 × 6]> <tibble [0 × 3]>
## 2 <split [84/10]> Repeat1 Fold02 <tibble [100 × 6]> <tibble [0 × 3]>
## 3 <split [84/10]> Repeat1 Fold03 <tibble [100 × 6]> <tibble [0 × 3]>
## 4 <split [84/10]> Repeat1 Fold04 <tibble [100 × 6]> <tibble [0 × 3]>
## 5 <split [84/10]> Repeat1 Fold05 <tibble [100 × 6]> <tibble [0 × 3]>
## 6 <split [84/10]> Repeat1 Fold06 <tibble [100 × 6]> <tibble [0 × 3]>
## 7 <split [85/9]> Repeat1 Fold07 <tibble [100 × 6]> <tibble [0 × 3]>
## 8 <split [85/9]> Repeat1 Fold08 <tibble [100 × 6]> <tibble [0 × 3]>
## 9 <split [86/8]> Repeat1 Fold09 <tibble [100 × 6]> <tibble [0 × 3]>
## 10 <split [86/8]> Repeat1 Fold10 <tibble [100 × 6]> <tibble [0 × 3]>
## # i 40 more rows
```

The resulting object "elastic_res" contains 50 rows (for 50 resamples) and 5 columns. Finally, by using the collect_metrics function, we can see the best mixture and penalty parameters.

```
elastic_res %>% collect_metrics() %>%
arrange(mean) %>%
flextable() %>% theme_box() %>%
set_caption(caption = "The mean accuracy of applying 100 combinations of mixture and penalty values on 50 resamples of stroke training data when using elastic net classification model")
```

The mean accuracy of applying 100 combinations of mixture and penalty values on 50 resamples of stroke training data when using elastic net classification model:

penalty	mixture	.metric	.estimator	mean	n	std_err	.config
1.00000000000000	0.2222222	accuracy	binary	0.5111111	50	0.003174603	Preprocessor1_Model030
1.00000000000000	0.3333333	accuracy	binary	0.5111111	50	0.003174603	Preprocessor1_Model040
1.00000000000000	0.4444444	accuracy	binary	0.5111111	50	0.003174603	Preprocessor1_Model050
1.00000000000000	0.5555556	accuracy	binary	0.5111111	50	0.003174603	Preprocessor1_Model060
1.00000000000000	0.6666667	accuracy	binary	0.5111111	50	0.003174603	Preprocessor1_Model070
1.00000000000000	0.7777778	accuracy	binary	0.5111111	50	0.003174603	Preprocessor1_Model080
1.00000000000000	0.8888889	accuracy	binary	0.5111111	50	0.003174603	Preprocessor1_Model090
1.00000000000000	1.0000000	accuracy	binary	0.5111111	50	0.003174603	Preprocessor1_Model100
1.00000000000000	0.1111111	accuracy	binary	0.5736667	50	0.017719796	Preprocessor1_Model020
0.00046415888336	0.7777778	accuracy	binary	0.6021667	50	0.016555618	Preprocessor1_Model077
0.00000000010000	0.2222222	accuracy	binary	0.6023889	50	0.016708001	Preprocessor1_Model021
0.00000000129155	0.2222222	accuracy	binary	0.6023889	50	0.016708001	Preprocessor1_Model022
0.00000001668101	0.2222222	accuracy	binary	0.6023889	50	0.016708001	Preprocessor1_Model023
0.00000021544347	0.2222222	accuracy	binary	0.6023889	50	0.016708001	Preprocessor1_Model024
0.00000278255940	0.2222222	accuracy	binary	0.6023889	50	0.016708001	Preprocessor1_Model025
0.00003593813664	0.2222222	accuracy	binary	0.6023889	50	0.016708001	Preprocessor1_Model026
0.00000000010000	0.3333333	accuracy	binary	0.6023889	50	0.016708001	Preprocessor1_Model031

0.00000000129155	0.3333333	accuracy	binary	0.6023889	50	0.016708001	Preprocessor1_Model032
0.00000001668101	0.3333333	accuracy	binary	0.6023889	50	0.016708001	Preprocessor1_Model033
0.00000021544347	0.3333333	accuracy	binary	0.6023889	50	0.016708001	Preprocessor1_Model034
0.00000278255940	0.3333333	accuracy	binary	0.6023889	50	0.016708001	Preprocessor1_Model035
0.00003593813664	0.3333333	accuracy	binary	0.6023889	50	0.016708001	Preprocessor1_Model036
0.00046415888336	0.3333333	accuracy	binary	0.6041667	50	0.016173593	Preprocessor1_Model037
0.00046415888336	0.4444444	accuracy	binary	0.6041667	50	0.016173593	Preprocessor1_Model047
0.00046415888336	0.5555556	accuracy	binary	0.6041667	50	0.016173593	Preprocessor1_Model057
0.00046415888336	0.8888889	accuracy	binary	0.6041667	50	0.016670682	Preprocessor1_Model087
0.00046415888336	1.0000000	accuracy	binary	0.6041667	50	0.016670682	Preprocessor1_Model097
0.00000000010000	0.4444444	accuracy	binary	0.6046111	50	0.016728647	Preprocessor1_Model041
0.00000000129155	0.4444444	accuracy	binary	0.6046111	50	0.016728647	Preprocessor1_Model042
0.00000001668101	0.4444444	accuracy	binary	0.6046111	50	0.016728647	Preprocessor1_Model043
0.00000021544347	0.4444444	accuracy	binary	0.6046111	50	0.016728647	Preprocessor1_Model044
0.00000278255940	0.4444444	accuracy	binary	0.6046111	50	0.016728647	Preprocessor1_Model045
0.00003593813664	0.4444444	accuracy	binary	0.6046111	50	0.016728647	Preprocessor1_Model046
0.00000000010000	0.5555556	accuracy	binary	0.6046111	50	0.016728647	Preprocessor1_Model051
0.00000000129155	0.5555556	accuracy	binary	0.6046111	50	0.016728647	Preprocessor1_Model052

0.00000001668101	0.5555556	accu-racy	binary	0.6046111	50	0.016728647	Preproces-sor1_Mod-el053
0.00000021544347	0.5555556	accu-racy	binary	0.6046111	50	0.016728647	Preproces-sor1_Mod-el054
0.00000278255940	0.5555556	accu-racy	binary	0.6046111	50	0.016728647	Preproces-sor1_Mod-el055
0.00003593813664	0.5555556	accu-racy	binary	0.6046111	50	0.016728647	Preproces-sor1_Mod-el056
0.00000000010000	0.6666667	accu-racy	binary	0.6046111	50	0.016728647	Preproces-sor1_Mod-el061
0.00000000129155	0.6666667	accu-racy	binary	0.6046111	50	0.016728647	Preproces-sor1_Mod-el062
0.00000001668101	0.6666667	accu-racy	binary	0.6046111	50	0.016728647	Preproces-sor1_Mod-el063
0.00000021544347	0.6666667	accu-racy	binary	0.6046111	50	0.016728647	Preproces-sor1_Mod-el064
0.00000278255940	0.6666667	accu-racy	binary	0.6046111	50	0.016728647	Preproces-sor1_Mod-el065
0.00003593813664	0.6666667	accu-racy	binary	0.6046111	50	0.016728647	Preproces-sor1_Mod-el066
0.00000000010000	0.7777778	accu-racy	binary	0.6046111	50	0.016728647	Preproces-sor1_Mod-el071
0.00000000129155	0.7777778	accu-racy	binary	0.6046111	50	0.016728647	Preproces-sor1_Mod-el072
0.00000001668101	0.7777778	accu-racy	binary	0.6046111	50	0.016728647	Preproces-sor1_Mod-el073
0.00000021544347	0.7777778	accu-racy	binary	0.6046111	50	0.016728647	Preproces-sor1_Mod-el074
0.00000278255940	0.7777778	accu-racy	binary	0.6046111	50	0.016728647	Preproces-sor1_Mod-el075
0.00003593813664	0.7777778	accu-racy	binary	0.6046111	50	0.016728647	Preproces-sor1_Mod-el076
0.00000000010000	0.8888889	accu-racy	binary	0.6046111	50	0.016728647	Preproces-sor1_Mod-el081
0.00000000129155	0.8888889	accu-racy	binary	0.6046111	50	0.016728647	Preproces-sor1_Mod-el082

0.00000001668101	0.8888889	accu-racy	binary	0.6046111	50	0.016728647	Preproces-sor1_Mod-el083
0.00000021544347	0.8888889	accu-racy	binary	0.6046111	50	0.016728647	Preproces-sor1_Mod-el084
0.00000278255940	0.8888889	accu-racy	binary	0.6046111	50	0.016728647	Preproces-sor1_Mod-el085
0.00003593813664	0.8888889	accu-racy	binary	0.6046111	50	0.016728647	Preproces-sor1_Mod-el086
0.00000000010000	1.0000000	accu-racy	binary	0.6046111	50	0.016728647	Preproces-sor1_Mod-el091
0.00000000129155	1.0000000	accu-racy	binary	0.6046111	50	0.016728647	Preproces-sor1_Mod-el092
0.00000001668101	1.0000000	accu-racy	binary	0.6046111	50	0.016728647	Preproces-sor1_Mod-el093
0.00000021544347	1.0000000	accu-racy	binary	0.6046111	50	0.016728647	Preproces-sor1_Mod-el094
0.00000278255940	1.0000000	accu-racy	binary	0.6046111	50	0.016728647	Preproces-sor1_Mod-el095
0.00003593813664	1.0000000	accu-racy	binary	0.6046111	50	0.016728647	Preproces-sor1_Mod-el096
0.00046415888336	0.1111111	accu-racy	binary	0.6061667	50	0.016286343	Preproces-sor1_Mod-el017
0.00046415888336	0.2222222	accu-racy	binary	0.6061667	50	0.016286343	Preproces-sor1_Mod-el027
0.00046415888336	0.6666667	accu-racy	binary	0.6061667	50	0.016033767	Preproces-sor1_Mod-el067
0.00000000010000	0.1111111	accu-racy	binary	0.6063889	50	0.016440117	Preproces-sor1_Mod-el011
0.00000000129155	0.1111111	accu-racy	binary	0.6063889	50	0.016440117	Preproces-sor1_Mod-el012
0.00000001668101	0.1111111	accu-racy	binary	0.6063889	50	0.016440117	Preproces-sor1_Mod-el013
0.00000021544347	0.1111111	accu-racy	binary	0.6063889	50	0.016440117	Preproces-sor1_Mod-el014
0.00000278255940	0.1111111	accu-racy	binary	0.6063889	50	0.016440117	Preproces-sor1_Mod-el015

0.00003593813664	0.1111111	accu-racy	binary	0.6063889	50	0.016440117	Preproces-sor1_Mod-el016
0.07742636826811	1.0000000	accu-racy	binary	0.6111667	50	0.022207973	Preproces-sor1_Mod-el099
1.00000000000000	0.0000000	accu-racy	binary	0.6140556	50	0.022972922	Preproces-sor1_Mod-el010
0.07742636826811	0.8888889	accu-racy	binary	0.6276667	50	0.023878203	Preproces-sor1_Mod-el089
0.07742636826811	0.4444444	accu-racy	binary	0.6286111	50	0.023325267	Preproces-sor1_Mod-el049
0.07742636826811	0.7777778	accu-racy	binary	0.6293889	50	0.023393063	Preproces-sor1_Mod-el079
0.07742636826811	0.3333333	accu-racy	binary	0.6308333	50	0.021087116	Preproces-sor1_Mod-el039
0.07742636826811	0.6666667	accu-racy	binary	0.6353889	50	0.024244026	Preproces-sor1_Mod-el069
0.00599484250319	1.0000000	accu-racy	binary	0.6385556	50	0.018808124	Preproces-sor1_Mod-el098
0.07742636826811	0.2222222	accu-racy	binary	0.6390556	50	0.020429597	Preproces-sor1_Mod-el029
0.00599484250319	0.8888889	accu-racy	binary	0.6427778	50	0.018858853	Preproces-sor1_Mod-el088
0.07742636826811	0.5555556	accu-racy	binary	0.6435556	50	0.026304638	Preproces-sor1_Mod-el059
0.00599484250319	0.7777778	accu-racy	binary	0.6447778	50	0.018654785	Preproces-sor1_Mod-el078
0.00599484250319	0.6666667	accu-racy	binary	0.6465556	50	0.018264759	Preproces-sor1_Mod-el068
0.00599484250319	0.5555556	accu-racy	binary	0.6466111	50	0.017182914	Preproces-sor1_Mod-el058
0.07742636826811	0.1111111	accu-racy	binary	0.6500556	50	0.019637444	Preproces-sor1_Mod-el019
0.00599484250319	0.2222222	accu-racy	binary	0.6508889	50	0.016869596	Preproces-sor1_Mod-el028
0.00599484250319	0.3333333	accu-racy	binary	0.6508889	50	0.016869596	Preproces-sor1_Mod-el038

0.00599484250319	0.4444444	accu-racy	binary	0.6511111	50	0.017299949	Preproces-sor1_Mod-el048
0.07742636826811	0.0000000	accu-racy	binary	0.6533333	50	0.018688412	Preproces-sor1_Mod-el009
0.00000000010000	0.0000000	accu-racy	binary	0.6538333	50	0.017976828	Preproces-sor1_Mod-el001
0.00000000129155	0.0000000	accu-racy	binary	0.6538333	50	0.017976828	Preproces-sor1_Mod-el002
0.00000001668101	0.0000000	accu-racy	binary	0.6538333	50	0.017976828	Preproces-sor1_Mod-el003
0.00000021544347	0.0000000	accu-racy	binary	0.6538333	50	0.017976828	Preproces-sor1_Mod-el004
0.00000278255940	0.0000000	accu-racy	binary	0.6538333	50	0.017976828	Preproces-sor1_Mod-el005
0.00003593813664	0.0000000	accu-racy	binary	0.6538333	50	0.017976828	Preproces-sor1_Mod-el006
0.00046415888336	0.0000000	accu-racy	binary	0.6538333	50	0.017976828	Preproces-sor1_Mod-el007
0.00599484250319	0.0000000	accu-racy	binary	0.6538333	50	0.017976828	Preproces-sor1_Mod-el008
0.00599484250319	0.1111111	accu-racy	binary	0.6551111	50	0.016749296	Preproces-sor1_Mod-el018

- We have 100 rows for 100 combinations of penalty and mixture values. Each row contains the mean accuracy across the 50 resamples (n = 50) for a single combination of penalty and mixture value.
- The lowest mean accuracy value (0.511) was achieved when using 1 penalty and different mixture values except the 0.111 mixture value.
- The highest mean accuracy value (0.655) was achieved when using 0.00599484250319 penalty and 0.1111111 mixture value.
- So, we recreate the elastic_model object using these values associated with the highest mean accuracy.

```
elastic_model<-multinom_reg(mixture = 0.1111111,
penalty = 0.00599484250319) %>%
set_engine("glmnet") %>%
set_mode("classification")
elastic_model
```

```
## Multinomial Regression Model Specification (classification)
##
## Main Arguments:
## penalty = 0.00599484250319
## mixture = 0.1111111
##
## Computational engine: glmnet
```

6.5.3. knn Model

We create knn_model by using the best combination determined by using the tune_grid function in Section 6.4.8 and contained in best_pen data frame.

```
best_pen
## # A tibble: 1 × 4
## neighbors weight_func dist_power .config
## <int> <chr> <dbl> <chr>
## 1 16 rectangular 1.41 Preprocessor1_Model082
knn_model<-nearest_neighbor(neighbors = 16, weight_func = “rectangular”,
dist_power = 1.41) %>%
set_engine(“kknn”) %>%
set_mode(“classification”)
knn_model
## K-Nearest Neighbor Model Specification (classification)
##
## Main Arguments:
## neighbors = 16
## weight_func = rectangular
## dist_power = 1.41
##
## Computational engine: kknn
```

6.5.4. Comparing the 3 Models

We create a list of the 1 created preprocessing recipe “preproc” by using the list function with the arguments:

- rec = rec to hold the recipe of the knn model that will be also used for other models.

```
preproc <- list(rec = rec)
preproc
## $rec
##
## ── Recipe ──────────────────────────────────────────────────────────────
##
## ── Inputs
## Number of variables by role
## outcome: 1
## predictor: 28
##
## ── Operations
## • Centering and scaling for: all_predictors()
```

We have a list of 1 recipe with a rec name.

We create a list of models "models" by using the list function with the arguments:

- lda = discrim_model to hold the linear LDA model.
- elastic = elastic_model to hold the elastic net model.
- knn = knn_model to hold the knn classification model.

```
models<-list(lda = discrim_model, elastic = elastic_model, knn = knn_model)
models
## $lda
## Linear Discriminant Model Specification (classification)
##
## Computational engine: MASS
##
##
## $elastic
## Multinomial Regression Model Specification (classification)
##
```

```
## Main Arguments:
## penalty = 0.00599484250319
## mixture = 0.1111111
##
## Computational engine: glmnet
##
##
## $knn
## K-Nearest Neighbor Model Specification (classification)
##
## Main Arguments:
## neighbors = 16
## weight_func = rectangular
## dist_power = 1.41
##
## Computational engine: kknn
```

We have a list of 3 models with lda, elastic, and knn names.

Then, we use the workflow_set functions to create a set of 3 workflows "class_models" by using the arguments:

- preproc which is the list of 1 recipe.
- models which is the list of 3 models.
- cross = TRUE so every model will be combined to the single recipe.

```
class_models <- workflow_set(preproc, models, cross = TRUE)
class_models
## # A workflow set/tibble: 3 × 4
## wflow_id info option result
## <chr> <list> <list> <list>
## 1 rec_lda <tibble [1 × 4]> <opts[0]> <list [0]>
## 2 rec_elastic <tibble [1 × 4]> <opts[0]> <list [0]>
## 3 rec_knn <tibble [1 × 4]> <opts[0]> <list [0]>
```

The class_models contains 3 workflows: rec_lda, rec_elastic, and rec_knn.

To fit all 3 workflows on 50 resamples of training data, we use the workflow_map function on the reg_models with the arguments:

- "fit_resamples" which is the function required to run on each workflow.
- seed = 123 for reproducibility.
- verbose = TRUE to monitor the fitting of 3 workflows.
- resamples = folds which contains the 50 resamples of training data.
- metrics = metric_set(accuracy) to extract the accuracy of each model on each resample.

```
fit_models <- class_models %>% workflow_map("fit_resamples",
seed = 123, verbose = TRUE,
resamples = folds,
metrics = metric_set(accuracy))
## i 1 of 3 resampling: rec_lda
## ✔ 1 of 3 resampling: rec_lda (2.2s)
## i 2 of 3 resampling: rec_elastic
## ✔ 2 of 3 resampling: rec_elastic (2.9s)
## i 3 of 3 resampling: rec_knn
## ✔ 3 of 3 resampling: rec_knn (3.5s)
fit_models
## # A workflow set/tibble: 3 × 4
## wflow_id info option result
## <chr> <list> <list> <list>
## 1 rec_lda <tibble [1 × 4]> <opts[2]> <rsmp[+]>
## 2 rec_elastic <tibble [1 × 4]> <opts[2]> <rsmp[+]>
## 3 rec_knn <tibble [1 × 4]> <opts[2]> <rsmp[+]>
```

The fit_models contains the results of applying the 3 models on 50 resamples of training data.

By using the collect_metrics function, we get the mean accuracy value for each model across the 50 resamples of training data.

```
fit_models %>% collect_metrics() %>% flextable() %>%
theme_box() %>% set_caption(caption = "The mean accuracy of linear discriminant analysis, elastic net, and k-nearest neighbors models on 50 resamples of stroke training data")
```

The mean accuracy of linear discriminant analysis (LDA), elastic net, and knn models on 50 resamples of stroke training data:

wflow_id	.config	pre-proc	model	.metric	.es-ti-ma-tor	mean	n	std_err
rec_lda	Pre-proces-sor1_Model1	reci-pe	dis-crim_linear	accuracy	bi-nary	0.6453889	50	0.01983629
rec_elas-tic	Pre-proces-sor1_Model1	reci-pe	multi-nom_reg	accuracy	bi-nary	0.6551111	50	0.01674930
rec_knn	Pre-proces-sor1_Model1	reci-pe	nearest_neigh-bor	accuracy	bi-nary	0.5791111	50	0.02362698

- The elastic net model has the highest accuracy value = 0.655 or 65.5%.

6.5.5. Plotting the Performance on Training Data

We can plot the 3 models' performances on the training data by using the following functions after collect_metrics:

- The ggplot function with the argument "aes(x = wflow_id, y = mean, color = wflow_id" to plot workflow name on x-axis, mean accuracy on y-axis, and a distinct color for each workflow name.
- The geom_point function to plot a scatter plot.
- The geom_errorbar function with the arguments:

+ aes(ymin = mean-std_err, ymax = mean+std_err) to plot an error bar with its minimum at the mean accuracy minus the corresponding standard error and its maximum at the mean accuracy plus the corresponding standard error.

+ width = 0.1 to decrease width of horizontal lines of the error bar to 0.1 its default.

- The labs function with the title argument to add a plot title, *x* argument to add *x*-axis title, y argument to add y-axis title, and color argument to add legend title.
- The theme_classic function as described before.

fit_models **%>% collect_metrics()** **%>% ggplot(aes**(x = wflow_id, y = mean, color = wflow_id))+

geom_point()+

geom_errorbar(aes(ymin = mean-std_err, ymax = mean+std_err), width = 0.1)+

labs(title = "The mean accuracy ± standard error of 3 models on 50 resamples of the stroke training data", x = "Model", y = "Mean accuracy", color = "Model")+

theme_classic()

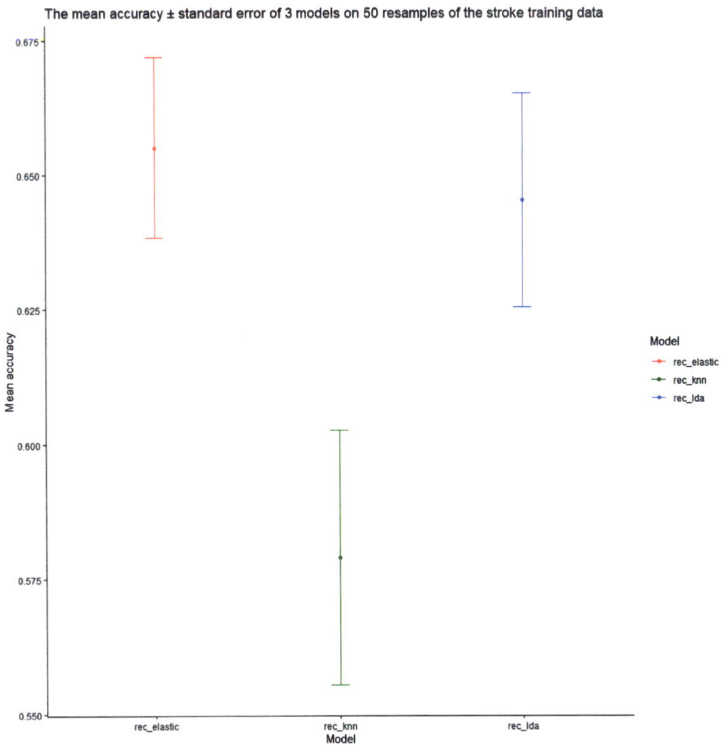

6.5.6. Comparing the Models Statistically

If we use the collect_metrics function with the argument summarize = FALSE, we will get the accuracy value of applying each model on each resample.

```
fit_models %>% collect_metrics(summarize = FALSE)
## # A tibble: 150 × 9
## wflow_id .config preproc model id id2 .metric .estimator .estimate
## <chr> <chr> <chr> <chr> <chr> <chr> <chr> <chr> <dbl>
## 1 rec_lda Preprocessor… recipe disc… Repe… Fold… accura… binary 0.8
## 2 rec_lda Preprocessor… recipe disc… Repe… Fold… accura… binary 0.5
## 3 rec_lda Preprocessor… recipe disc… Repe… Fold… accura… binary 0.7
## 4 rec_lda Preprocessor… recipe disc… Repe… Fold… accura… binary 0.7
## 5 rec_lda Preprocessor… recipe disc… Repe… Fold… accura… binary 0.5
## 6 rec_lda Preprocessor… recipe disc… Repe… Fold… accura… binary 0.6
## 7 rec_lda Preprocessor… recipe disc… Repe… Fold… accura… binary 0.778
## 8 rec_lda Preprocessor… recipe disc… Repe… Fold… accura… binary 0.667
## 9 rec_lda Preprocessor… recipe disc… Repe… Fold… accura… binary 0.625
## 10 rec_lda Preprocessor… recipe disc… Repe… Fold… accura… binary 0.625
## # i 140 more rows
```

The result is 150 rows because we have 50 resamples × 3 different models. We can do a t-test to see if the mean accuracy value in the .estimate column is different across the 3 models by using the function t_test, from the rstatix package, with the arguments:

- .estimate ~ wflow_id to see if the mean accuracy value in the .estimate column is different across the 3 models in the wflow_id column.
- paired = TRUE because we are comparing the same 50 resamples across the 3 models.
- p.adjust.method = "fdr" to adjust the p-values for pairwise comparison using the false discovery rate (FDR) method.

```
library(rstatix)
fit_models %>% collect_metrics(summarize = FALSE) %>%
t_test(.estimate ~ wflow_id, paired = TRUE,
p.adjust.method = "fdr") %>%
flextable() %>% theme_box() %>%
```

set_caption(caption = "t-test results comparing the accuracy of 3 models on 50 resamples of stroke training data")

t-test results comparing the accuracy of 3 models on 50 resamples of stroke training data:

.y.	group1	group2	n1	n2	statistic	df	p	p.adj	p.adj. signif
.estimate	rec_ elastic	rec_ knn	50	50	2.937 3299	49	0.005	0.015	*
.estimate	rec_ elastic	rec_lda	50	50	0.8107 384	49	0.421	0.421	ns
.estimate	rec_knn	rec_lda	50	50	–2.21 12255	49	0.032	0.048	*

- The elastic net model has significantly higher accuracy than the knn model with a significant adjusted p-value = 0.015.
- The LDA model has significantly higher accuracy than the knn model with a significant adjusted p-value = 0.048.
- The linear LDA model has equivalent accuracy to that of the elastic net model because the adjusted p-value is insignificant (> 0.05) = 0.421.

BIBLIOGRAPHY

1. Benjamini, Y., & Hochberg, Y. (1995). Controlling the false discovery rate: A practical and powerful approach to multiple testing. *Journal of the Royal Statistical Society: Series B (Methodological)*, *57*, 289–300. https://doi.org/10.1111/j.2517-6161.1995.tb02031.x.
2. De Cock, D. (2011). Ames, Iowa: Alternative to the Boston Housing Data as an end of semester regression project. *Journal of Statistics Education*, *19*(3). https://doi.org/10.1080/10691898.2011.11889627.
3. Friedman, J., Hastie, T., & Tibshirani, R. (2010). Regularization paths for generalized linear models via coordinate descent. *Journal of Statistical Software*, *33*(1), 1–22. https://doi.org/10.18637/jss.v033.i01.
4. Gohel, D. (2022). *flextable: Functions for Tabular Reporting* (R package version 0.7.0). https://CRAN.R-project.org/package=flextable (accessed on 20 May 2025).
5. Hvitfeldt, E., & Kuhn, M. (2023). *Discrim: Model Wrappers for Discriminant Analysis* (R package version 1.0.1). https://CRAN.R-project.org/package=discrim (accessed on 20 May 2025).
6. James, G., Witten, D., Hastie, T., & Tibshirani, R. (2014). *An Introduction to Statistical Learning: With Applications in R*. Springer Publishing Company.
7. Kassambara, A. (2019). *Datarium: Data Bank for Statistical Analysis and Visualization* (R package version 0.1.0). https://CRAN.R-project.org/package=datarium (accessed on 20 May 2025).
8. Kassambara, A. (2022). *rstatix: Pipe-Friendly Framework for Basic Statistical Tests* (R package version 0.7.1). https://CRAN.R-project.org/package=rstatix (accessed on 20 May 2025).

9. Kuhn, M., & Johnson, K. (2019). *Feature Engineering and Selection: A Practical Approach for Predictive Models*. Chapman and Hall/CRC.
10. Kuhn, M., et al. (2020). Tidymodels: A collection of packages for modeling and machine learning using tidyverse principles. https://www.tidymodels.org (accessed on 20 May 2025).
11. Lakshika, J. P. G., & Talagala, T. S. (2021). Computer-aided interpretable features for leaf image classification. *arXiv preprint arXiv:2106.08077*. https://doi.org/10.48550/arXiv.2106.08077.
12. Waring, E., Quinn, M., McNamara, A., Arino de la Rubia, E., Zhu, H., & Ellis, S. (2022). *skimr: Compact and Flexible Summaries of Data* (R package version 2.1.4). https://CRAN.R-project.org/package=skimr (accessed on 20 May 2025).
13. Wickham, H., Averick, M., Bryan, J., Chang, W., McGowan, L. D. A., François, R., & Yutani, H. (2019). Welcome to the tidyverse. *Journal of Open-Source Software*, *4*(43), 1686. https://doi.org/10.21105/joss.01686.
14. Wickham, H., Pedersen, T., & Seidel, D. (2023). *Scales: Scale Functions for Visualization* (R package version 1.3.0). https://CRAN.R-project.org/package=scales (accessed on 20 May 2025).

INDEX

A

accuracy 95, 97, 98, 99, 100, 101, 102, 103, 116, 117, 118, 119, 120, 121, 122, 123, 124
add_model function 13, 32, 51, 62
add_recipe function 13, 32, 51, 62
add_significance function 14, 33, 52, 63
advertising budget 1, 2, 10, 15, 53
advertising experiment 1
advertising media 1
age 317, 318, 319, 324, 325, 326
Alley 126, 129, 133, 143, 145, 150, 156, 182, 197, 218
apex 222, 224, 226, 233, 235, 242, 246, 271, 272, 273, 291, 292, 294, 295
area 223, 225, 228, 229, 234, 238, 240, 245, 294
area_convexity 223, 225, 229, 234, 240, 245, 294
area_ratio_convexity 223, 225, 229, 234, 240, 245, 294
artifical data 73
aspect_ratio 223, 225, 229, 234, 239, 245, 294
assessment data 98, 99, 118, 119
atrial_fibrillation 367, 368, 371, 376, 378, 380
average value 5

B

base 222, 224, 226, 233, 235, 243, 246, 267, 272, 291, 292, 295, 312
Bedroom_AbvGr 128, 131, 138, 144, 149, 155, 181, 195, 217
blast_furnace_slag 318, 319, 323, 324, 325, 326
Bldg_Type 127, 130, 134, 145, 151, 156, 181, 196, 217
Bsmt_Cond 127, 130, 134, 146, 152, 157, 182, 197, 218
Bsmt_Exposure 127, 130, 135, 146, 152, 157, 180, 181, 195, 216, 217, 218
BsmtFin_SF_1 127, 130, 137, 144, 148, 155, 182, 194, 197, 218
BsmtFin_SF_2 127, 130, 137, 143
BsmtFin_Type_1 127, 130, 135, 146, 152, 153, 157, 180, 182, 183, 194, 195, 196, 197, 216, 218, 219
BsmtFin_Type_2 127, 130, 135, 146, 153, 157, 182, 197, 219
Bsmt_Full_Bath 128, 131, 137, 144, 148, 155, 181, 195, 217
Bsmt_Half_Bath 128, 131, 137, 144, 148, 155, 182, 197, 218
Bsmt_Unf_SF 127, 130, 137, 144, 148, 155, 182, 196, 218

C

calc_vol 366, 367, 370, 375, 377, 379

caption argument 4
carotid artery blockages 365
categorical columns 5, 6
cells 4, 14, 33, 52, 63
cement 318, 319, 323, 324, 325, 326
characterization 365
cholesterol 3, 7, 8, 29, 30, 31, 34, 35, 36, 37, 39, 40, 41, 42, 43, 46, 47, 48, 49, 61, 62, 63, 64, 65, 66, 67, 68, 71
cholesterol concentration 3
circularity 223, 225, 229, 234, 239, 245, 295
classification model 95
clumpy_contour 222, 224, 228, 233, 237, 244, 273, 293, 294
clumpy_polar 222, 224, 228, 233, 236, 244, 270, 290, 293, 294, 315
coarse_aggregate 318, 319, 324, 325, 326
code 2
collect_metrics function 24, 27, 43, 46, 60, 71, 100, 101, 122
column classes 2
column names 2, 18, 29, 37, 48
compactness 223, 225, 229, 234, 239, 245, 272, 273, 294
complete_rate 4, 5, 6, 7, 8, 76, 77, 78, 79, 80, 84, 86
compressive_strength 318, 319, 321, 322, 324, 325, 326, 327, 344, 345, 346, 356
computed tomography angiography (CTA) 365
concrete mixture 317, 318
Condition_1 126, 129, 134, 145, 150, 156, 181, 195, 196, 217
confusion matrix 96, 97, 98, 102, 116, 117, 123
contrast 223, 225, 229, 235, 241, 245, 273, 295
convex_contour 223, 225, 228, 234, 238, 244, 273, 294
convex_polar 222, 224, 228, 233, 237, 244, 270, 290, 293, 294, 315
coronary_artery_disease 367, 368, 371, 376, 378, 380
correlation 224, 225, 226, 229, 235, 241, 242, 245, 246, 291, 295
correlation_texture 224, 225, 229, 235, 241, 245, 295
cross-validation 9, 12, 19, 29, 31, 38, 54, 61, 65, 71

D

data 1, 2, 3, 4, 5, 6, 7, 8, 9, 10, 11, 12, 14, 15, 16, 17, 18, 19, 20, 21, 24, 27, 28, 29, 30, 31, 32, 33, 34, 36, 37, 38, 39, 40, 43, 46, 47, 48, 49, 50, 51, 52, 53, 54, 55, 57, 60, 61, 63, 64, 65, 67, 68, 71
data analysis 2, 8, 74
data columns 4, 5
data dimensions 10, 30
data exploration 4
data function 2, 3, 74, 75
data modeling 126, 132
datarium package 2, 3
datasets package 75
decimals 2, 3
decision tree 9
denate_edge 222, 224, 227, 233
diabetes_history 367, 368, 371, 376, 378, 380
diameter 223, 225, 228, 229, 234, 238, 239, 240, 244, 245, 274, 294, 295
discrim_model 87, 88, 109
dollars 1, 3
drug 3, 6, 7, 61, 63, 64
dummification 8

E

eccentriciry 223, 225, 229, 235, 240, 245, 273, 294
Electrical 128, 131, 135, 146, 153, 158, 183, 197, 219
Enclosed_Porch 128, 132, 138
entropy 224, 225, 229, 235, 241, 245, 295

equation 90
Exter_Cond 127, 130, 134, 146, 152, 157, 182, 196, 197, 218
Exterior_1st 127, 130, 134, 145, 151, 157, 181, 182, 194, 195, 196, 217, 218
Exterior_2nd 127, 130, 134, 145, 146, 151, 152, 157, 181, 182, 183, 195, 196, 197, 218, 219

F

Facebook 1, 2, 50, 53
facet_wrap function 23, 42, 56, 66
Fence 129, 132, 135, 147, 154, 158, 182, 196, 197, 218
fine_aggregate 318, 319, 324, 325, 326
Fireplaces 128, 131, 138, 144, 149, 155, 180, 194, 216
First_Flr_SF 128, 131, 137, 144, 148, 155, 180, 196, 216
fit_resamples function 18, 38, 53, 65
Flavia species 221
flextable 74, 76, 77, 78, 79, 83, 84, 85, 90, 92, 100, 113, 119
flextable function 4, 5, 14, 33, 52, 63
flextable package 2
fly_ash 318, 319, 324, 325, 326
Foundation 127, 130, 134, 146, 152, 157, 181, 195, 196, 217
Full_Bath 128, 131, 137, 144, 148, 155, 181, 196, 217
Functional 128, 131, 135, 146, 153, 158, 180, 195, 217

G

Garage_Area 128, 131, 138, 144, 149, 156, 180, 196, 217
Garage_Cars 128, 131, 138, 144, 149, 156, 180, 194, 216
Garage_Cond 128, 131, 135, 147, 153, 154, 158, 182, 183, 196, 197, 218, 219
Garage_Finish 128, 131, 135, 146, 147, 153, 158, 181, 183, 195, 197, 217, 219
Garage_Type 128, 131, 135, 146, 153, 158, 181, 182, 183, 196, 197, 218, 219
gender 3, 5, 6, 7, 29, 30, 31, 34, 35, 36, 38, 43, 46, 49, 61, 63, 64, 68
gender values 47
geom_abline function 23, 42, 55, 66
geom_jitter function 93
geom_point function 15, 23, 34, 42, 55, 66, 114
geom_smooth function 15, 34
geom_vline function 93, 114
ggplot function 15, 23, 34, 41, 55, 66, 93, 114
glimpse function 2, 3
Gr_Liv_Area 128, 131, 137, 144, 148, 155, 180, 183, 194, 197, 216

H

Half_Bath 128, 131, 137, 144, 149, 155, 181, 197, 218
Heating 128, 130, 135, 146, 153, 158, 181, 182, 195, 196, 217, 218
Heating_QC 128, 130, 135, 146, 153, 158, 181, 182, 195, 196, 217, 218
histogram plot 5
House_Style 127, 130, 134, 145, 151, 156, 180, 182, 194, 195, 216, 218
hypercholesterolemia_history 367, 368, 371, 376, 378, 380
hypertension_history 367, 371, 376, 378, 380

I

id 3, 7, 8, 12, 19, 20, 21, 23, 24, 31, 32, 38, 39, 40, 41, 42, 43, 54, 55, 56, 57, 65, 66, 67, 68
information 4, 5, 7, 9
initial_split function 10, 29, 30
integer column 3
inverse_difference_moments 224, 225, 229, 235, 241, 245, 274, 292, 294
iris data 75, 78, 79, 104, 105, 107, 108

Iris setosa 75
ischemic_stroke 366, 368, 369, 372, 373

K

Kitchen_AbvGr 128, 131, 138

L

labs function 16, 23, 34, 42, 56, 66
Land_Contour 126, 129, 133, 145, 150, 156, 182, 197, 218
Land_Slope 126, 129, 133
Latitude 129, 132, 138, 141, 142, 143
lda_res 98, 99, 100, 101
library function 2, 4, 10, 15, 74, 76, 87
linear combinations 80
linear discriminant analysis (LDA) 9
linear discriminants 80, 90, 111
linear model 10, 15, 18, 19, 20, 27, 29, 34, 38, 39, 46, 49, 51, 53, 54, 55, 60, 64, 65, 71
linear_reg function 13
linear regression 9, 10, 13, 14, 15, 16, 18, 33, 34, 35, 38, 49, 51, 52, 54, 62, 63, 65
lipid-rich necrotic core 365
lm_model 13, 32, 50, 51, 61, 62
loading 2
lobed_edge 222, 224, 227, 235, 243, 246, 272, 292, 295
logistic regression 9
Longitude 129, 132, 138, 141, 142, 143
Lot_Area 126, 129, 137, 143, 144, 148, 155, 181, 196, 218
Lot_Config 126, 129, 133, 145, 150, 156, 181, 182, 195, 197, 217, 218
Lot_Frontage 126, 129, 137, 143, 144, 148, 155, 182, 197, 218
Lot_Shape 126, 129, 133, 145, 150, 156, 181, 196, 217
lrnc_vol 366, 367, 370, 375, 377, 379

M

Machine Learning (ML) 8, 13, 32, 50, 61
male 367, 368, 371, 376, 378, 380
marketing 2, 4, 5, 10, 11, 15, 21, 24, 52, 57
marketing data 2, 10, 11
Mas_Vnr_Area 127, 130, 137, 144, 148, 155, 180, 194, 216
Mas_Vnr_Type 127, 130, 134, 146, 152, 157, 181, 182, 183, 194, 195, 217, 218, 219
matx_vol 366, 367, 370, 375, 377, 379
max_calc_area 366, 367, 370, 375, 377, 379
max_lrnc_area 366, 367, 368, 370, 375, 377, 379
max_matx_area 366, 367, 370, 375, 377, 379
max_max_wall_thickness 367, 368, 371, 375, 378, 379
max_remodeling_ratio 367, 368, 371, 375, 378, 380
max_stenosis_by_area 367, 368, 371, 376, 378, 380
max_stenosis_by_diameter 367, 368, 371, 376, 378, 380
max_wall_area 367, 368, 371, 376, 378, 380
mean 4, 5, 7, 8, 9, 16, 27, 46, 49, 60, 71
mean_blue_val 224, 225, 229, 235, 241, 246, 294, 295
mean_green_val 224, 225, 229, 235, 241, 245, 274, 294
mean_red_val 224, 225, 229, 235, 241, 245, 274, 294
Misc_Feature 129, 132, 135
Misc_Val 129, 132, 138
modeldata package 74, 126, 317
model performance 89, 98, 118
monotonic_contour 223, 225, 228, 234, 238, 244, 295
monotonic_polar 222, 224, 228, 233, 237, 244, 270, 274, 290, 293, 295, 315
Mo_Sold 129, 132, 138, 144, 149, 156, 182, 197, 219
MS_SubClass 126, 129, 133, 143, 144, 149, 156, 181, 182, 196, 217, 218

MS_Zoning 126, 129, 133, 143, 145, 150, 156, 181, 182, 195, 196, 217, 218
Multiple Linear Regression 49, 50, 61

N

narrow_factor 223, 225, 229, 234, 239, 245, 274, 294
nascet_scale 366, 367, 370, 375, 377, 379
Neighborhood 126, 129, 134, 145, 150, 156, 180, 181, 182, 183, 194, 195, 196, 216, 217, 218
newspapers 1
n_missing 4, 5, 6, 7, 8, 76, 77, 78, 79, 80, 84, 86
normalization 82, 83, 84, 85, 88, 89, 91, 98, 105, 107, 109, 110, 112, 118
num_convex_points 223, 225, 229, 234, 240, 245, 295
numeric column 2, 3, 8
num_max_ponits 223, 225, 228, 234, 238, 244, 295
num_min_points 223, 225, 228, 234, 238, 244, 295
n_unique 5, 6

O

Open_Porch_SF 128, 132, 138, 144, 149, 156, 182, 196, 218
outlying_contour 222, 224, 228
outlying_polar 222, 224, 228, 233
Overall_Cond 127, 130, 134, 145, 151, 156, 157, 180, 181, 182, 195, 217, 218

P

Packages 2
Paved_Drive 128, 131, 135, 147, 154, 158, 182, 197, 219
percentile 5
performance metrics 9, 20, 24, 39, 43, 57, 68
perimeter 223, 225, 228, 229, 234, 238, 239, 240, 245, 272, 274, 292, 294, 295
perimeter_convexity 223, 225, 229, 234, 240, 245, 294
perimeter_ratio_length 223, 225, 229, 234, 240, 245, 292, 294
perimeter_ratio_lw 223, 225, 229, 234, 240, 245, 272, 292, 295
petal length 75
Petal.Length 75, 80, 105, 106, 107, 110, 111, 112, 113, 115
Petal.Width 75, 80, 105, 106, 107, 110, 111, 112, 113, 115
physiological_length 223, 225, 228, 234, 239, 245, 294
physiological_width 223, 225, 229, 234, 239, 245, 274, 294
plot title 16, 23, 34, 42, 56, 66
Pool_Area 128, 132, 138
Pool_QC 128, 132, 135
predictors 9, 49, 50, 51, 53, 54, 57, 60, 61, 62, 64, 65, 68, 71
predictor variables 80, 90, 111
prep_rec 82, 83, 84, 85
preprocessing steps 8, 13, 14, 18, 32, 33, 38, 51, 62
p-value significance 14, 33, 52, 63

R

rectangularity 223, 225, 229, 234, 239, 245, 272, 292, 295
resample number 12, 32
risk 3, 6, 7, 61, 63, 64
rmse function 18, 29, 37, 48
Roof_Matl 127, 130, 134
Roof_Style 127, 130, 134, 145, 151, 157, 180, 183, 194, 195, 217, 219
R programming 75
R session 2, 3
R studio 2

S

Sale_Condition 129, 132, 136, 147, 154, 158, 181, 195, 196, 217

Sale_Price 129, 132, 138, 140, 141, 142, 144, 149, 156, 158, 159, 183, 184, 198, 219
sales 1, 2, 3, 4, 10, 11, 12, 13, 15, 16, 17, 18, 19, 20, 21, 22, 23, 24, 27, 28, 29, 38, 49, 50, 51, 52, 53, 54, 55, 56, 57, 60
Sale_Type 129, 132, 136, 147, 154, 158, 180, 182, 195, 197, 217, 219
Screen_Porch 128, 132, 138
Second_Flr_SF 128, 131, 137, 144, 148, 155, 180, 194, 216
sepal length 75
Sepal.Length 75, 79, 105, 106, 107, 110, 111, 112, 113, 115
Sepal.Width 75, 80, 105, 106, 107, 110, 111, 112, 113, 115
set_caption function 4, 15, 33, 52, 63
set_caption functions 100
set_engine function 13, 87
set_mode function 13, 87
setosa 75, 79, 104, 107, 110, 112, 113, 114, 116, 123
set.seed function 10, 12, 30, 31
shape 222, 224, 227, 233, 235, 243, 246, 272, 274, 292, 294, 295
skewed_contour 222, 224, 228, 233, 237, 244, 270, 290, 293, 295, 315
skewed_polar 222, 224, 228, 233, 236, 244, 270, 274, 290, 293, 295, 315
skim function 75, 76, 77, 78, 79, 84, 85
skimr package 4
skim_variable 4, 5, 6, 7, 8
skinny_contour 223, 225, 228, 234, 238, 244, 294
skinny_polar 222, 224, 228, 233, 237, 244, 270, 274, 290, 293, 295, 315
smoking 366, 367, 368, 371, 376, 378, 380
smoking_history 367, 368, 371, 376, 378, 380
smooth_edge 222, 224, 227, 235, 243, 246, 292, 295
sparse_contour 222, 225, 228, 233, 237, 244, 295
sparse_polar 222, 224, 228, 233, 236, 244, 270, 290, 293, 295, 315
species 222, 224, 226, 227, 230, 231, 232, 235, 246, 247, 248, 271, 272, 273, 275, 276, 277, 279, 291, 292, 293, 295, 296, 297, 298, 315
split_iris object 104
split_market 10, 11
standard deviation 5
std_blue_val 224, 226, 229, 235, 242, 246, 294
std_green_val 224, 226, 229, 235, 242, 246, 295
std_red_val 224, 226, 229, 235, 241, 246, 294
step_normalize function 82, 83, 105
Street 126, 129, 133, 143
striated_contour 223, 225, 228, 234, 237, 244, 274, 294
striated_polar 222, 224, 228, 233, 236, 244, 270, 275, 290, 293, 294, 295, 315
stringy_contour 223, 225, 228
stringy_polar 222, 224, 228, 233, 237, 244, 270, 275, 290, 293, 294, 315
structure 74, 75, 84, 85, 106, 107
superplasticizer 318, 319, 324, 325, 326

T

table title 4
test_class 81, 85, 102, 103
testing data 8, 9, 10, 11, 14, 27, 28, 30, 47
test_market 10, 11, 27, 28, 29, 50, 60
theme_box 76, 77, 78, 79, 83, 84, 85, 90, 92, 100, 113, 119
theme_box function 4, 14, 33, 52, 63
theme_classic function 16, 23, 34, 42, 56, 67, 93, 114
three-dimensional visualization 365
Three_season_porch 128, 132, 138
tibble 12, 17, 18, 19, 20, 21, 27, 28, 29, 31, 36, 37, 38, 39, 40, 46, 47, 48, 49, 53, 54, 55, 60, 64, 65, 66, 71
tidymodels package 74, 126, 221

tidyverse package 2, 74
Tools 2
toothed_edge 222, 224, 227, 235, 243, 246, 272, 292, 295
top_counts 5, 6
Total_Bsmt_SF 127, 130, 137, 144, 148, 155, 180, 194, 216
TotRms_AbvGrd 128, 131, 138, 144, 149, 155, 182, 196, 218
training 8, 9, 10, 11, 12, 14, 15, 16, 17, 18, 20, 21, 24, 27, 29, 30, 32, 33, 34, 36, 38, 39, 40, 43, 46, 50, 51, 52, 53, 54, 55, 57, 60, 61, 63, 64, 65, 67, 68, 71
training data 9, 10, 14, 16, 17, 20, 27, 29, 30, 36, 39, 46, 50, 51, 60, 61, 71
train_iris 104, 105, 107, 108, 110, 112, 113, 115, 116, 117
transformation 8
two_class_dat 74, 76, 77, 81

U

undulate_edge 222, 224, 227
unnest function 20, 21, 22, 39, 40, 41, 55, 65, 66
Utilities 126, 129, 133

V

values 1, 2, 3, 5, 6, 7, 8, 12, 15, 16, 17, 18, 19, 27, 28, 29, 32, 34, 35, 36, 37, 38, 43, 46, 47, 48, 54, 65
versicolor 75, 79, 104, 110, 113, 114, 116, 123
V-Fold Cross-Validation 8
virginica 75, 79, 104, 110, 113, 114, 116, 123

W

wall_vol 367, 368, 371, 376, 378, 380
water 318, 319, 324, 325, 326
wflow 13, 14, 15, 18, 19
Wood_Deck_SF 128, 131, 138, 144, 149, 156, 181, 196, 217
workflow 9, 13, 14, 18, 32, 33, 38, 51, 54, 62, 65

X

x-axis 15, 22, 23, 34, 41, 42, 55, 56, 66

Y

yank function 4, 5, 7, 75, 76, 77, 78, 79, 84, 85
y-axis 15, 22, 23, 34, 41, 42, 43, 55, 56, 66
Year_Built 127, 130, 137, 144, 148, 155, 180, 194, 217
Year_Remod_Add 127, 130, 137, 144, 148, 155, 180, 194, 216
Year_Sold 129, 132, 138, 144, 149, 156, 181, 196, 218
YouTube 1, 50, 53